CONTENTS

To the Student

Since your grade in this course depends on your understanding of economic theory and its applications, you are probably reluctant to spend more than a minute or two reading this preface — let's get on to chapter one, you may be thinking. That's a good attitude to have, but brains and energy are not always enough. Focus is also important. Unless you focus your energies on the right thing, you will waste valuable hours of study time. That is one of the things we have tried to help you do in this study guide. Rather than look at the guide as a series of questions and exercises, think of it as a tool to help focus your thoughts and energies on the most relevant issues contained in the text.

In each chapter, Part 1 provides a general overview of the topics examined in the corresponding chapter of the text. The overview does not examine every detail, but introduces the reader to the subject matter and places it in its proper perspective. What are the three or four most important ideas in this chapter? How is material from earlier chapters used in this one? What makes the material worth studying in the first place? Without clear answers to these questions, many students get lost in the details of economic theory and never quite grasp the point of it all.

Part 2 is an exercise calling for you to match key terms used in previous chapters to their definitions or meanings. Because these terms were discussed earlier in the course, any difficulty here is a signal that your understanding of that material may be somewhat less complete than you previously believed. This may also prevent you from fully grasping the material in the present chapter, so you should review the meaning and use of any "problem" terms before proceeding. A word to the wise is sufficient.

Ideally, Parts 1 and 2 should be read prior to reading the corresponding chapter of the text.

Part 3 should be completed after you read the text. The fill-in-the-blank questions in Part 3 help to develop your understanding of key terms, as well as your ability to manipulate the theoretical concepts from which economic models are constructed. The questions in Part 3 are among the most important in the guide, because by answering them you build your economic vocabulary — which is important not only in the current chapter, but in future ones.

Part 4 includes a handful of problems and exercises that vary so much from one chapter to the next that it is difficult to describe them all with a single term or phrase. What the exercises share in common is their purpose — all were designed to get you more involved with the subject matter presented in the text, either by graphing data, drawing curves, calculating answers to problems, or conducting your own economic analysis. We believe the exercises in Part 4 will develop a depth of understanding that simply isn't possible by matching a term to its meaning or picking the correct answer from four possible choices. In Part 4 there are no answers from which to select — the answers are for you to provide.

Part 5 contains a variety of questions similar to those administered in most university-level economics courses. Use these questions as a self-test, after you have read the text and completed the other parts in the study guide. By taking the self-test in advance of an in-class examination, you can spot your weaknesses in advance and administer the appropriate remedy — which is study.

Finally, review your errors from Parts 3, 4, and 5 for possible patterns. By spotting similarities between questions you missed, you will have a better idea of the topics on which to concentrate your final (pre-test) hours of study.

We hope you enjoy your economics course, and especially hope that this study guide proves useful. If you have suggested improvements for later editions, either of us would be delighted to hear from you.

T.L.W.
R.A.A.

Chapter 1
What Economics Is About

Part 1. Introduction and Purpose
Consider the following points as you read chapter 1 in the text.

What is economics? Economics is many things to many people, as illustrated by three definitions discussed in the text. A constant theme in economics is that **incentives** have an impact on human behavior. This is most obvious in the study of **microeconomics** -- the economics of the consumer, the seller, the worker -- but also underlies much of **macroeconomic** thinking as well. Economists take it as given that men and women make the choices that provide themselves with the greatest net gain, and your study of economics will be far more productive if *you* pay particular attention to the role played by incentives throughout this course. (Because paying attention to incentives will help your grade, we predict you will do it.)

So if you read that a higher price causes people to buy less of some item, ask yourself what incentive they have to behave that way. Economists believe consumers who react that way gain more **utility**, or satisfaction, than they would if they behaved differently. This issue will appear in a later chapter.)

That is not to say that people are totally self centered or unwilling to lift a finger to help others. People give gifts and perform charitable acts every day, and these activities are all the proof one needs that narrow self interest does not rule our every action. But charity does not conflict with the view that self interest is *one* of the things that motivate people, or with the prediction that an increase in the incentive to do something makes it more likely that people will do it, **ceteris paribus**. Other things being equal, higher wages give people more incentive to work, whether the individual is self interested or charitable. Even a very charitable person may work longer and harder for a higher wage, since that would mean more income to donate to worthy causes. But in any event, predicting that workers will react to a higher wage by working more is not the same as saying that other considerations -- personal wealth, family responsibilities, laziness -- cannot also be influential. Incentives are important, but they are not everything.

Each of these observations is relevant to the study of economics. From the perspective that human action is influenced by incentives, each change in real-world conditions which affects personal incentives will also affect the behavior of consumers, workers, company managers, and government officials. If the earth's atmosphere warms, crops may fail and push crop prices up. Higher crop prices in turn provide an incentive to irrigate dry lands, which would increase profits for companies that drill wells and thousands of dollars' worth of irrigation equipment.

Scarcity is the fundamental fact of life which forces people to make economic choices. Since Adam and Eve left the Garden of Eden, people's desires have exceeded the goods made freely available by nature. Scarcity makes it necessary to trade off some desires against others if one hopes to satisfy his or her most urgent wants instead of other, lower-priority urges. It would be nice to have a new car every year, but few people are willing to give up their summer vacation every year and work every Saturday in order to get it. When people are faced with scarcity, economists **predict** that they will buy items that provide the most utility for the smallest sacrifice, or **cost**.

Such predictions are the subject of **positive economics**. In conducting a positive analysis, economists do not concern themselves with the desirability or undesirability of individual behavior. Instead they concentrate on the circumstances and motivations which explain it. Typically, economic **theories** are statements about the effect of incentives on behavior -- statements that have been shown to be effective predictors of behavior over a wide range of circumstances.

Judging the effectiveness of a theory by **testing** it against actual behavior or events -- the empirical method -- is an important aspect of scientific inquiry. Because **logical errors** sometimes creep into scientific analysis (the belief that association implies causation, the fallacy of composition), the conclusions arrived at may be erroneous. Putting predictions beside facts is a proven way of rejecting false and ultimately worthless theories, and of building on those that show the most promise.

Part 2. Key Concepts in this Chapter
After reading chapter 1 in the text, answer the following questions.

1. The happiness or satisfaction individuals receive from consuming goods is called _____ .

2. Economics studies the actions of _____ that are directed toward meeting certain _____ in a world where goods and resources have _____ uses.

3. _____ makes it necessary to choose between alternatives.

4. The highest valued alternative foregone as a result of making a choice is its _____ cost.

5. Focusing on a limited number of factors to explain an event is called _____.

6. A _____ is an "if-then" statement about the relationship between two or more variables.

7. According to Milton Friedman, theories should be judged successful on the basis of their ability to _____ behavior or events.

8. _____ economics is value-free economic analysis. _____ economics includes the personal goals and values of the analyst.

9. A good made available by nature in sufficient quantity to satisfy all wants is a _____ good.

10. _____ is a Latin phrase that means other things remain constant.

11. The _____ of a $500 television set is the foregone opportunity to buy $500 worth of other goods.

12. True or false? _____ A theory should be rejected if there is an inconsistency between its assumptions and real-world conditions.

13. "Whatever is good for General Motors is good for America." This statement commits which fallacy of logic? The fallacy of _____.

14. _____ is the study of economics that deals with the entire economy.

15. _____ is the study of economics that deals with consumers, sellers, workers, and other segments of the economy.

16. If event A occurs immediately before event B, then A probably caused or contributed to B. This logic assumes that association implies _____.

17. High _____ costs prevent many fashion models, rock stars, and actors from going to college.

18. The economic conditions included in an economic theory are referred to as _____.

19. For most purposes the words "model" and _____ are interchangeable.

20. Because of _____, "more resources for education mean fewer resources for defense."

Part 3. Problems and Exercises
After reading chapter 1 you should be able to work the following problems.

1. Clint and Cindi plan to travel from New York to Tampa. Clint has a job paying $6 an hour; Cindi has a job paying $15 an hour. Which of the two do you predict will be most likely to prefer taking the trip by car? _____ By air? _____
   Use incentives to explain your prediction: _____
   _____

2. Examine the table at right. Do workers react to incentives as economist predict? _____
   Explain your conclusion:_____
   _____

Wage	Hours Worked Per Week
$ 3.50	16
4.00	20
4.50	25
5.00	28

3. Indicate with a check mark (√) which of the following are costs of attending college. Recall that costs result from making a particular decision.

_√_Tuition and other fees	$_____
___Room and board	_____
___Textbooks and other class materials	_____
___Extra income that you could have earned by working full time rather than attending college	_____
___The cost of clothing	_____
TOTAL	$_____

4. Estimate the annual cost associated with each √ item above and write it in the space provided at right. Multiply by four (4) to estimate the total cost of a college education: $_____.

5. "If colleges would eliminate their tuitions, everyone could afford to go college." Explain why this statement is false:_____

_____

6. Assume high school graduates have an average monthly income of $450, but then wages among this group rise to $500. Explain how this affects the cost of attending college.

_____

7. If you stopped studying at this instant, what would you do instead? _____
   What do economists call the opportunities you forego to study ?_____

8. Adam Smith, the father of modern economics, wrote more than 200 years ago about the children in Britain's American colonies. "The labor of each child," he said, "before it can leave their house, is computed to be worth a hundred pounds clear gain to them" [the child's parents].
Do you feel that children provide a "clear gain" (income in excess of expenses) to parents today? _____
   Comparing the situation 200 years ago with that today, what has happened to the incentive to get married and have children?_____

9. Indicate whether particular topics are more closely related to <u>macro</u>economics or <u>micro</u>economics.
•the price of gasoline	macro / micro		•the general price level	macro / micro
•the unemployment rate	macro / micro		•the wages of teachers	macro / micro
•national output	macro / micro		•total car production	macro / micro

10. In 1974, the interstate highway speed limit was reduced from 70 to 55 mph to improve gas mileage in order to reduce the nation's demand for petroleum a. If gas mileage rose from 15 to 18 mpg at the lower speed, how much gasoline would be saved on a 250-mile trip? _____ gal. At the 1974 price of 60¢ per gallon, about $_____ worth of gasoline was conserved by the lower speed limit. b.How much extra time is required to make the 250-mi. trip at the lower speed limit? _____ If a car has 2 passengers and each values their time at $4 an hour, what did the lower speed limit cost in terms of time lost? $ _____ c. Compare the benefits in (a) with the costs in (b). Did the law conserve fuel at a low cost? _____

Part 4. Self Test
Multiple Choice Questions

1. Milton Friedman defined economics as:

a. the science of how a particular society solves its economic problems
b. the science which studies human behavior as a relationship between ends and scarce means which have alternative uses
c. a study of mankind in the ordinary business of life
d. the science of exchange

Answer: _____

2. Scarcity exists:

a. in only poor countries of the world
b. in all countries of the world
c. only when society does not employ all its resources in an efficient way
d. only when society produces too many frivilous or silly goods

Answer: _____

3. Which of the following statements is true?

a. Both a millionaire and a poor person must deal with scarcity.
b. People would have to make choices even if scarcity did not exist.
c. Scarcity is a relatively new problem in the world's history; it has not always existed.
d. It is likely that one day scarcity will no longer exist.

Answer: _____

4. Which of the following statements is true?

a. Coca-Cola is a good for everyone, even someone who has an allergy to Coca-Cola.
b. If you pay someone to take X off your hands, then it is likely that you consider X a bad.
c. It is possible, but not likely, that someone can obtain both utility and disutility from a bad.
d. If there is more of good A than people want at zero price, then good A is an economic good.

Answer: _____

5. If the air is cleaner in Blacksburg, Virginia than in Washington, D.C., and relatively clean air is an economic good, it follows that:

a. real estate prices in Blacksburg will be lower than real estate prices in Washington
b. real estate prices in Blacksburg will be higher than real estate prices in Washington
c. real estate prices in Blacksburg will be lower than real estate prices in Washington, ceteris paribus
d. real estate prices in Blacksburg will be higher than real estate prices in Washington, ceteris paribus

Answer: _____

6. Kristin Taylor attends the University of North Carolina at Chapel Hill. The opportunity cost of her attending college is:

a. equal to the salary she will earn when she graduates
b. equal to the money she spends on college tuition
c. the highest valued alternative she forfeits to attend college
d. the least valued alternative she forfeits to attend college

Answer: _____

7. Frank is 19 years old and in the movies. He earns $500,000 a picture. Cassandra is 19 years old and works in a clothing store at the nearby shopping mall. She earns $5 an hour. Which of the two persons is more likely to attend college and for what reason?

a. Cassandra, because she is smarter.
b. Frank, because he has higher opportunity costs of attending college than Cassandra.
c. Cassandra, because she has lower opportunity costs of attending college than Frank.
d. Frank, because he earns a higher income than Cassandra.

Answer: _____

8. A theory is:

a. a simplified abstract representation of the real world
b. built on critical factors or variables
c. an accurate and complete description of reality
d. a and b
e. a, b, and c

Answer: _____

9. Which of the following is the best example of a hypothesis?

a. If a person eats too many fatty foods, then his or her cholesterol level will rise.
b. If it is 12 noon in New York City, it is 9 a.m. in Los Angeles.
c. The daytime temperature is often over 100 degrees in Las Vegas in the summer.
d. If someone yells "fire" in a crowded theater and everyone runs to the exit, you will be worse off than had everyone walked but you.

Answer: _____

10. Evidence can:

a. prove a theory but never disprove it
b. disprove (or reject) a theory but never prove it
c. both prove and disprove a theory (although not at the same time)
d. change the assumptions of the theory to fit the facts

Answer: _____

11. If an economist tests his or her theory and finds that it predicts accurately, he or she would likely say:

a. the evidence fails to reject the theory
b. the theory has been proved correct
c. the theory is true
d. the theory is a good theory

Answer: _____

12. When an economist says that association is not causation, he or she means:

a. that event X and Y can be related in time (say one occurs a few minutes before the other) without X causing Y or Y causing X
b. that if X occurs close in time to Y it must be that either X is the cause of Y or Y is the cause of X
c. that what is good for one person is good for all persons
d. that what is good for one person is usually bad for all persons

Answer: _____

13. Ceteris paribus means:

a. the correct relationship specified
b. there are too many variables considered in this theory
c. all other things held constant
d. assuming that people are rational human beings

Answer: _____

14. Which of the following is an example of a positive statement?

a. If you drop a quarter off the top of the Sears building in Chicago, it will fall to the ground.
b. The minimum wage should be raised to $6 an hour.
c. There is too much crime in the United States; something should be done about it.
d. People should learn to love each other.

Answer: _____

15. Which of the following topics is a microeconomics topic?

a. the study of what influences the nation's unemployment rate
b. the study of how changes in the nation's money supply affect the nation's output
c. the study of prices in the automobile market
d. the study of what affects interest rates

Answer: _____

True-False

16. A good is anything from which individuals   T F
receive utility.

17. If there is no explicit charge for a good,   T F
the good is definitely a free good.

18. Scarcity implies that choices will be made.   T F

19. The higher a person's opportunity cost of time,   T F
the more likely a person will stand in a long line
to buy a ticket to a concert or some other event,
ceteris paribus.

20. According to Milton Friedman, theories are   T F
better judged by their assumptions than by their
predictions.

Fill in the blank

21. If one person talks louder than others at a cocktail party, he or she is heard better. If everyone talks louder at a cocktail party, everyone is heard better. This is an illustration of the _____ .

22. Stephen believes that those things which come first necessarily cause those things that come later. Stephen believes that _____ .

23. If calorie intake causes weight gain and there are numerous things that cause weight loss, then the more cookies you eat, the more weight you will gain, _____ .

24. _____ is the branch of economics that deals with highly aggregated markets or the entire economy.

25. If the evidence is consistent with a theory, economists do not say the theory has been proved correct. Instead, they say that the evidence _____ the theory.

Part 4. Answers to Self Test

1. a 2. b 3. a 4. b 5. d 6. c 7. c 8. d 9. a 10. b
11. a 12. a 13. c 14. a 15. c
16. T 17. F 18. T 19. F 20. F
21. fallacy of composition 22. association is causation
23. ceteris paribus 24. Macroeconomics 25 fails to reject

Part 5. Answers

Part 2 Key Concepts
1. utility   2. individuals, ends (goals), alternative   3. scarcity   4. opportunity cost   5. abstraction
6. hypothesis   7. predict accurately   8. positive economics, normative economics   9. free   10. ceteris
paribus   11. cost   12. false   13. composition   14. macroeconomics   15. microeconomics
16. causation   17. opportunity costs   18. variables   19. theory   20. scarcity

Part 3 Problems and exercises
1. Clint by car and Cindi by air; Cindi's time is more valuable, so the cost of travel time is higher for her.
2. Yes. Higher wages provide an incentive to work more, and the worker does that as the wage increases.
3-4. Checks should go before tuition, textbooks, and lost income. You would have eaten and bought
    clothes anyway, so no extra cost is incurred in these areas due to the decision to attend college.

5. For most students foregone earnings are the largest components of college costs, and those would remain even if tuition were zero. Consequently the statement is false.

6. The opportunity cost of going to college would rise by about $50 per month, times 9 months, times 4 years -- or $1800.

7. Watch "Alf" on television; opportunity cost.

8. As children have gone from being a source of income to a costly "consumption good," the incentive to have children has declined.

9. left column: micro, macro, macro   right column: macro, micro, micro

10. a. 2.78 gal. with a market value of $1.67, b. 0.97 hours with a value of $7.79   c. no

Chapter 2
Fundamentals of Economic Thinking

Part 1. Introduction and Purpose
Consider the following points as you read chapter 2 in the text.

What makes economics a difficult subject for many people is the complexity of our $5 trillion economy and the conflicting explanations analysts offer for every twist and turn it makes. With so much going on at the same time, many surrender to the feeling that economic "theory" is just too abstract and confusing to learn.

That is largely a case of not seeing the forest for the trees. Fortunately, economists don't have to design an economy or examine every economic transaction to understand economic behavior or major trends underway in the economy. As you gain experience in economic thinking you should gradually come to see that economic analysis uses a half-dozen **tools**, or economic **principles**, in many different areas of inquiry. There is not one set of economic theories for the breakfast cereal market, a different one for labor markets, and still another for the herion market; the same handful of principles apply in all three situations.

This helps explain why a few students in your class will be able to earn high grades with little apparent effort. Those who excel may not be more intelligent overall or study harder than those who struggle to earn Bs. But those who find economics "easy" will have discovered the few important principles and how to apply them to a variety of different situations. Before the discovery, economics is a mass of theories and definitions too large to manage; afterwards, it is a manageable handful of economic principles that become easier to manipulate with practice.

The message is that students who familiarize themselves with — who ponder — each of the major themes raised in this chapter will be better prepared for material later in the course than those who don't. **Decision making at the margin** may strike you as a rather boring subject that you would rather not spend much time reading about. Taken alone, the part of the chapter which discusses marginal thinking is no big deal — but you may think it more important when you consider how many times marginal thinking is discussed elsewhere in the text: marginal cost, marginal benefit, marginal revenue, marginal productivity, marginal resource cost, marginal utility, marginal propensity to consume, marginal propensity to save, marginal tax rate. Fail to understand marginal thinking now and much of the material in later chapters will remain beyond your grasp.

The same can be said of the other economic fundamentals examined in chapter 2. Since economists assume that consumers, workers, business managers, investors, government bureaucrats, voters, and elected officials usually exhibit **rational behavior** — a tendency to do things for which the benefits of elected officials usually exhibit **rational behavior** — a tendency to do things for which the benefits of taking action exceed the costs — then students will be more successful if they learn about the rational behavior assumption now and learn to recognize it in later chapters.

As noted a moment ago, economic theories are usually formulated in general terms so they can be used in a variety of different applications. Rather than talking about the methods used to assemble steel and various materials into automobiles, economists discuss the **production** process in more general terms: production is the transformation of economic resources (**land**, **labor**, **capital**, and **entrepreneurship**) into goods and services. Resources are being used **efficiently** if as much output as possible is produced from a given amount of resources (and if not, resources are used inefficiently).

In many ways this is pretty obvious stuff. The hard part is becoming so familiar with these ideas that they come to mind when the evening news is discussing the economics of medical care or farm economics. If they do, that is a sign you're learning the economic way of thinking.

Among the most important concepts discussed in chapter 2 is **exchange**. Exchange occurs when rational buyers and sellers agree on terms for a trade which each considers to be in his or her own best interest. The fact that traders are motivated by self interest should not conceal the fact that voluntary exchange is a form of **social cooperation** that results in a major increase in everyone's standard of living. The most prosperous nations in the world encourage relatively free and uncontrolled exchange; the least prosperous typically have man-made or natural barriers, that prevent trade from being carried out in the same free and easy manner.

If you're in the advice-taking mood, we suggest that you read chapter 2 twice and spend a couple of minutes reflecting on each of the economic principles it examines. Whenever possible, try to think of an example from your own experience that illustrates the key point under consideration. Practice and familiarity underlie excellence in any field of endeavor, and economics is no exception.

Part 2. Review of Concepts from Earlier Chapters
Prior to reading chapter 2, match statements at left with the appropriate concept at right.

__1. Benefits in excess of costs.   a. scarcity
__2. Satisfaction from consuming goods.   b. good
__3. Assuming that other things remain unchanged.   c. incentive
__4. When desires exceed the ability to produce goods. d. ceteris paribus
__5. Whatever is foregone as a result of taking an action. e. utility
__6. Something that gives consumers happiness.   f. cost

Part 3. Key Concepts in this Chapter
After reading chapter 2 in the text, answer the following questions.

1. The act of trading one thing for another is also called _____.

2. A __PPF / cost / demand__ curve describes combinations of goods that an economy can produce using all of its _____ and existing technology.

3. The generic names for all resources used to produce goods and services are: _____
_____ _____ and _____.

4. _____ is the term economists use to describe air, water, and other natural resources used in production.

5. One <u>considers</u> taking action before the fact, or ex <u>post / ante</u> and <u>reflects</u> on having taken it after the fact, or ex <u>post / ante</u>.

6. A person whose actions are influenced by a comparison of benefits and costs <u>is / is not</u> said to be a utility maximizer.

7. "I can earn another $5 by working for one more hour, but I wouldn't do it for less than $10." This <u>does / does not</u> reflect marginal decision making

8. The economy is operating _____ when production occurs at a point below the PPF. When production occurs at a point along PPF, the economy is using resources _____.

9. An _____ identifies unfulfilled consumer demands and profitable ways to organize goods and resources to satisfy those demands.

10. There is no such thing as a _____ _____ means that all scarce goods are costly.

11. Things that "might have been" are _____ costs.

12. _____ costs are historical costs or past costs.

13. Because resources are _____ in particular uses, the production possibilities frontier will be curved. A PPF that is bowed outward illustrates the law of increasing _____ _____.

14. If it is impossible to increase the production of one good without reducing that of another, resources are currently being used _____.

15. If the cost of taking some action increases, rational self interest suggests that an individual will be <u>more / less / equally</u> likely to take the action than before.

16. _____ refers to knowledge about how to use resources to produce goods.

17. Economic growth can occur when the PPF shifts <u>rightward and up / leftward and down</u>.

18. Every economic system must answer the same four questions:
a) _____ goods will be produced with the scarce resources available? b) _____ will produce those goods, and c) _____ will they will produced? d) For _____ are those goods produced?

19. Economist Gary Becker believes that people attempt to maximize their _____ whether they are buying goods in the marketplace or engaging in "nonmarket" activities such as allocating leisure time.

20. It is not the _____ of the butcher, the brewer, or the baker that provides us our meals, but their regard to their own _____.

21. Economic _____ refers to extending the economic way of thinking into traditionally non-economic areas.

Part 4.   Problems and Exercises
After reading chapter 2 in the text you should be able to work the following problems.

1. Use the accompanying grid to draw a PPF curve. Point out one unattainable combination of goods and label it **U**. Point out a combination of goods that is inefficient and label it **I**. Point out a combination of goods produced that is efficient and label it **E**.

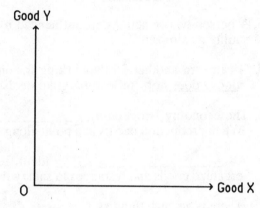

2. Use the accompanying grid to draw a PPF curve. Show what happens when the economy experiences economic growth. (Use arrows, curves, points, or whatever graphing technique you feel illustrates economic growth.)

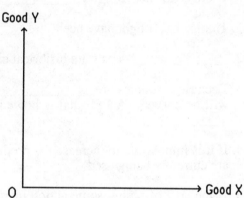

3. Rob requires the same amount of water, effort, and land to grow 10 pounds of tomatoes at 22 pounds of cucumbers. The opportunity cost of 1 pound of tomatoes is _____ pounds of cucumbers.

4. Visiting the dairy section of the local supermarket, you notice that a 14-ounce block of cheese is priced at $1.79 while a 16-ounce block is $1.99. The marginal cost of cheese is _____ per ounce in this instance. What was the average cost of each of the first 14 ounces? _____ What is the average cost per ounce for all 16 oz.? _____

5. The table below gives values for two
   variables, C and Y. Graph each C,Y
   combination in the grid on your right.

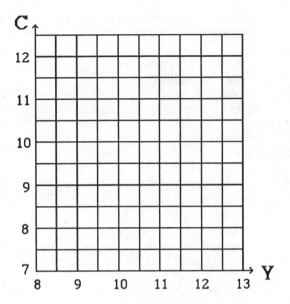

Observation	Y	C
1	8.4	7.6
2	9.2	8.3
3	9.7	8.8
4	10.3	9.5
5	11.3	10.3
6	11.9	11.0
7	12.5	11.6
8	13.0	12.2

Next, use a ruler to <u>draw</u> a <u>straight</u> <u>line</u>
through the points you just graphed. This
straight line should be as close as possible
to all of the points in your graph, and will
represent the general relationship between
C and Y.

Finally, <u>compute</u> <u>the slope of the straight line</u> you just drew. To do that, pick two points on the line
(not the data points graphed earlier, but two imaginary points on the straignt line) and divide the vertical
distance between the points by the horizontal distance between them. (See the appendix to chapter 2
for a discussion of this procedure.) Slope = _____.

You may be interested to know that the data in the table were taken from the 1988 Economic Report of
the President, table B-27 (which can be found in most college libraries). The "C" column represents
per capita consumption spending, 1980-87; the "Y" column represents personal income per capita over
the same period. (All figures are expressed as thousands of dollars.) The straight line you have drawn
is known as a consumption function, and its slope is the marginal propensity to consume.

Part 5. Self Test
Multiple choice questions

1. Which of the following statements is true?

a. Rational self-interested behavior is the same as selfish behavior.
b. Not all people exhibit self-interested behavior.
c. To act in a rational self-interested manner means to act to maximize the difference between (subjectively
evaluated) benefits and costs; it means to maximize utility.
d. Rational self-interested persons do not change their behavior when benefits and costs change.

Answer: _____

2. If you decide whether to buy an additional pair of shoes by evaluating the additional costs and benefits associated with the pair of shoes, then you are:

a. deciding at the margin
b. deciding at the peak
c. allowing sunk costs to influence your decision
d. doing something that most people do not do

Answer: _____

3. Which of the following is not a resource or factor of production?

a. land
b. labor
c. entrepreneurship
d. a final good

Answer: _____

4. If there is always a constant tradeoff between goods A and B, the production possibilities frontier between A and B is:

a. circular
b. a downward-sloping curve
c. a downward-sloping straight line
d. a downward-sloping straight line that is broken at one point

Answer: _____

5. The unattainable region of the production possibilities frontier (PPF) includes:

a. the points below and above the PPF
b. the points above the PPF
c. the points below the PPF
d. the points on the PPF

Answer: _____

6. Which of the following statements is true?

a. Scarcity is represented by the frontier of the production possibilities frontier.
b. Capital includes stocks and bonds.
c. The attainable region of the production possibilities frontier (PPF) includes the points on and above the PPF.
d. There are four maximum or end points on a PPF.

Answer: _____

7. If a new discovery of some resource is made, the production possibilities frontier will:

a. shift outward
b. shift inward
c. remain where it is
d. there is not enough information to answer the question

Answer: _____

8. Consider two points on the production possibilities frontier: point X, at which there are 100 cars and 78 trucks, and point Y, at which there are 90 cars and 79 trucks. If the economy is currently at point X, the opportunity cost of moving to point Y is:

a. 12 cars
b. 1 truck
c. 10 cars
d. 79 trucks
e. none of the above

Answer: _____

9. Which of the following illustrates constant opportunity costs?

a. people pay higher prices for cars the higher the costs of cars
b. as more cars are produced, the opportunity cost of each additional car is the same as for the preceding unit
c. as more cars are produced, the opportunity cost of each additional car is less than for the preceding unit
d. as more cars are produced, the opportunity cost of each additional car is greater than for the preceding unit

Answer: _____

10. If currently it is possible to produce more of one good without getting less of another, then:

a. the economy is operating efficiently
b. the economy is sluggish
c. the economy is operating inefficiently
d. the economy is operating at technological inferiority

Answer: _____

11. Efficiency implies that:

a. there are too few resources
b. there are too many resources
c. it is possible to obtain gains in one area without losses in another
d. it is impossible to obtain gains in one area without losses in another

Answer: _____

12. If you are thinking about buying (but have not yet bought) a new jacket, then you are in:

a. the ex post position
b. a rational position
c. the ex ante position
d. a holding position
e. none of the above

Answer: _____

13. A telephone answering machine sells for $100, therefore:

a. the terms of exchange are 1 answering telephone machine for $100
b. we know there will be an exchange
c. we know there will not be an exchange
d. the terms of exchange are in the seller's favor
e. none of the above

Answer: _____

14. Which of the following statements exhibits an awareness that there is no such thing as a free lunch?

a. My children go to school for free.
b. It costs nothing to cross the bridge.
c. It costs nothing to drive on the highways.
d. I have more X, but now I can't have Y.
e. a, b, and c

Answer: _____

15. If a buyer says he was "ripped off" by a seller, the buyer means:

a. that he was cheated and that if he had it over to do again he would not make the   exchange
b. the terms of exchange were in the seller's favor
c. it could be either a or b
d. neither a nor b

Answer: _____

True-False

16. Because scarcity exists, individuals and   T F
societies must make choices.

17. If the production of good X comes in terms   T F
of increasing costs of good Y, then the production
possibilities frontier between the two goods is a
downward-sloping straight line.

18. Economic growth shifts the production   T F
possibilities frontier inward.

19. In the ex ante (exchange) position,   T F
everyone believes he or she will benefit
from an exchange.

20. Without scarcity, there would be no   T F
production possibilities frontier.

Fill in the blank

21. The four questions (economists say) that all societies must answer are: What to produce? How to
produce? Who produces it? and _____ ?

22. _____ implies it is possible to obtain gains in one area without loses in another.

23. Increasing opportunity costs exist when resources are _____ .

24. _____ implies it is impossible to obtain gains in one area without loses in another.

25. At point A on a production possibilities frontier there are 50 apples and 60 oranges. At point B there
are 49 apples and 68 oranges. If the economy is currently at point B, the opportunity cost of moving to
point A is _____ oranges.

Part 5. Answers to Self Test

1. c 2. a 3. d 4. c 5. b 6. a 7. a 8. c 9. b 10. c
11. d 12. c 13. a 14. d 15. c
16. T 17. F 18. F 19. F 20. T
21. For whom is it produced 22. Inefficiency
23. specialized 24. Efficiency 25. 8

Part 6.   Answers

Part 2
1.c   2.e   3.d   4. a   5. f   6.b

Part 3
1. exchange
2. PPF, resources
3. land, labor, capital, entrepreneurship
4. land
5. ex ante, ex post
6. is
7. does
8. inefficiently, efficiently
9. entrepreneur

10. free lunch
11. opportunity costs
12. sunk
13. specialized, opportunity cost
14. efficiently
15. less
16. technology
17. rightward & up
18. What, Who, How, For Whom
19. utility
20. benevolence, interest
21. imperialism

Part 4

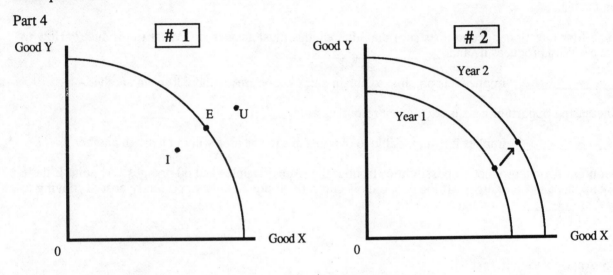

3. 2.2   4. 20-cents more ÷ 2 more ounces = 10-cents per extra ounce
5.

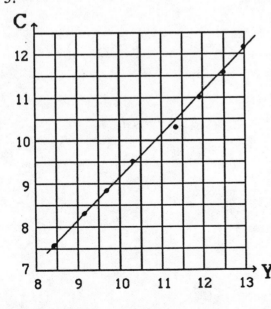

In this case observations
1 & 3 are both on the straight
line. Using data at those
points shows:

Vertical distance = 7.6 → 8.8
                  = 2.2 units

Horizontal distance = 8.4 → 9.7
                    = 2.3 units

Slope = 2.2 ÷ 2.3 = 0.957

For each 1-unit increase
in Y there is an increase
in C of 0.96 units

Chapter 3
Supply, Demand, and Price: Theory

Part 1. Introduction and Purpose
Consider the following points as you read chapter 3 in the text.

Chapter 3 presents one of the most powerful tools in economics, and one that most economics students will remember and use throughout their lives. Fortunately, a little practice is all that is required to master the supply and demand model. Your common sense probably tells you that the price of something will rise when the demand for it increases or when the supply of it decreases — and in a way the supply and demand model is just a formalized version of what most people consider common sense. The work you do in chapter 3 is just a way of exercising and disciplining your common sense so that it's a little less common than the next guy's.

The author of the text and your instructor have a few specific goals for you to achieve in this chapter, and their goals influence their presentation of the material. Later in the chapter they want to investigate the forces that determine market **prices** and **quantities**. Consequently, the first part of the chapter discusses terms (like demand and quantity demanded, supply and quantity supplied) that are used in the larger supply and demand model.

Here's where it is important to discipline your common sense. Demand and quantity demanded mean different things to an economist, and you should always listen (or read) carefully enough to know which is being used at any point in the discussion. Changes in **demand** (shifts in the curve) *affect* market price, but changes in **quantity demanded** don't. Changes in quantity demanded are the *result* of price changes, not their cause. If you recall that your instructor wants you to understand the forces that determine market **prices**, then you see why it is important to distinguish between something that will influence price (a change in demand) and something that won't (a change in quantity demanded).

The same is true of the distinction between changes in **supply** (shifts in the curve) and changes in **quantity supplied** (moving along a single curve). A change in supply will *affect* market price, but changes in quantity supplied *result* from price changes that originated elsewhere.

Common sense also tells you that when there is a shortage of something its price will rise, and that when there's a surplus its price will fall. For example a surplus of apartments will cause rents in your town to fall.

Falling apartment rents affect the market in two ways. First, lower prices cause quantity demanded to increase. Second, they cause quantity supplied to decline. These effects of falling prices both help to reduce the surplus of housing. Once rents have fallen by enough, the surplus will disappear entirely. This suggests another important idea that you should understand, that of a market in **equilibrium** -- a market clearing situation where there's neither surplus nor shortage, nor any reason for price to change from its current level.

In that sense, an equilibrium situation is a state of affairs in which sellers aren't forced to keep unsold units of something they'd like to sell, and in which buyers aren't forced to do without something they'd like to have.

A market equilibrium is also an important **reference point** that you'll use in this and in later chapters. If someone asks, "What is the effect of an increase in event X on the market price?" the implicit assumption is that the market is initially in equilibrium, and the analysis should trace the event's impact until a new equilibrium is reached.

Finally, a market **equilibrium is determined jointly by buyers and sellers** -- by demand and supply working together rather than by one or the other working alone. While some observers emphasize the importance of supply in the marketplace, others believe demand is the dominant factor. Both points of view are incorrect to the degree they overlook the role played by the other side of the market.

In this chapter more than most, it will be helpful to keep **paper and pencil** nearby. Each time the text mentions an example where demand or supply shifts, sketch the graph that illustrates that case. When two curves shift simultaneously, be on your guard! It is important to consider which curve shifts by more to accurately predict the impact on equilibrium price and quantity. Common sense won't tell you much about these cases, but they are easy when you see them on paper.

Part 2. Review of Concepts from Earlier Chapters
Prior to reading chapter 3, match statements at left with the appropriate concept at right.

__1. Wants exceed what limited resources can produce.   a. terms of exchange
__2. All other things remaining constant.   b. marginal
__3. Something that gives consumers utility (happiness).   c. resources
__4. Additional or incremental (as in "additional costs").   d. opportunity cost
__5. Land, labor, capital, and entrepreneurship.   e. good
__6. How much of one thing is traded for another.   f. scarcity
__7. What must be foregone when a choice is made.   g. ceteris paribus

Part 3. Key Concepts in this Chapter
After reading chapter 3 in the text, answer the following questions.

1. Exchanges between buyers and sellers occur in a _____-place.

2. When the price of a good declines, consumers will purchase more / less / the same amount of the good. This change in consumption is a change in demand / quantity demanded .

3. The law of _____ says that as the price of a good rises, more of it is produced and offered for sale.

4. When price is below the equilibrium price, there will be a surplus / shortage .

5. A _____ price is the price of one good expressed in units of another.

6. An increase in consumer income will cause demand to increase for _____ goods, but will cause demand to decrease for _____ goods.

7. Alfred _____ said that market price is determined by demand and supply working together, much as it takes both scissor blades to cut something.

8. If two goods are used jointly (in combination) by consumers, the goods are said to be substitutes / compliments. Consume more of good X, and you will consume more / less of good Y, a compliment to X.

9. An excess of quantity supplied over quantity demanded is a surplus / shortage .

10. If the price of good X rises, what happens to the demand for good Y, which is a substitute for good X? The demand for X will rise / fall .

11. When price exceeds / equals / is less than the equilibrium price, quantity supplied equals quantity demanded.

12. The _____ demand curve is the sum of quantities demanded by all consumers, at each given price.

13. When the price of a good rises, firms will produce more / less / the same amount of the good. This change in production is called a change in supply / quantity supplied .

14. An improvement in technology shifts the market supply curve right / left / in circles .

15. If it is expected that the price of good X will rise in the future, the current demand curve for the good will increase / decrease .

16. The supply curve for Stradivarius violins is a horizontal / vertical curve.

17. Taxis in New York pay approximately _____ for a license to operate.

18. A decrease in demand causes the equilibrium price to rise / fall and the equilibrium quantity to rise / fall .

19. An increase in supply causes the equilibrium price to rise / fall and the equilibrium quantity to rise / fall .

20. How will a simultaneous increase in consumer income and an increase in the price of good X affect the total consumption of X? (Assume X is a normal good.) _____

Part 4. Problems and Exercises
After reading chapter 3 in the text you should be able to work the following problems.

1.Refer to the paragraph.
   a. What happens to the demand for good X if consumers' income rises and X is a <u>normal</u> good? Draw the new demand curve and label it D2.

   b. What happens to the demand for good X if consumers' income rises and X is an <u>inferior</u> good? Draw the new demand curve and label it D3.

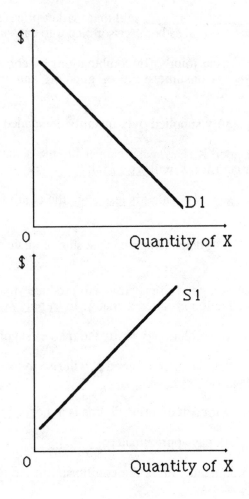

2. Refer to the paragraph.

   a. What happens to the supply of X if a new <u>technology</u> is introduced which increases labor productivity in producing X? Draw the new supply curve and label it S2.

   b. What happens to the supply of X if a $1 per unit tax is imposed on those who produce X? Draw the new demand curve and label it S3.

3. Consider the equilibrium point in the accompanying graph. Starting at this equilibrium, show what happens if supply declines by **3** units at every price and demand declines by **1** unit at every price. (Draw the new supply and demand curves, and indicate the new price.)

From this example can you conclude that a simultaneous reduction in supply and demand will result in a price increase every time?   <u>yes/no</u>   Explain your answer:_____
_____
_____

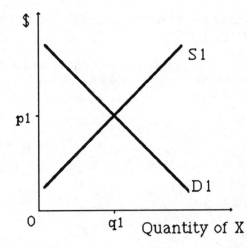

4. It takes Robinson Crusoe 1 day to trap (catch) a wild goat but 2 days to trap a beaver. In this case, the relative price of a beaver is _____ goats. The relative price of a goat is _____ beavers.

5. Indicate whether the paired items below are complements (C), substitutes (S), or unrelated (U) goods.

Pick One	
C / S/ U	tires and gasoline
C / S/ U	chicken soup and tennis shoes
C / S/ U	Fords and Chevys
C / S/ U	personal computers and floppy disks
C / S/ U	bacon and eggs
C / S/ U	bus rides and taxi rides

6. Here are demand schedules for movie tickets by 3 consumers. Use this information to draw the market demand curve in the grid at right.

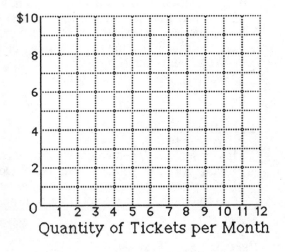

Quantity of Tickets per Month

Market Price	Quantity Demanded per month			
	Al	Bob	Cindi	Total
$10	0	1	0	__
8	1	2	0	__
6	2	3	1	__
4	3	4	2	__
2	3	5	3	__

7. Consider the following quote: "Now that the adult population is growing, the demand for homes will rise. That will push home prices up. But higher prices reduce the demand for homes, which will push prices back down. All in all, it is impossible to say whether home prices should go up or down because of the increase in demand."
Cross out those parts of the statement above that make it incorrect.

8. Events may affect either the current supply or demand for good X. In the boxes at right indicate which is affected by particular events. Write "increase" or "decrease" in the space provided. (Only one curve shifts in each case.)

Event	ΔDemand	ΔSupply
a. Labor productivity rises for producers of X		
b. Price of substitute good rises		
c. Consumer incomes fall (normal good)		
d. Sales tax increases from 0% to 5% rate		
e. Raw material prices decline		
f. Price of complementary good declines		
g. Raw material prices rise		
h. Consumers expect X prices to decline tomorrow		

9. An important objective of chapter 3 is to develop your ability to apply the supply and demand model to various situations. In each of the cases listed below, predict how the equilibrium price or quantity will be affected. (Assume ceteris paribus in each instance.) Fill in the blanks, then compute your score below.

    a. Gasoline is produced from crude oil. When oil prices increase, the quantity of gasoline bought and sold will __.
    b. A decline in the price of VCR players and tapes will __ the price of movie tickets.
    c. If the price of personal computers declines, the price of "floppy" disks will __.
    d. Rising consumer incomes will cause the price of hotdogs, an inferior good, to __.
    e. An increase in IBM computer prices will __ the price of Macintosh computers.
    f. Low rainfall will __ the price of corn, wheat, and other grains.
    g. If airplane tickets become less expensive, the price of gasoline will __.
    h. An increase in the demand for Stradivarius will __ the supply.
    i. A significant decline in the number of births in the U.S. will __ wages in various occupations about 20-25 years later.
    j. A policy that provides subsidies to families that buy homes will cause housing prices to __.

Answers: Rise or increase: c, e, f, i, and j; Fall or decrease: a, b, d, and g; Not affect: h

•If you score 0-5, you've earned the treasured Econowimp rating. Read the chapter again.
•If you score 6-7, you've got what it takes -- to be a C student.
•If you score 8-9, you're almost there. Don't forget that practice makes perfect.
•If you score 10, you're on your way to becoming a Grand Master of Economics. That entitles you to party the night before your next test.

Part 5. Self Test
Multiple choice questions

1. The law of demand states that:

a. price and quantity demanded are inversely related
b. price and quantity demanded are directly related
c. price and quantity demanded are directly related, ceteris paribus
d. price and quantity demanded are inversely related, ceteris paribus

Answer: _____

2. The price of a Toyota is $15,000 and the price of a TV set is $3,000, therefore the relative price of a Toyota is:

a. 5 TV sets
b. 1/5 Toyota
c. 3 TV sets
d. $15,000
e. none of the above

Answer: _____

3. If the absolute price of a big screen TV rises, then the relative price of a big screen TV:

a. falls
b. rises
c. rises, ceteris paribus
d. falls, ceteris paribus
e. none of the above, since there is no relationship between the relative and absolute price of a good

Answer: _____

4. Which of the following statements is true?

a. A demand schedule is the same thing as a demand curve.
b. A downward-sloping demand curve is the graphical representation of the law of demand.
c. Quantity demanded is a relationship between price and demand.
d. "Quantity wanted" comes closer to meaning "quantity demanded" than does "quantity purchased."

Answer: _____

5. In year 1 the price of good X is $20 and the price of good Y is $5. In year 2 the price of good X is $30 and the price of good Y is $15. It follows that:

a. the absolute price of both goods increased but only the relative price of X increased
b. the absolute price of both goods increased but only the relative price of Y increased
c. the absolute price of good X increased and the relative price of good Y decreased
d. the absolute price of good Y increased and the relative price of good Y increased

Answer: _____

6. If W1 is the equilibrium wage rate and W2 is a wage rate above equilibrium, then at W2:

a. there are more people who want to work and more people working than at W1
b. there are fewer people who want to work and more people working than at W1
c. there are fewer people who want to work and fewer people working than at W1
d. there are more people who want to work and fewer people working than at W1

Answer: _____

7. If you have the ability to buy more of a particular good:

a. it necessarily follows that you will buy more of that good
b. it doesn't necessarily follow that you will buy more of that good
c. it necessarily follows that suppliers will produce more of that good
d. it necessarily follows that the price of that good will increase
e. none of the above

Answer: _____

8. If an increase in income leads to an increase in the demand for sausage, then sausage is:

a. an essential good
b. a normal good
c. a luxury good
d. a discretionary good

Answer: _____

9. Which of the following can shift the demand curve rightward?

a. an increase in income
b. an increase in the price of a substitute good
c. a decrease in the price of a complementary good
d. a and b
e. a, b, and c

Answer: _____

10. Which of the following cannot increase the demand for good X?

a. an increase in income
b. a decrease in the price of good X
c. an increase in the price of a substitute good
d. more buyers
e. a change in preferences in favor of good X

Answer: _____

11. The law of supply states that:

a. price and quantity supplied are directly related
b. price and quantity supplied are inversely related
c. price and quantity supplied are inversely related, ceteris paribus
d. price and quantity supplied are directly related, ceteris paribus

Answer: _____

12. A change in the quantity supplied of a good is directly brought about by a:

a. change in the good's own price
b. decrease in income
c. technological advance
d. fall in the price of resources needed to produce the good
e. none of the above

Answer: _____

13. Five dollars is the equilibrium price for good Z. At a price of $2, there is:

a. a shortage
b. a surplus
c. excess supply
d. aggregate demand

Answer: _____

14. If supply rises by a greater amount that demand rises:

a. equilibrium price rises and equilibrium quantity falls
b. equilibrium price falls and equilibrium quantity falls
c. equilibrium price rises and equilibrium quantity rises
d. equilibrium price falls and equilibrium quantity rises

Answer: _____

15. If supply rises and demand is constant:

a. equilibrium price rises and equilibrium quantity falls
b. equilibrium price falls and equilibrium quantity falls
c. equilibrium price rises and equilibrium quantity rises
d. equilibrium price falls and equilibrium quantity rises

Answer: _____

True-False

16. If the absolute price of a good rises, it   T F
necessarily follows that the relative price of the
good rises, too.

17. Demand is more important to the determination   T F
of price than supply.

18. At the equilibrium price for good X, good X is   T F
scarce.

19. Quantity supplied is a specific amount of a   T F
good, such as 50 units of good Y.

20. There is a tendency for price to rise when the   T F
quantity demanded of a good is greater than the
quantity supplied.

Fill in the blank

21. As price rises, quantity demanded _____ and quantity supplied
_____ .

22. A _____ is any arrangement by which people exchange goods and services.

23. If Harry's demand for motorcycles rises as his income falls, then motorcyles are a(n)
_____ good for Harry.

24. If demand rises more than supply falls, then equilibrium quantity _____ .

25. At equilibrium, the quantity demanded of a good _____ the
quantity supplied of the good.

Part 5. Answers to Self Test

1. d 2. a 3. c 4. b 5. b 6. d 7. b 8. b 9. e 10. b
11. d 12. a 13. a 14. d 15. d
16. F 17. F 18. T 19. T 20. T
21. falls, rises 22. market 23. inferior 24. increases
25. equals

Part 6.   Answers

Part 2. Review of Concepts
1. f 2. g 3. e 4. b 5. c 6. a 7.d

Part 3. Key Concepts in this Chapter
1. market 2. more, quantity demanded 3. supply 4. shortage 5. relative price
6. normal, inferior 7. Marshall 8. complements, more 9. surplus 10. rise   11. equals
12. market   13. more, quantity supplied 14. right 15. increase
16. vertical 17. $65k 18. fall, fall 19. fall, rise 20. impossible to say w/o more information

Part 4. Problems and Exercises
1. D2 is to the right of D1; D3 is to the left of D1.
2. S2 is to the right of S1; S3 is to the left of S1
3. Supply shifts left 3 units, demand shifts left by 1 unit. Price rises and quantity falls. No. Price would
    have fallen if the decrease in demand had been larger than the decrease in supply. The actual change in
    price is determined by the relative size of the two shifts.
4. 2, 1/2
5. C,U,S,C,C,S
6. 1 @ $10, 3 @ $8, 6 @ $6, 9 @ $4, 11 @ $2
7. Cross out everything starting with "But higher prices reduce demand. . ." They don't.
8. increase supply: a,e,   increase demand: b,f   decrease supply: d,g   decrease demand: c,h

Chapter 4
Supply, Demand, and Price: Applications

Part 1. Introduction and Purpose
Consider the following points as you read chapter 4 in the text.

The supply and demand model developed in chapter 3 provides a useful framework for looking at trading agreements between utility-maximizing consumers and profit-maximizing sellers. Properly applied, it is one of the most powerful tools available for analyzing the effects of various government policies and natural events.

In almost every application of the supply-and-demand model, the analysis is *triggered* by one of three events. Either **demand shifts, supply shifts,** or something happens to **prevent price from adjusting** to reflect market conditions. The first two events cause the market to move from one equilibrium to another, with corresponding changes in prices, profits, and production. In the third case, the market is prevented from adjusting to equilibrium, so shortages or surpluses result. As you read each application and as you consider your own experiences with supply and demand, *consciously* ask yourself which of these three things originally triggered the problem or situation you want to analyze.

Once you can say, "This situation was triggered by a shift in demand," or "That law is making it impossible for the price of corn to decline below a certain level," then you are on your way to developing an intuition into the way markets work. The same analysis applies to a number of situations, so there really are only a few theoretical tools to remember. Other details of the case being analyzed — specifics about the identity of the buyer or seller, the nation where exchange takes place, the product being traded, and so forth — are of secondary importance for our purposes. Rising demand implies a rising price, and seldom will the details of a particular situation change that result.

What the details of a situation can do however, is divert your attention from the question posed above: Did demand shift, did supply shift, or did something prevent price from adjusting to equilibrium? In economics as in sports, you've got to keep your eye on the ball.

Aside from the impact of shifting curves or that of price inflexibilities, chapter 4 also raises another important issue. With millions of buyers and sellers all pursuing their own self interest, *there is a need for some mechanism to make the actions of a large number of people consistent with the actions of others.* If eight million people want to eat dinner in New York City tonight, there must be some way of ensuring that food is sent there, and moreover that just the right amount is sent to each restaurant and each grocery store. A coordinating mechanism is needed.

While economists once debated whether a large computer filled with vast amounts of information could perform this function, it is now fairly apparent that a computer or any other form of centralized control of the economy provides an inferior method of allocating goods and resources to their highest valued uses. Even if the problem were not far larger than any computer could manage, few people would be willing to surrender their freedom to the decisions of a computer when they prefer to do something else. This is one of the major lessons learned from the Soviet Union's 70-year experience with central planning.

In practice, the "price mechanism" is a very efficient allocator of resources. A shortage of some good will cause its price to rise, but higher **prices signal producers** that they should increase output and signal **customers** that they should reduce consumption. These actions make more of the good available than before, and make it possible to cope with whatever created the original shortage. Prices fall during periods of surplus, and the ways buyers and sellers react to lower prices help eliminate the surplus.

Not only are shortages filled and surplusses eliminated by the price mechanism — equally significant is the fact that no buyer or seller may even be aware of what originally caused the shortage or surplus. One can react to a rising price without knowing what caused it to rise, and that's usually how things work in our economy. Unlike a centrally planned economy then, there is no need for anyone to collect large amounts of information before the proper reaction can be formulated. The **price mechanism economizes on information**, so the economy operates more smoothly and at lower cost.

Part 2. Review of Concepts from Earlier Chapters
Prior to reading chapter 4, match statements at left with the appropriate concept at right.

__1. Exchanges between buyers and sellers occur here.	a. change in demand
__2. Changes in these cause supply curve to shift.	b. change in quantity demanded
__3. Market price tends to move toward this.	c. change in quantity supplied
__4. Rising prices discourage consumption.	d. equilibrium
__5. For these goods consumption rises when income rises.	e. market
__6. What results when price is held above equilibrium.	f. shortage
__7. Higher prices cause greater production.	g. surplus
__8. Consumption falls when consumer income rises.	h. resource prices
__9. Price is held below equilibrium.	i. inferior good
__10. If consumer tastes change.	j. normal good

Part 3. Key Concepts in this Chapter
After reading chapter 4 in the text, answer the following questions.

1. An effective price ceiling maintains the price of a good _above / below_ its equilibrium level.

2. _Production / rationing / consuming_ is used to decide who will receive scarce goods.

3. A higher _____ signals companies to increase output in a market economy

4. A price _floor / ceiling_ can create a shortage.

5. If tolls were used to reduce freeway congestion, they would be highest during what part of the day? _____ When would tolls be lowest? _____

6. The minimum wage is an example of a price _floor / ceiling_ applied to the market for labor.

7. If a price _floor / ceiling_ causes a shortage of some good, non-_____ _____ devices are used to decide who gets the available quantity.

8._____ were once used as money in a World War II Prisoner-of-War camp.

9. Price _____ for agricultural products result in surplusses. The government incurs additional expenses when it has to _____ the surplus.

10. A surplus of labor is called _____.

11. If a price ceiling is _above / below_ the equilibrium price, it will not affect the market's operation.

12. A _____ _____ is an illegal market.

13. _____ transmit information to buyers and sellers regarding shortages and surplusses, and provide them an incentive to help _enlarge / reduce_ the shortage or surplus.

14. Markets that rely on nonprice rationing devices necessarily treat people more fairly than those that use price as the sole rationing device. _true / false_

15. A surplus exists when _____ supplied exceeds quantity _____.

16. A price _floor / ceiling_ can create a waiting line of customers.

17. To avoid losing too many students, a college that increases its tuition by a large amount may decide to _raise / lower_ its SAT and ACT admission requirements.

18. Price floors and price ceilings _increase / reduce_ the quantity of exchange between buyers and sellers.

19. The price ceiling on gasoline and oil in the 1970s _increased / reduced_ the amount of fuel desired by consumers. Did prices signal consumers that oil was in short supply in the '70s? _yes / no_

20. The existence of an ongoing surplus in the market for X suggests that a price _floor / ceiling_ is preventing the market price from _rising / falling_ toward equilibrium.

Part 4. Problems and Exercises
After reading chapter 4 in the text you should be able to work the following problems.

1. The text pointed out that there is a shortage of good seats in Las Vegas showrooms, and that as a result patrons offer tips to be seated in desirable locations. Suppose tips were prohibited,while ticket prices remained unchanged. Then who do you think would be most likely to receive the best seats? (To answer this question, suppose you are the showroom employee who actually assigns seats. Who would you place in the best seats?)_____
_____
_____

2. In the diagram at right, suppose a $2 price ceiling is imposed on the market for good X.

   a. Show the new quantity supplied and quantity demanded. Label them Q1 and Q2, respectively.

   b. What quantity will actually be exchanged in the marketplace in this instance? Q1 / Q2 .

   c. In this case there is a surplus / shortage.

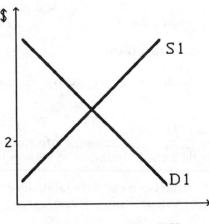

Quantity of Good X

3. In the diagram at right, suppose a $40 price floor is imposed on the market for good X.

   a. Show the new quantity supplied and quantity demanded. Label them Q1 and Q2, respectively.

   b. What quantity will actually be exchanged in the marketplace in this instance? Q1 / Q2 .

   c. In this case there is a surplus / shortage.

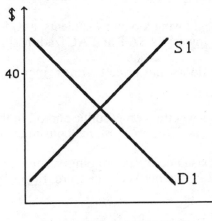

Quantity of Good X

4. Refer to the previous two exercises. Price floors and price ceilings _____ the quantity of goods actually exchanged in the marketplace compared to the equilibrium quantity.
   a) increase   b) decrease   c) do not affect

5. List 2 places on your campus where prices are not used to ration scarce goods. Do shortages arise in these areas? (Briefly explain.)
Example: Classroom space for next semester is rationed to seniors first, freshmen last. Freshmen often can't get in the best classes at the best time of the day, which implies a shortage.
   a._____

   _____

   b._____

   _____

6. Suppose the government eliminates a number of tax laws. It has previously required 20,000 full-time accountants to comply with these laws.

a. This law causes the <u>supply / demand</u> curve to shift to the <u>right / left</u>.

b. Draw the new demand curve in the graph and label the curve D2.

c. Label the original equilibrium price (wage) and quantity P1 and Q1. Label the new price and quantity P2 and Q2.

d. How will the wage change affect college students who are selecting a college major?
_____

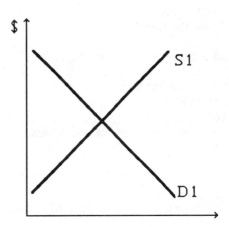

Number of Accountants

7. What fundamental economic "problem" makes the rationing of goods necessary? _____
What other ways besides price can be used to ration goods?_____
_____

Are these other methods less cruel or dehumanizing than rationing goods to the highest bidder? (Explain your answer.)_____
_____

8. At many colleges there is a shortage of classroom space during "prime time" (mid morning to early afternoon) and a surplus of classroom space in the late afternoon and evening. Describe the tuition policy that would induce students to take more afternoon and evening classes, and fewer prime time classes: _____

9. In August 1971, President Nixon imposed a wage and price "freeze" that prohibited increases in workers' pay or in the prices of most consumer goods. In the space provided at right, show how the price freeze would affect a market that was originally in equilibrium, but which later experienced an increase in demand. <u>Show:</u>

a) the initial equilibrium price and label it P1
b) the shift on demand, and label the new curve D2
c) quantities demanded and supplied after demand shifts to D2, and label them Q1 and Q2 respectfully.

How do you describe the situation?_____
_____

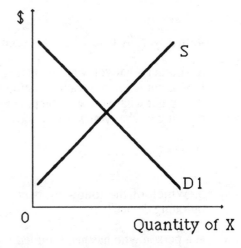

Quantity of X

10. Airport runways are particularly congested with takeoffs and landings during some times of the day, but much less crowded at other times. How might landing and takeoff fees for planes be changed to reduce the shortage of runway space during high-demand periods, and to convince some travelers to fly at different times of the day?_____
_____

Part 5. Self Test
Multiple choice questions

1. Which of the following statements is false?

a. Prices transmit information.
b. Wants are limited.
c. Resources are limited.
d. Prices ration scarce resources and goods.

Answer: _____

2. Which of the following could be used as a rationing device?

a. brute force
b. price
c. religion
d. a and b
e. a, b, and c

Answer: _____

3. If need were the rationing device, which of the following problems would likely arise?

a. there would be little incentive to produce
b. there would be disagreements over what people need
c. there would be disagreements over who or what would determine need
d. a, b, and c

Answer: _____

4. In a world where religion is used as a rationing device:

a. you get what you want by taking what you want from others
b. you get what you want by being the "right" religion as determined by those persons in power
c. you get what you want by paying people with money
d. you get what you want by showing other people how smart you are

Answer: _____

5. Which of the following persons would be least likely to prefer first-come-first-served (FCFS) as a rationing device?

a. a person who has just returned from visiting a busy city
b. a person who has just returned from visiting a small town
c. a person with low opportunity cost of time
d. a person with high opportunity cost of time

Answer: _____

6. Which of the following statements is true?

a. All societies use rationing devices because scarcity exists in all societies.
b. Price serves as a rationing device.
c. All societies use rationing devices because it is usually mandated by government.
d. a and b
e. a and c

Answer: _____

7. Suppose bad weather in California wipes out one-quarter of the orange crop. As a result, the price of oranges rises. The rising price of oranges conveys what information?

a. that the gap between people's wants for oranges and the amount of oranges available to satisfy those wants has widened
b. that the gap between people's wants for oranges and the amount of oranges available to satisfy those wants has narrowed
c. that people do not like oranges as much as they once did
d. that people like oranges more than they once did

Answer: _____

8. At a price ceiling (below equilibrium price):

a. there is a surplus
b. quantity supplied is greater than quantity demanded
c. quantity demanded equals quantity supplied
d. supply equals demand
e. quantity demanded is greater than quantity supplied

Answer: _____

9. Which of the following effects may occur as a result of a price ceiling?

a. fewer exchanges
b. an increase in supply
c. an increase in demand
d. a surplus
e. a and c

Answer: _____

10. Because of a price ceiling on lightbulbs, the quantity demanded of lightbulbs exceeds the quantity supplied. The owner of lightbulbs decides to sell them on a first-come-first-served basis. This is an example of:

a. a surplus
b. a tie-in sale
c. a nonprice rationing device
d. a black market
e. none of the above

Answer: _____

11. Which of the following statements is true?

a. Price ceilings cause surpluses.
b. Shortages cause price ceilings to be imposed.
c. Neither a price ceiling nor a shortage is an effect of the other.
d. Price ceilings cannot be imposed for longer than a week.
e. none of the above

Answer: _____

12. The minimum wage is an example of a(n):

a. price floor
b. price ceiling
c. equilibrium wage
d. subequilibrium wage

Answer: _____

13. One of the consequences of the minimum wage is:

a. fewer people will work than at the equilibrium wage
b. some members of the unskilled labor market earn higher wages
c. there is a surplus of labor
d. a and c
e. a, b, and c

Answer: _____

14. Driving on a non-toll freeway comes with:

a. a cost and zero money price
b. zero cost and (positive) money price
c. a cost and a (positive) money price
d. zero cost and zero money price

Answer: _____

15. At University X, the tuition that students pay is below the equilibrium level. We can expect:

a. a shortage of places at the university and some nonprice rationing device (such as GPAs, etc.) being used to decide who gets one of the available spaces at the university
b. a surplus of places at the university and some nonprice rationing device (such as SATs, etc.) being used to decide who gets one of the available spaces at the university
c. unusually nice instructors at the university
d. unusually rude instructors at the university
e. a and c

Answer: _____

True-False

16. A rationing device serves to determine who gets   T F
what of the available limited resources and goods.

17. All rationing devices will benefit some people   T F
more than others.

18. A price ceiling is a government-mandated minimum   T F
price below which legal trades cannot be made.

19. One of the effects of a price floor (above   T F
equilibrium price) is that higher quality goods are
produced.

20. In a competitive labor market, the wage rate is   T F
determined by the government deciding who should be
paid what amount.
Fill in the blank

21. The number of persons who want to work at the minimum wage is _____ than the number of persons who want to work at the equilibrium wage.

22. Price acts to transmit _____ and _____
resources and goods.

23. In the article by R.A. Radford about a POW camp, _____ were used as money.

24. First-come-first-served is an example of a _____ rationing device.

25. Suppose you live in New York City and are required to rent the furniture in an apartment before you can rent the apartment. This is described as a _____ sale.

Part 5. Answers to Self Test.

1. b 2. e 3. d 4. b 5. d 6. d 7. a 8. e 9. a 10. c
11. e 12. a 13. e 14. a 15. a
16. T 17. T 18. F 19. F 20. F
21. higher 22. information, ration 23. cigarettes
24. nonprice 25. tie-in

Part 6. Answers

Part 2 Review of Concepts
1. e   2. h   3. d   4. b   5. j   6. g   7. c   8. i   9. f   10. a

Part 3. Key Concepts in the Chapter
1. below   2. rationing   3. price   4. ceiling   5. rush hours, late night   6. floor
7. ceiling, nonprice rationing   8. cigarettes   9. supports (floors), stores   10. unemployment
11. above   12. black market   13. prices, reduce   14. false   15. quantity, demanded
16. ceiling   17. lower   18. reduce   19. increased, no   20. floor, falling

Part 4. Problems and Exercises
1. Friends, family, those offering bribes or favors, people you like being around
2. Q2>Q1. The quantity sold is Q1, since sellers will not send any more than Q1 to market at P=$2.
   Shortage.
3. Q1>Q2. The quantity sold is Q2, since consumers will not buy any more than Q2 to market at P=$40.
   Surplus.
4. decrease
5. student clinic, parking spaces, library books
6. a. demand, left
      b-c. The equilibrium wage and employment level decline due to the shift in demand.
      d. Some accounting students will interpret falling wages as a signal to major in other subjects.
7. scarcity; political preference, religious preference, good looks, friendly personality, first-come first-
   served, physical strength, alphabetical order of last name. Many of these methods make it impossible
   for the average person to acquire desired goods and services, while rationing by price permits anyone
   with the required number of dollars to have whatever they would like.
8. Raise fees during prime time, lower fees at other times.
9. A shortage will develop at the original price level.
10. Raise landing and takeoff fees during rush hours, lower them at other times.

Chapter 5
Macroeconomic Issues

Part 1. Introduction and Purpose
Consider the following points as you read chapter 5 in the text.

Chapter 5 is the first of several chapters that examine the operation of the macroeconomy -- the economy as a whole. Macroeconomists look at broad trends in the economy that influence most industries in the same general way. An economic recession is bad for the automobile industry, but it is also bad for the construction industry and banking. To some extent, all share the same macroeconomic fate. Decisions to change production and price are important at the microeconomic level, but so are macroeconomic conditions which often influence a person's situation as much as ability, ambition, and hard work.

The average citizen's common-sense understanding of economics is often fairly accurate. It seems reasonable that an increase in taxes would slow down the pace of economic activity, and in fact it would. In many instances however, amateur macroeconomists get lost in the issues by falling prey to the **fallacy of composition** and other logical errors. You will recall that the fallacy of composition is a flawed way of thinking, the result of automatically concluding that "what is true for the parts" of the economy are also "true for the whole" economy. Because macroeconomics is more than just adding together a large number of microeconomic markets, conclusions drawn from everyday (microeconomic) experiences often provide a bad guide for macroeconomic policy.

For example, below-normal normal rainfall in the midwest depressed the production of many crops by up to one-fourth in 1988. With supplies falling, food prices rose rapidly. It seems obvious that bad weather was a cause of price inflation that year.

Obvious perhaps, but not necessarily correct. What is true for part of the economy (wheat) is not necessarily true for the entire economy. If rising food prices mean customers pay more to grocers, food processors, and farmers, then consumers have *fewer* dollars than before to spend on other goods.

Do you see it coming? If consumers spend less on non-food goods, there is downward pressure on their prices. The net effect may be for the overall price level -- the price of crops averaged in with the prices of all other goods -- to show little if any change due to the drought. Relative prices would be different than before, but if the overall price level is unchanged the bad weather wasn't inflationary.

The amateur economist's problem was forgetting to look outside the food market to see what **secondary or longer-run effects** rising wheat prices might have. The macroeconomist cannot afford to overlook these wider effects.

We're all familiar with a few phrases like unemployment, inflation, and economic growth -- all macroeconomic issues. But familiarity with terms does not mean familiarity with the workings of the economy. We live our lives in the microeconomy -- looking for jobs, buying breakfast cereal, selling a used car -- so our everyday experience may not be a very good guide for understanding macroeconomic phenomena. It is not always a bad guide either. Each case has to be examined individually.

There are important differences between macro- and microeconomic problems which require the use of distinct **theories** and in many cases a different **vocabulary**. And as suggested before, macroeconomic analysis may lead to conclusions that clash with ideas formed during a lifetime of transacting in the microeconomy.

Chapter 5 in your text was written with all of this in mind. As you read the chapter it is less important for you to memorize details from the charts and tables than to see the **turning points** and **trends** which they illustrate. Notice that many of the topics raised in the chapter — the business cycle, the federal budget deficit, the general price level — are outside your own personal experience, although you may have been hearing or reading about them for many years. Finally, pay attention to the **links** (or relationships) between some macroeconomic conditions and others. Later chapters in the text will develop theories to explain *how* a rising money supply can cause prices to increase, or *how* higher taxes may lead to a recession.

Part 2. Review of Concepts from Earlier Chapters
Prior to reading chapter 5, match statements at left with the appropriate concept at right.

__1. Rightward shift in the production possibilities frontier.   a. ceteris paribus
__2. A surplus of workers at the current wage.   b. fallacy of composition
__3. The level toward which price gravitates.   c. money
__4. Event A may precede B without having caused it.   d. opportunity cost
__5. To attain one goal it is necessary to sacrifice another.   e. economic growth
__6. What is true of the parts is true of the whole.   f. association not causation
__7. Something generally used to buy other goods.   g. unemployment
__8. Assuming other things remain unchanged.   h. equilibrium

Part 3. Key Concepts in this Chapter
After reading chapter 5 in the text, answer the following questions.

1. As the economy expands from its low point, reaches a peak, and returns to another low it has gone through one business _____.

2. Sometimes policy makers _____-off more inflation for a reduction in the amount of unemployment.

3. Government taxing and spending policies are called monetary / fiscal / trade policy.

4. The top of a business cycle is known as its _____; the bottom, as its _____.

5. A weighted average of a basket of goods is a price _____.
6. When government spends more than its tax revenues it runs a budget surplus / deficit .

7. The _____ rate is the percent of the labor force seeking but not finding jobs.

8. Keynesian macroeconomics stresses the use of monetary / fiscal policy to stabilize the economy.

9. Economists who believe the national money supply exerts a strong influence on economic conditions are known as ____ _____.

10. John Maynard _____ wrote *The General Theory of Employment, Interest, and Money* in 1936.

11. If a particular economic statistic moves in one general direction for a long time, a _____ is established.

12. A budget surplus implies that government <u>receipts / expenditures</u> exceed <u>receipts / expenditures</u>.

13. A _____ _____ philosophy says that government should play a minimal role in the economy.

14. The _____ _____ conducts U.S. monetary policy.

15. A two-quarter decline in national output is often referred to as an economic _____.

16. Between 1800 and 1940, the general price level trended <u>up / down / in neither direction</u>.

17. During the past generation, interest rates have reached their highest point when the inflation was <u>higher than average / lower than average / about average</u>.

18. Keynesian economists believe that the economy may in equilibrium even though a substantial amount of <u>employment / unemployment</u> exists.

19. More inflationary policies may not help reduce the unemployment rate in the <u>long / short</u> run.

20. Two statistical measures of the money supply are M-___ and M-___.

Part 4. Problems and Exercises
After reading chapter 5 in the text you should be able to work the following problems.

1. Examine exhibit 5-5 in the text (regarding the federal budget deficit). When does it appear that policy makers adopted the view that federal budget deficits aren't such a bad thing for the economy?

Identify 3 periods:
a) deficits are undesirable   prior to 19____
b) transition period   19____ - 19____
c) deficits are acceptable   after about 19____

2. The table below shows the number of people working in the U.S. between 1978 and 1987 (employment in millions). Graph these figures in the grid at right.

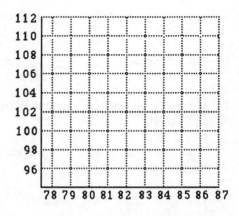

Year	Employment
1978	96.0
1979	98.8
1980	99.3
1981	100.4
1982	99.5
1983	100.8
1984	105.0
1985	107.2
1986	109.6
1987	112.4

3. Refer to your diagram for exercise 2. Total employment reached a <u>trough</u> in 19____. Total employment reached a <u>peak</u> in 19____. Does 1987 qualify as a trough or peak year? _____

4. Examine exhibit 5-1 in the text. What general impression do you get about the US inflation rate during:
        a) the Civil War (1860s)   _____
        b) the Great Depression (1930s)   _____
        c) World War II (mid 1940s)   _____
        d) the 1960s and 1970s   _____
        e) the 1980s   _____

5. In enacting the Employment Act of 1946, Congress pledged to stabilize the economy, including the unemployment rate (which it would prevent from rising to unacceptable levels). Examine exhibit 5-2 and describe the unemployment rate's general trend since 1946._____

6. Two of the nation's leading macroeconomic goals are price stability and full employment. What do exhibits 5-1 and 5-2 indicate about the overall performance of the economy since passage of the Employment Act of 1946?_____

Part 5. Self Test
Multiple choice questions

1. What does it mean if someone says there is no particular trend in the price level between year 1 and 100?

a. It means that the price level was the same in each year 1 through 100.
b. It means that the price level was lower each year than the previous year.
c. It means that the price level was higher each year than the previous year.
d. It means that the price level might have gone up in some years and down in other years, but on average over the 100 years it did not exhibit any noticeable rise or fall.

Answer: _____

2. Which of the following statements is false?

a. From one year to the next, there is more likely to be a tradeoff between unemployment and inflation than over a period of 10 years.
b. The unemployment rate has trended downward since the late 1940s.
c. Between 1900 and 1947 there was no distinct trend in the unemployment rate.
d. b and c
e. none of the above

Answer: _____

3. Someone observes that high inflation rates are associated with high interest rates. From this he or she knows:

a. that high inflation rates cause high interest rates
b. that high interest rates cause high inflation rates
c. that both high inflation rates and high interest rates are effects of some other factor
d. nothing more than that high inflation rates are associated with high interest rates

Answer: _____

4. The federal budget has been in deficit in each year starting with:

a. 1964
b. 1970
c. 1975
d. 1981

Answer: _____

5. The federal budget is balanced when:

a. federal government expenditures outstrip tax receipts
b. federal government tax receipts outstrip expenditures
c. fiscal policy is in effect
d. federal government expenditures equal tax receipts
e. none of the above

Answer: _____

6. A recession is:

a. an increase in real output that lasts for two consecutive months
b. an increase in real output that lasts for six consecutive months
c. a decrease in real output that lasts for two consecutive months
d. a decrease in real output that lasts for twelve consecutive months
e. none of the above

Answer: _____

7. Which of the following statements is true?

a. A business cycle is sometimes called a business trough.
b. There appears to be no relationship between recessions and political developments.
c. The United States has experienced no more than 5 recessions since 1865.
d. A business cycle is defined as the recurrent swings in the level of (general) economic activity.

Answer: _____

8. The budget deficit and inflation rate are:

a. directly related
b. inversely related
c. independent
d. sometimes directly related and sometimes inversely related

Answer: _____

9. The economist cited in the text who has argued that the central issue in macroeconomic theory is the extent to which the economy, or at least its market sectors, may properly be regarded as a self-regulating system is:

a. Axel Leijonhufvud
b. Milton Friedman
c. John Maynard Keynes
d. Anna Schwartz

Answer: _____

10. The institution that has the ability to change the nation's money supply is the:

a. Congress
b. U.S. Treasury
c. Supreme Court
d. governors of different states
e. Federal Reserve System

Answer: _____

True-False

11. John Maynard Keynes wrote A Monetary History of   T F
the United States, 1867-1960.

12. Monetarists stress the importance of the money   T F
supply when discussing the economy.

13. Fiscal policy is concerned with government   T F
spending and taxation.

14. Keynesian economists are more likely than   T F
monetarists to advocate laissez-faire.

15. John Maynard Keynes was responsible for the   T F
revolution in economic thinking that occurred during
the 1930s.

Fill in the blank

16. _____ is best described as a government policy of
noninterference with market activities.

17. A revolution in economic thinking occurred in the 1960s as a result of the monetary research of
_____ .

18. Keynesian economists feel that stabilization policies should focus on _____ policy.

19. A _____ occurs when federal government expenditures outstrip tax receipts.

20. The _____ is the weighted average of the prices of all goods and services in the economy.

Part 5. Answers to Self Test.

1. d 2. b 3. d 4. b 5. d 6. e 7. d 8. d 9. a 10. e
11. F 12. T 13. T 14. F 15. T
16. Laissez-faire 17. Milton Friedman 18. fiscal
19. budget deficit 20. price level

Part 6. Answers

Part 2 Review of Concepts
1. e   2. g   3. h   4. f   5. d   6. b   7. c   8. a

Part 3 Key Concepts
1. cycle   2. trade-off   3. fiscal   4. peak, trough   5. level   6. deficit   7. unemployment rate
8. fiscal   9. monetarists   10. Keynes   11. trend   12. receipts, expenditures   13. laissez faire
14. Federal Reserve ("Fed")   15. recession   16. in neither direction   17. higher
18. unemployment   19. long   20. M1, M2

Part 4 Problems and Exercises

1. a) prior to about 1960   b) 1960-70   c) after about 1970
2. See graph at right
3. 1982, 1981, no (the rise hadn't ended in '87)
4. a) high inflation   b) deflation   c) very high inflation
   d) inflation e) moderating inflation
5. the unemployment rate has trended upward
6. Both unemployment and prices have increased
    significantly since 1946.

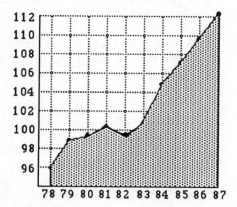

Chapter 6
Macroeconomic Measurements

Part 1. Introduction and Purpose
Consider the following points as you read chapter 6 in the text.

What would a picture of the macroeconomy look like? The first half of chapter 6 presents several snapshots of major sectors of the economy and the transactions between them. Each transaction has **real goods** or resources moving in one direction (from seller to buyer), and **money** moving in t'.. other (from buyer to seller) -- so in the end money and real goods **circulate** through the economy in opposite directions.

These dollars don't remain in their new destination for long. If received by businesses, they are used to hire additional resources and expand production. If received by households, they are spent for consumption goods or put to some other use (such as paying taxes). The actions of one sector influence the others, and they in turn influence it. All of this is indirectly related to the supply and demand model we discussed in chapters 3 and 4. Where supply and demand described the operation of individual markets, the **circular flow** diagrams in chapter 6 show how the different markets are connected.

The circular flow model also shows how government, the Federal Reserve, and foreign producers and consumers are able to influence the private economy. By injecting themselves into the flow, their decisions may either speed up the flow of dollars or slow it down -- often with noticeable effects on employment, prices, and income.

Speaking of which, the second part of chapter 6 defines and discusses the most commonly used measures of economic activity. You have undoubtedly noticed one or more of these measures in the news -- does **Gross National Product** (GNP) sound familiar?

If you've always wondered what the GNP actually measures, you're in luck. Chapter 6 points out that GNP is the most comprehensive measure of U.S. economic activity, and includes the market value of all final goods produced during the year. In practice there are two methods of measuring GNP that yield identical answers-the **expenditure approach** and the **income approach**. The value of total production (which we want to measure) equals total spending for newly produced goods, and it also equals the total amount of income earned by owners of the factors of production and others who have a claim on the sellers' revenues.

Throughout the chapter it is important to keep the distinction clear in your mind between **stock** and **flow** concepts. As used here, a stock is an outstanding quantity of something measured at a point in time -- such as the number of shirts or blouses currently in your closet. While this number reveals something about your wardrobe, it does not reveal how modern and fashionable it is. How many new shirts or blouses have you added to your wardrobe this year? Flows refer to changes or events that occur over time, a "moving picture" rather than a snapshot.

It is the flow of newly produced goods,services, and income that we will mainly concern ourselves with in future chapters, rather than the stock of homes and cars accumulated in past years. Since we desire goods and services daily (food, clothing, shelter, transportation), our national prosperity hinges on the ability to produce a continuing flow of output. No matter how great our existing stock of wealth may be, it will eventually be consumed if nothing is done to augment it on a daily basis. For these reasons, policy makers and economists typically pay more attention to the flow of income and production (GNP, disposable income) than to other measures of economic well-being (such as national wealth).

Finally, chapter 6 examines some of the procedures used to construct a **price index**, an average price level for a "basket" of goods. In this instance two baskets are priced -- one containing the goods consumed by the typical urban household, the other containing a broad sample of all final goods produced in the economy. The price of the former is widely known as the **consumer price index**, while the price of the latter is the GNP **price deflator**. Among other things, these indexes indicate whether a speed-up in economic activity (a rising GNP) is due to rising prices (bad) or to real increases in annual production (good).

Although chapter 6 introduces several new concepts, it is absolutely essential that you learn the vocabulary of macroeconomics now, before moving on to study macroeconomic theories. To meaningfully discuss whether a particular policy is inflationary or likely to stimulate household consumtion, one must first have an idea what inflation and consumption refer to.

Part 2.   Review of Concepts from Earlier Chapters
Prior to reading chapter 6, match statements at left with the appropriate concept at right.

__1. An outward shift in the production possibilities frontier.	a. capital good
__2. The average level of prices for a given basket of goods.	b. recession
__3. Used to produce goods and services.	c. fiscal policy
__4. Two-quarter decline in real output.	d. economic growth
__5. Non-human factor of production.	e. price index
__6. Government spending and taxing policies.	f. factor of production

Part 3.   Key Concepts in this Chapter
After reading chapter 6 in the text, answer the following questions.

1. A more official-sounding term for the value of capital goods lost due to depreciation while being used to produce other goods is called the _____ _____ allowance.

2. The total market value of all final goods and services produced in the economy this year is the _____ _____ product. If this same production is expressed in terms of prices prevailing in some benchmark (base) year, it is referred to as _____ GNP.

3. In the circular flow diagran, the value of total output produced equals total _____ earned by the factors of production.

4. In the national income accounts, corporate profits are / are not regarded as a payment to a factor of production.

5. As economists use the term, which of these qualifies as "investment spending"?
   a. buy corporate bonds
   b. purchase computer for office
   c. buy gold on the expectation that its price will increase

6. The _____ price index is a price index for a basket of goods purchased by urban households.

7. The price _____ for GNP is a price index for a basket that contains all final goods produced in the U.S.

8. Which of the following utilizes a stock measure and which utilizes a flow measure?
   a. I have ten shirts in my closet. Stock / Flow
   b. I earned $300 this week. Stock / Flow
   c. The money supply is about $800 billion. Stock / Flow
   d. Ford will produce 1.5 million cars this year. Stock / Flow

9. _____ payments are payments to someone for which no good or services are given in return.

10. Disposable income minus spending for consumption goods equals _____.

11. The illegal economy is also called the _____ economy.

12. True or false? _____ Net national product is occasionally greater than GNP.

13. The two approaches used to compute GNP are the _____ approach and the _____ approach.

14. The Measure of _____ _____ is a measure of economic well being.

15. The underground economy tends to become larger as income tax rates are raised / lowered .

16. The underground economy in the U.S. is estimated at about _____% of gross national product.

17. The expenditure approach to calculating Gross National Product calls for summing (adding) consumption, gross _____, government _____, and net _____.

18. _____ income consists of all payments to the suppliers of the factors of production.

19. "Net taxes" equal taxes minus _____ payments.

20. Net exports equal _____ minus _____.

21. _____ of employees is the largest component of national income, contributing about 73% to the total.

22. True or false? _____ National income must exceed Personal Income.

23. True or false? _____ Transfer payments to individuals are not included in the spending flow called "government expenditures."

24. According to Deputy Barney Fife, gypsies are _____.

Part 4. Problems and Exercises
After reading chapter 6 in the text you should be able to work the following problems.

1. An important objective of chapter 6 is to develop your ability to identify income and expenditure flows that are included in the economy's Gross National Product (GNP) In each of the cases listed below, indicate whether the income or expenditure contributes to GNP.
Mark Y for yes and N for no in the blanks provided at left, then compute your score below.

___ a. $2000 paid for a used car
___ b. Unemployment compensation
___ c. Daily newspaper
___ d. Crops sold by farms with less than $10,000 in annual sales
___ e. Earnings of the president of the U.S.
___ f. Corporate profits
___ g. $8 paid to a barber for a haircut
___ h. A $5 million stock purchase
___ i. $1 million worth of timber used to produce lumber used in home construction
___ j. Marijuana sold by foreign producers to U.S. consumers
___ k. Marijuana sold by U.S. producers to U.S. consumers
___ l. Intermediate goods

Answers : Yes (c,d,e,f,g) No (a,b,h,i,j,k,l)
•If your score was 0-6, you probably haven't read the chapter yet. If you have, try reading it again with your stereo turned off
•If you scored 7-8, don't despair. You may still earn that C.
•If you scored 9-11, you've been paying attention. Pay a little more and that A may be yours.
•If you scored 12, the Commerce Department could use your talents. Tell them we sent you.

2. Use the following figures to compute national income first, then calculate the other income and product measures indicated at right.

Compensation of emplyees	1050	National income =
Social insurance (Social Security) taxes	105	
Corporate profits	120	Personal income =
Transfer payments	102	
Personal taxes	204	Disposable income =
Indirect business taxes (incl. statistical discrepancy)	71	
Corporate profits taxes	20	Net National Product =
Capital consumption allowance (depreciation)	90	
Undistributed profits	10	Gross National Product =
Net interest income	20	
Proprietor's income	55	
Rental income	60	

3. In 1986, the Texas share of gross national product was equal to $303.5 billion. The Texas population that year was 16.7 million. According to these figures, per capita GNP in Texas was $_____.

4. Match the descriptions on your left with the appropriate concepts at right.
   ___Income received by households, whether earned or not.
   ___Income earned by the owners of the factors of production.
   ___Total output of all final goods & services during the year.
   ___After-tax (spendable) income.
   ___Total production minus the value of capital goods used up in production.

   a. GNP
   b. NNP
   c. NI
   d. PI
   e. DI

5. The following data were published in a recent issue of the Survey of Current Business (from the U.S. Commerce Department; all figures in billions of dollars). Use this information to compute the income measures called for at right.

Personal consumption expenditures	3128
Indirect business taxes (incl. statistical discrepancy)	375
Gross private domestic investment	763
Government purchases of goods & services	945
Total exports of goods & services	488
Compensation of employees	2816
Total imports of goods & services	600
Capital consumption allowance	498
Personal saving	150

Net exports = _____

GNP = _____

NNP = _____

National income = _____

6. Suppose the typical basket of goods purchased by urban consumers in the base year costs $245, while it costs $261 to purchase the same basket in the following year. In this second year the consumer price index (CPI) equals _____.

7. Suppose in 2004 the market value of all final goods and services produced in the economy is $6,128 billion. The same goods evaluated at prices prevailing in 1998 would have sold for $5,405 bil. The GNP price deflator in 2004 equals _____ (where 1998 index=100).

8. Here is a simple circular flow diagram, where the economy has no credit market, government, or foreign sector. Match terms at right with the parts of the diagram to which they correspond.

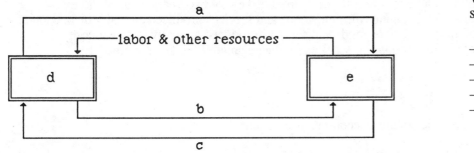

Write a,b,c,d,or e in the space provided

___Households
___Goods and services
___Business firms
___National income
___Consumption
   spending

9. Suppose GNP equals $5,250 bil. in 1991, while the GNP deflator equals 123 (1982=100). Then the 1991 GNP valued at prices prevailing in 1982 would be $_____ bil.

Part 5. Self Test
Multiple choice questions

1. The four factor payments are:

a. money, capital, salaries, and income
b. wages, rent, interest, and profits
c. money, power, prestige, and wealth
d. wages, interest, salaries, and income
e. none of the above

Answer: _____

2. In economics, investment refers to:

a. firms buying stocks and bonds
b. firms constructing and purchasing capital goods
c. governments purchasing consumer items
d. a and b
e. a and c

Answer: _____

3. Which of the following is a transfer payment?

a. payment of college tuition
b. a Social Security payment
c. an interest payment
d. payment for a leased car

Answer: _____

4. Gross national product is:

a. the total market value of all final goods and services produced every two years in an economy
b. the total market value of all final and intermediate goods and services produced annually in an economy
c. the total market value of all intermediate goods and services produced annually in an economy
d. the total market value of all final goods and services produced annually in an economy

Answer: _____

5. To avoid the problem of double counting, economists take only:

a. final goods and services into account when calculating GNP
b. intermediate goods and services into account when calculating GNP
c. labor income into account when calculating GNP
d. labor and capital income into account when calculating GNP (they omit profits)

Answer: _____

6. A television set purchased by someone in a retail store is an example of:

a. an intermediate good
b. a capital good
c. a final good
d. a surplus good
e. none of the above

Answer: _____

7. Which of the following is counted in GNP?

a. a used car sale
b. the purchase of 100 shares of Apple stock
c. a radio that is produced this year but not sold
d. the leisure people consume
e. none of the above

Answer: _____

8. The following figures are for year X: consumption = $3,010 billion; investment = $731 billion; exports = $400 billion; imports = $408 billion; government
expenditures = $766 billion; spending on durable goods = $400 billion; personal income = $3, 575 billion.
What was GNP in year X?

a. $4,499 billion
b. $4,899 billion
c. $4,507 billion
d. $4,675 billion

Answer: _____

9. Net exports equal:

a. exports x imports
b. exports + imports
c. exports - imports
d. exports during the year
e. none of the above

Answer: _____

10. The expenditure approach to measuring GNP sums:

a. consumption, gross private domestic investment (or simply, investment), government expenditures, and net exports
b. consumption, gross private domestic investment, government expenditures, and exports
c. compensation of employees, rental income, net interest, and profits
d. net exports, consumption, wages, salaries, and tips
e. consumption, government expenditures, personal income, and taxes

Answer: _____

11. The largest component of national income is:

a. proprietors' income
b. rental income
c. compensation of employees
d. corporate profits
e. net interest

Answer: _____

12. Which of the following taxes is considered a factor payment?

a. sales taxes
b. property taxes
c. corporate profits taxes
d. b and c
e. a and b

Answer: _____

13. Undistributed profits are considered:

a. income earned but not received
b. income received but not earned
c. income earned and received
d. income neither earned nor received

Answer: _____

14. Net national product (NNP) measures:

a. the total value of all final goods and services produced in the economy in one year
b. the total value of only intermediate goods produced in the economy in one year
c. the total value of all final goods and services produced in the economy in one year minus gross private domestic investment
d. the total value of only intermediate goods produced in the economy in one year plus gross private domestic investment
e. the total value of all final goods and services produced in the economy in one year minus capital consumption allowance

Answer: _____

15. The CPI in the base year is:

a. always 100
b. sometimes 100
c. somewhere between 1 and 100
d. usually over 200

Answer: _____

True-False

16. The CPI is based on a representative group of   T F
goods purchased by a typical "consumer unit" or
household in 1982-84.

17. If the total dollar expenditure on the market   T F
basket in the current year is $500 and the total
dollar expenditure on the market basket in the
base year is $200, the CPI in the current year
is 250.

18. If the CPI was 117.5 in 1970 and 340 in 1986,   T F
prices had risen by approximately 189 percent
during that time period.

19. If we were to value this year's output at   T F
current prices, we would have real GNP.

20. In 1982, the GNP deflator was 100 and   T F
GNP was $3,166 billion, therefore real GNP was
$3,099 billion.

Fill in the blank

21. The circular-flow diagram illustrates that there are two ways to measure the level of economic activity of the economy. These two measurements include _____ and

_____ .

22. Expenditures made by households are called _____ .

23. _____ is that part of a person's income that is not consumed.

24. _____ equals compensation of employees + proprietors' income + corporate profits + rental income + net interest.

25._____ is the amount of income that individuals actually receive.

Part 5. Answers to Self Test

1. b 2. b 3. b 4. d 5. a 6. c 7. c 8. a 9. c 10. a
11. c. 12. c 13. a 14. e 15. a
16. T 17. T 18. T 19. F 20. F
21. total output, total income 22. consumption (expenditures) 23. Saving 24. National income
25. Personal income

Part 6.   Answers

Part 2 Review of Concepts
1. d   2. e   3. f   4. b   5. a   6. c

Part 3. Key Concepts
1. capital consumption   2. gross national, real   3. income   4. are   5. b   6. consumer
7. deflator   8. S,F,S,F   9. Transfer   10. saving   11. underground   12 False
13. Income, Expenditure   14. Economic Welfare   15. raised   16. 8%
17. investment, purchases, exports   18. National   19. transfer   20. exports, imports
21. Compensation   22. False   23. True   24. moody

Part 4. Problems and Exercises
2. NI=1305, PI=1272, DI=1068, NNP=1376, GNP=1466   3. $18,174   4. d, c, a, e, b
5. -112, 4724, 4226, 3851   6. 106.5   7. 113.4   8. e,b,d,a,c   9. $4268.3

Chapter 7
Money and Banking

Part 1. Introduction and Purpose
Consider the following points as you read chapter 7 in the text.

Chapter 7 explores the nature and origin of money. What is money? Where did it originate? Who creates money? Why do people use money? Since few remember a time when money wasn't a part of their everyday lives, we may consider ourselves to be experts on the subject. Yet there is more to money than meets the eye, as you will see when reading this chapter and the next one.

Money has a certain mystique about it that makes people thing it is more complicated than it really is. Money originated when people found themselves inconvenienced by the alternative — **barter**, or the trade of goods for goods. When there is money, anything you want to buy or sell can be priced in money and can be directly exchanged for money. That's easy compared to what took place under barter, where people had to spend a lot of time searching for someone to trade with (barter requires a **double coincidence of wants** between buyer and seller), and had to **express the value** of each good in terms of all others that they might be in the market for. The high **cost of transacting** reduced the profitability of exchange, and without exchange each of us is left to satisfy his or her own needs. By facilitating exchange, money permits a greater volume of trade to take place and contributes greatly to our prosperity.

These ideas were not as clearly understood back when money was first used — recall that Fred and Barney bought things with rocks in the town of Bedrock ("A place right out of history"). But it isn't necessary to be a monetary theorist to realize that barter is inconvenient, and a basic human trait is to try and accomplish things with less effort or expense. Once it was realized that certain items were more acceptable in trade than other goods, it was only natural to always try and trade one's daily production for that one good. That initial trade having been accomplished, the individual was in possession of generalized purchasing power, in theory not very different from what we call money today.

European-style **banks**, after which our own banks are patterned, emerged from a similar process. Traders found it inconvenient to lug around and protect large quantities of gold, particularly when traveling over long distances. To cope, they left their gold with goldsmiths (craftsmen who worked with gold) and carried around paper **warehouse receipts** signed by the goldsmiths instead. Before long people were exchanging these receipts rather than the underlying precious metals. Those warehouse receipts were not much different from the currency issued by U.S. banks in the 1800s and the checks we carry around today. In each case an initial deposit entitles the depositor to a piece of spendable paper that buyers find convenient to use and sellers find convenient to accept.

Although a number of technical issues have been raised by researchers regarding the "best" definition of money, probably the best definition for you to keep in mind is the simplest: **Money is anything that is generally used to buy goods and services.** Anything means just that — anything that people use as money *is* money. It doesn't take an act of Congress for some item to serve as money, and the item doesn't have to look like money either. Anything that is is **generally acceptable** to a large segment of the population in exchange for goods is money.

In our own day and time, this includes coins and **currency, checking deposits** at banks and a few other financial institutions, and **traveler's checks.** A few generations back, before checks gained wide use, the money supply would only have included coins and currency, including the gold coins that circulated until the 1930s. In the early 1980s, savings and loan associations and credit unions began offering new types of checking accounts — NOW accounts, share draft accounts — so economists and policy makers broadened their definition of money to include these. Looking into the future, it is likely that some new financial "instrument" will gain wide acceptance among buyers and sellers, and at that point the definition of what is included in the money supply will change again. Officially, the spendable money supply is known as **M1** ("em-one"). This is the measure of money most often referred to by economists and financial commentators. Although the total amount of M1 money changes from one day to the next, the total is approaching $800 billion as this is written — or about $3300 per capita. Unless specifically noted, you should **always assume** that the money an economist is talking about is the **M1** variety.

Part 2.   Review of Concepts from Earlier Chapters
Prior to reading chapter 7, match statements at left with the appropriate concept at right.

__1. These economists stress the importance of money on the economy.	a. credit
__2. Using goods rather than money to buy other goods.	b. monetarists
__3. This was money in a World War II prisoner-of-war camp.	c. barter
__4. Loans are extended in this market.	d. interest
__5. The reward for taking some action.	e. cigarettes
__6. Income received by those who lend funds.	f. incentive

Part 3.   Key Concepts in this Chapter
After reading chapter 7 in the text, answer the following questions.

1. The first modern bankers were _____ who held gold for clients and gave them _____ receipts as evidence of their "deposits."

2. The sum of all currency, checking account balances, and checking accounts is called M1 / M2 / M3 .

3. First and foremost, money serves as a medium of _____.

4. When money is held to preserve wealth (or purchasing power) over time it is serving as a _____ of _____.

5. Fractional reserve banking means that bank reserves are greater / less than the value of their deposit liabilities.

6. Before barter can occur there must be a double _____ of _____ between buyer and seller.

7. A unit of _____ serves as a common unit for measuring the values of goods.

8. Gresham's Law states that _good / bad_ money drives _good / bad_ money out of circulation (as money).

9. The paper currency now circulating in the U.S. are _____ _____ Notes.

10. The _M1 / M2 / M3_ money supply includes savings & small time deposits, but not large time deposits.

11. The cost of searching for and completing an exchange is a _____ cost. These costs are _higher / lower_ in a barter economy than in a money economy.

12. The _____ _____ is the central bank of the U.S.

13. Total bank reserves equals bank deposits _at the Fed / received from customers_ plus vault cash.

14. True or false? _____ Credit card credit is included in the money supply (M1).

15. Total bank reserves minus required reserves equal _average / marginal / excess / legal_ reserves.

16. A bank can expand loans if it has _____ reserves.

17. A _M / T / J / C_ account records changes in the assets and liabilities of a bank.

18. The simple money multiplier equals one divided by the _____ _____ ratio.

19. A ___-___-___ is the name of a secret number used to gain access to one's bank account from a remote location.

20. True or false? _____ If total bank reserves decrease by $1 million, the money supply reacts in the opposite direction but by the same amount as if bank reserves increase by $1 mil.
near money

Part 4. Problems and Exercises
After reading chapter 7 in the text you should be able to work the following problems.

1. Suppose it takes 1 lb. of copper to manufacture 100 pennies (each penny contains 1/100 oz. of copper).
   a. In this case, the official price of copper is $_____ per pound.
   b. If the market price of copper is $1 per pound, then pennies are _more / less / equally_ valuable as money than they are as a commodity.
   c. If the market price of copper is $1.25 per pound, then pennies are _more / less / equally_ valuable as a commodity than they are as money.
   d.. If the market price of copper is $0.75 per pound, then pennies are _more / less / equally_ valuable as a commodity than they are as money.
   e. If the market price of copper is _above / below / equal to_ the official price, pennies will be melted for their value as a commodity.

2. The figures below were current in August 1988 (amounts in billions). According to your calculations the value of the M1 money supply was $ _____ billion.

Currency $207.2
Traveler's checks   7.2
Savings deposits   190.6
Demand deposits   290.0
NOW accounts plus other checkable deposits $278.1

3. Use the following information to calculate the simple money multiplier.

	required reserve ratio (r)	simple money multiplier (m)
a.	0.10	_____
b.	0.333	_____
c.	0.4	_____
d.	0.20	_____
e.	0.25	_____
f.	0.5	_____

Part 5. Self Test
Multiple choice questions

1. If chalk is widely accepted for purposes of exchange, then:

a. chalk is money
b. chalk is less valuable than it was before it was widely accepted for purposes of exchange
c. we would observe people using chalk to buy their weekly groceries
d. a and b
e. a and c

Answer: _____

2. Money is valuable because:

a. it is backed by gold
b. the government says it is valuable
c. people are willing to accept it in payment for goods and services
d. it is backed by silver
e. none of the above

Answer: _____

3. Gresham's law says that:

a. good money drives bad money out of circulation
b. both bad and good money are important in everyday business transactions
c. bad money drives good money out of circulation
d. bad money is more valuable than good money in certain circumstances
e. none of the above

Answer: _____

4. M1 is comprised of:

a. currency held by the nonbanking public, demand deposits, other checkable deposits, Visa and MasterCard
b. currency held by the nonbanking public, demand deposits, other checkable deposits, traveler's checks
c. currency held by the nonbanking public, demand deposits, other checkable deposits
d. currency held by the nonbanking public, demand deposits, other checkable deposits, savings deposits

Answer: _____

5. A credit card is:

a. considered money
b. not considered money
c. under certain circumstances considered money
d. the same as a repurchase agreement
e. none of the above

Answer: _____

6. Reserves equal:

a. demand deposits + vault cash - traveler's checks
b. currency in the hands of the nonbanking public + savings deposits + vault cash
c. bank deposits at the Fed + vault cash + currency in the hands of the nonbanking public
d. bank deposits at the Fed + vault cash

Answer: _____

7. If deposits in Bank A total $15 million and the required-reserve ratio is 10 percent, then excess reserves equal:

a. $13.5 million
b. $ 1.5 million
c. $10.5 million
d. $ 2.5 million
e. none of the above

Answer: _____

8. Which of the following required-reserve ratios would allow a bank the least amount of loanable funds?

a. 5 percent
b. 10 percent
c. 12 percent
d. 15 percent

Answer: _____

9. The banking system increases the money supply by:

a. printing its own currency
b. creating demand deposits
c. creating demand deposits and currency
d. creating Federal Reserve Notes
e. none of the above

Answer: _____

10. Suppose that the excess reserves in Bank A increase by $3,000. If the required-reserve ratio is 20 percent, what is the maximum change in demand deposits brought about by the banking system?

a. $15,000
b. $12,000
c. $10,000
d. $ 8,500
e. none of the above

Answer: _____

11. Which of the following statements is false?

a. A change in the composition of the money supply always decreases the money supply.
b. If Smith takes $1,000 out of her wallet and deposits it in a bank, the composition of the money supply changes.
c. If Jones takes $1,000 out of his checking account in the bank and puts it in his wallet, the composition of the money supply changes.
d. A change in the composition of the money supply can change the size of the money supply.
e. a and c

Answer: _____

12. The simple deposit multiplier is:

a. the required-reserve ratio
b. always 1
c. the reciprocal of the required-reserve ratio
d. different from bank to bank even if the required-reserve ratio is the same for all banks

Answer: _____

13. If there is a change in the composition of the money supply such that there is more currency in the hands of the nonbanking public and less demand deposits, then this will cause the money supply to:

a. fall
b. rise
c. stay constant
d. first fall and then sharply rise

Answer: _____

14. If the required-reserve ratio is 20 percent, the simple deposit multiplier is:

a. 3
b. 4
c. 5
d. 6
e. none of the above

Answer: _____

15. Bank A has deposits of $10,000 and reserves of $3,600. If the required-reserve ratio is .20, the bank has excess reserves of:

a. $2,000
b. $3,600
c. $1,200
d. $1,600
e. none of the above

Answer: _____

True-False

16. A unit of account is a common measurement in   T F
which values are expressed.

17. Money is unique in that it is the only good   T F
that serves as a store of value.

18. Bad money drives good money out of   T F
circulation if the two monies have the same face
value, different intrinsic values, and the exchange
rate between the two monies is not fixed at 1 for 1.

19. The more new reserves that enter the banking   T F
system, the greater the money supply will be,
ceteris paribus.

20. Money did not exist before formal governments   T F
existed.

Fill in the blank

21. Money reduces the _____ costs of making exchanges.

22. Two people have a _____ if what the first person wants is what
the second person has, and what the second person wants is what the first person has.

23. About 99 percent of the paper money in circulation is _____ .

24. Under a _____ banking system, banks create money by holding on reserve only a fraction
of the money deposited with them and lending the remainder.

25. If the required-reserve ratio is 10 percent, the simple deposit multiplier is _____ .

Part 5. Answers to Self Test

1. e 2. c 3. c 4. b 5. b 6. d 7. a 8. d 9. b 10. a
11. a 12. c 13. a 14. c 15. d
16. T 17. F 18. F 19. T 20. F
21. transaction 22. double coincidence of wants
23. Federal Reserve Notes 24. fractional reserve 25. 10

Part 6.   Answers

Part 2 Review of Concepts
1. b   2. c   3. e   4. a   5. f   6. d

Part 3 Key Concepts
1. goldsmiths, warehouse   2. M1   3. exchange.   4. store of value   5. less
6. coincidence of wants   7. account   8. bad, good   9. Federal Reserve   10. M2
11. transaction, higher   12. Federal Reserve   13. at the Fed   14. false   15. excess   16. excess
17. T   18. required reserve   19. P-I-N   20. True

Part 4 Problems and Exercises
1. a. $1   b. equally   c. more   d. less   e. above
2. $782.5
3. a. 10   b. 3   c. 2.5   d. 5   e. 4   f. 2

Chapter 8
The Federal Reserve System

Part 1. Introduction and Purpose
Consider the following points as you read chapter 8 in the text.

Many people consider the Federal Reserve to be the nation's most powerful economic policy making institution. To say that does not necessarily mean that Congress or the president do not have considerable powers of their own, or even that monetary policy is more powerful than fiscal policy. Instead, elected officials are often occupied with political matters, foreign policy, or unexpected emergencies to focus their energies on economic policy making the way the Fed can. It's (almost) single minded devotion to economic issues and the strong influence of money on the economy combine to make the Fed a potent force with the power to stabilize (or destabilize) the economy.

So, "Who is this Fed?" you may be asking yourself. First of all, it is *not* a regular branch of the government. The Federal Reserve was originally created by legislation passed in 1913, but to insulate monetary policy from political influence, it was made **independent** of government. In practice, ownership shares in the Federal Reserve are held by member (commercial) banks, but members of the Fed's governing board are appointed by the U.S. president with the advice and consent of the Senate. Thus the Fed is a semi-private and semi-public organization that conducts U.S. monetary policy and engages in related activities (bank regulation, serving as the federal government's bank, clearing checks, etc.).

The ability to create money "out of thin air" — as the Fed can — places the Fed in a key position in the economy. If you recall the **circular flow** diagram of the economy (chapter 6), the Fed can "inject" more dollars into the flow of funds through the economy. Depending on the channel chosen, such an injection may cause firms to increase their output or raise their prices, or it may cause interest rates to decline to borrowers, or it may may cause government tax revenues to increase (which would reduce the deficit). Even if only one of these sectors is initially affected, the new dollars are spent and re-spent, so eventually almost everyone is affected by the Fed's action.

As all Fed watchers are aware, the Federal Reserve System has three main components. At the top of the Fed is the seven-member **Board of Governors**, whose members are appointed by the president for 14-year terms. (Replacements for those who resign serve out the remainder of the original term.) Long terms are a second way of reducing the influence of politicians on Fed policy. At a lower level in the Fed are the 12 regional **Federal Reserve Banks**, located in major cities around the country. Each Fed Bank has a president who, in addition to his or her "local" duties, attends meetings with the Board of Governors and helps set monetary policy. Finally, about 6,000 privately owned commercial banks have elected to join the Federal Reserve System and are referred to as **member banks**. The largest commercial banks tend to be member banks, though that is not universally the case.

The Federal Reserve performs several functions, but for our purposes the most important is **monetary policy**. You may recall reading in chapter 5 that monetary policy consists of controlling the national money supply to stabilize economic conditions — to prevent inflation from rising to unacceptable levels, to prevent unemployment and interest rates from rising too high, and so forth.

The Fed has three main monetary policy tools. First, it engages in **open market purchases and sales** of government securities. When the Fed pays for the securities it buys, it pays with funds that did not previously exist, and the money supply increases. Through a sort of chain reaction that may take several weeks to complete, the Fed's injection of new funds will increase bank **reserves**, the **monetary base,** and the money supply. Exactly the opposite happens when the Fed sells government securities to someone in the private economy. When it collects its payment for the securities, the Fed takes the dollars out of circulation and causes the money supply to decline. Open market policy is conducted by a 12-member **Federal Open Market Committee**, made up of the seven Fed Governors plus five of the 12 Reserve Bank presidents.

Another way the Fed injects funds into the economy is by lending dollars to banks. Member banks occasionally borrow funds at the Fed's "discount window," and when they do the total volume of bank reserves is increased. The money supply will also increase in such cases.

The policy used by the Fed to influence the amount member banks borrow at the discount window is known as **discount rate policy**. By raising or lowering the interest rate it charges at the discount window (relative to other interest rates), the Fed can reduce or increase the incentive of banks to borrow. Ceteris paribus, a higher discount rate discourages banks from borrowing at the discount window so bank reserves and the money supply decline. A lower discount rate causes banks to seek more Fed loans, which will cause reserves and the money supply to grow.

Finally, the Fed can raise or lower the **required reserve ratio** on bank deposits. An increase in the ratio reduces the amount of excess reserves resulting from each customer deposit, which in turn reduces the volume of new loans the bank can make. That reduces the quantity of money in the economy. This process also works in reverse, so a reduction in the required reserve ratios implies more bank loans and a larger money supply.

Of the three, open market policy is the most often used. Open market operations of one type or another occur every few days. The Fed changes the discount rate a few times each year, and changes required reserve ratios only once every few years.

Part 2.   Review of Concepts from Earlier Chapters
Prior to reading chapter 8, match statements at left with the appropriate concept at right.

___1. The central bank of the U.S.

a. M1

___2. Shows the movement of goods and money through the economy.

b. monetary policy

___3. Spending money.

c. Federal Reserve

___4. Vault cash and bank deposits at the Fed.

d. Federal Reserve Notes

___5. One divided by the required reserve ratio on checking accounts.

e. circular flow

___6. Manipulation of money supply to stabilize the economy.

f. simple multiplier

___7. Official U.S. currency.

g. bank reserves

Part 3. Key Concepts in this Chapter
After reading chapter 8 in the text, answer the following questions.

1. A person who monitors Fed policies to predict what it might do next is called a Fed _____.

2. The _____ of _____ is the governing body of the Federal Reserve System. This group has _____ members.

3. The _____ can create money "out of thin air."

4. The percent of a deposit that banks must hold on reserve is the _____ _____ ratio.

5. The monetary base equals the sum of bank _____ and _____ held by the nonbanking public.

6. The Fed is the lender of last _____ for commercial banks.

7. Purchases and sales of government _____ is the most often used tool of monetary policy.

8. The current chairman of the Board of Governors is Alan _____.

9. The _____ rate is the interest rate the Fed charges banks for short term loans.

10. The Federal _____ _____ Committee decides whether the Fed should buy or sell government securities.

11. The Federal Reserve Act was passed into law in 19___.

12. There are approximately _____ member banks in the Federal Reserve System.

13. The typical $1 bill has an average life of _____ months.

14. Of the past four chairmen of the Fed Board of Governors, ___ have been economists.

15. The Federal Reserve's major responsibility is to control the _____ _____ in order to stabilize the economy.

16. True or false? _____ The monetary base is larger than the money supply.

17. A full term on the Board of Governors is __ years.

18. The _____ _____ rate is the interest rate banks charge each other on short term loans of reserves.

19. Since 1980, which banks have been subject to the Fed's required reserve ratios? _____

20. The FOMC has ____ members, including ____ Federal Reserve bank presidents and ____ members of the Board of Governors.

21. Since passage of DIDMCA in 1980, interest rates on checking accounts have risen/fallen.

22. An increase / A decrease in the discount rate relative to the federal funds rate will reduce bank borrowing at the discount window.

23. In 1985 it cost the Federal Reserve _____ cents to have a Federal Reserve Note produced.

24. True or false? _____ The Fed must request Congressional approval before making major changes in monetary policy.

25. Each $1 increase in the monetary _____ increases the _____ _____ by a multiple of that amount.

26. If the Fed reduces required reserve ratios the money multiplier will increase / decrease in value; consequently the money supply will rise / fall .

27. According to former chairman Volcker the Fed's "vegetables" _____.

Part 4. Problems and Exercises

After reading chapter 8 in the text you should be able to work the following problems.

1. An important objective of chapter 8 is to understand the impact of various policies and conditions on the money supply. In each of the cases listed below, indicate whether M1 will rise or fall as a result of the event listed. Indicate the direction of change in the blanks provided at left, then compute your score below.

__a. The required reserve ratio on checking deposits increases.
__b. The required reserve ratio on checking deposits decreases.
__c. The fed funds rate rises (while the discount rate is constant).
__d. Lower the discount rate (while the federal funds rate is constant).
__e. Raise the discount rate (while the federal funds rate is constant).
__f. The fed funds rate falls (while the discount rate is constant).
__g. The Fed purchases $10 million worth of government securities from private investors.
__h. The Fed sells $1 million worth of government securities to private investors.
__i. An individual moves $100 from her checking account to her savings account.
__j. An individual receives a $100 loan from his bank.

Answers: Rise (b,c,d,g,j)   Fall(a,e,f,h,i)

•If your score was 0-6, you probably understand nuclear physics better than monetary policy. The same was true for a recent U.S. president.
•If you scored 6-7, you may be confused on one or two main points. Review them in the textbook before proceeding.
•If you scored 8-9, you probably understand all of the main issues but tend to be a little careless. Don't do that!
•If you scored 10, you deserve a prize. Call your parents tonight and ask them to send you $10.

2. Examine the map in exhibit 8-2 in the text.

   a. In which Fed district do you live? _____

   b. Examine the currency in your pocket or purse. Out of ____ Federal Reserve notes in your possession, ____ were issued by the Federal Reserve Bank in whose district you reside.

3. Suppose banks hold $15 mil. in their vaults and have another $120 mil. in reserve deposits at the Fed.

   a. In this setting the monetary base equals $_____ mil. If the money multiplier equals 2.75, M1 = $_____ million.

   b. If the Fed wants to increase the money supply by another $10 mil., then it should increase the monetary base by $_____ mil.

4. Sam deposits $300 in the First National Bank, and the bank's required reserve ratio is 12% (0.12). Assuming the bank holds no excess reserves, it will hold $_____ of the deposit on reserve and will make $_____ worth of loans.

5. Fill in blank spaces in the table below.

	multiplier	ΔMonetary Base	ΔM1
a.	____	$200	$900
b.	4.2	____	$500
c.	6.0	$100	____
d.	____	$150	____

6. The ABC Bank has $1 million in its vault and $12 mil. in its account at the Fed. Its total reserves are $___ mil. If the bank holds $110 mil. in customer deposits and the required reserve ratio is 9%, it is required to hold $_____ mil. on reserve. The ABC Bank's excess reserves equal $_____ mil.

7. In December 1987 the money supply (M1) was $753.2 bil. and the monetary base was $256.7 bil. At that time, the money multiplier must have been _____. If the Fed wanted to increase the money supply by $10 bil., it would have had to increase the monetary base by $_____ bil.

8. Suppose the federal funds rate rises while the discount rate remains unchanged. If other things are unchanged, bank borrowing at the Fed will _rise / fall_. That will cause bank reserves and the monetary base to _rise / fall_, so the money supply will _rise / fall_.

9. If r (the required reserve ratio against checking accounts) is 7% (0.07), the simple money multiplier equals _____. If r is 10% (0.10), the money multiplier is _____. If r is 15% (0.15), the money multiplier is ____. You conclude that larger values of r correspond to a _larger / smaller_ multiplier.

Part 5. Self Test
Multiple choice questions

1. The Federal Reserve System began operations in:

a. December 1903
b. November 1913
c. November 1914
d. September 1945

Answer: _____

2. The principal components of the Federal Reserve System are:

a. the Board of Governors, the 12 Federal Reserve District Banks, and approximately 6,000 member commercial banks
b. the Board of Governors, the 12 Federal Reserve District Banks, and the Office of Management and Budget
c. the Board of Governors, the 12 Federal Reserve District Banks, and the Treasury
d. the Board of Governors, the Treasury, and the Senate Banking and Finance Committee

Answer: _____

3. Which of the following statements is true?

a. The Federal Open Market Committee (FOMC) is responsible for providing check-clearing services for checks that have been written by the public.
b. The FOMC controls and coordinates all the activities of the Federal Reserve System.
c. The FOMC is responsible for collecting taxes.
d. The FOMC is responsible for buying and selling government securities.

Answer: _____

4. Anytime the Fed buys or sells something:

a. currency in the hands of the nonbanking public necessarily remains constant
b. the monetary base changes
c. there are fewer Federal Reserve Notes in circulation
d. a and b
e. none of the above

Answer: _____

5. The reserves of the banking system increase:

a. if the Fed purchases government securities from commercial banks
b. if the Fed sells government securities to commercial banks
c. if one commercial bank borrows from another commercial bank
d. if one commercial lends funds to another commercial bank
e. c and d

Answer: _____

6. In order to finance a budget deficit, the U.S. Treasury:

a. creates money "out of thin air"
b. orders the Fed to purchase government securities
c. borrows money from the public by issuing securities
d. prints more Federal Reserve Notes
e. b or d

Answer: _____

7. The monetary base is comprised of:

a. bank deposits at the Fed and currency held by the nonbanking public
b. reserves and currency held by the nonbanking public
c. bank deposits at the Fed and vault cash
d. currency held by the nonbanking public and currency held by banks

Answer: _____

8. The money multiplier:

a. is equal to the simple deposit multiplier minus the cash leakage
b. measures the actual change in the money supply for a dollar change in the monetary base
c. equals the money supply times the monetary base
d. equals the monetary base divided by 2
e. none of the above

Answer: _____

9. If the Fed sells $5 billion of government securities and the money multiplier is 3.50, then the money supply will:

a. increase by $10.5 billion
b. decrease by $11.5 billion
c. increase by $17.5 billion
d. decrease by $19.5 billion
e. none of the above

Answer: _____

10. If the money multiplier is 2.40 and the money supply is $825 billion, then the monetary base is:

a. approximately $344 billion
b. approximately $277 billion
c. approximately $432 billion
d. approximately $295 billion

Answer: _____

11. If the money supply is $500 billion and the monetary base is $125 billion, then the money multiplier is:

a. 1/5
b. 5
c. 4
d. 2

Answer: _____

12. If the Fed wants to decrease the money supply through an open market operation, it would:

a. sell government securities
b. raise the required-reserve ratio
c. purchase government securities
d. create money out of thin air
e. a or b

Answer: _____

13. If the Fed wants to increase the money supply it would:

a. raise the required-reserve ratio
b. sell government securities
c. raise the discount rate above the federal funds rate
d. lower the required-reserve ratio
e. a, b, or c

Answer: _____

14. Open market operations is the Fed tool:

a. used most often to increase but not decrease the money supply
b. used most often to change the money supply
c. used least often to decrease the money supply
d. used least often to change the money supply

Answer: _____

15. If one bank borrows reserves from another commercial bank:

a. the reserves of the banking system remain constant
b. the reserves of the banking system increase
c. the reserves of the banking system decrease
d. the money supply rises
e. b and d

Answer: _____

True-False

16. The major policy-making group within the Fed   T F
is the Federal Open Market Committee (FOMC).

17. Alan Greenspan is currently the chairman of   T F
the Board of Governors of the Federal Reserve
System.

18. An open market sale will increase the money   T F
supply.

19. The discount rate is the interest rate one   T F
commercial bank pays another commerical bank for
a loan.

20. The money multiplier times the monetary base   T F
equals the money supply.

Fill in the blank

21. Another name for the monetary base is _____ .

22. A decrease in the required-reserve ratio will _____ the money supply.

23. An open market purchase will _____ the money supply.

24. The Board of Governors is made up of _____members, each appointed to _____ year terms.

25. Old money is sent to _____ to be exchanged for new.

Part 5. Answers to Self Test

1. c 2. a 3. d 4. b 5. a 6. c 7. b 8. b 9. e 10. a
11. c 12. a 13. d 14. b 15. a
16. T 17. T. 18. F 19. F 20. T
21. high-powered money 22. increase 23. increase
24. seven, 14 25. Federal Reserve District Banks

Part 6. Answers

Part 2 Review of Concepts
1. c   2. e   3. a   4. g   5. f   6. b   7. d

Part 3 Key Concepts
1. watcher   2. Board of Governors, 7   3. Fed   4. required reserve   5. reserves, currency
6. resort   7. securities   8. Greenspan   9. discount   10. Open Market (FOMC)   11. 1913
12. 6,000   13. 18   14. 3   15. money supply   16. false   17. 14   18. federal funds   19. all
20. 12, 5, 7   21. risen (NOW accounts)   22. An increase   23. 2.6   24. false
25. base, money supply   26. decrease, fall   27. can order lunch for themselves (see footnote 1)

Part 4 Problems and Exercises
3. a. $135, $371.25,   b. $3.64
4. $36, $264
5. a 4.5 b. $119.05 c. $600 d. impossible to answer
6. 13, 9.9, 3.1
7. 2.934, $3.41
8. rise, rise, rise
9. 14.3, 10.0, 6.67, smaller

Chapter 9
The Income-Expenditure and MV-PQ Frameworks

Part 1. Introduction and Purpose

Consider the following points as you read chapter 8 in the text.

Back in chapter 6 we saw that real goods and services flow through the economy from sellers to buyers, and that dollars flow in the opposite direction when buyers pay for the things they have purchased. Where we previously used the circular flow model to illustrate broad trends in economic activity, *in chapter 9 we want to use the model to examine policies and events that can increase or reduce the rate at which goods and dollars flow through the economy.*

Think of the total flow of dollars as gross national product (GNP). Macroeconomists often want to know how large GNP will be this year or next, and have developed several different — sometimes conflicting — models to answer that question. For example, one very simple model assumes that the same number of goods and dollars will flow through the economy this year as did last year. A slightly more sophisticated version of that model predicts that GNP this year will be 2.5% above last year's GNP — due to the belief that over the longer run GNP will grow at that average rate.

Unfortunately these simplest models are not particularly accurate, so more sophisticated models have been developed to provide more accurate predictions. The two approaches examined in chapter 9 are the **income-expenditure** model and the **MV-PQ** model. So that you do not lose sight of what you are doing this chapter, keep in mind that *the basic purpose of each economic model is to explain how many dollars and goods will circulate through the circular flow* that we call our economy.

The income-expenditure (I-E) model provides a graphical representation of the spending habits of households (**consumption**) and businesses (**investment**). A more complex version of the model, presented in a later chapter, includes spending by governments and foreign consumers. The fundamental assumption of the I-E model is that businesses attempt to produce whatever quantity of goods is needed to satisfy the total demand for them. With production passively responding to the **demand** for goods, the model's emphasis is on the conditions that influence each group's spending behavior, and on correctly adding up total spending by all groups to determine what quantity of goods business will be able to sell.

A second key feature of the I-E model is its **feedback mechanism** which helps the economy move toward its equilibrium. If businesses produce more goods than they can sell, at the end of the year they will have excessive inventories of goods. The unprofitability of these **unplanned inventories** leads businesses to cut back production in the future to avoid making the same mistake again. In short, excessive production in one year provides businesses an incentive to eliminate the surplus, which represents a movement toward equilibrium. If companies produce too little to satisfy current demands, sellers reduce their inventories of goods below desired levels. In this case an **unplanned reduction of inventories** provides an incentive to increase production. The extra production helps eliminate the shortage and moves the economy toward equilibrium.

The other macroeconomic model introduced in chapter 9 is the MV-PQ model, originally developed by economists about 150 years ago. You are already familiar with some of the components of the MV-PQ model. **M** is the money supply, **P** is the general price level, and **Q** is the real quantity of goods produced during the year (real GNP). That leaves **V** — the velocity of money, or the average number of times dollars are spent each year to purchase newly produced goods and services.

The MV-PQ model is a mathematical formulation of the circular flow that, like the I-E model, emphasizes total spending for goods. Rather than concentrating on the groups that spend dollars however, the MV-PQ model pays more attention to the dollars themselves and how rapidly they are spent. For example, if the money supply is $100 and if each dollar is spent 5 times during the year then total spending on goods that year will be $500.

By adding one additional assumption to the model it can tell us how many dollars will actually flow through the economy during the year. The assumption is that the velocity of money remains unchanged from one year to the next. In this case, total spending will equal the money supply multiplied by a constant number, such as 5. This says that each $1 change in the money supply causes total spending and sales within the economy to rise by $5. This is a **quantity theory of money**. The dollar value economic activity (GNP) rises and falls in **proportion** to the money supply.

If the economy is already using all available factors of production — that is, if the economy is already operating along its production possibilities frontier — then any GNP growth is reflected in rising prices rather than in a higher rate of production. In terms of the formula, the increase in M is matched by a proportional increase in P and no change in Q.

In reality, **V** is not perfectly constant and the economy only occasionally operates at "full" employment. Consequently more refined versions of the theory examine the specific conditions that cause V to vary and the circumstances that determine whether fluctuations in GNP occur as changes in P or Q (or both). Partly because the quantity theory of money did a good job forecasting the high inflation rate of the late 1960s and '70s every macroeconomist has this theory in his or her tool kit.

Part 2.   Review of Concepts from Earlier Chapters
Prior to reading chapter 9, match statements at left with the appropriate concept at right.

__1. Diagram showing the flow of money and goods in the economy.

__2. Total market value of all newly produced goods for the year.
__3. Total income of the factors of production.
__4. A stable situation, away from which there is no tendency to move.
__5. Consumption, investment, government purchases, plus net exports.
__6. The inflation-adjusted value of total national output.
__7. New plant and equipment acquired by companies.
__8. Newly acquired structures, equipment, and inventories.
__9. Household spending for goods and services.
__10. An indicator of the general price level.
__11.Disposable income that is not spent.
__12. Increases in the cigarette supply caused prices to rise here.

a. expenditure approach to
    GNP
b. equilibrium
c. national income
d. real GNP
e. capital good
f. GNP
g. POW camp
h. saving
i. circular flow
j. consumption expenditures
k. price index
l. investment

Part 3.   Key Concepts in this Chapter
After reading chapter 9 in the text, answer the following questions.

1. In the MV-PQ model, the letter V represents the _volume / velocity_ of money, while Q is real _____.

2. An _injection / leakage_ slows down the flow of dollars and goods through the economy.

3. Increases in total planned expenditures can also be described as an _injection / leakage_ into the circular flow model.

4. Planned consumption plus planned investment equals total planned _____
   (_T_ _P_ ___) .

5. Actual consumption plus actual investment equals total _____ _____
   (_T_ ___ ___) .

6. If total planned expenditures are _greater / less_ than total planned production, then some goods will go unsold and will be added to sellers' inventories.

7. If TPE>TPP, then _more / fewer_ goods will be sold than are produced. In this situation, sellers' inventories will _exceed / fall short of_ desired levels.

8. P multiplied by Q equals gross _____ _____.

9. In equilibrium, total _actual / planned_ expenditures equal total production.

10. The presence of unplanned inventory investment signals that the economy _is / is not_ in equilibrium under the present circumstances.

11. If companies' inventories fall below desired levels they will _increase / reduce_ their production.

12. The income-_____ model places primary emphasis on who is spending dollars and their reasons for doing so, while the _____-_____ model emphasizes the number of dollars available for spending.

13. _An increase / A decrease_ in planned spending causes a leakage from the circular flow of spending and income.

14. An increase in MxV will cause _____ or Q to rise (or both).

15. If companies' inventories rise above desired levels they will _increase / reduce_ their production.

16. If the TPE curve lies currently above the TPP curve, national income and output will _rise / fall_ from its present level.

17. Household consumption spending is _positively / negatively / un-_ related to national income.

18. "Autonomous consumption" is the level of consumption that would occur when income equals _____.

19. If total planned saving exceeds total planned investment, TPE is _greater than / less than / equal to_ TPP. Consequently, sellers' inventories will _rise above / fall below / equal_ desired levels.

20. If the velocity of money is 4 and GNP equals $800, the money supply must be $_____.

21. The simple quantity theory of money says that a 10% increase in the money supply should cause the general price level to rise by _____%.

22. If GNP equals $5,000 and the money supply equals $800, the velocity of money is _____.

23. The "classical economists" used the _____-_____ macroeconomic model to analyze the economy.

24. Total planned expenditures plus _planned / unplanned_ inventory changes equal total actual expenditures.

25. True or false? _____ If total planned saving equals total planned investment, TPE equals TPP.

Part 4. Problems and Exercises

After reading chapter 9 in the text you should be able to work the following problems.

1. The table below gives values for two variables, per capita consumption spending (C) and per capita disposable income (Y) for 1980-1987 (amounts in thousands of dollars). Graph each combination of C and Y in the grid at right.

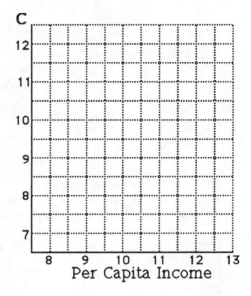

Year	Y	C
80	8.4	7.6
81	9.2	8.3
82	9.7	8.8
83	10.3	9.5
84	11.3	10.3
85	11.9	11.0
86	12.5	11.6
87	13.0	12.2

Next, use a ruler to <u>draw</u> <u>a</u> <u>straight</u> <u>line</u> through the points you just graphed. This straight line should be as close as possible to all of the points in your graph. It represents the general relationship between C and Y.

2. Higher interest rates <u>increase / reduce</u> the cost of purchasing goods on credit. If the interest rate rises, what impact do you think this will have on consumer spending at any given income level? _____ (Recall the Law of Demand.)

3. Refer to the diagram at right.

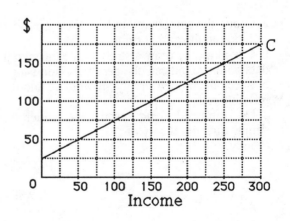

a. A consumer whose income is $200 purchases _____ worth of goods.
b. Suppose higher interest rates reduce consumption spending by $25 for this consumer. Indicate the new level of spending by the consumer whose income is still $200. (Place a dot at the appropriate consumption-income point.)
c. Draw a new consumption curve through the dot you just drew and parallel to the original consumption curve (exactly $25 below the original C curve at each income level.) Label the curve C'.

4. Suppose the sum of autonomous consumption and autonomous planned investment equals $200 while the slope of the consumption curve is 0.5.
a. The equilibrium level of national income will be $_____.
b. If autonomous spending increases to $210, equilibrium national income will be $_____.
c. National income rose by $____ for each $1 increase in autonomous spending.

5. Suppose initially the money supply is rising at a 2% annual rate, but then accelerates to a new (permanantly higher) growth rate of 5%. Those who subscribe to the simple quantity theory of money would predict that the new inflation would be ____% higher than before.

6. Complete the following table on the MV-PQ model.

	M	V	P	Q	Y
a.	$400	2.0	6	____	$____
b.	$____	4.0	____	$500	$1000
c.	$700	____	3	$900	$____
d.	$____	3.5	5	$____	$2500

7. The table below shows the annual rate of money supply expansion during 1979-84 for 10 nations, and the inflation rates experienced by each.

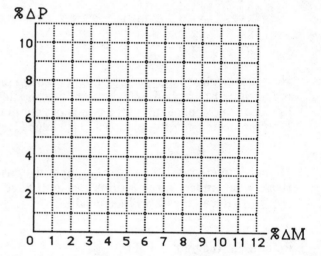

Country	%ΔM	%ΔP
United States	7.5	6.5
United Kingdom	11.8	9.5
Japan	4.0	2.2
Germany	4.7	3.7
France	10.9	10.3
Kenya	7.4	10.0
Australia	8.9	9.6
Thailand	8.0	6.3
Panama	4.8	5.2
Morocco	9.5	8.3

a. Graph the combinations of money growth and inflation in the grid at right.

b. Use a ruler to draw a straight line through the data points to indicate the general relationship between the money supply growth rate and the inflation rate.

c. Do your results tend to support or undercut the simple quantity theory of money?_____

8. Examine the income-expenditure model at right.

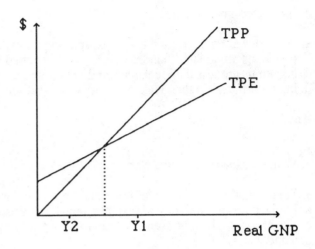

a. At income level Y_1 the production of goods is _greater / less_ than total planned expenditures. Inventories will be _above / below_ desired levels, so companies will _increase / reduce_ their output.

b. At income level Y_2 the production of goods is _greater / less_ than total planned expenditures. Inventories will be _above / below_ desired levels, so companies will _increase / reduce_ their output.

Part 5. Self Test
Multiple choice questions

1. In terms of the circular flow diagram, an injection is:

a. an inflow of expenditures into the circular flow stream
b. an outflow of expenditures from the circular flow stream
c. the same as a leakage
d. anything that reduces total expenditures

Answer: _____

2. What firms plan to invest:

a. always equals what households plan to save
b. sometimes equals what firms plan to invest
c. is always greater than what firms plan to invest
d. is always less than what firms plan to invest

Answer: _____

3. In terms of the circular-flow diagram, saving is:

a. an injection
b. a planned expenditure
c. a leakage
d. an inventory change

Answer: _____

4. If planned investment is greater than planned saving, then:

a. injections are greater than leakages, and unplanned inventory changes will be positive
b. injections are greater than leakages, and unplanned inventory changes will be negative
c. injections are less than leakages, and unplanned inventory changes will be positive
d. injections are less than leakages, and unplanned inventory changes will be negative

Answer: _____

5. Which of the following statements is false?

a. Total actual production does not equal total actual expenditures.
b. Planned production may not equal planned expenditures.
c. The amount which households plan to save may not equal the amount that business firms plan to invest.
d. a and c
e. none of the above

Answer: _____

6. Consider the following data: planned production on consumer goods is $5,000; planned production on capital goods is $2,000; planned expenditures on consumer goods is $6,000; planned expenditures on new capital goods is $4,000; and firms plan $0 in inventory changes. Given this:

a. total planned production (TPP) is greater than total planned expenditures (TPE)
b. TPE > TPP
c. TPP = TPE
d. total planned saving is greater than total planned investment

Answer: _____

7. If households plan to purchase $100,000 worth of consumer goods and firms plan to produce $90,000 worth of consumer goods, then:

a. unplanned inventory changes is -$10,000
b. unplanned inventory changes is +$10,000
c. new capital goods expenditures is $5,000
d. saving equals $190,000
e. none of the above

Answer: _____

8. Planned investment plus unplanned investment equals:

a. concrete investment
b. economic investment
c. composite investment
d. actual investment

Answer: _____

9. Which of the following statements is false?

a. Unplanned inventory changes can be negative but not positive.
b. Unplanned inventory changes can be positive but not negative.
c. Unplanned inventory changes cannot be zero.
d. a and c
e. a, b, and c

Answer: _____

10. When total planned production is greater than total planned expenditures:

a. there is a tendency for total output to fall
b. there is a tendency for total output to rise
c. there is a tendency for total output to remain constant
d. there will be negative unplanned inventory changes
e. a and d

Answer: _____

11. If total planned production is greater than total planned expenditures, then:

a. there are positive unplanned inventory changes
b. total planned saving is greater than total planned investment
c. there is a tendency for total output to rise
d. a and b
e. b and c

Answer: _____

12. In a simple economy with no government and no foreign sector, if autonomous consumption equals $400, planned investment equals $1,200, and the slope of the consumption function equals .80, equilibrium national income is:

a. $8,000
b. $6,000
c. $7,000
d. $9,000

Answer: _____

13. If GNP is $3,000 billion and the average money supply (for the year) is $500 billion, then velocity for the year is:

a. 1
b. 5
c. 6
d. 7

Answer: _____

14. The simple quantity theory of money assumes that:

a. velocity and the price level are constant
b. velocity and real GNP are constant
c. the money supply is constant
d. velocity and the money supply are constant

Answer: _____

15. The simple quantity theory of money predicts that:

a. changes in the money supply lead to nearly proportional changes in the price level
b. changes in the price level bring about changes in the money supply
c. increases in real GNP are greater than changes in the price level if the money supply has fallen
d. changes in velocity lead to nearly proportional changes in the money supply
e. none of the above

Answer: _____

True-False

16. The condition for economy-wide equilibrium is   T F
total planned production equals total planned
expenditures.

17. If total planned production is greater than   T F
total planned expenditures, it follows that
total planned saving is less than total planned
investment.

18. Velocity is the average number of times a   T F
dollar is spent to buy final goods and services.

19. The equation of exchange says that total   T F
spending must equal the total sales revenues
of business firms.

20. The equation of exchange and the simple   T F
quantity theory of money are one and the same.

Fill in the blank

21. Total actual production equals total actual expenditures because firms _____ any goods they
produce that cannot be sold to households.

22. According to the simple quantity theory of money, if the money supply rises by 10 percent, the price
level _____ by _____ percent.

23. If GNP is $1,000 billion and velocity is 5, it follows that the money supply is_____ billion.

24. The difference between what firms produce and what households actually purchase is
_____.

25. If total planned expenditures are greater than total planned production, there are _____
unplanned inventory changes, which signal firms that they have
_____ .

Part 5. Answers to Self Test

1. a 2. b 3. c 4. b 5. a 6. b 7. a 8. d 9. e. 10. a
11. d. 12. a 13. c 14. b 15. e
16. T 17. F 18. T 19. T 20. F
21. purchase 22. rises, 10 23. $200 24. unplanned inventory changes 25. negative, underproduced

Part 6.   Answers

Part 2 Review of Concepts
1. i 2. f 3. c 4. b 5. a 6. d 7. e 8. 1 9. j 10. k 11. h 12. g

Part 3 Key Concepts
1. velocity, GNP   2. leakage   3. injection   4. expenditures (TPP)   5. actual expenditures (TAE)
6. less   7. more, fall short of   8. national product   9. planned   10. is not   11. increase
12. -expenditure, MV-PQ   13. decrease   14. P   15. reduce   16. rise   17. positively   18. zero

19. less than, rise above   20. $200   21. 10%   22. 6.25
23. MV-PQ (or the quantity theory of money)   24. unplanned inventory changes   25. true

Part 4 Problems and Exercises

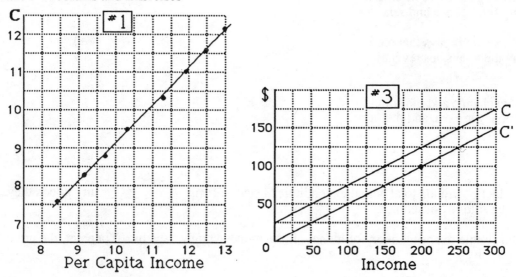

2. reduce, it should decline
4. $400   b. $420   c. $2
5. 3%
6. a. Q=$133.33, Y=$800   b. M=$250, P=2   c. V=3.86, Y=$2700   d. M=$714.29, Q=$500

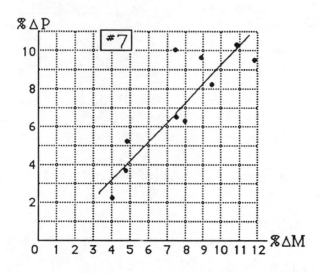

7. c. support

8. a. greater than, above, reduce   b. less than, below, increase

Chapter 10
The Aggregate Demand -
Aggregate Supply Framework

Part 1. Introduction and Purpose
Consider the following points as you read chapter 10 in the text.

The two economic models you read about in the previous chapter (income-expenditure and MV-PQ) were developed to show how certain events and policies affect economic activity — or in more familiar terms, to explain the flow of goods and dollars through the circular flow or the economy. (It may be helpful to briefly review exhibits 6-1 and 6-2 in the text.)

For many years, the I-E and MV-PQ models were the only ones used to interpret events and predict future conditions in the macroeconomy. About 15 years ago however, it became apparent that both models concentrated almost exclusively on the demand side of the economy — to total spending on goods. Consumption spending, business investment spending, and the velocity of money tell us something about **aggregate demand**, but very little about the willingness of producers to supply goods (**aggregate supply**).

In chapter 10, a more sophisticated and more useful model of the economy is sketched. The Aggregete Demand-Aggregate Supply (AD-AS) framework shows that the pace of economic activity can be influenced by the actions of producers as well as aggregate spending. Where earlier we pictured the circular flow as a number of dollars and goods moving from one sector to the other, *here we see the flow speeding up or slowing down because of decisions by buyers or sellers*. For example if workers bargain for (and receive) **higher wages** this year than last, then companies may decide to hire fewer workers and to produce less output. That **reduces** the **aggregate supply** of goods produced that year. Goods flow more slowly through the circular flow, so real GNP declines.

But by how much? The circular flow diagram shows the links between households, businesses, and other sectors of the economy, but isn't very useful for making specific dollar estimates of one sector's impact on the others. The AD-AS model in chapter 10 permits more precise estimates, but at the cost of moving to a somewhat higher level of abstraction.

Fortunately, the AD-AS model is similar in some ways to the microeconomic supply and demand model you studied in chapter 3. The AD curve slopes downward to the right, just as the demand curve for an individual good does; the AS curve slopes upward, just as the demand for an individual good does. Macroeconomic equilibrium occurs at the price and output level where AD and AS intersect, just as before.

Not everything carries over from the earlier model however, so you should not attempt to read things into the AD-AS framework that are not really there. The demand curve for a single good slopes downward because of diminishing marginal utility by consumers, while the AD curve slopes downward because of the **real balance** effect.

There is also a great deal of similarity between the supply curve for a particular good and the aggregate supply curve for the entire economy. In both models higher prices increase the profitability of supplying more output, so both curves slope upward and to the right. The major difference between the two situations is that most companies can continue increasing their output almost without limit. Just hire more workers, rent a larger building, buy more tools and machinery, arrange to have additional materials sent in each month. That cannot happen in the macroeconomy, which encompasses *all* of the particular goods and services supplied by the nation. In the long run, national output can't be expanded by shifting resources from one industry to another, because the two effects are offsetting in the GNP accounts. This suggests that the economy's **long run aggregate supply** curve is (approximately) **vertical**. Higher prices (P) do not stimulate production (Q) in the long run. It follows that increases in aggregate demand can only temporarily increase real national output.

When policy makers and others overlook or deny this longer run constraint (limit) on national output, they often advocate policies that have disastrous consequences. As noted in the text, policy makers in the 1960s attempted to expand national output with policies that stimulated aggregate demand. Defense spending rose, new social spending programs were created, and the money supply grew more rapidly. Real economic activity increased all right — right up until inflation increased to an unacceptable rate. Policy makers spent the next decade combatting inflation with on again-off again "tight" monetary policies, higher taxes, and price controls. If a stimulative aggregate demand policy could permanantly increase real output above natural GNP (or permanantly lower unemployment below the natural rate of unemployment), we would have found out about it in the 1960s and '70s.

One result has been for economists and policy makers to devote more time to increasing aggregate supply while holding demand in check. You will learn more about these matters in a later chapter. . . .

Part 2.   Review of Concepts from Earlier Chapters
Prior to reading chapter 10 , match statements at left with the appropriate concept at right.

___1. Additions to the flow of dollars through the economy.
___2. A reduction in spending in the circular flow model.

___3. Planned consumption and investment expenditures
___4. Business purchases of structures, equipment, and inventories

___5. The quantity of newly produced goods and services.
___6. Emphasizes impact of spending by consumers, businesses, others.

___7. Examines impact of money supply on the macroeconomy.
___8. Household spending that occurs at a zero income level.

a. investment spending
b. income-expenditure model
c. MV-PQ model
d. total planned expenditures
e. real GNP
f. autonomous consumption
g. injection
h. leakage

Part 3. Key Concepts in this Chapter
After reading chapter 10 in the text, answer the following questions.

1. The aggregate supply / demand curve shows the quantity of national output people would buy at various price levels.

2. The aggregate supply / demand curve shows the quantity of national output offered for sale at various price levels.

3. A rightward shift in aggregate demand indicates that injections / leakages have increased.

4. The real _____ effect says that individual wealth and spending will increase if all prices and wages decline by an equal percentage amount.

5. A beneficial supply shock shifts the aggregate supply curve to the right / left .

6. Ceteris paribus, rising / declining wages will cause the aggregate supply curve to shift leftward.

7. Other than a changing price level, anything that causes a downward shift in total planned expenditures (in the income-expenditure model) will cause the aggregate demand curve to shift rightward / leftward .

8. During 1966-69, aggregate demand in the U.S. increased / decreased significantly. Consequently the unemployment rate rose / fell and the inflation rate rose / fell .

9. If unemployed workers do not have the skills needed to fill available jobs, structural / cyclical unemployment is observed.

10. The aggregate demand curve indicate that people will buy more goods as the general price level declines because the real value of their income / money balances is greater at the lower price level.

11. Structural / Frictional unemployment exists when a person is in the process of changing jobs.

12. "Full employment" indicates that the actual unemployment rate equals the cyclical / natural / zero rate of unemployment.

13. Higher income tax rates increase / reduce the willingness of workers and other factor owners to supply their services. Therefore higher tax rates imply a leftward / rightward shift in the economy's aggregate supply curve.

14. The natural rate of unemployment probably is about _____ to _____%.

15. The long-run aggregate supply curve is horizontal / vertical / circular / a 45-degree line .

16. When the unemployment rate exceeds the natural rate, real GNP exceeds / is less than the natural real GNP.

17. The natural rate of unemployment is the sum of the cyclical / frictional unemployment rate and the structural / seasonal unemployment rate.

18. If workers believe the general price level will rise in the near future, they will bargain for higher / lower wages. That will cause the aggregate supply curve to shift to the right / left .

19. An inflationary gap exists whenever real GNP _exceeds / is below_ natural real GNP.

20. Exhibit 10-8 in the text indicates that there is _a positive / an inverse_ relationship between the unemployment rate and real GNP.

21. In a stable, self-equilibrating economy actual real GNP tends to move toward _____ real GNP.

22. Ceteris paribus, a leftward shift in the aggregate demand curve will cause the general price level to _rise / fall_. Ceteris paribus, a leftward shift in the aggregate supply curve will cause the general price level to _rise / fall_.

23. An increase in the general price level will cause the TPE curve to shift _upward / downward_. This shift in TPE _does / does not_ cause the aggregate demand curve to shift leftward. If anything else causes the TPE curve to shift, that _will / will not_ cause the aggregate demand curve to shift.

24. If labor productivity increases, the aggregate supply curve will shift to the _right / left_.

25. If actual unemployment is less than the natural rate, market wages will tend to _rise / fall_. That will shift the short run aggregate supply (SRAS) curve to the _right / left_.

26. A long run equilibrium for the economy occurs at the intersection of the aggregate _____ curve and the _short / long_ run aggregate _____ curve.

Part 4. Problems and Exercises
After reading chapter 10 in the text you should be able to work the following problems.

1. Examine the following events or policies and indicate with a check mark (√) whether they affect aggregate demand, aggregate supply, or neither; and indicate whether the effect is positive, negative, or zero in each instance.

Agg. Demand		Agg. Supply		Neither	Event
+	-	+	-	0	
					a. Income tax rates are increased
					b. Autonomous consumption declines
					c. Increase in business investment spending
					d. Decline in labor productivity
					e. A reduction in wage rates
					f. Decrease in expected rate of inflation
					g. Beneficial supply shock
					h. Increase in manufacturers' utility costs
					i. A spending injection into the circular flow
					j. A decrease in government purchases of goods
					k. An increase in net exports from the U.S.
					l. A reduction in the U.S. money supply
					m. The working age population increases

2. The table below shows the U.S. unemployment rate, 1980-87.

Year	Unemp. Rate (%)
1980	7.1
1981	7.6
1982	9.7
1983	9.6
1984	7.5
1985	7.2
1986	7.0
1987	6.2

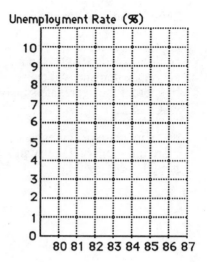

Unemployment Rate (%)

a. Graph the data in the grid provided at right.

b. Assume the natural rate of unemployment is 6% and draw a horizontal line indicating that amount.

c. What happened to the <u>difference</u> between the actual unemployment rate and the natural rate during the 1980s?

_____

_____

3. In the graph at right, notice that equilibrium real GNP exceeds Q_n.

a. The unemployment rate is currently
 <u>above / below</u> the natural rate of unemployment.

b. In this situation wages will tend to
 <u>rise / fall</u>, which will push the SRAS curve to the <u>right / left</u>.

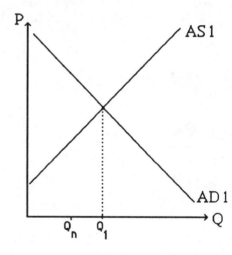

4. Refer to the diagram at right.

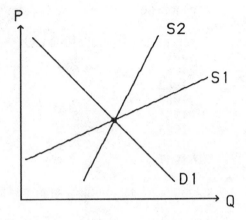

    a. Starting at the initial macroeconomic
equilibrium (at P1-Q1), an increase in
aggregate demand will cause output to expand
by more if the aggregate supply curve is
 S1 / S2 .

    b. An increase in aggregate demand will be
more inflationary if the aggregate supply curve
is S1 / S2 .

5. In the graph at right, notice that Qn exceeds
equilibrium real GNP.

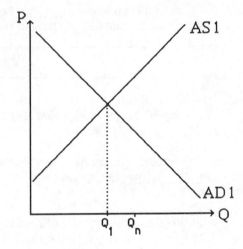

    a. The unemployment rate is currently
 above / below the natural rate of unemployment.

    b. In this situation wages will tend to rise / fall ,
which will push the SRAS curve to the right / left .

6. The following table includes data from the text regarding U.S. inflation and unemployment during the 1960s.

Year	Unemp. Rate	Infl. Rate
1964	5.0%	1.3%
1965	4.4	1.7
1966	3.7	2.9
1967	3.7	2.9
1968	3.5	4.2
1969	3.4	5.4

a. Graph this data in the grid provided at right, then sketch a straight line through the points that shows the general relationship between the two variables during the time period under consideration.

b. The curve you have drawn is a short run Phillips curve. According to the short run Phillips curve, reducing the unemployment rate means the nation will have a _higher / lower_ inflation rate.

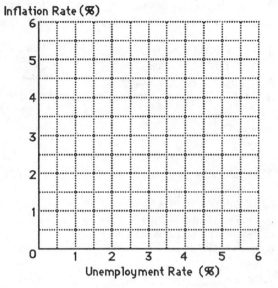

Part 5. Self Test
Multiple choice questions

1. Suppose total planned expenditures (TPE) is composed of consumption and investment. The TPE curve shifts downward and the economy moves up the aggregate demand (AD) curve. Which of the following events would bring this about?

a. a rise in investment
b. a fall in the price level
c. a rise in the price level
d. a fall in investment
e. c and d

Answer: _____

2. Suppose total planned expenditures (TPE) is composed of consumption and investment. The TPE curve shifts upward and the economy moves down the aggregate demand (AD) curve. Which of the following events would bring this about?

a. a rise in investment
b. a fall in the price level
c. a rise in the price level
d. a fall in investment
e. a and b

Answer: _____

3. Since the total planned expenditure curve is made up of consumption and investment at a particular price level, what happens to real GNP if consumption falls?

a. Real GNP increases
b. Real GNP decreases
c. Real GNP does not change
d. Real GNP either increases or decreases, depending upon what causes the price level to change

Answer: _____

4. What curve shows the real output people are willing to buy at different price levels, ceteris paribus?

a. the aggregate investment curve
b. the aggregate supply curve
c. the aggregate demand curve
d. both b and c

Answer: _____

5. The real balance effect refers to:

a. the change in the purchasing power of dollar-denominated assets
b. the real changes in GNP that occur because of changes in nominal aggregate supply
c. the situation of aggregate demand and aggregate supply in equilibrium
d. the interest rate effect produced by changes in the value of nonmonetary assets

Answer: _____

6. If the price level rises, the value of your cash holdings will _____ , so you will _____ consumption, which causes the total planned expenditure curve to shift _____ .

a. fall, decrease, downward
b. rise, increase, upward
c. fall, decrease, upward
d. rise, decrease, downward
e. none of the above

Answer: _____

7. The total planned expenditure (TPE) curve shifts upward at a constant price level. What could have caused this?

a. a fall in autonomous consumption
b. a leftward shift in the aggregate demand curve
c. the real balance effect
d. a rise in autonomous consumption
e. c and d

Answer: _____

8. Which of the following statements is false?

a. A change in net exports can shift the aggregate demand (AD) curve.
b. A change in government expenditures can shift the AD curve.
c. A change in autonomous consumption can shift the AD curve.
d. A change in the price level can shift the AD curve.
e. c and d

Answer: _____

9. A rise in wage rates:

a. causes the short-run aggregate supply (SRAS) curve to shift leftward
b. causes the aggregate demand (AD) curve to shift rightward
c. causes the SRAS curve to shift rightward
d. causes the AD curve to shift leftward

Answer: _____

10. Smith, who is searching for a job, thinks that every wage offer he is offered has less purchasing power than it actually has. We would say that:

a. Smith has an expected inflation rate higher than the actual inflation rate
b. Smith has an expected inflation rate lower than the actual inflation rate
c. Smith has too much wealth
d. the economy is in short-run equilibrium
e. b and d

Answer: _____

11. The frictional rate of unemployment plus the structural rate of unemployment is equal to the:

a. basic rate of unemployment
b. natural rate of unemployment
c. super-normal unemployment rate
d. efficient unemployment rate

Answer: _____

12. If the natural rate of unemployment is 5 percent, and the current unemployment rate is 6 percent, then the economy:

a. is producing more real GNP than it does at full employment
b. is in an inflationary gap
c. is producing less real GNP than it does at full employment
d. a and b
e. b and c

Answer: _____

13. If the economy is in long-run equilibrium it is:

a. producing real GNP at a level at which the long-run aggregate supply (LRAS) curve intersects the aggregate demand (AD) curve
b. producing real GNP at a level at which there exists an inflationary gap
c. producing real GNP at a level at which there exists a recessionary gap
d. producing real GNP at a level at which the natural rate of unemployment is greater than the (actual) unemployment rate
e. none of the above

Answer: _____

14. Most economists estimate the natural rate of unemployment to be somewhere between:

a. 4.0 and 6.9 percent
b. 3.8 and 6.6 percent
c. 4.0 and 6.5 percent
d. 3.9 and 6.0 percent

Answer: _____

15. The unemployment that arises whenever available workers do not match available jobs in terms of skills required is called:

a. frictional unemployment
b. structural unemployment
c. concrete unemployment
d. non-matching unemployment

Answer: _____

True-False

16. The real balance effects always works to   T F
move the total planned expenditure curve upward.

17. An increase in autonomous consumption moves   T F
the economy from one point on an aggregate demand
curve to another point on the same curve.

18. Some economists believe that the economy   T F
cannot cure itself of a recessionary gap because
wages are sticky in the downward direction.

19. If the economy is in long-run equilibrium,   T F
there is no recessionary gap.

20. If real GNP is less than natural real GNP,   T F
the economy is in an inflationary gap.

Fill in the blank

21. That portion of total consumption that is independent of the level of income is called _____ .

22. A fall in wage rates causes the short-run aggregate supply curve to shift
_____ .

23. If a person searching for a job has an expected inflation rate lower than the actual inflation rate, he will search _____ than if his expected inflation rate equals the actual inflation rate.

24. Natural real GNP is the same as _____ real GNP.

25. If real GNP is greater than natural real GNP, the economy is in a(an) _____ .

Part 5. Answers to Self Test

1. c 2. b 3. b 4. c 5. a 6. a 7. d 8. d 9. a 10. a
11. b 12. c 13. a 14. c 15. b
16. F 17. F 18. T 19. T 20. F
21. autonomous consumption 22. rightward 23. less
24. full-employment 25. inflationary gap

Part 6.   Answers

Part 2 Review of Concepts
1. g 2. h 3. d 4. a 5. e 6. b 7. c 8. f

Part 3 Key Concepts
1. demand   2. supply   3. injections   4. balance   5. right   6. rising   7. leftward
8. increased, fell, rose   9. structural   10. money   11. frictional   12. natural
13. reduce, leftward   14. 4.0 and 6.5   15. vertical   16. is less than   17. frictional, structural
18. higher, left   19. exceeds   20. an inverse   21. natural   22. fall, rise
23. downward, does not, will   24. right   25. rise, left   26. demand, long, supply

Part 4 Problems and Exercises

1. a. AS- b. AD- c. AD+ d. AS- e. AS+
   f. AS+ g. AS+ h. AS- i. AD+ j. AD-
   k. AD+ l. AD- m. AS+
2c. It rose at first, but declined rapidly in 1985-87.
3. below, rise, left
4. a. S1   b. S2
5. a. above   b. fall, right
6. a. see graph below   b. higher

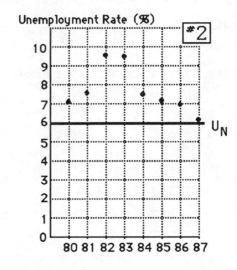

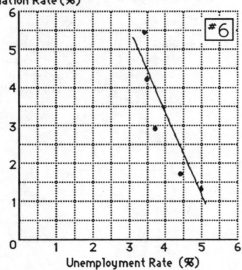

Chapter 11
From Classical to Keynesian Theory

Part 1. Introduction and Purpose
Consider the following points as you read chapter 11 in the text.

Some 50 years ago, economics was going through a **Keynesian Revolution**. The prevailing macroeconomic theory — the **classical** economists' **quantity theory** of money, discussed in chapter 9 — relied heavily on the idea that large and ongoing surpluses of goods and labor (unemployment) would be prevented from arising by the operation of supply and demand. A surplus of labor should cause wages to decline, thereby eliminating the surplus.

To be sure, the classical economists (Say, Pigou, Marshall, and others) recognized that difficulties might arise. Since it takes a little time for labor contracts to be revised and for people to move from communities where jobs are scarce to where they are plentiful, it could take several months or maybe a year for the economy to move to equilibrium following a supply or demand "shock" that disturbed the initial equilibrium.

The classical logic was widely accepted until well after World War I. But the U.S. suffered with massive unemployment throughout the **Great Depression** of the 1930s, Britain suffered throughout the two decades of the 1920s and '30s, and most other industrialized nations went through a similar traumatic experience. Many interpreted these events as empirical proof that the world does not operate the way the classical economists had claimed.

Although a number of economists were discussing possible solutions at the time, Keynes' model was the most fully developed and provided perhaps the clearest answers. According to Keynes, inadequate investment spending by businesses reduced income by workers and other factor owners, so most households reduced consumption spending. (The consumption function illustrates this idea.) The reduction in consumption outlays constitutes yet another leakage from the circular flow, so business sales and factor incomes decline yet again — putting even more downward pressure on economic activity. Once started, the economy may spiral downward and not arrive at an equilibrium until large surplusses of labor and other goods are observed.

Having concluded that under-investment by the business community caused aggregate demand to be inadequate to provide employment and other aspects of economic stability, Keynes suggested one remedy — an offsetting policy of **government spending**. If business investment falls by $1 million, then let government spend another million to prevent the economy from faltering. Analysts later showed that policy makers could achieve the same result by transferring dollars to or away from households (**transfers** and **taxes**), thereby causing household spending to offset fluctuations in investment.

With a **large marginal propensity to consume (MPC)**, any initial reduction in investment spending by businesses will lower worker incomes and trigger a reduction in consumption spending by households. That is important, because the decline in consumption spending causes more companies to lay off workers so household incomes decline again. With a **smaller MPC**, the initial drop in investment would have triggered relatively smaller spending cuts by households, and that would have reduced the second-round decline in total spending. The downturn in overall economic activity would have been smaller with an equal reduction in investment spending.

Adding the initial decline in GNP resulting from the decline in investment spending to the second-, third-, and later-round declines produces a result that surprises some people — namely that shifts in autonomous spending can cause total income in the economy to change by a <u>multiple</u> of the original shift. This is the famous Keynesian **multiplier** (m). *The total stimulus to GNP and national income is found by multiplying the initial change in autonomous spending by the Keynesian multiplier.*

Critics of Keynesian analysis have emphasized one shortcoming of his theory — namely that the demand for goods determines the pace of economic activity while factors that might influence the supply of goods are neglected. In the original Keynesian model, the aggregate supply curve is horizontal so the entire impact of the spending increase falls on employment and output; none is transmitted into rising prices. More recently, economists have downplayed the horizontal (no-inflation) segment of the aggregate supply curve and have made increasing use of its upward-sloping and vertical segments. This change in emphasis has resulted in major changes in the policy prescriptions of economists in the past decade, as you will learn in later chapters.

Part 2. Review of Concepts from Earlier Chapters
Prior to reading chapter 11, match statements at left with the appropriate concept at right.

___1. Combinations of goods produced with all available resources.
___2. Total earnings of labor and the other factors of production.
___3. Frictional plus structural unemployment.
___4. Desired consumption plus planned investment.
___5. Aggregate demand equals aggregate supply.
___6. Addition to the flow of dollars through the economy.
___7. Diagram showing flow of dollars & goods through the economy.
___8. Spending that is unrelated to the level of income.
___9. Believe the money supply exerts a strong influence on the economy.
___10. Total planned production exceeds total planned expenditures.
___11. Real GNP exceeds natural real GNP.
___12. Natural real GNP exceeds actual real GNP.
___13. Rising real money balances increases total spending.

a. full employment
b. circular flow
c. inflationary gap
d. PPF curve
e. equilibrium
f. national income
g. monetarists
h. unplanned inventories
i. injection
j. TPE curve
k. recessionary gap
l. autonomous
m. real balance effect

Part 3. Key Concepts in this Chapter
After reading chapter 11 in the text, answer the following questions.

1. _____ wrote *The General Theory of Employment, Interest, and Money* in 1936.

2. The Keynesian spending multiplier equals one divided by the marginal propensity to save / consume .

3. The _____ propensity to _____ is the fraction of an extra dollar's worth of income that will be spent on consumption goods.

4. According to Say's Law, demand / supply creates its own demand / supply .

5. The analysis of classical economists included the assumption that prices, _____, and the _____ rate were flexible both upward and downward. Keynes accepted / rejected this assumption.

6. According to the classical / Keynesian theory, the economy is always operating on or near its production possibilities frontier.

7. During the Great Depression of the 1930s, the unemployment rate in the U.S. rose to about ____%.

8. The model developed by Keynes / Say showed that it was possible for total planned spending to fall short of total production.

9. As interest rates rise, household saving should normally rise / fall as a percentage of income. This implies that household consumption expenditures probably increase / decrease as the interest rate increases.

10. The _____ function gives the relationship between consumption spending and disposable household income.

11. Which of the following do not cause the consumption function to shift?___
    a. increases in consumer wealth   c. increase in consumer disposable income
    b. decline in expected rate of inflation   d. rise in the market interest rate

12. In Keynes' basic model, the aggregate supply curve is horizontal / vertical / upward sloping .

13. True or false? _____ Keynes believed that a market economy contains a self-correcting mechanism that will cause the economy to reach equilibrium.at or near the point of full-employment.

14. The average / marginal propensity to consume is the slope of the consumption function.

15. If the TPE curve shifts downward, the equilibrium level of income will rise / fall by an equal amount / less than / more than the initial shift in TPE.

16. Low-income consumers probably have a higher / a lower / about the same average propensity to consume as high-income consumers.

17. A lower interest rate will probably cause the consumption function to shift _____.

18. Suppose a $5000 downward shift in the total planned expenditures curve causes equilibrium GNP to decline by $30,000. Then the multiplier equals _____.

19. Changing expectations generally exert a _greater / smaller_ influence on consumption spendingthan on investment spending.

20. If there are substantial idle resources the aggregate supply curve is _horizontal / vertical_.

21. Any level of income that equates total planned expenditures and total planned production is the _equilibrium / full employment / maximum possible_ income.

22. The passive supply hypothesis is consistent with a _horizontal / vertical_ aggregate supply curve.

23. If the economy moves to a less-than-full-employment equilibrium, the policy Keynes advocated for moving the economy toward full employment was to stimulate _TPE / aggregate supply_.

24. The Keynesian explanation of what caused the Great Depression was an autonomous reduction in _consumption / investent / government_ spending.

25. President _____'s administration utilized Keynesian economies to stabilize the economy.

26. According to the interview with Professor Paul Samuelson, the Keynesian economic model is constructed upon _solid / insecure_ microeconomic foundations.

27. Professor Samuelson tends to _accept / reject / be indifferent toward_ the Keynesian macro model.

28. True or false? _____ Samuelson tends to believe that the U.S. will go through another depression like that of his childhood (the 1930s).

29. The view that current consumption is influenced more by one's lifetime income than income in the current year is embodied in the _____ income hypothesis.

30. True or false? _____ According to the permanant income hypothesis, if your income temporarily doubles in a given year your consumption will also tend to double.

Part 4. Problems and Exercises
After reading chapter 11 in the text you should be able to work the following problems.

1. Consider the following consumption function:

    $C = 50 + 0.75\ Yd,$

    where C represents dollars' worth of consumption spending and Yd represents dollars worth of disposable income. Use this function to calculate household spending and complete the table.

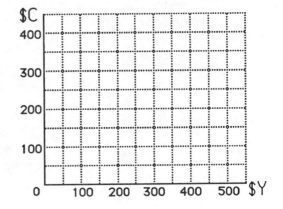

Yd	$0	$100	$200	$300	$400	$500
C	$__	$___	$___	$___	$___	$___

Once you have completed the table, plot the values you calculated for C against those for Yd in the grid at right. Connect the points with a straight line.

2. Since Yd = C + S, then it must also be true that:

a.   Yd - _____ = S   (fill in the blank).

b. Carry out the mathematical exercise called for in the equation to compute household saving. Use the figures from exercise 1 above.

Yd	$0	$100	$200	$300	$400	$500
S	$__	$___	$___	$___	$___	$___

c. Once you have completed the table, plot the values you calculated for S against those for Yd in the grid above. Connect the points with a straight line.

3. Fill in the blank spaces in the table at right. Knowledge of any one of the three variables (MPC, MPS, m) is sufficient to calculate the other two. This exercise will develop your ability to compute Keynesian spending multipliers.

	MPC	MPS	m
a.	0.5	____	____
b.	0.6	____	____
c.	____	0.25	____
d.	____	____	3
e.	____	0.1	____
f.	____	____	4.5

4. Fill in missing values in the table at right. In each instance an autonomous spending change triggers a shift in TPE, which triggers a multiplier impact on GNP.

	ΔCo or ΔIo	m	ΔY
a.	$10	2	$___
b.	$20	___	$50
c.	$___	5	$500
d.	$50	___	$200
e.	$90	8	$___
f.	$___	4	$240

5. Examine the following events and indicate with a check mark (√) whether they affect autonomous consumption, autonomous investment, or neither; and indicate whether the effect is positive, negative, or zero in each instance.

Event	ΔCo +	ΔCo -	ΔIo +	ΔIo -	Neither 0
a. Increase in interest rates					
b. A decrease in household wealth					
c. Increase in the corporate profits tax rate					
d. A rise in household income					
e. Increased optimism about future sales					
f. Increased optimism about future income					
g. Rise in utilization rate of capital capacity					

6. Use the grid at right to draw two aggregate supply curves.

   Curve 1 should reflect the situation where there are substantial supplies of idle resources (factors of production). Label this curve S1.

   Curve 2 should reflect the situation where resources are fully employed. Label this curve S2.

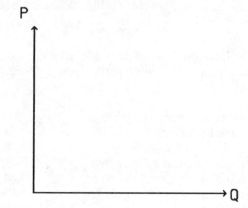

7. The following table shows consumption spending at various levels of income. Indicate in the spaces provided the amount of autonomous and induced consumption spending at each income.

Yd	$0	$100	$200	$300	$400
C	$50	$125	$200	$275	$350
Autonomous C					
Induced C					

8. See the diagram at right.

a. If the interest rate is i_1, then leakages _equal / exceed / are less than_ injections into the circular flow of the economy.

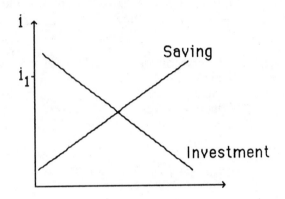

b. Classical economists felt that if $i = i_1$ the interest rate would _rise / fall_. This change in interest rates would tend to _increase / reduce_ leakages and to _increase / reduce_ injections, both of which would cause the economy to move _toward / away from_ full employment.

c. In the Keynesian model, the real interest rate _will / will not_ decline to the equilibrium level. Consequently real income may remain _above / below_ full employment real income.

9. _Classical / Keynesian_ economists tend to support laissez faire economic policies while _Classical / Keynesian_ economists tend to support activist fiscal policies.

Part 5. Self Test
Multiple choice questions

1. The economy always operates close to or on its producton possibilities frontier. This is a position held by:

a. Keynesian economists
b. classical economists
c. Marxist economists
d. all economists
e. no economists

Answer: _____

2. Say's law says:

a. supply creates itself
b. demand creates itself
c. demand creates its own supply
d. supply creates its own demand
e. none of the above

Answer: _____

3. According to classical economists, the relationship between the amount of funds firms plan to invest and the interest rate is _____ ; the relationship between the amount of funds households plan to save and the interest rate is _____ .

a. inverse, direct
b. direct, inverse
c. direct, direct
d. inverse, inverse

Answer: _____

4. Keynes believed that:

a. there would be no involuntary unemployment
b. the economy would always be near or on its production possibilities frontier
c. that the Great Depression was proof that classical economics was right
d. that total spending is always sufficient to purchase all the goods produced
e. none of the above

Answer: _____

5. If income rises from $600 to $700 and consumption rises from $300 to $380, the marginal propensity to consume is:

a. .54
b. .80
c. 1.00
d. .65

Answer: _____

6. If income rises from $10,000 to $10,700 and consumption rises from $8,000 to $8,525, the marginal propensity to save is:

a. .25
b. .30
c. .75
d. .50
e. none of the above

Answer: _____

7. If autonomous consumption rises by $600 and as a result real national income rises by $3,000, the the marginal propensity to consume is:

a. .90
b. .80
c. .70
d. .60
e. none of the above

Answer: _____

8. In the basic Keynesian theory, a decrease in wealth will:

a. raise autonomous consumption, shift the consumption function upward (in the I-E framework), and raise real national income by more than the change in autonomous consumption
b. raise autonomous consumption, shift the consumption function downward (in the I-E framework), and lower real national income by more than the change in autonomous consumption
c. lower autonomous consumption, shift the consumption function upward (in the I-E framework), and lower real national income by more than the change in autonomous consumption
d. lower autonomous consumption, shift the consumption function downward (in the I-E framework), and lower real national income by more than the change in autonomous consumption

Answer: _____

9. A firm is not likely to alter its investment expenditures if:

a. the firm has excess productive capactity and current sales increase
b. the firm does not have excess productive capacity and current sales increase
c. the firm has excess productive capacity and current sales remain constant
d. a and c
e. b and c

Answer: _____

10. In the basic Keynesian theory, if the MPC = .80 and autonomous investment increases by $10 million, then real national income:

a. falls by $40 million
b. rises by $50 million
c. falls by $100 million
d. rises by $100 million

Answer: _____

11. No matter what demand is, supply rises to meet it. This is known as:

a. the passive supply hypothesis
b. Say's law
c. the first law of Keynesian economics
d. the equation of exchange
e. none of the above

Answer: _____

12. Hyman Minsky believes that the central message of the General Theory by Keynes is:

a. changes in the money supply are important to changes in interest rates and investment
b. businessmen are greedy
c. it is necessary to model an economy with a Wall Street
d. it is necessary to model an economy with a Main Street

Answer: _____

13. The first American economist to win the Nobel Prize in Economics was:

a. John Maynard Keynes
b. Paul Samuelson
c. Milton Friedman
d. David Ricardo

Answer: _____

14. In the basic Keynesian theory, a less optimistic expecation of futures sales will:

a. lower autonomous investment, shift the investment function downward (in the I-E framework), and lower real national income by more than the change in autonomous investment
b. raise autonomous investment, shift the investment function upward (in the I-E framework), and raise real national income by an amount equal to the change in autonomous investment
c. raise autonomous investment, shift the investment function upward (in the I-E framework), and raise real national income by more than the change in autonomous investment
d. lower autonomous investment, shift the investment function upward (in the I-E framework), and raise real national income by an amount less than the change in autonomous investment

Answer: _____

15. In the basic Keynesian theory, it is assumed that:

a. there are no idle resources
b. there are few idle resources
c. prices and wages are completely flexible
d. idle resources come into the picture after full-employment output has been achieved
e. none of the above

Answer: _____

True-False

16. According to classical economists, there could   T F
be a general overproduction of goods in a money
economy but not in a barter economy.

17. Classical economists believed in laissez-faire.   T F

18. Keynes believed that the internal structure of   T F
the economy is extremely competitive and that
wage-price flexibility exists.

19. The marginal propensity to consume is   T F
necessarily greater than the marginal propensity
to save.

20. The relationship between wealth and consumption   T F
is expected to be inverse.

Fill in the blank

21. The larger the marginal propensity to save, the _____ the multiplier.

22. Consumption spending that changes in response to changes in income is called _____.

23. 1/1-MPC is the _____ .

24. Most economists would agree that the stock market crash of 1929 was an _____ not a
_ _____ of the Great Depression.

25. Say's law implies that there cannot be either a general _____ or _____ of goods.

Part 5. Answers to Self Test

1. b 2. d 3. a 4. e 5. b 6. a 7. b 8. d 9. d 10. b
11. a 12. c 13. b 14. a 15. e
16. F 17. T 18. F 19. F 20. F
21. smaller 22. induced consumption 23. multiplier
24. effect, cause 25. overproduction, underproduction

Part 6. Answers

Part 2 Review of Concepts
1. d 2. f 3. a 4. j 5. e 6. i 7. b 8. 1 9. g 10. h 11. c 12. k   13. m

Part 3 Key Concepts
1. Keynes   2. save   3. marginal consume   4. supply, demand   5. wages, interest, rejected
6. classical   7. 25%   8. Keynes   9. rise, decrease   10. consumption   11. c
12. horizontal   13. false   14. marginal   15. fall, more than   16. a higher   17. upward
18. 6   19. smaller   20. horizontal   21. equilibrium   22. horizontal   23. TPE   24. investment
25. Kennedy   26. insecure   27. accept   28. false   29. permanant   30. false

Part 4 Problems and Exercises

1. C=$50, 125, 200, 275, 350, 425
   also see grid at right

2. a. Yd - C = S
   b. S=$-50, -25, 0, 25, 50, 75
   c. see grid at right

3. a. 0.5, 2   b. 0.4, 2.5   c. 0.75, 4
   d. 0.6667, 0.3333   e. 0.9, 10
   f. 0.7778, 0.2222

4. a. $20   b. 2.5   c. $100
   d. 4   e. $720   f. $60

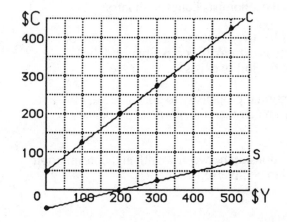

5. a. C-, I-   b. C-   c. I-
   d. 0   e. I+   f. C+   g. I+

6. See graph at right.

7. Auto. C always equals $50;
   Induced C: $0, $75, $150, $225, $300

8. a. exceed
   b. fall, reduce, increase, toward
   c. will not, below

9. Classical, Keynesian

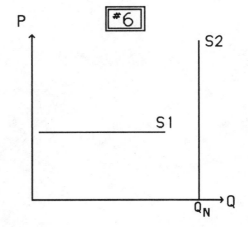

Chapter 12
Monetarism

Part 1. Introduction and Purpose
Consider the following points as you read chapter 12 in the text.

Back in chapter 6 you learned about the circular flow of income and product. The Keynesian economic model presented in chapter 11 examined how many dollars and how many goods will actually flow through the economy in a given year; the answer was autonomous spending by households, businesses, government, and foreigners, multiplied by k, the spending multiplier.

Chapter 12 will present a different answer to the same question. **Monetarists** believe that the total volume of economic activity is better predicted with a model that incorporates the money supply and money demand. Stripped to the bare essentials, the **monetarist model** says that the aggregate demand for goods rises and falls because of changes in the quantity of excess money balances. That is, if money supply exceeds money demand there is an **excess supply of money**. Households, businesses, and others attempt to rid themselves of the extra money by exchanging it for other goods and services (of which they have too few). By trading their "extra" money for goods, people increase aggregate demand and cause GNP to rise.

In the other direction, if for any reason people have **deficient money balances** — if money demand exceeds money supply — they reduce their rate of spending in the hope of accumulating more money. The reduced rate of spending implies a decline in aggregate demand.

What causes money supply to exceed money demand, or vice versa? Glad you asked. We saw back in chapters 7 and 8 that the money supply rises and falls with changes in the monetary base and the money multiplier. In chapter 12 we will see that money demand will shift because of changes in the level of **interest rates** or in the **expected rate of inflation**. Increases in the interest rate or in the expected inflation rate lower money demand, as does a reduction in the **period between paychecks** for the typical American. The demand for money increases if interest or expected inflation declines, or if the period between paychecks lengthens.

Much of the material in chapter 12 — money supply, aggregate demand, aggregate supply — is a review of topics examined in earlier chapters. The only really new ideas are (1) the **analysis of money demand** and (2) the emphasis on **excess (or deficient) money balances as the primary determinant of aggregate demand**.

We touched on (2) just a minute ago. When people hold more of one asset (money) than they want to hold, they trade the excess for other assets (goods). The asset-shuffling causes an increase in total spending for goods — an increase in aggregate demand. In a similar way, a deficiency of money balances will cause people to reduce spending so aggregate demand will decline.

The analysis of money demand is the other new feature on the macroeconomic landscape. Several mathematical manipulations are required to arrive at the conclusion that money demand (Md) is related to k, P, and Q:

Md = k x P x Q,

where k is the inverse of velocity (1/V). The value of k will increase whenever velocity decreases, and vice versa. In general, k rises whenever money becomes a more attractive asset to hold, relative to other assets. People also seek to hold larger money balances if their incomes rises, which accounts for the PxQ entry in the above equation.

Although k, P, and Q all influence the amount of money people wish to hold, there is an important difference between changes in desired money balances that result from changes in k and those resulting from changes in PxQ (or nominal income). A change in k (or V) will cause GNP to change, but changes in desired money balances caused by rising or falling household incomes (PxQ) will not.

Today's **monetarists** are the modern day equivalents of the **classical** economists. Most monetarists believe the economy tends toward a full employment equilibrium and that the government should play only a minor role in the economy (rather than follow the activist prescriptions of Keynesian economists).

Actually there are **two main differences** between the monetarists' macroeconomic model and that of the classical economists. Where classical economists considered V (the **velocity** of money) to be a fixed number over considerable periods of time, monetarists believe that V changes, but in predictable ways. Therefore there is a clear and predictable link between M and PxQ (or Y), although not the precise 1-to-1 relationship about which the classical economists wrote.

Second, many monetarists accept the view that the short run **aggregate supply** curve is upward sloping, rather than vertical as predicted by their classical forerunners Monetarists argue that increases in aggregate demand may increase Q as well as P in the short run (within a year or two), but agree that over longer periods the full impact of a change in aggregate demand is reflected in higher prices rather than greater real output. What classical economists believed would be the immediate effect of an expanding money supply, monetarists believe will only eventually come to pass.

Part 2. Review of Concepts from Earlier Chapters
Prior to reading chapter 12, match statements at left with the appropriate concept at right.

__1. The number of times per year each dollar is spent on newly produced goods.   a. monetarists
__2. A belief that government should not interfere in the private economy.   b. MV=PQ
__3. An index of total real output produced.   c. real GNP
__4. What one foregoes in order to acquire something.   d. GNP
                                                                                            (nominal)
__5. Macroeconomic model used by classical economists.   e. flow
__6. Shape of aggregate supply curve in a non-inflationary economy.   f. stock
__7. Quantity supplied exceeds amound desired.   g. velocity
__8. Economic statistic measured at a point in time.   h. opportunity
                                                                                            cost
__9. Economic activity measured over a time interval (e.g., one year).   i. laissez faire
__10. Shape of aggregate supply curve in an economy with no idle resources.   j. surplus
__11. Economists who emphasize impact of money on the economy.   k. vertical
__12. Real GNP multiplied by general price level.   l. horizontal
__13. Expected inflation causes aggregate supply to shift in this direction.   m. leftward

Part 3. Key Concepts in this Chapter
After reading chapter 12 in the text, answer the following questions.

1. The cost of holding money balances is the _____ foregone from not holding other assets instead.

2. If M^{AH} > M^d, there is a surplus / shortage / equilibrium amount of money in the economy.

3. Monetarists believe that the short run aggregate supply curve is
 horizontal / vertical / upward sloping . Monetarists believe that the long run aggregate supply
curve is horizontal / vertical / upward sloping .

4. A decline in the velocity of money implies that the demand for money has increased / decreased .

5. An increase in the velocity of money will cause aggregate demand to increase / decrease .

6. Three factors that can change the velocity of money (or k) are changes in the _____ rate,
the expected _____ rate, and the period between _____.

7. Increases in the general price level and real GNP cause people to hold larger / smaller money
balances. Increases in P and Q do / do not cause V (or k) to change.

8. Suppose money balances begin to pay interest while interest rates on other assets remain unchanged.
This should cause money demand to rise / fall , which would tend to create a shortage / surplus
of money to develop. The result would be for aggregate demand to increase / decrease .

9. If M^{AH} < M^d, there is a surplus / shortage / equilibrium amount of money in the economy.

10. True or false? _____ Monetarists believe price and wage flexibility keeps the economy operating
near its production possibilities frontier.

11. Monetarists do not believe V is constant, but they do believe it moves in a _____ way.

12. Ceteris paribus, a decrease in the money supply causes aggregate demand to _rise / decline_. Ceteris paribus, an increase in money demand causes aggregate demand to _rise / decline_.

13. In the interview with Professor Allan Meltzer, he says the money supply _can / cannot_ be used to "steer" the economy where policy makers want it to go because the relationship between money and real output _is / is not_ strong enough to use for that purpose.

14. Allan Meltzer and other monetarists believe that stable, long-term growth in real economic activity requires a monetary policy that is _steady & reliable / flexible & adaptable_.

15. In the interview with Professor Karl Brunner, he notes that in every dis-inflationary episode the velocity of money _rises / declines_. This implies that dis-inflation causes the demand for money to _increase / decrease_.

16. True or false? _____ Karl Brunner believes that the Federal Reserve's monetary policies are highly predictable three to six months in advance.

17. Suppose the money supply rises by $10 billion, and on the same day the demand for money rises by the same amount. In combination these two events _will / will not_ cause the aggregate demand curve to shift.

18. Starting at a point of equilibrium, if people begin to anticipate less inflation in upcoming months and years than previously, the velocity of money will _rise / fall_. This will cause aggregate demand to _increase / decrease_, which in turn will tend to cause the general price level to _rise / fall_.

19. If individuals desire to hold $650 billion in money balances but actually hold $720 bil., they will _hold / spend_ the excess. That will cause nominal GNP to _rise / fall_, which in turn will _increase / reduce_ the amount of money people desire _above / below_ $650 bil. This effect will cause the surplus of money to _grow larger / shrink_.

20. If GNP is $5,000 and M1 is $800, the value of k (or 1/V) is _____.

Part 4. Problems and Exercises

After reading chapter 12 in the text you should be able to work the following problems.

1. The table at right contains information used in the monetarist macro model. Use the information that is provided plus the theory you have learned to fill in the missing values.

	M^d	Y	V	k
a.	$100	$400	____	____
b.	$____	$1000	5	____
c.	$500	$____	____	0.5
d.	$____	$2000	10	____
e.	$600	$3000	____	____

2. Assume the following money demand function:
   $M^d = kY$, where k=0.25.

a. With this information fill in values for M^d in the table below for each income level indicated.

Y	$0	$100	$200	$300	$400	$500
M^d	___	___	___	___	___	___

b. Use information from your table to graph the relationship at right between nominal income and desired money balances. Use a ruler to sketch the general relationship between M^d and Y.

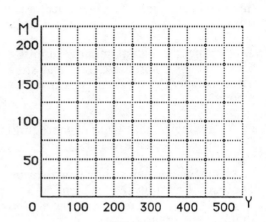

3. Refer to the previous question. Assume the value of k rises to 0.30.

a. recalculate the amount of desired money balances at each income level, and graph your results in the graph for question 1.

Y	$0	$100	$200	$300	$400	$500
M^d	___	___	___	___	___	___

b. As k rose from 0.25 to 0.3, the amount of desired money balances has increased / decreased at each income level.

4. The table below shows the U.S. money supply in 1929-33.

Year (Dec.)	M1 (billions)
1929	$26.2
1930	$24.6
1931	$21.9
1932	$20.4
1933	$19.8

a. Graph these values in the grid at right.

b. Assume _desired_ money balances were equal to the 1929 money supply, and remained at that level over the next four years. This implies there was a shortage / surplus of money at the time.

c. According to the monetarist analysis, monetary policy in 1929-33 caused aggregate demand to increase / decrease .

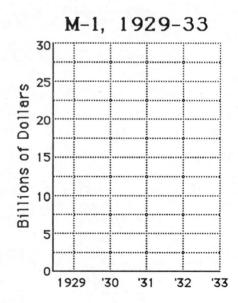

M-1, 1929-33

5. The graph at right contains a curve that depicts the relationship between GNP (income) and the desired amount of money balances.

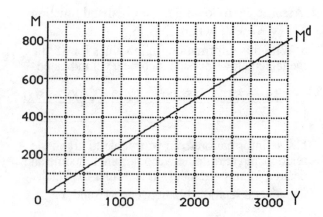

a. Assume the actual money supply equals $500. Draw a horizontal line that shows the money supply (which is the same at all levels of income).

b. According to the diagram the equilibrium GNP in this economy is $_____.

c. Assume the money supply now rises to $600. The equilibrium level of income will now be $_____. (Hint: draw the new money supply curve in the graph.)

6. In the left-hand column of the following table are listed a series of events that can change money demand or money supply. Indicate by placing a check mark (√) in the appropriate box whether the event causes money demand or money supply to rise (+) or fall (-).

Then indicate whether the change in money demand or supply will increase (+) or decrease (-) aggregate demand.

Event	ΔMd +	ΔMd -	ΔMs +	ΔMs -	ΔAD +	ΔAD -
a. Interest rates on bonds increase						
b. Interest rate earned on money balances increases						
c. The required reserve ratio is lowered						
d. The expected inflation rate declines						
e. Monetary base is lowered						
f. Time between paychecks is lengthened						
g. Money multiplier falls						
h. Fed purchases government securities from banks						

Part 5. Self Test
Multiple choice questions

1. Monetarists:

a. agree with classical economists that the economy is a self-regulating mechanism that settles into equilibrium at full-employment output
b. disagree with classical economicsts that the economy is a self-regulating mechanism that settles into equilibrium at full-employment output
c. agree with Keynesians that the economy is a self-regulating mechanism that settles into equilibrium at full-employment output
d. do not believe that the economy is a self-regulating mechanism that settles into equilibrium at full-employment output

Answer: _____

2. Which of the following statements is true?

a. In the modern quantity theory of money velocity is assumed to be constant but real GNP is not.
b. In the modern quantity theory of money real GNP is assumed to be constant but velocity is not.
c. In the modern quantity theory of money velocity and real GNP are assumed to be constant.
d. In the modern quantity theory of money velocity and real GNP are not assumed to be constant.

Answer: _____

3. Monetarists are interested in knowing:

a. what Keynesians are interested in knowing, namely what the multiplier equals and whether it is stable
b. what Keynesians are interested in knowing, namely what velocity equals and whether it is stable
c. what the multiplier equals and whether it is stable, whereas Keynesians are interested in knowing what velocity equals and whether it is stable
d. what velocity equals and whether it is stable, whereas Keynesians are interested in knowing what the multiplier equals and whether it is stable

Answer: _____

4. When an economist says that an individual is holding too little money, he means that:

a. the individual has little money and should try to get more from others
b. the individual is keeping too little money in the bank
c. the individual is literally holding too little money in his or her hands
d. the individual has too little of his or her wealth in money form and too much in nonmoney form

Answer: _____

5. A decrease in the price level (P) will:

a. increase the quantity supplied of money
b. decrease the quantity demanded of money
c. decrease the quantity supplied of money
d. increase the quantity demanded of money

Answer: _____

6. There has been an increase in the quantity demanded of money. Which of the following events could have brought this about?

a. an increase in real GNP
b. a decrease in real GNP
c. an increase in the price level
d. a and c
e. b and c

Answer: _____

7. Individuals desire to hold a smaller fraction of their incomes in money balances:

a. as the interest rate (return) on close substitutes for money rises
b. as the interest rate (return) on close substitutes for money falls
c. the more wealth they have
d. the less wealth they have
e. b and d

Answer: _____

8. As the interest rate (return) on close substitutes for money rises:

a. the money demand line rotates downward
b. the money demand line rotates upward
c. the quantity demanded of money rises
d. the money supply expands

Answer: _____

9. An expected increase in the inflation rate will:

a. decrease velocity and rotate the money demand line upward
b. increase velocity and rotate the money demand line upward
c. decrease velocity and rotate the money demand line downward
d. increase velocity and rotate the money demand line downward

Answer: _____

10. Which of the following describes money market equilibrium? (Ms = quantity supplied of money, MAH = quantity of money people actually hold, Md = quantity demanded of money.)

a. Ms > MAH = Md
b. Ms = MAH > Md
c. Ms < MAH = Md
d. Ms/MAH = Md
e. none of the above

Answer: _____

11. Which of the following statements is true?

a. If individuals desire to hold $350 billion at a nominal national income of $1,000 billion and they desire to hold $400 billion at a nominal national income of $1,333, then the fraction of their incomes they desire to hold at the two income levels is the same.
b. If individuals desire to hold $400 billion at a nominal national income of $1,250 billion and they desire to hold $500 billion at a nominal national income of $1,333, then the fraction of their incomes they desire to hold at the two income levels is the same.
c. If individuals desire to hold $600 billion at a nominal national income of $1,000 billion and they desire to hold $400 billion at a nominal national income of $1,333, then the fraction of their incomes they desire to hold at the two income levels is the same.
d. If individuals desire to hold $500 billion at a nominal national income of $1,000 billion and they desire to hold $400 billion at a nominal national income of $1,333, then the fraction of their incomes they desire to hold at the two income levels is the same.
e. none of the above

Answer: _____

12. Which of the following statements is true?

a. The demand for money is the same as the demand for income.
b. The demand for money is the same as the demand for credit.
c. The demand for money is the same as the demand for wealth.
d. a and c
e. none of the above

Answer: _____

13. The person who coined the term monetarism is:

a. Allan Meltzer
b. Milton Friedman
c. Karl Brunner
d. Adam Smith
e. unknown

Answer: _____

14. A decrease in money demand, ceteris paribus, will likely result in people holding _____ money at the current nominal income level and _____ in expenditures on goods and services.

a. too much, an increase
b. too little, a decrease
c. too much, a decrease
d. too little, an increase

Answer: _____

15. Milton Friedman is a:

a. monetarist
b. Keynesian
c. Marxist economist
d. classical economist

Answer: _____

True-False

16. The modern quantity theory of money is the same   T F
as the simple quantity theory of money.

17. Monetarists believe in laissez-faire.   T F

18. Keynesians believe that a change in autonomous   T F
spending will be transmitted to real GNP through
the multiplier.

19. Money is a flow.   T F

20. An increase in the price level will increase   T F
the quantity supplied of money.

Fill in the blank

21. Monetarists believe that the velocity of money is highly _____ .

22. A _____ represents the direct relationship between the quantity demanded of money and
nominal national income.

23. An expected decrease in the inflation rate will _____ velocity.

24. If the quantity supplied of money is greater than the quantity demanded of money, the money market is
in _____ .

25. If the quantity supplied of money is greater than the quantity demanded of money, then people are
holding _____ money.

Part 5. Answers to Self Test

1. a 2. d 3. d 4. d 5. b 6. d 7. a 8. a 9. d 10. e
11. e 12. e 13. c 14. a 15. a
16. F 17. T 18. T 19. F 20. F
21. stable 22. money demand line 23. decrease
24. disequilibrium 25. too much

Part 6. Answers

Part 2 Review of Concepts
1. g   2. i   3. c   4. h   5. b   6. 1   7. j   8. f   9. e   10. g   11. a   12. d   13. m

Part 3 Key Concepts
1. interest   2. surplus   3. upward sloping, vertical   4. increased   5. increase
6. interest, inflation, paychecks   7. larger, do not   8. rise, shortage, decrease   9. shortage
10. True   11. predictable   12. decline, decline   13. cannot, is not   14. steady & reliable
15. declines, increase   16. false   17. will not   18. fall, decrease, fall
19. spend, rise, increase, above, shrink   20. 0.16 (V=6.25)

Part 4 Problems and Exercises

1. a. 4, 0.25   b. $200, 0.20   c. $1000, 2
   d. $200, 0.10   e. 5, 0.20

2. $0, $25, $50, $75, $100, $125

3. a. $0, $30 $60 $90 $120 $150
   b. See graph at right
   c. increase

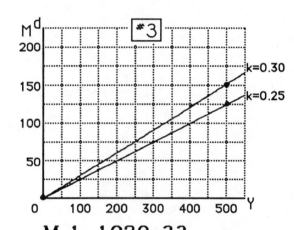

4. a. Graph at right
   b. shortage ($M^d > M^{AH}$ by about 25%)
   c. decrease

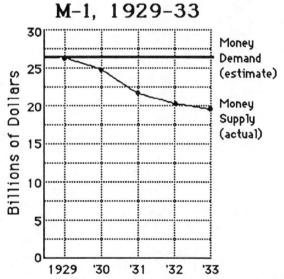

5. a. See graph at right.
   b. $2000
   c. $2400

6. a. Md-, AD+   b. Md+, AD-
   c. Ms+, AD+   d. Md+, AD-
   e. Ms-, AD-   f. Md+, AD-
   g. Ms-, AD-   h. Ms+, AD+

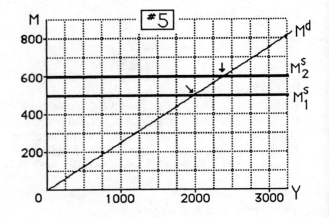

Chapter 13
Inflation

Part 1. Introduction and Purpose

Consider the following points as you read chapter 13 in the text.

The two most widely discussed economic problems in recent years have been inflation and unemployment. The present chapter examines the first of these, and unemployment is the subject of the next. Because inflation and unemployment are such (un)popular topics, what you learn from these chapters will largely determine how well you understand other people's views on the macroeconomy, and whether other people will respect your own opinions on these matters.

For many years inflation has been popularly described as a situation where *too many dollars are chasing too few goods*. This oversimplified view of inflation is subject to criticism on several points, but conveys the general nature of the problem. Expressed in terms of the circular flow model, inflation can result when the spending flow accelerates without a corresponding increase in national production. The general price level can also increase if total spending remains constant, but fewer goods are produced. With the same number of dollars chasing fewer goods, the average unit of output will exchange for more dollars than before.

More generally though, economists discuss inflation within the context of an aggregate demand-aggregate supply framework that provides a more useful picture of economic activity than the circular flow model. In the AD-AS model, **inflation is a supply and demand phenomenon** that arises either because of increases in the aggregate demand or decreases in the aggregate supply of goods.

Before continuing, let's pause for a couple of definitions of inflation. In general, inflation refers to an increase in the general level of prices. Some analysts use the **CPI** as a measure of the general price level, while others refer to the **GNP price deflator**. The text mainly uses the CPI, though in practice it does not usually make much difference which specific index one uses. Inflation comes in two types: **temporary** or **sustained**. That is, the overall price level may display a one-shot increase that begins and ends within a few months. Alternatively, prices may continue to rise for an extended period, perhaps for many years or even decades. The U.S. began flirting with sustained inflation beginning in about 1965, and even with the anti-inflation successes of the early 1980s it is still an open question whether the U.S. will return to overall price stability anytime soon.

In general, many events and policies that cause inflation have a one-shot (temporary) effect. Bad weather can reduce crop harvests and oil cartels can withhold energy from the marketplace, and both will push the price index up somewhat. Experience has shown that such difficulties often reverse themselves, rather than continuing to grow worse (and to stimulate inflation) year after year. One thing that can cause sustained inflation is an ongoing increase in the **money supply**. There are seldom any natural limits on the amount of money that a nation's central bank can create, and political will-power is not always sufficient to constrain growth in the money supply.

Since we use a supply and demand model to understand inflationary impulses in the economy, in any discussion of inflation it is a good idea to place each inflation-causing event into one of these two categories. If someone claims that event X causes inflation, immediately ask yourself whether event X would have increased aggregate demand or decreased aggregate supply. If event X doesn't have one of these effects, it's unlikely that it causes inflation. You have read about the circumstances that can cause aggregate demand and supply to shift in the past few chapters, so we need not review them here.

The aggregate demand-aggregate supply model will seem fairly obvious if you have been doing your homework this semester. In practice things aren't quite so simple — partly because it is so easy to commit the **fallacy of composition** when thinking about the macroeconomy. You will recall that it is a mistake to automatically assume that the best way to understand an issue (or object) is to analyze its individual parts. In the present case, the danger is in observing the circumstances that cause one price or a few individual prices to increase, and then projecting the same explanation onto the entire economy.

For example, it may be true that increasing demand for a particular good X will increase its price. Although to some the price increase will appear inflationary, other things will also happen that are equally important. If they spend more of their dollars on X, now consumers have fewer dollars to spend on other goods. Falling demands for these other goods will cause their prices to decline relative to X's price — so in the end the overall price level is (approximately) unchanged. The lesson is that isolated events are not inflationary if they affect individual markets rather than aggregate demand and supply.

Aside from economists, few people are interested in studying inflation just out of curiosity Most of the interest in inflation is due to its capacity to injure or benefit various groups in society. Given the reality of a major economic trend, it is always better to understand what is taking place and make the appropriate adjustments to one's circumstances.

In general, unforseen **inflation redistributes wealth** within society *from* those who have contracted to receive fixed payments of dollars *to* those who have contracted to pay fixed amounts. This is sometimes expressed by saying that unexpected inflation redistributes wealth from creditors to debtors (from lenders to borrowers). Because unforseen — or **unanticipated** — inflation has the ability to redistribute wealth, people attempt to predict it in advance and arrange their financial affairs so as not to be on the losing end of these redistributions. If it is thought that prices are likely to rise by 10% over the coming year, workers may bargain for a $10 wage today plus a 10% inflation premium to compensate for the rising cost of living later in the year. Lenders behave in much the same way. They will require borrowers to pay a certain amount of real interest for a loan, plus an inflation premium to compensate for the lost purchasing power of the dollars by the time they are repaid. Once lenders add the inflation premium onto their interest charges, a 10% inflation no longer redistributes wealth from lenders to borrowers. A similar conclusion applies to workers and others who will incorporate expected inflation rates into their long-term contracts. The inflation that redistributes wealth is the unanticipated variety, when the dollar has more or less purchasing power than had been planned on.

Many of the economic difficulties experienced in the 1980s have been the result of fighting the inflation of the 1960s and '70s. You will learn more about some of these effects in the next chapter.

Part 2. Review of Concepts from Earlier Chapters
Prior to reading chapter 13, match statements at left with the appropriate concept at right.

__1. An index of the price of goods purchased by the typical household.
__2. The predicted rate of price increase.
__3. Real output when workers are fully employed.
__4. A dollar amount that has been adjusted for changes in the price level.
__5. If money supply exceeds money demand.

__6. Higher wages and other factor prices shift this curve leftward.
__7. A dollar amount not adjusted for changes in the general price level.
__8. An index of the price of all newly produced goods and services.

__9. The quantity of national output purchased at various price levels.

a. real
b. aggregate supply
c. aggregate demand
d. GNP price deflator
e. excess money
   balances
f. natural real GNP
g. CPI
h. expected inflation
   rate
i. nominal

Part 3. Key Concepts in this Chapter
After reading chapter 13 in the text, answer the following questions.

1. Inflation can result from a leftward shift (decrease) in the aggregate demand / supply curve.

2. A one-shot increase in the price level is known as _____ inflation.

3. If expected inflation causes workers to bargain for higher wages, the aggregate supply curve will shift
   to the right / left .

4. When inflation pushes a person into a higher tax bracket, then inflation has caused _____ creep.

5. _____-inflation is an extreme case of inflation.

6. The observed market interest rate published in the daily newspaper equals the nominal / real interest
   rate plus the expected rate of _____.

7. True or false? _____ According to the text, unions are a major cause of inflation in the U.S.

8. Inflation redistributes wealth away from creditors / debtors and toward creditors / debtors .

9. The real interest rate is positive / negative / zero if the expected rate of inflation exceeds the nominal
   interest rate.

10. If the government issues bonds to finance its spending programs and the Fed purchases / sells
    bonds in the marketplace to prevent interest rates from rising, the Fed's policy is "accomodative."

11. An increase / decline in the inflation rate is called disinflation.

12. Refer to exhibits in the text and compare two five-year periods, 1975-80 and 1980-85. The inflation
    rate fell / rose in the second period compared to the first. The ratio of federal deficits to GNP
     fell / rose from the first period to the second.

13. A continuing increase in the general price level is known as hyper- / sustained / dis- inflation.

14. Inflation can result from a rightward shift in the aggregate _supply / demand_ curve.

15. An increase in the money supply causes interest rates to _rise / fall_ because of the liquidity effect.

16. An increase in the money supply causes interest rates to increase because of the _liquidity / income_ effect and the expectations effect.

17. Within about _1 / 6 / 12 / 24_ month(s), the net effect of an expanding money supply is likely to cause interest rates to move higher than they were originally.

18. If a person's expectations about next year's inflation rate are formed by looking at past inflation, then that person has _rational / adaptive / sluggish_ expectations.

19. If a person's expectations about next year's inflation rate are formed by looking at past inflation as well as current monetary and fiscal policies (and other conditions), then that person has _____ expectations.

20. As a practical matter, an expanding _____ supply is the most likely cause of a sustained inflation.

21. The practice of lowering tax rates to offset the effects of bracket creep is referred to as tax _____.

22. Buying gold or other assets whose real value is maintained during periods of inflation is called _accomodating / hedging against / indexing_ inflation.

23. In speaking about continued inflation, Milton Fiedman has written that, "Inflation is always and everywhere a _fiscal / supply side / monetary_ phenomenon."

Part 4. Problems and Exercises
After reading chapter 13 in the text you should be able to work the following problems.

1. An important objective of chapter 13 is to understand the impact of various events and policies on the inflation rate. In each of the cases listed below, decide whether the general price level will rise or fall. Indicate the direction of change in the blanks provided at left, then compute your score below. (Hint: To do well at this exercise, ask yourself how each event affects aggregate demand or aggregate supply.)

__a. Income tax rates are increased (other policies keep total tax collections from changing)
__b. Autonomous consumption declines
__c. Business investment spending increases (but capital goods are not yet used in production)
__d. Labor productivity declines
__e. Wage rates are reduced
__f. An adverse supply shock occurs
__g. A beneficial supply shock occurs
__h. Manufacturers' energy costs increase
__i. Additional spending is injected into the circular flow
__j. Government purchases of goods decline (with no change in tax collections)
__k. Net exports of goods from the U.S. increase
__l. The U.S. money supply is reduced

Answers: Rise (a,c,d,f,h,i,k) Fall (b,e,g,j,l)

- If your score was 0-6, you are probably genetically related to a Treasury Secretary or Federal Reserve chairman who served during the 1970s. Scientists have found a cure for this: Stay home in bed and re-read chapters 10 and 13 of your text.
- If you scored 7-9, you understand the basics but are are weak when it comes to translating events into aggregate demand-aggregate supply terms. Draw a diagram for each of the cases listed above.
- If you scored 10-11, you've got potential. The bad news is that it's hard to live up to your potential.
- If you scored 12, you qualify as a Grand Master of Inflation. This title used to be valuable, but rising prices have reduced its real value to near zero.

2. The following table contains information about the consumer price index duing the 1980s. Use this data to calculate the inflation rate using the formula in your text. [That is, subtract column (3) from (2), divide the result by col (3), and multiply by 100.]

(1) Year	(2) Current CPI	(3) CPI Previous Year	(4) Change in CPI	(5) ΔCPI÷Previous CPI	(6) x100
1980	82.4	72.6	9.8	0.135	13.5%
1981	90.9	82.4	____	____	____%
1982	96.5	90.9	____	____	____%
1983	99.6	96.5	____	____	____%
1984	103.9	99.6	____	____	____%
1985	107.6	____	____	____	____%
1986	109.6	____	____	____	____%
1987	113.6	____	____	____	____%
1988	118.3	____	____	____	____%

3.   a. Graph the inflation figures you calculated in problem 2 (above) in the grid provided at right. Connect the points in your graph to show the general trend of inflation in the 1980s.

b. Beginning with 1980 as the peak inflation rate, it appears to have taken about ____ years to lower inflation to a mild and sustained rate.

c. The adaptive expectations theory suggests that the inflation rate people expect for 1989 and '90 might be about _____%.

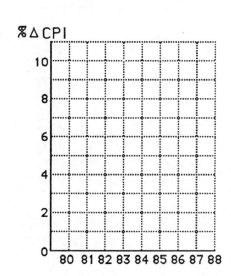

4. The following table contains hypothetical information on interest rates and the anticipated rate of inflation. Fill in blank spaces in the table by using the interest rate relationship identified by Irving Fisher (whose biography can be found in the text).

	Nominal Interest Rate	Real Interest Rate	Expected Inflation Rate
a.	____%	4%	2%
b.	9%	____%	6%
c.	8%	5%	____%
d.	____%	2%	12%
e.	21%	____%	16%
f.	7%	3%	____%

5. a. An expanding money supply initially causes interest rates to _rise / fall_ due to the liquidity effect, but later interest rates _rise / fall_ due to the income and expectations effects.

b. If people have adaptive expectations, the expectations effect (above) will occur _earlier / later_ than if they had rational expectations.

Part 5. Self Test
Multiple choice questions

1. Inflation is:

a. an increase in the prices of services, but not goods
b. an increase in the prices of oil, steel, and food
c. an increase in the general level of prices
d. a rise in the interest rates

Answer: _____

2. The CPI in year 1 was 80 and the CPI in year 2 was 96. The annual inflation rate between year 1 and year 2 was:

a. approximately 20 percent
b. approximately 15.4 percent
c. approximately 14.5 percent
d. approximately 16.9 percent

Answer: _____

3. The economy starts off producing natural real GNP. Next, aggregate supply falls, ceteris paribus. As a result, the price level _____ in the short run. If in the long run the economy has moved back to producing natural real GNP, the price level will be _____.

a. rises, higher than it was in short run equilibrium
b. falls, lower than it was in short run equilibrium, but higher than it was originally (before aggregate supply fell)
c. rises, lower than it was originally (before aggregate supply fell)
d. rises, equal to what it was originally (before aggregate supply fell)

Answer: _____

4. Can an increase in the demand for money cause temporary inflation?

a. yes, because it shifts the aggregate demand curve rightward
b. no, because it shifts the aggregate demand curve leftward
c. yes, because it shifts the aggregate demand curve leftward
d. yes, because it shifts the aggregate supply curve leftward

Answer: _____

5. The nominal interest rate equals:

a. the real interest rate times the expected inflation rate
b. the real interest rate plus the expected inflation rate
c. the real interest rate minus the expected inflation rate
d. twice the real inerest rate

Answer: _____

6. Suppose Vernon and Alice place $15,000 into a savings account on January 1, 1981. If the inflation rate was 15% over the year, and the expected inflation rate was 0%, what dollar amount would Vern and Alice have needed to receive from their savings account on January 1, 1982 to maintain their purchasing power?

a. $17,250
b. $18,000
c. $18,800
d. $17,875
e. None of the above

Answer: _____

7. Suppose Dave and Nicole placed $10,000 into a savings account on January 1, 1979 that paid an interest rate of 8%. If the inflation rate was 10% over the year, then what was the overall interest rate return Dave and Nicole received on their savings account over the year?

a. + 2 percent
b. - 2 percent
c. + 18 percent
d. - 18 percent

Answer: _____

8. Suppose the nominal interest rate is 11 percent, the expected inflation rate is 5 percent, and the (actual) inflation rate turns out to be 7 percent. It follows that:

a. the ex ante real interest rate is 6 percent and the ex post real interest rate is minus 2 percent
b. the ex ante real interest rate is 5 percent and the ex post real interest rate is minus 3 percent
c. the ex ante real interest rate is 6 percent and the ex post real interest rate is 4 percent
d. the ex ante real interest rate is 4 percent and the ex post real interest rate is 7 percent

Answer: _____

9. For the ex post real interest rate to be less than the ex ante real interest rate:

a. the inflation rate has to turn out to be less than the expected inflation rate
b. the inflation rate has to turn out to be greater than the expected inflation rate
c. the inflation rate has to turn out to be equal to the expected inflation rate
d. individuals have to borrow more at lower interest rates than at higher interest rates
e. individuals have to borrow less at lower interest rates than at higher interest rates

Answer: _____

10. An indexed progressive income tax structure combined with inflation can:

a. push taxpayers into higher tax brackets even though their real income has remained constant
b. pull taxpayers into lower tax brackets even though their real income has remained constant
c. redistribute buying power away from taxpayers to government
d. a and c
e. none of the above

Answer: _____

11. Economists usually refer to periods of extreme inflation as:

a. inflationary highs
b. hyperinflations
c. confederacy inflations
d. superinflations
e. none of the above

Answer: _____

12. The change in the real and nominal interest rates due to a change in the supply of loanable funds is referred to as the:

a. income effect
b. expectations effect
c. the liquitity effect
d. real effect

Answer: _____

13. The change in the real and nominal interest rates brought on by a change in nominal national income is referred to as the:

a. liquitity affect
b. expectations affect
c. income affect
d. nominal affect

Answer: _____

14. The change in the nominal interest rate due to a change in the expected inflation rate is called the:

a. expectations affect
b. income affect
c. liquitity affect
d. nominal affect
e. none of the above

Answer: _____

15. Disinflation is:

a. a rise in the general level of prices
b. a decrease in the rate of inflation
c. a fall in the general level of prices
d. an increase in the rate at which inflation is occurring

Answer: _____

True-False

16. Temporary inflation can originate only on the demand side   T F
    of the economy.

17. A decrease in the demand for money can cause temporary   T F
    inflation.

18. A rise in a single price is inflation.   T F

19. There was hyperinflation in Germany in the early 1920s.   T F

20. The nominal interest rate is always higher than the real   T F
    interest rate

Fill in the blank

21. _____ redistributes buying power from lenders to borrowers.

22. If the expected inflation rate is formed adaptively, then it is _____ to change
    than if it is formed rationally.

23. Suppose the government incurs a budget deficit and the Fed allows the money supply
    to increase. This is referred to as _____ monetary policy.

24. A decrease in the rate of inflation is referred to as _____ .

25. _____ invented the visible part index system.

Part 5. Answers to Self Test

1. c 2. a 3. d 4. b 5. b 6. a 7. b 8. c 9. b 10. e
11. b 12. c 13. c 14. a 15. b
16. F 17. T 18. F 19. T 20. F
21. Unanticipated inflation 22. slower 23. accomodative
24. disinflation 25. Irving Fisher

Part 6. Answers

Part 2 Review of Concepts
1. g   2. h   3. f   4. a   5. e   6. b   7. i   8. d   9. c

Part 3 Key Concepts
1. supply   2. temporary   3. left   4. bracket   5. Hyper   6. real, inflation   7. False
8. creditors (lenders), debtors (borrowers)   9. negative   10. purchases   11. decline   12. fell, rose
13. sustained   14. demand   15. fall   16. income   17. one   18. adaptive   19. rational
20. money   21. indexation   22. hedging   23. monetary

Part 4 Problems and Exercises

2. 81: 10.3%   82: 6.2%   83: 3.2%
   84: 4.3%   85: 3.6%   86 :1.9%
   87 :3.6%   88: 4.1%

3. a. See graph at right.
   b. three years (1980-83)
   c. 4%

4. a. 6%   b. 3%   c. 3%
   d. 14%   e. 5%   f. 4%

5. a. fall, rise   b. later

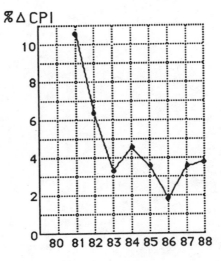

Chapter 14
Unemployment

Part 1. Introduction and Purpose

Consider the following points as you read chapter 14 in the text.

Almost everyone has been out of work at one time or another, and those who have been know that the period between jobs can be an agonizing experience filled with uncertainty and self doubt. The Great Depression of the 1930s, when about one worker in four was out of work, was such a traumatic experience that full employment has remained a top priority for policy makers ever since.

Economists like to look at unemployment on two different levels. First, unemployment may result from what are essentially microeconomic decisions or events. If you are lazy and don't look for a job or don't work hard at the job you have, you are likely to be unemployed. If business managers decide to supply products that customers don't want to buy, they will soon go out of business and workers will be thrown out of jobs. At another level, unemployment may result from events that no individual worker or business manager can influence. These are the macroeconomic causes of unemployment which are also the subject of the present chapter. To put the point a little differently, we are interested in the forces which tend to create (or reduce) unemployment on an economy-wide basis.

Fortunately, it is possible to use the same basic AD-AS model to analyze unemployment that we used in the previous chapter on inflation. Whereas increases in aggregate demand may be inflationary, **decreases in aggregate demand** may lead to unemployment. **Reductions in aggregate supply** (caused by adverse supply shocks) may also eliminate job opportunities and contribute to unemployment.

The analysis of unemployment is fairly simple. *Events that reduce equilibrium real GNP in the AD-AS model simultaneously reduce the demand for workers* and other factors of production. Ford Motor Company may need 300,000 workers to produce 1.5 million cars, but if it reduces output to 1 mil. units then somewhat fewer workers are needed. Either workers will be laid off in such circumstances, or the company's owners will realize smaller profits (or larger losses) than otherwise. Given the choice between laying off workers and earning smaller profits, many shareholders prefer layoffs. The inverse relationship between real GNP and unemployment is used in several of the AD-AS diagrams included in the chapter, so it is worthwhile to keep the relationship in mind as you read.

As always, it is important to distinguish what happens in one part of the economy from what happens to the overall economy. For example, if workers in the steel industry strike for higher wages, the cost of producing steel increases so steel producers raise their prices. The Law of Demand tells us that less steel will be sold at the higher price, so steel companies will lay off some of their workers. Unemployment? Maybe for few weeks or months while displaced steel workers search for jobs elsewhere, but eventually they will move to other occupations so employment and unemployment will return to their original levels. Because displaced workers can work elsewhere, what's true for the steel industry (unemployment) may not be true for the overall economy.

It also follows that different policies are appropriate to deal with different kinds of unemployment. If deficient aggregate demand results in unemployment, then a policy to stimulate aggregate demand is called for. But if a large number of steel workers are out of work while the rest of the economy is operating normally, it is impossible to manipulate aggregate demand in a way that will put steel workers back to work without over-stimulating the rest of the economy and triggering inflation. Unemployment in the steeel industry is a microeconomic event that cannot effectively be dealt with by monetary and fiscal policy makers.

Broadly speaking, unemployment that results from inadequate aggregate demand is referred to as **cyclical unemployment**. The term comes from cycle, as in business cycle. Cyclical unemployment reflects ups and downs in general business activity.

You may recall reading about two other kinds of unemployment back in chapter 11 — frictional unemployment and structural employment. **The natural rate of unemployment** is found by adding together the frictional and structural unemployment rates. The natural rate can be thought of the unemployment rate that aggregate demand policies are ineffective against — that is, unemployment which cannot be reduced by monetary and fiscal policies without triggering inflation. These policies are only effective when the total unemployment rate is above the natural rate — when cyclical unemployment is positive. Many economists estimate the natural unemployment rate at about 5.5%, so aggregate demand policies should be stimulative only when the unemployment rate is above that figure. It is standard practice for economists to speak of **full employment** when the unemployment rate equals the natual rate. It may seem strange to speak of full employment when several million people are out of work, but once unemployment has fallen to that level there is little that expansionary monetary and fiscal policies can do to put people back to work. Further reductions in unemployment require policies to improve the functioning of individual markets — essentially a microeconomic problem.

To recap, monetary and fiscal policy are mainly effective against cyclical unemployment — which means unemployment in excess of the natural rate. These policies operate by stimulating aggregate demand, which causes companies to hire more workers in order to produce more output (to satisfy the new demand). Stimulative policies are recommended only when inadequate aggregate demand or adverse supply shocks reduce national output significantly below natural real GNP.

Part 2. Review of Concepts from Earlier Chapters
Prior to reading chapter 14, match statements at left with the appropriate concept at right.

__1. Real output when there is full employment.
__2. The anticipated increase in prices.
__3. Rising real GNP means this will decline.
__4. Full employment rate of unemployment.
__5. Curve showing maximum output with all factors fully employed.
__6. When the unemployment rate is high this tends to decline.

a. unemployment rate
b. PPF curve
c. real wage
d. 4-6.5%
e. natural real GNP
f. expected inflation rate

Part 3. Key Concepts in this Chapter
After reading chapter 14 in the text, answer the following questions.

1. The _____ _____ force includes virtually everyone who has a job plus everyone looking for a job.

2. The unemployment rate equals the number of people unemployed added to / minus / divided by the civilian labor force.

3. The employment rate equals the number of employed people divided by the noninstitutional adult civilian _____ .

4. True or false? _____ The unemployment rate plus the employment rate add up to 100%.

5. An optimistic / discouraged / unhappy worker is one who could not find work, and eventually left the labor force rather than continue looking.

6. Structural / frictional unemployment results when workers with transferable skills move between jobs.

7. The natural rate of unemployment equals structural / cyclical unemployment plus long term / frictional unemployment.

8. There is a positive relationship between the duration of job search / seniority and the unemployment rate.

9. When unemployment equals the natural rate, the economy is / is not operating along its institutional PPF curve.

10. Structural / frictional / cyclical / long term unemployment is the difference betwen the actual unemployment rate and the natural rate of unemployment.

11. There are four ways a person may be counted as unemployed. She may be a job loser, a job _____, a _____ back into the labor force, or a new _____ into the labor force

12. An increase in aggregate demand will cause the wage offer curve to shift upward / downward .

13. More generous unemployment compensation benefits will cause the reservation wage curve to shift upward / downward . This tends to cause the duration of job search (and unemployment) to shorten / lengthen .

14. If a worker is on strike, he is officially counted as employed / unemployed .

15. The sum of the unemployment rate and the inflation rate is called the comfort / discomfort index, or sometimes the _____ index.

16. Okun's Law says that a _____% rise in real output is associated with a 1% reduction in the unemployment rate.

17. If workers expect inflation to increase in coming months, they will tend to bargain for higher / lower nominal (money) wages. This implies that the reservation wage curve will shift upward / downward .

18. The optimal search time for unemployed workers is determined by comparing wage offers to the _____ wage. If the former is less than the latter, then it is rational to _extend / shorten_ the period of job search.

19. If the optimal search time lengthens, the unemployment rate tends to _rise / fall_. That _increases / reduces_ total employment and production, which shifts the aggregate supply curve to the _left / right_.

20. A rightward shift in the aggregate demand curve should cause real GNP to _rise / fall_ and should cause unemployment to _rise / fall_.

Part 4. Problems and Exercises
After reading chapter 14 in the text you should be able to work the following problems.

1. The following table contains a variety of related unemployment rates. Use available information to fill in the missing figures.

	Actual	Frictional	Structural	Natural	Cyclical
a.	8%	2%	__%	__%	4%
b.	9%	__%	2%	6%	__%
c.	__%	3%	3%	__%	2%
d.	5%	__%	4%	6%	__%
e.	__%	4%	__%	6%	3%
f.	12%	2%	4%	__%	__%

Unemployment Rates (%)

2. Use the following data to compute the Misery Index, then graph your results in the grid at right.

Year	%ΔCPI	U. Rate%	Misery Index
1980	13.5%	7.1	___
1982	6.2%	9.7%	___
1984	4.3%	7.5%	___
1986	1.9%	7.0%	___
1988	4.1%	5.5%	___

What general trend do you observe?

_____

_____

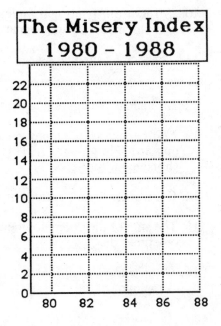

The Misery Index
1980 – 1988

3. Use data in the table to fill in missing values.

	Employed	Unemployed	Civ. Labor Force	Unemployment Rate
a.	5,500	500	_____	____%
b.	_____	1,000	20,000	____%
c.	_____	_____	100,000	10%
d.	103,000	_____	109,000	____%

4. Which of the following add to <u>cyclical</u> unemployment? Place a check mark (√) next to each event or policy that causes the cyclical unemployment rate to <u>increase</u>.

___a. Autonomous consumption spending increases.
___b. The money supply expands from $800 to $900.
___c. Oil and other energy costs increase.
___d. The aggregate demand curve shifts leftward
___e. The natural unemployment rate rises while the actual unemployment rate is unchanged.
___f. Personal taxes are increased by $100 on each citizen.
___g. Planned investment spending by business declines.
___h. The number of workers who voluntarily move between jobs increases.

5. The following table provides information on real GNP (in trillions of 1982 dollars) and the civilian unemployment rate.

Year	Real GNP	Unempl. Rate
1980	3.19	7.1%
1981	3.25	7.6
1982	3.17	9.7
1983	3.28	9.6
1984	3.50	7.5
1985	3.62	7.2
1986	3.72	7.0
1987	3.85	6.2
1988	3.99	5.5

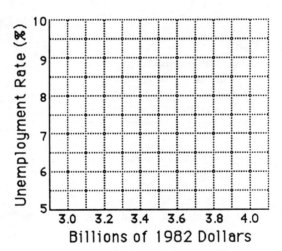

a. Graph the data in the table at right, then use a ruler to draw a straight line through the observations to indicate the approximate relationship between real GNP and the unemployment rate.

b. There is a _positive / inverse_ relationship between real GNP and the unemployment rate.

Part 5.   Self Test
Multiple choice questions

1. Everyone in the population who is not 16 years of age, in the armed forces, or institutionalized is:

a. part of the labor force
b. part of the noninstitutional adult civilian population
c. employed
d. unemployed

Answer: _____

2. Which of the following persons would be considered not in the labor force?

a. a retired person
b. a person engaged in own-home housework
c. a prison guard
d. a and b
e. a, b, and c

Answer: _____

3. If a person worked at least 15 hours per week as an unpaid member of a family farm or business, how is he or she classified?

a. as an unemployed person
b. as not in the labor force
c. as an employed person
d. as a potential worker
e. none of the above

Answer: _____

4. If a person did not work during the survey week, is currently available for work, but did not actively look for work within the past four weeks, how is he or she is classified?

a. as part of the population
b. as not in the labor force
c. as an unemployed person
d. as an employed person
e. none of the above

Answer: _____

5. The unemployment rate equals:

a. the number of unemployed persons divided by the civilian labor force
b. the number of unemployed persons divided by the noninstitutional adult civilian population
c. the number of employed persons divided by the number of unemployed persons
d. the sum of unemployed persons plus discouraged workers divided by the civilian labor force

Answer: _____

6. Suppose the noninstitutional adult civilian population equals 200,000, the civilian labor force equals 150,000, there are 120,000 employed persons and 30,000 unemployed persons. How many people are not in the labor force?

a. 50,000
b. 90,000
c. 20,000
d. 30,000

Answer: _____

7. Suppose the noninstitutional adult civilian population equals 150,000, the civilian labor force equals 130,000, there are 110,000 employed persons and 20,000 unemployed persons. If 5,000 persons who are currently "not in the labor force" decide to join the civilian labor force, and 2,000 of this group become employed and 3,000 are unemployed, then:

a. both the unemployment rate and employment rate rise
b. both the unemployment rate and employment rate fall
c. the unemployment rate rises and the employment rate falls
d. the unemployment rate falls and the employment rate rises

Answer: _____

8. If discouraged workers were classified as unemployed:

a. the unemployment rate would be lower
b. the unemployment rate would be higher
c. the unemployment rate would be no different than when discouraged workers are not classified as unemployed
d. there is not enough information to answer the question

Answer: _____

9. The discomfort index equals the:

a. unemployment rate
b. inflation rate
c. unemployment rate + inflation rate
d. unemployment rate - inflation rate
e. there is no such thing as the discomfort index

Answer: _____

10. If the unemployment rate is greater than its natural rate, then:

a. positive cyclical unemployment exists
b. negative cyclical unemployment exists
c. either positive or negative cyclical unemployment could exist, but certainly one of the two does
d. neither positive nor negative cyclical unemployment exists

Answer: _____

11. If negative cyclical unemployment exists, the economy:

a. is operating beyond its institutional production possibilities frontier (PPF) but below its physical PPF
b. is operating below its institutional PPF and real GNP is lower than natural real GNP
c. is operating on its institutional PPF and real GNP is lower than natural real GNP
d. is operating beyond its physical PPF

Answer: _____

12. Alphie was employed in the civilian labor force and was fired. Alphie is classified as a:

a. job loser
b. job leaver
c. reentrant
d. new entrant

Answer: _____

13. The average duration of unemployment and the unemployment rate:

a. are always inversely related
b. are usually inversely related
c. are usually directly related
d. are unrelated

Answer: _____

14. The lowest wage a person will accept at any time in the job search process is that person's:

a. reservation wage
b. concrete wage
c. floor wage
d. lowest acceptable wage
e. none of the above

Answer: _____

15. A decrease in optimal search time:

a. lowers wage offers
b. raises the unemployment rate
c. lowers the unemployment rate
d. raises wage offers
e. none of the above

Answer: _____

True-False

16. A discouraged worker is considered unemployed.   T F

17. An economy can operate beyond its institutional   T F
production possibilities frontier.

18. It is possible for the unemployment rate to   T F
go up at the same time the employment rate goes up.

19. If a wage offer exceeds a person's reservation   T F
wage, then the person will probably continue the
job search.

20. An increase in the unemployment rate will be   T F
followed by an increase in the optimal search time for
a job.

Fill in the blank

21. The noninstitutional adult civilan population consists of _____ and
_____ .

22. If positive cyclical unemployment exists, real GNP is _____
than it otherwise could be.

23. George used to work but quit to go to school. He has recently reentered the civilian labor force and is
looking for a job. He is classified as a _____ .

24. If the optimal search time falls, the unemployment rate _____ .

25. Higher unemployment benefits would probably _____ job search time.

Part 5. Answers to Self Test

1. b 2. d 3. c 4. e 5. a 6. a 7. a 8. b 9. c 10. a
11. a 12. a 13. c 14. a 15. c
16. F 17. T 18. T 19. F 20. F
21. persons not in the labor force, persons in the civilian labor force 22. less 23. reentrant
24. falls 25. increase

Part 6. Answers

Part 2 Review of Concepts
1. e   2. f   3. a   4. d   5. b   6. c

Part 3 Key Concepts
1 civilian labor   2. divided by   3. population   4. false   5. discouraged   6. frictional 4)
7. structural, frictional   8. search   9. is   10. cyclical   11. leaver, reentrant, entrant
12. upward   13. upward, lengthen   14. employed   15. discomfort, misery
16. 3% (this can be found in a footnote)   17. higher, upward   18. reservation, extend
19. rise, reduces, left   20. rise, fall

Part 4 Problems and Exercises

1. a. 2%, 4%   b. 4%, 3%   c. 8%, 6%   d. 2%, -1%
   e. 9%, 2%   f. 6%, 6%

2. See the graph at right
   '80: 20.6   '82: 15.9   '84: 11.8   '86: 8.9   '88:9.6;
   The Misery Index trend has been downward

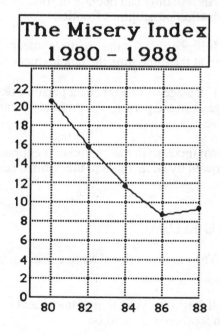

The Misery Index 1980 – 1988

3. a. 6000, 8.33%   b. 19,000, 5%
   c. 90,000, 10,000   d. 6000, 5.5%

4. √ c,d,f, g

5. a. See the graph at right
   b. inverse (as real GNP rises,
      unemployment falls)

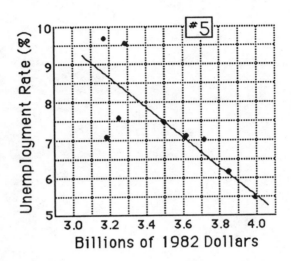

Chapter 15
The Phillips Curve and Expectations Theory

Part 1. Introduction and Purpose
Consider the following points as you read chapter 15 in the text.

Chapter 15 uses a different method to present economic concepts and theories than previous chapters. Where earlier chapters concentrated on presenting economic theories, chapter 15 is also a lesson in the **history of economic thinking**.— how our ideas have developed over the years. By discussing theories of the Phillips curve from a historical perspective you will be able to see how objections to earlier theories led to the discovery of new theories that are more useful for understanding economic phenomena.

Among the highlights of the chapter are the interviews with economists Paul Samuelson and Robert Lucas. Samuelson has long been a leading Keynesian economist, and along with Robert Solow was personally responsible for bringing the Phillips curve to America. Some twenty years later, Lucas was a leader of the movement to revise the Phillips curve analysis, and his approach to the inflation-unemployment tradeoff is now highly regarded (though not completely accepted) by the majority of economists.

Recall that a Phillips curve describes the relationship between the inflation rate and unemployment rate for a given economy. As Phillips saw it, expansionary aggregate demand policies would cause companies to hire more labor and other resources, and as they did both employment and wages would increase. His conclusion was that rising wages and decreasing unemployment should occur simultaneously, and the evidence he gathered on Britain seemed to support his prediction.

According to Paul Samuelson, on this side of the Atlantic economists wondered whether Phillips' work would be useful for predicting the inflation rate. They took Phillips' analysis one step further: rising wages (wage inflation) increase business costs, which causes suppliers to raise their prices. So if Phillips was right that declining unemployment means wage inflation, then declining employment should also mean more price inflation. Early evidence for the U.S. tended to support this **Americanized version of the Phillips curve** too, so it wasn't long until most economists were using the Phillips curve to represent the tradeoff between inflation and unemployment that every economy faced. The view was that policy makers faced a **menu of choices** such that any decision to reduce unemployment meant higher inflation had to be tolerated, and any decision to reduce inflation meant that higher unemployment had to be tolerated.

Although it was understood, the significance of one key idea was overlooked — namely that the *Phillips curve analysis concentrated exclusively on fluctuations in inflation and unemployment caused by shifts in aggregate demand.* The aggregate supply side of the economy was ignored, presumably because it would respond passively to demand shifts. Each of the refinements made to the Phillips curve analysis shows what happens when resource owners and product suppliers play a more active role than the one alloted them in the Keynesian model. If workers expect more inflation they will bargain for higher wages and if savers expect more inflation they will demand more interest for the use of their funds. These events and others shift the aggregate supply curve to the left — fewer goods are supplied at any given price, or higher prices will be charged for any given quantity of output.

Although several prominent economists were discussing these issues in the late 1960s, Milton Friedman is resposible for bridging the gap between inflation expectations, the aggregate supply curve, and the vertical Phillips curve in his 1967 presidential address to the American Economics Association. While Friedman's **natural rate hypothesis** argued that the long run Phillips curve is vertical, he continued to support the downward sloping Phillips curve for shorter periods. The poor performance of the economy in the 1970s seemed to support Friedman's analysis, so it gained many adherents in the 1970s and '80s.

Another group picked up where Friedman left off. In the **rational expectations** model, workers and other factor owners incorporate their predictions of current and anticipated policies into their inflation expectations. In this setting the economy moves to Friedman's long-run (vertical) Phillips curve very quickly, so it is impossible for policy makers to exert more than a minor influence on real GNP and unemployment unless their policies come as a complete surprise to suppliers of factors of production and goods.

Some people accept the basic idea of the **rational expectations** (ratex) model, but doubt that circumstances permit suppliers to adjust wages and prices rapidly enough to completely offset the effects of expansionary and contractionary policies. Because of fixed contracts and other costs of adjusting prices instantaneously, a fourth model was developed in which wage and price inflexibilities slow down the adjustment process but not the ultimate outcome predicted by Friedman and the ratex economists. This fourth model is a **nonclassical ratex** model — where nonclassical means that wages and prices are not perfectly flexible.

Although there are still some unsettled issues in this area, most revolve around how long it takes for expectations to adjust sufficiently to return the economy to its long-run Phillips curve following a shift in aggregate demand. Today many economists believe that (aggregate) demand management policies have only limited effectiveness for stabilizing the economy. This group often advocates microeconomic policies to reduce frictional and structural unemployment rather than active monetary and fiscal policies. While many disagree with that prescription, nearly all recognize the importance of expectations in macroeconomic analysis, and few believe demand management policies can keep the unemployment below the natural rate for very long without triggering an inflation problem.

Part 2. Review of Concepts from Earlier Chapters
Prior to reading chapter 15, match statements at left with the appropriate concept at right.

__1. The annual percentage increase in the general price level.

__2. Frictional plus structural unemployment.

__3. Anticipated rate of change in prices.

__4. A tradeoff between inflation and the unemployment rate.

__5. Expectations formed by looking at past events.

__6. Expectations formed by looking at past & current events & policies.

__7. Wage increases push the aggregate supply curve in this direction.

__8. His model assumes agg. supply responds passively to agg. demand.

__9. The unemployment rate when "full employment" prevails.

__10. Unemployment in excess of the natural rate.

a. adaptive
b. Keynes
c. left (decrease)
d. natural rate
e. inflation rate
f. rational
g. expected inflation
     rate
h. cyclical
     unemployment
i. 4-6.5%
j. Phillips curve

Part 3. Key Concepts in this Chapter
After reading chapter 15 in the text, answer the following questions.

1. Keynesian economists believed that a _straight / Phillips_ curve provided policy makers with a menu of choices concerning _____ and inflation.

2. The economist Phillips was from _the US / Britain / Canada_ . He believed there was an inverse relationship between unemployment and the rate of _price inflation / interest / wage inflation_ .

3. In the American version of the Phillips curve, a diagram is drawn with the unemployment rate measured along the horizontal axis and the _____ rate along the vertical axis.

4. The theoretical explanation for the original Phillips curve assumed a shift in aggregate _demand / supply_ curve was responsible for changes in unemployment and prices. The aggregate _demand / supply_ curve was assumed not to shift.

5. If the aggregate supply curve is horizontal, an increase in aggregate demand will cause real GNP to _rise / fall_ and will cause unemployment to _rise / fall_ . Prices will _increase / decrease / remain unchanged_ because of the shift in agg. demand. These events imply that the Phillips curve is _horizontal / vertical / upward sloping_ .

6. When the aggregate supply curve is vertical, an increase in aggregate demand _will / will not_ cause real GNP to rise and _will / will not_ cause unemployment to decline. Prices will generally _increase / decrease / remain unchanged_ following a shift in aggregate demand. These events imply that the Phillips curve is _horizontal / vertical / upward sloping_ .

7. _Monetarist / Keynesian_ economists advocate fine tuning the economy by the use of fiscal and monetary policy.

8. The long-run Phillips curve is _horizontal / vertical / downward sloping_ .

9. Early Phillips curve users did not consider the effects of changing inflation _____ .

10. Stagflation is a period of _high / low_ unemployment and relatively _high / low_ inflation.

10. Stagflation is a period of _high / low_ unemployment and relatively _high / low_ inflation.

11. If people expect a higher inflation rate than before, workers will bargain for _higher / lower_ wages than before. That will tend to _increase / decrease_ aggregate supply. As a result, the actual unemployment rate is likely to _rise / fall_ and the general price level will tend to _rise / fall_. (Hint: Draw an AD-AS diagram and shift AS in the direction indicated by your answer.)

12. The _____ rate hypothesis states that in the long run the unemployment rate will return to its natural rate, regardless of how high or low the actual inflation rate happens to be.

13. The ratex theory is a combination of two words: _____ and _____.

14. The nonclassical ratex model assumes that wages and prices are _flexible / inflexible_ in the short run.

15. In the interview with Professor Lucas, an imaginary student (Ernie) asks, "How on earth are people supposed to anticipate the effects of_____?" Lucas replied that it is in peoples' interest to _____ what is going on in their area, to forecast the effects of policy, and also to try to _____ them. People probably have better information in their own area of interest than they could get from an _____ model of the economy.

16. Professor Lucas believes that the ratex analysis _increases / diminishes / has nothing to do with_ the difference between microeconomics and macroeconomic analysis.

17. In the original Phillips curve analysis, a _rightward / leftward_ shift in the aggregate demand curve causes unemployment to _rise / fall_ and causes prices to _rise / fall_.

18. Matching: Draw a line ---> connecting the names at left to the economic model which each helped develop.

       Milton Friedman   American (Keynesian) Phillips Curve

       Robert Lucas   Natural Rate Hypothesis (adaptive expectations)

       Paul Samuelson   Ratex model (rational expectations)

19. In the natural rate hypothesis, increases in aggregate demand will at first move the economy along its _short / long_ run Phillips curve. This will decrease the _unemployment / inflation_ rate and increase in the _unemployment / inflation_ rate. Eventually people revise their expected inflation rate _upward / downward_, which leads them to bargain for higher wages.

20. The optimum duration of job search and unemployment is indicated by an intersection between the wage _offer / demand_ curve and in the _reservation / real / market_ wage curve.

21. If there is an increase in aggregate demand, the wage offer curve shifts _upward / downward_, and the optimum duration of job search (and unemployment) will _rise / fall_.

22. If people begin to expect higher inflation than before, workers' reservation wage curve will shift _upward / downward_. That will tend to _prolong / shorten_ the optimum duration of job search and unemployment.

23. If the actual inflation rate rises above the expected inflation rate, then wages (and other factor prices) will probably rise _at the same rate as / faster than / slower than_ the general price level. Consequently the real wage will _rise / fall_ and employers will attempt to hire _more / fewer_

24. Along the long run Phillips curve, the actual inflation rate always equals / exceeds / is less than the expected inflation rate.

25. According to the interview with Professor Samuelson, an expansionary monetary or fiscal policy could lower _____ for a year or two, but later the inflation / interest rate would increase when the unemployment rate falls below the market / natural / cyclical rate.

Part 4.   Problems and Exercises

After reading chapter 15 in the text you should be able to work the following problems.

1. Here are unemployment and inflation observations from the 1960s. Graph the data in the grid at right.

Year	Unemp. Rate	Inflation Rate
1964	5.0%	1.3%
1965	4.4	1.7
1966	3.7	2.9
1967	3.7	2.9
1968	3.5	4.2
1969	3.4	5.4

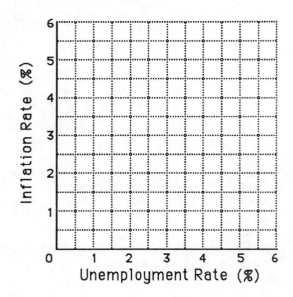

a. From your diagram does it appear that all of the points lie along a single Phillips curve? ____

b. Sketch the short-run Phillips curve that prevailed during the 1960s in your graph.

c. Does the 1960s experience seem to support the original Phillips curve model or the natural rate hypothesis? _____

2. Refer to data in the table to answer a-c below.

Year	%ΔCPI	U. Rate %
1980	13.5%	7.1%
1981	10.4%	7.6%
1982	6.1%	9.7%
1983	3.2%	9.6%
1984	4.3%	7.5%
1985	3.6%	7.2%
1986	1.9%	7.0%
1987	3.7%	6.2%
1988	4.1%	5.5%

a. Graph the first three observations (1980-82) in the grid at right, and sketch the short-run Phillips curve for those years.

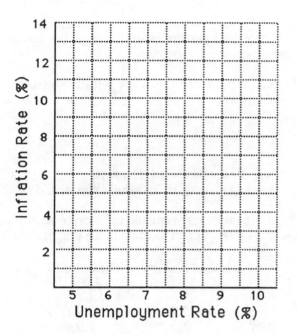

b. Graph the last three observations (1986-88) in the grid at right, and sketch the short-run Phillips curve for those years.

c. Between 1982 and 1986 the inflation rate and unemployment rate both _rose / fell_ every year. This indicates that the short-run Phillips curve was shifting _upward / downward_ as people lowered their inflation expectations and workers _raised / lowered_ their reservation wage demands.

3. What happens to the economy after aggregate demand increases? According to the original (American Keynesian) **Phillips curve model** the demand increase causes firms to employ more workers and to raise their prices.

Fill in the blanks and answer the questions below. Because we are dealing with a larger process of economic adjustment, each part of the exercise logically follows earlier parts. As you answer each question, think of the material that preceded it. (Hint: draw a series of diagrams to illustrate each case. The suggested diagrams are: 1) AD-AS and 2) Phillips curve.)

a. Starting at a point of long run equilibrium for the economy, suppose **aggregate demand increases**. Companies will satisfy new demands by selling from their inventories. As their inventories _rise above / fall below_ desired levels, companies will _increase / reduce_ production.

b. As production _rises / falls_, companies will hire _more / fewer_ workers than before.

c. If it is costly to expand production rapidly to keep up with the increasing demand, companies will probably _raise / lower_ their prices.

d. With prices _rising / falling_ and nominal wages remaining at previous levels, real wages will _increase / decline_. This reinforces the desire by companies to hire _more / fewer_ workers than they did before demand increased.

e. Compared to the situation before AD increased, the unemployment rate is _higher / lower_ than before and the inflation rate is _higher / lower_ than before. Thus the Phillips curve is _upward / downward_ sloping in this model.

f. A decrease in aggregate demand would have the _same / opposite_ effect as those listed above. The unemployment rate would _rise / fall_, and the inflation rate would _rise / fall_.

4. What happens to the economy if aggregate demand increases? According to **Friedman's natural rate model** there is a short run response, followed by a revision of inflation expectations, followed by a return to long-run equilibrium (where inflation expectations equal actual inflation).

Fill in the blanks and answer the questions below. Because we are dealing with a larger process of economic adjustment, each part of the exercise logically follows earlier parts. As you answer each question, think of the material that preceded it. (Hint: draw a series of diagrams that will help you in areas where you can't think your way through the problem. The suggested diagrams are: 1) AD-AS, 2) Phillips curve (short run & long run), and 3) Wage offer-Reservation wage.)

The Short Run

a. Starting at a point of long run equilibrium for the economy, suppose **aggregate demand increases**. This will cause companies to _increase / reduce_ production, which causes them to hire _more / fewer_ workers than before.

b. This is also reflected in a _higher / lower_ wage offer curve, which means the duration of job search will _lengthen / shorten_ and the unemployment rate will _increase / decline_.

c. As demand for their products rises above the predicted amount, companies satisfy new demands by selling from their inventories. Companies will then _raise / lower_ their prices.

d. To this point, the increase in aggregate demand has caused the unemployment rate to _rise / fall_ and the inflation rate to _rise / fall_.

Adaptive Expectations

e. After prices have been _rising / falling_ for a while, workers' real wages _rise / fall_ compared to their previously bargined level. To maintain their standard of living, workers bargain for _higher / lower_ nominal wages. If it appears the inflation rate has accelerated by 5%, workers seeking to maintain their standard of living will bargain for annual pay increases of ____%.

f. If workers bargain for nominal (money) wages that match the inflation rate, this will be reflected in an _upward / downward_ shift in the reservation wage curve, which implies that the duration of job search and unemployment will _lengthen / shorten_.

The Long Run

g. With nominal wages _rising / falling_ and the duration of unemployment growing _longer / shorter_, companies will tend to hire _more / fewer_ workers than a moment ago.

h. This change in total employment will _increase / reduce_ real output in the economy, which means the aggregate supply curve shifts _right / left_.

i. Once the aggregate supply curve shifts to the _right / left_ by as much as the aggregate demand curve originally shifted to the right, the economy will return to a _short / long_-run equilibrium. Real GNP will equal natural real GNP, and the unemployment rate will equal the _____ rate.

j. Compared to the original equilibrium which prevailed before aggregate demand shifted, the unemployment rate now _exceeds / equals / is less than_ the original unemployment rate. The current inflation rate _exceeds / equals / is less than_ the original inflation rate. The long-run Phillips curve is _horizontal / vertical_.

Part 5. Self Test
Multiple choice questions

1. According to the short-run Phillips curve:

a. high inflation and high unemployment can occur together
b. high inflation and low unemployment can occur together
c. low inflation and low unemployment can occur together
d. low inflation and high unemployment can occur together
e. b and d

Answer: _____

2. The Phillips curve Samuelson and Solow fitted to the data was:

a. upward-sloping
b. vertical
c. downward-sloping
d. horizontal

Answer: _____

3. The simultaneous occurrence of high inflation and high unemployment is called:

a. reflation
b. stagflation
c. the Phillips curve paradox
d. the kinked aggregate supply curve

Answer: _____

4. Milton Friedman argued that there:

a. are two Phillips curves, a short-run one and a long-run one
b. are three Phillips curves, a short-run one, a long-run one, and one during high inflation
c. is one Phillips curve, and it is vertical
d. is one Phillips curve, and it is nearly flat or horizontal

Answer: _____

5. According to Milton Friedman, if the expected inflation rate is less than the actual inflation rate:

a. the economy is not in long-run equilibrium
b. the economy is in long-run equilibrium
c. the economy is definitely in short-run equilibrium
d. a and c
e. none of the above

Answer: _____

6. According to the natural rate hypothesis, there is:

a. no short-run tradeoff between inflation and unemployment
b. a short-run tradeoff between inflation and unemployment
c. no long-run tradeoff between inflation and unemployment
d. a and b
e. b and c

Answer: _____

7. The short-run aggregate supply curve will shift leftward at the same time the aggregate demand curve shifts rightward, so that there will be no change in real GNP. This is a point that would be made by:

a. rational expectationists, assuming aggregate supply is correctly anticipated
b. rational expectationists, assuming aggregate demand is correctly anticipated
c. economists that believe in adaptive expectations theory
d. economists that believe that wages are sticky in the downward direction
e. both b and d

Answer: _____

8. Starting from long-run equilibrium, if the public anticipates that policymakers will increase aggregate demand by less than in fact policymakers do increase aggregate demand, and if the short-run aggregate supply curve adjusts to the (incorrectly) anticipated increase in aggregate demand, then:

a. real GNP will rise and the price level will rise
b. real GNP will decline and the price level will fall
c. real GNP will stay constant and the price level will rise
d. real GNP will fall and the price level will rise

Answer: _____

9. Which of the following statements is true?

a. In nonclassical ratex theory the short-run aggregate supply curve is vertical and in new classical ratex theory the short-run aggregate supply curve is upward-sloping.
b. In new classical ratex theory wages are assumed to be somewhat sticky and in nonclassical ratex theory wages are assumed to be flexible.
c. Adaptive expectations is the dominant expectations theory in new classical ratex theory and rational expectations is the dominant expectations theory in nonclassical ratex theory.
d. In new classical ratex theory wages are assumed to be flexible and in nonclassical ratex theory wages are assumed to be somewhat sticky.

Answer: _____

10. Thomas Sargent is probably best known as:

a. an adaptive expectations theorist
b. a monetarist
c. a Keynesian
d. a rational expectations theorist

Answer: _____

True-False

11. The original Phillips curve plotted price   T F
inflation and unemployment rates in the United Kingdom.

12. According to the long-run Phillips curve there   T F
is a tradeoff between unemployment and inflation.

13. If the public does not correctly anticipate a   T F
given policy, there could be adverse economic
results according to new classical macroeconomists.

14. Nonclassical ratex theorists argue that prices   T F
and wages are free to adjust to policy changes.

15. According to Paul Samuelson, rational   T F
expectations theory does a good job of explaining
the Great Depression.

Fill in the blank

16. The short-run Phillips curve holds that inflation are unemployment are _____ related.

17. A kinked aggregate supply curve which is horizontal up to full employment output and _____
thereafter implies that there is no tradeoff between unemployment and inflation.

18. According to the new classical macroeconomists, if policy is correctly anticipated there may be a
change in the price level but not in _____ .

19. According to Milton Friedman, if the expected inflation rate is equal to the actual inflation rate the
economy is in _____ .

20. According to new classical ratex theory, the short-run Phillips curve can be_____ at times.

Part 5. Answers to Self Test

1. e 2. c 3. b 4. a 5. a 6. e 7. b 8. a 9. d 10. d
11. F 12. F 13. T 14. F 15. F
16. inversely 17. vertical 18. real GNP
19. long-run equilbrium 20. vertical

Part 6. Answers

Part 2 Review of Concepts
1. e   2. d   3. g   4. j   5. a   6. f   7. c   8. b   9. i   10. h

Part 3 Key Concepts
1. Phillips, unemployment   2. Britain, wage inflation   3. unemployment, inflation
4. demand, supply   5. rise, fall, remain unchanged, horizontal   6. will not, will not, increase, vertical
7. Keynesians/Phillips curve advocates   8. vertical   9. expectations   10. high, high
11. higher, decrease, rise, rise   12. natural   13. rational expectations   14. inflexible (or sticky")
15. policy, follow, influence, econometric   16. diminishes   17. rightward, fall, rise
18. Friedman-->Natural Rate Hypothesis   Lucas-->Ratex   Samuelson-->American Phillips Curve
19. short, unemployment, inflation, upward   20. wage, reservation   21. upward, fall
22. upward, prolong   23. slower than, fall, more, reduces   24. equals
25. unemployment, inflation, natural

Part 4 Problems and Exercises
1. a. yes (approximately)
   b. see graph
   c. original Phillips curve

2. a. See the graph.
   b. See the graph.
   c. fall, downward, lowered

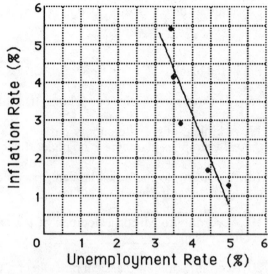

3. a. rise above
   b. rises, more
   c. raise
   d. rising, decline, more
   e. lower, higher, downward
   f. opposite, rise, fall

4. a. increase, more
   b. wage, shorten, decline
   c. raise
   d. fall, rise
   e. rising, fall, higher, 5%
   f. upward, lengthen
   g. rising, longer, fewer
   h. reduce, left
   i. left, long, natural
   j. equals, exceeds, vertical

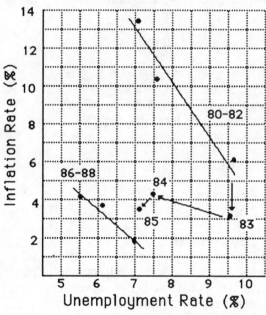

Chapter 16
Business Cycles

Part 1. Introduction and Purpose
Consider the following points as you read chapter 16 in the text.

The U.S. will move through several business cycles in your lifetime, or alternating periods of expansion and contraction which seem to exert a similar effect on most sectors of the economy. In fact, after you've observed a couple of business cycles you'll get the feeling that they're all pretty much alike — where inflations are followed by recessions, and recessions are followed by turnaround that eventually become inflationary. Although there is considerable similarity between most business cycles, they aren't all the same. Unemployment will always be unemployment and inflation will always be inflation, but knowing what triggers a particular business cycle is important for predicting its likely effects and for devising policies to deal with it.

A recent example illustrates the importance of knowing about the specific cause of an economic expansion. In 1983, many economists and business managers assumed that expansionary aggregate demand policies had been used to end the recent recession. Having concluded that the economy's upturn originated on the demand side of the economy, they predicted that within a couple of years the inflation rate would be higher than in 1982 — and on that basis, they entered into contracts that reflected fairly high inflation expectations for 1983-85. For example, some farmers bought new tractors and more land in the belief that their crops would sell for higher prices in the future. Several other industries did much the same thing.

As later events showed however, the economic expansion beginning in late 1982 was greatly affected by the supply side of the economy. Lower tax rates encouraged workers and investors to increase the supply of labor and capital, so aggregate supply increased. Because of high unemployment in the 1970s workers were prepared to accept lower wages and corporate bankruptcies caused companies to adopt more efficient production techniques, so aggregate supply rose. Deregulation helped oil prices to decline and encouraged previously regulated industries to expand. The economy expanded, but rather than the predicted upward pressure on prices, the inflation rate fell because of the increasing aggregate supply. Farmers and others who had been counting on rising prices to help them pay their bills were often forced out of business.

So all business cycles aren't alike, and it is important to understand the forces that dominate the business cycle at any given moment in time.

Fortunately the aggregate demand-aggregate supply (AD-AS) framework provides a useful model for analyzing business cycles. Any event that triggers a business cycle must either shift the AD or the AS curve — to the right (increase) to trigger an expansion, to the left (decrease) to trigger a contraction.

Once aggregate demand or supply shifts, the challenge facing economists is to explain what initially triggered the expansion or contraction, and to predict what path the economy will follow as it responds to the initial stimulus. As we saw a moment ago in regard to the 1982-83 economic upturn, expansions triggered by shifts in aggregate demand result in more inflation, whereas supply side expansions are actually disinflationary. So it is necessary to understand the forces that dominate the macroeconomic landscape in order to predict where the economy is heading.

Having information about the initial stimulus that pushed the economy above or below its natural growth path (natural real GNP) is helpful, but something else is necessary to forecast how the economy is likely to perform — an economic model. Models range from extremely simple to extremely complicated, and often yield conflicting predictions at any point in time.

One fairly simple model, the **real business cycle theory**, predicts that the economy will grow at a constant 2.5-3% rate per year, except when disturbed by an adverse or beneficial **supply shock** which shifts the aggregate supply curve to the right or left.

Most macroeconomic models examine business cycles that are triggered by fluctuations in aggregate demand. For example in the **Keynesian income-expenditure model** a decline in autonomous spending in the economy (by consumers, businesses, or foreign purchasers) will induce a reduction in the output of goods and in the number of jobs — an economic recession. Friedman's **natural rate theory** also suggests that the business cycle is a demand-side phenomenon, resulting when the money supply grows significantly more or less rapidly than a moderate rate. In the short run, excess money balances increase total spending in the economy, leading to temporary increases in employment and output and some increase in prices.

In the **new classical (rational expectations) theory**, people correctly anticipate most policies that affect aggregate demand, and adjust quickly enough to cancel out most of the short-run effects described by Keynesians, monetarists, and natural rate economists. Whatever business cycle we observe is caused by **unpredictable** shifts in aggregate demand or supply — similar to the conclusion of those holding to the real business cycle theory (above).

A few other theories are also mentioned in the text, but we will leave it to you to discover them on your own. The most important thing to keep in mind as you read the text is that the main topic is the business cycle, where several different models of the business cycle are discussed. If different models seem to disagree on key points, that's not just your imagination — they do disagree. Don't let that throw you — it can be fun finding out why the different theories disagree on particular points.

To make certain you always know where you are in the discussion, it may help to write short notes in the margin of the text listing: a) Which <u>model</u> is being applied in the current situation? b) Was the business cycle under consideration triggered by a shift in aggregate <u>demand</u> or aggregate <u>supply</u>? c) Was the shift in aggregate demand or supply <u>expected</u> or <u>unexpected</u>? (In the "long run" the shift is fully anticipated.) By keeping these issues clearly in mind, you will avoid some of the confusions associated with jumping back and forth between conflicting models.

Part 2. Review of Concepts from Earlier Chapters

Prior to reading chapter 16, match statements at left with the appropriate concept at right.

__1. A business cycle top, after which the economy contracts.
__2. Real GNP at full employment.
__3. Another word for expected or predicted.
__4. An originator of the natural rate hypothesis.
__5. Classical economists believed this guaranteed full employment.
__6. Keynesians believe wages and prices have this characteristic.
__7. In their model policies and events are anticipated in advance.
__8. Bottom of the business cycle.

a. new classical economists
b. trough
c. wage & price flexibility
d. anticipated
e. natural real GNP
f. Friedman
g. peak
h. inflexible

Part 3. Key Concepts in this Chapter

After reading chapter 16 in the text, answer the following questions.

1. Business cycles have 4 phases: expansion, _____, _____, and _____.

2. An unanticipated event or policy _can / cannot_ trigger a business cycle in Friedman's natural rate theory. It _can / cannot_ trigger a business cycle in the (old) classical model. It _can / cannot_ trigger a business cycle in the Keynesian theory.

3. If a <u>large</u> increase in aggregate demand is expected for this year but only a <u>small</u> increase actually occurs, then the new classical (ratex) theory predicts that real GNP _will / will not_ be affected by the surprise.

4. In Friedman's natural rate theory an unexpected increase in aggregate demand will cause the inflation rate to _rise / fall_ and will cause real wages to _rise / fall_ compared to their intended level.

5. In the _Ratex / Keynesian_ theory, if aggregate demand declines then real GNP will _rise / fall_, and will remain at its new level indefinitely. At this point unemployment _will / will not_ exceed its natural rate.

6. The Keynesian business cycle is largely the result of _flexible / inflexible_ wages and prices.

7. Wages might be unable to adjust downward in response to a fall in demand are _long / short_ -run labor contracts or a desire by companies to pay _more / less_ than the market clearing (equilibrium) wage to encourage high worker productivity.

8. U.S. labor contracts are for _longer / shorter / about the same_ periods than labor contracts in Japan. The U.S. unemployment rate is usually _higher / lower_ than Japan's.

9. Suppose the business cycle reaches a peak in September. An economic indicator that peaks in July and turns down after that is a _leading / lagging_ indicator; an indicator that peaks in November is a _leading / lagging_ indicator; an indicator that peaks in September is a _leading / coincident_ indicator.

10. _Monetarists / Keynesians_ believe that economic contractions are caused by a decline in the money supply (or in its rate of growth).

11. _Monetarists / Keynesians_ believe that autonomous changes in investment or consumption spending are major causes of the business cycle.

12. The accelerator principle says that if 5% of all capital goods must be replaced each year due to depreciation, then a 10% increase in aggregate demand that is perceived as permanant will cause capital goods orders to rise by _____% this year.

13. In the real _____ _____ theory, changes in measured aggregate demand are the effect rather than the cause of business cycles.

14. A _____ business cycle is one that results when policies are manipulated to improved the reelection chances of incumbent officials.

15. In the real business cycle theory, business downturns begin when the aggregate _supply / demand_ curve shifts to the left. As a result real GNP _rises / falls_ and real wages _rise / fall_, and unemployment _rises / falls_.

16. Schumpeter's theory of the business cycle emphasizes the role of new _____. He called this a process of creative _production / destruction_, where new goods and methods replace old ones in the marketplace. Initially this substitution of new for old causes existing industries and the macroeconomy to _contract / expand_, but once the new goods or methods have gained wider use the economy _contract / expand_.

17. According to the interview with Professor Barro, some new classical economists have lately been de-emphasizing the role played by _fiscal / monetary_ in triggering a business cycle, and giving more emphasis to shocks which affect technology and the position of the aggregate _supply / demand_ curve.

18. Professor Akerlof (see interview) suggests five reasons companies may not lower the wages they pay workers even if the demand for goods (and labor) declines. a) to raise worker morale; b) to lower worker _____ rates; c) to stop workers from joining _____; d) to give workers an incentive not to _____ their work responsibilities; and e) to _ _____ higher quality workers.

19. Akerlof's theories suggest that wages may be _flexible / inflexible_. This tends to support the _Monetarist / Keynesian_ analysis of the business cycle.

Part 4. Problems and Exercises

After reading chapter 16 in the text you should be able to work the following problems.

1. Refer to the diagram at right. It shows the trend of real GNP and actual real GNP at various points in time.

   a. Draw points on the curve to show business cycle peaks (P) and troughs (T).

   b. Label periods of expansion and contraction along the horizontal (time) axis.

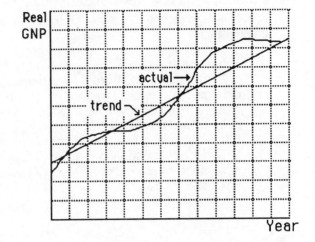

2. In the graph at right, consider a fully anticipated increase in the money supply within the natural rate theory.

   a. The aggregate demand curve shifts _right / left_ because the _____ supply _increased / decreased_ .

   b. The aggregate supply curve shifts _right / left_ because wages _rise / fall_ in anticipation of _more / less_ inflation.

   c. In the theory, which curve shifts first (or do they shift simultaneously)? _____

   d. Does the expansionary monetary policy cause real GNP to rise above Q_n? _yes / no_

   e. Draw the new aggregate demand and supply curves in the graph. Label them AD2 and SRAS2.

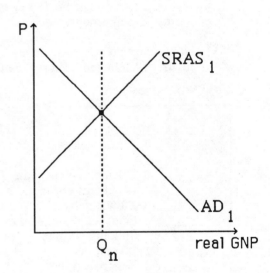

3. An important objective of chapter 16 is to understand the forces that might trigger a business cycle expansion or contraction in each of the economic models. In the cases listed below, decide whether the indicated event or policy will cause real GNP to accelerate or slow down relative to its normal growth rate. Use the <u>symbols</u> (↑, ↓ or 0) to indicate accelerations, slowdowns, and neutral effects (answers on next page).

___a. In the Keynesian model, a rise in autonomous investment spending.
___b. In the natural rate theory, an anticipated rise in the money supply.
___c. In the new classical (ratex) theory, a new tax depresses consumer spending.
___d. In the real business cycle theory, a decrease in the money supply.
___e. In the real business cycle theory, an economy-wide decrease in labor productivity.
___f. In the natural rate theory, an unexpected decline in the money supply.
___g. In the Keynesian model, a rise in government spending.
___h. In the real business cycle theory, a decrease in energy prices.
___i. In the Keynesian model, an increase in net exports.
___j. In the political business cycle theory, an increase in the money supply.

4. The table shows net changes in the components of the index of leading economic indicators (LEI).

a. For each component listed at left, indicate whether the observed index change (Δ) is signaling a turn up (U) or a turn down (D). [<u>Warning</u>: a negative change in the index does not necessarily mean the economy is being depressed, nor does a positive change necessarily indicate economic strength.]

b. How many up (U) components do you count? _____ How many down (D) components? _____ Is the list of leading indicators pointing up or down for the overall economy in this case? _____

U / D	Component	ΔIndex	Description of Component
_____	a. Workweek	+0.10	Average hours worked by manufacturing workers
_____	b. Unemployment claims	-0.39	New claims for unemployment compensation
_____	c. Orders for consumer goods	-0.23	New orders
_____	d. Slower deliveries	-0.11	Time needed to fill back orders
_____	e. Plant and equipment orders	-0.01	New orders for capital goods
_____	f. Building permits	-0.20	Permits taken out to construct new buildings
_____	g. Inventories	-0.10	Value of businesses inventories
_____	h. Materials prices	+0.05	Price of raw materials used by manufacturers
_____	i. Stock prices	-0.05	Corporate stock prices
_____	j. Money supply	-0.05	M-1 money supply
_____	k. Credit	+0.11	Total outstanding credit

Answers to Exercise 3

p'ɔ'q :0   ɟ'ə :ʇ   ɟ'ǀ'ɥ'ɓ'ɐ :ʇ

•If your score was 0-5, you are probably confused by jumping from one economic model
   to another. Try analyzing the cases again in a different order: first all of the
   Keynesian questions, then all of the natural rate questions, etc.
•If you scored 6-7, you may have difficulty distinguishing the effects of anticipated and
   unanticipated policies (questions b,c,f) or you may be confused by the real business
   cycle theory, which emphasizes the supply side of the economy and deemphasizes demand.
•If you scored 8-9, you're doing pretty good. It's difficult to work with so many different
   theories in a single chapter.
•If you scored 10, Congratulations! Have you considered majoring in economics?

Part 5. Self Test
Multiple choice questions

1. The four stages of the business cycle are:

a. expansion, peak, contraction, and trough
b. expansion, high, low, and middle
c. expansion, contraction, middle, low
d. inflation, unemployment, recession, depression
e. none of the above

Answer: _____

2. The classical theory:

a. does not provide an explanation of the business cycle
b. provides the same explanation of the business cycle as the new classical ratex theory under the condition
of unanticipated policy
c. provides the same explanation of the business cycle as the Friedman natural rate theory
d. provides the same explanation of the business cycle as the Keynesian theory

Answer: _____

3. If the economy is always on its production possibilities frontier (PPF):

a. there is no inflation
b. there are fewer business cycles than if the economy weren't on its PPF
c. there are no business cycles
d. there are more business cycles than if the economy weren't on its PPF

Answer: _____

4. A change in aggregate demand will be completely offset by a change in aggregate supply, therefore real GNP will not change. This is consistent with what business cycle theory?

a. classical theory
b. new classical ratex theory under the condition of incorrectly anticipated policy
c. the Friedman natural rate theory
d. the multiplier-accelerator theory
e. none of the above

Answer: _____

5. In the _____ the business cycle occurs because there is a difference between individuals' expected inflation rate and the actual inflation rate.

a. Keynesian theory
b. Friedman natural rate theory
c. new classical ratex theory under the condition of correctly anticipated policy
d. classical theory

Answer: _____

6. Which of the following statements is false?

a. In the Keynesian theory the economy does not always return to its natural real GNP level.
b. In the Friedman natural rate theory the economy always returns to its natural real GNP level.
c. In the new classical ratex theory under the condition of unanticipated policy the economy always returns to its natural real GNP level.
d. In the Keynesian theory the economy can get stuck at a level of real GNP lower than natural real GNP.
e. none of the above

Answer: _____

7. In the Keynesian theory the economy sometimes gets "stuck" at a level of real GNP below the natural level because:

a. sticky (downward) nominal wage rates exist
b. workers will not accept higher nominal wages
c. government manages the economy and at times does not want the economy to move up to natural real GNP
d. the money supply has grown too rapidly

Answer: _____

8. If shirking increases, monitoring costs for the firm will rise. The theory this statement is associated with is the:

a. new classical theory under all conditions
b. Friedman natural rate theory
c. efficiency wage theory
d. multiplier-accelerator theory
e. none of the above

Answer: _____

9. Monetarists contend that:

a. typically money supply growth drops before or during economic contractions and is constant before or during expansions
b. typically money supply growth rises before or during economic contractions and falls before or during expansions
c. typically money supply growth drops before or during economic contractions and rises before or during expansions
d. there is no relationship between the business cycle and the money supply

Answer: _____

10. The accelerator principle captures the idea that:

a. investment depends upon the growth of output
b. investment depends upon interest rates
c. the money supply causes the economic boom and bust
d. entrepreneurship is on the decline

Answer: _____

11. Public choice economists are known for:

a. applying the tools of economics to the study of the public sector
b. studying the economies of foreign countries
c. proposing that the Fed be abolished and replaced with a gold standard
d. b and c
e. none of the above

Answer: _____

12. Robert Barro is a:

a. monetarist
b. Keynesian
c. Schumpterian
d. new classical macroeconomist
e. none of the above

Answer: _____

13. George Akerlof is a:

a. efficiency wage model theorist
b. real business cycle theorist
c. political business cycle theorist
d. monetarist
e. none of the above

Answer: _____

14. The theory that holds that business cycles originate on the supply side of the economy is the:

a. multiplier-accelerator theory
b. political business cycle theory
c. Friedman natural rate theory
d. real business cycle theory
e. none of the above

Answer: _____

15. According to the multiplier-accelerator theory of the business cycle:

a. the private economy is inherently stable
b. the private economy is inherently unstable
c. individuals correctly anticipate policies and events
d. firms do not maximize profits
e. a and c

Answer: _____

True-False

16. Business cycles range from 1 to 100 years.   T F

17. Monetarists believe that business cycles are   T F
caused by inappropriate and destabilizing monetary
policy.

18. Following a decrease in aggregate demand, the   T F
economy may not equilibrate at full-employment
output or natural real GNP if wages are sticky
in the downward direction.

19. In explaining the business cycle, Keynesians   T F
focus on political factors.

20. According to the efficiency wage models,   T F
wages and productivity may be directly related.

Fill in the blank

21. The accelerator principle assumes that there is a constant relationship between the _____ and
_____ .

22. According to the accelerator principle, investment spending is a function of the rate of growth in
_____ .

23. We would expect a _____ indicator to rise before a boom and fall before a bust.

24. _____ developed a theory of the business cycle which emphasized creative destruction.

25. Many Keynesian economists argue that wages are sticky in the downward direction because workers
and management enter into _____ for mutually advantageous reasons.

Part 5. Answers to Self Test

1. a 2. a 3. c 4. e 5. b 6. e 7. a 8. c 9. c 10. a
11. a 12. d 13. a 14. d 15. b
16. F 17. T 18. T 19. F 20. T
21. capital stock, output 22. output 23. leading economic
24. Schumpeter 25. long-term contracts

Part 6.   Answers

Part 2 Review of Concepts
1. g   2. e   3. d   4. f   5. c   6. h   7. a   8. b

Part 3 Key Concepts
1. peak, contraction, trough   2. can, cannot, can   3. will   4. rise, fall   5. Keynesian, fall, will
6. inflexible ("sticky")   7. long, more   8. longer, higher   9. leading, lagging, coincident
10. Monetarists   11. Keynesian   12. 200%   13. business cycle   14. political
15. supply, falls, fall, rises   16. innovations, destruction, contract, expands   17. monetary, supply
18. quit, unions, shirk, attract   19. inflexible (or "sticky"), Keynesian

Part 4 Problems and Exercises

2. a. right, money, increased
b. left, rise, more
c. simultaneously
d. no
e. See graph below.

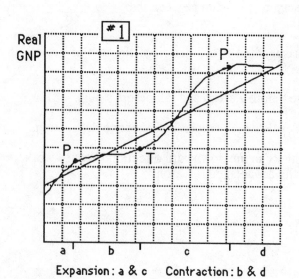

Expansion: a & c   Contraction: b & d

4. Up: a,b,g,h,k
Down: c,d,e,f,i,j
Overall LEI: down

To some extent, whether indicators point up
or down depends on which model one uses.
If you disagree with the answers given here,
mention what model or assumption will make
your answer correct.

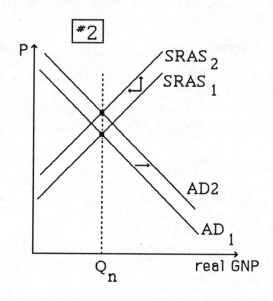

Chapter 17
Fiscal Policy

Part 1. Introduction and Purpose
Consider the following points as you read chapter 17 in the text.

Fiscal policy is the name given to government spending and taxing policies, in particular those used to achieve macroeconomic goals like price stability, full employment, and the like. Fiscal policies result from legislation passed by Congress and signed into law by the president. In the ideal case, such laws deal with the most pressing needs of the nation and do so at minimal cost, but most observers agree that fiscal policy is also used to promote the goals of policy makers themselves — reelection.

It has always been that way to some degree, but earlier practices tended to limit the role played by politics in policy decisions. Under the **old time fiscal religion**, the dominant thinking among policy makers until about 1960, it was generally assumed that government should refrain from running **budget deficits** during normal times. The budget's net position is calculated by subtracting government expenditures from government revenues. If the difference is negative, so that spending exceeds revenues, a deficit occurs. This requires the Treasury to borrow from the private sector here and overseas to finance the excess of spending over receipts. On the other hand, if public sector revenues exceed spending a **budget surplus** occurs that allows the Treasury to pay off some of the debt accumulated from earlier deficits. The last budget surplus occurred in fiscal year 1969.

Under the **new fiscal religion**, policy makers believe it is appropriate to incur deficits or run surpluses as a way of stabilizing the macroeconomy. The theory is that deficits stimulate the economy by injecting more dollars of spending into the circular flow than they withdraw through tax leakages. A budget surplus causes leakages from the circular flow (taxes) to exceed injections into it (spending). By lowering aggregate demand, a budget surplus slows down the economy when inflation threatens.

Fiscal policy may affect aggregate demand indirectly too, by causing interest rates to change. If government increases its spending and finances the new outlay by borrowing from the private sector, the demand for loanable funds increases and interest rates are pushed upward. Higher interest rates have at least two effects on total planned spending in the private sector. First, higher interest rates reduce the willingness of companies to borrow to construct new plants or invest in new equipment, which reduces the demand for new output. Second, higher interest rates cause households to save more of their disposable incomes and to spend less. The result is for government spending to be a less powerful policy tool than originally thought. In an extreme case the crowding out of private spending would equal the original increase in government spending — a case of **complete crowding out**. The opposite may also happen, where reductions in government spending lower interest rates and actually stimulate private spending. This is called **crowding in** — private spending rises when public spending falls.

A different perspective of fiscal policy emphasizes its impact on the aggregate supply curve. All of the issues discussed above relate to its use as a demand management policy, but in recent years **supply-side fiscal policies** have captured the headlines. A supply side fiscal policy is one that alters **incentives** to work, invest, and produce. The change in incentives shifts the aggregate supply curve rightward (if incentives have been strengthened) or leftward (if incentives have been reduced).

The tax laws passed in 1981 and 1986 were endorsed by supply-side economists who believed that high tax rates (and other economic regulations) had lowered the economy's ability to grow during the 1970s. At the beginning of 1981 the maximum tax rate was 70%, which meant that for some people another dollar's worth of profits or interest income would only mean another 30¢ in disposable income. After the **Tax Reform Act of 1986** was enacted, marginal tax rates fell to 28% or lower. The same dollar's worth of income then translated into 72¢ in disposable income — about 240% as much as the earlier figure. This provides more incentive for starting new businesses, introducing innovations, and investing in capital goods. All should eventually shift the production possibilities frontier (PPF) outward and shift the aggregate supply curve to the right.

Tax rates were broadly reduced twice in the 1980s to stimulate the economy's supply side. Tax policy is potentially very important since expansionary supply side policies can increase employment and real GNP without stimulating inflation. This appears to be consistent with most of our macroeconomic goals rather than presenting us with the inflation-unemployment tradeoff associated with demand-side policies.

Part 2. Review of Concepts from Earlier Chapters
Prior to reading chapter 17, match statements at left with the appropriate concept at right.

__1. An injection into the circular flow.	a. Great Depression
__2. Government taxing and spending policies.	b. deflationary gap
__3. Another name for full employment.	c. government spending
__4. The planned spending curve in the income-expenditure model.	d. natural rate of unemployment
__5. An income level from which there is no tendency to change.	e. TPE curve
__6. A leakage out of the circular flow.	f. inflationary gap
__7. A general increase in prices.	g. fiscal policy
__8. Unemployment over and above the natural rate.	h. inflation
__9. Period in the 1930s with very high unemployment.	i. taxes
__10. If real GNP exceeds natural real GNP.	j. cyclical unemployment
__11. If real GNP is less than natural real GNP.	k. equilibrium

Part 3. Key Concepts in this Chapter
After reading chapter 17 in the text, answer the following questions.

1. If government spending exceeds taxes and other revenues, the budget will be in _surplus / deficit_. If taxes and revenues _exceed / equal / are less than_ government spending, the budget will be in surplus.

2. The Old Time Fiscal Religion said that the budget should be deficit only during _____ and other emergencies. At other times a small _surplus / deficit_ was appropriate so that over the long run the budget was balanced.

3. The New Fiscal Religion says that budget _____ and _____ should be used to promote full employment and other macroeconomic goals.

4. Expansionary fiscal policies shift the aggregate demand curve to the _right / left_.

5. If autonomous spending rises by $1 and national income rises by $3, then autonomous spending has a _leveraged / multiplier / powerful_ effect.

6. If there is a recessionary gap, the appropriate fiscal policy is a _contractionary / expansionary_ one. If policy is used to change aggregate demand, policy makers will either increase _spending / taxes_ or reduce _spending / taxes_.

7. If the government spending multiplier equals 4, the MPC must equal _____.

8. If the MPC = 0.75, then the tax multiplier equals _____.

9. According to the balanced budget theorem, if government spending and taxes both increase by $50 million, then national income will _rise / fall_ by $ _0 / 1 / 25 / 50 / 100_ million.

10. If officials take deliberate action to change government spending or taxes, this is an example of _discretionary / automatic_ fiscal policy. If economic conditions trigger spending or tax changes because of programs instituted in the past, this is an example of _discretionary / automatic_ fiscal policy.

11. According to the interview with Professor Walter Heller, prior to the tax cuts of 1964 the top marginal tax rate was _____%.

12. The interview with Professor Heller indicated that the main difficulty facing fiscal policy makers is the long _____ between the time a policy is needed and the time it is finally implemented.

13. Crowding out refers to the reduction in _public / private_ spending that occurs when government spending is _increased / reduced_.

14. Suppose government spending rises while taxes remain unchanged. This should cause the total planned expenditures curve (TPE) to shift _upward / downward_ and should cause the aggregate demand curve (AD) to shift _rightward / leftward_. Crowding out _increases / reduces_ the size of the shifts relative to the case when no crowding out occurs.

15. David Ricardo and Robert Barro believe that when government spends dollars it has borrowed (debt), then people will anticipate that their future tax burden will be _higher / lower_ than today. Consequently they will save _more / less_ out of their current income than before and will consume _more / less_ than before.

16. If crowding out is complete, a new debt-financed government spending program _will / will not_ stimulate total planned expenditures and aggregate demand. The policy _will / will not_ reduce unemployment.

17. If the nation imports more goods and services than before and exports less, then aggregate demand for U.S. goods and services is _greater / less_ than before.

18. There are five time lags in conducting fiscal policy, including the time required to collect relevant data, a _____- and-see lag as policy makers try to interpret the data and decide if it accurately describes what the economy is experiencing, a _____ lag associated with the time required to pass appropriate spending or tax laws, a _____ lag during which time an authorized policy is being implemented, and a _____ lag for the policy to impact the economy.

19. A _revenue / Heller / Laffer_ curve shows the relationship between the tax rate levied on incomes and the actual tax revenues collected by government.

20. The marginal tax rate equals the change in a person's tax liability divided by a change in her _wealth / income / purchases_. For example if the marginal tax rate is 20% and your income rises by $1000, then your tax bill will rise by $_____.

21. _Higher_ marginal tax rates will probably cause people to work _more / less_ than before and cause them to _increase / lower_ their investment income. _Lower_ marginal tax rates will probably cause people to earn _more / less_ income.

22. Lower marginal tax rates should cause the aggregate supply curve to shift _right / left_.

23. Total tax collections equal the tax _revenue / rate_ multiplied by the tax _base / rate_.

24. Suppose tax rates are lowered. Government tax receipts will _fall_ if the (positive) percentage change in the tax _base / rate_ is less than the (negative) percentage change in the tax _base / rate_. Tax receipts will _rise_ when rates are lowered if the percentage change in the tax _base / rate_ is greater than the percentage change in the tax _base / rate_..

25. The Tax Reform Act of 1986 _increased / reduced_ the highest regular marginal tax rate to ___%.

26. In the Arthur Laffer interview, he says supply-side economics is the economics of _____.

27. In the interview with Arthur Laffer, he suggests that the ability of tax rate changes to directly contribute to household income is less important than the incentive they provide to work and invest _more / less_. According to his analysis, the income effects are _more / less_ important than the substitution effects of lower tax rates.

Part 4. Problems and Exercises
After reading chapter 17 in the text you should be able to work the following problems.

1. Use the information provided to fill in missing values in the table. Each is used extensively in the income-expenditure model to estimate the impact of fiscal policies on aggregate demand.

	MPC	MPS	m	m_{T^-}
a.	0.5	___	___	___
b.	0.6	___	___	___
c.	___	0.25	___	___
d.	___	___	3	___
e.	___	0.1	___	___
f.	___	___	4.5	___

2. Some people claim that the tax multiplier is can be computed by subtracting one from the government spending multiplier, then placing a negative sign in front of the answer. So if the government multiplier is 4, the tax multiplier equals: -(4-1) = -3. Do your calculations in problem #1 confirm or deny this claim?

_____

3. Changes in autonomous government spending (G) affect national income (Y) in the income-expenditure model, or affect aggregate demand in the AD-AS model. Fill in the table below with the appropriate values for ΔG, m, and ΔY (or ΔAD).

	ΔG	m	ΔY
a.	$10	2	$___
b.	-$20	2.5	$___
c.	$100	___	$500
d.	-$50	___	-$200
e.	$90	8	$___
f.	$___	4	$240

4. Changes in autonomous government spending (T) affect national income (Y) in the income-expenditure model, or affect aggregate demand in the AD-AS model. Fill in the table below with the appropriate values for ΔT, m, and ΔY (or ΔAD).

	ΔT	m_{T^-}	ΔY
a.	$10	-2	$___
b.	-$20	-1.5	$___
c.	$100	___	-$300
d.	-$50	___	$125
e.	-$90	-3	$___
f.	$___	-5	$250

5. Suppose your current income is $1000 and you pay $150 in taxes. When your income rises to $1100, your tax bill rises to $175. Under these conditions your marginal tax rate equals _____%.

6. Suppose your current income is $5000 and you pay $500 in taxes. If your income rises to $6000 and your marginal tax rate is 20%, your total tax bill will rise to $_____.

7. Refer to the grid at right.

   a. The equilibrium income equals $_____.

   b. In this case total autonomous spending
equals $_____ and the spending
multiplier equals _____.

   c. Assume full employment is achieved when
GNP=$500. Draw the appropriate TPE
curve in the diagram to make $500 the
equilibrium level of income.

   d. To bring income to $500, autonomous
spending must _rise / fall_ by $_____.
This could be achieved by lowering
government spending by $_____. After
the change in policy, total autonomous
spending will equal $_____.

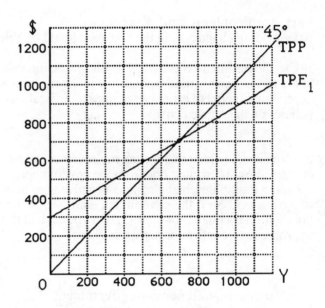

8. Fill in the table below.

	Tax Base	Tax Rate	Tax Revenue
a.	$10,000	0%	$_____
b.	$ _____	10%	$ 900
c.	$ 8500	20%	$_____
d.	$ 7000	__%	$2100
e.	$ 6000	40%	$_____
f.	$_____	50%	$2000
g.	$ 3000	__%	$1800
h.	$_____	80%	$1200
i.	$ 1000	90%	$_____
j.	$_____	100%	$ 0

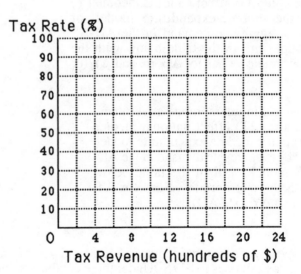

9. Once you have completed the table above,
plot government tax revenues against the tax
rate in the grid at right.

If you connect points in the graph, the
resulting curve is a _____
curve.

Part 5. Self Test
Multiple choice questions

1. Which of the following statements is false?

a. Federal spending was a smaller percentage of GNP in 1962 when John Kennedy was president than in 1987 when Ronald Reagan was president.
b. The deficit-GNP ratio trended upward between the early 1960s and the early-to-mid 1980s.
c. The national debt-GNP ratio trended upward in the early 1980s.
d. The largest percentage of federal spending goes to national defense.

Answer: _____

2. If federal expenditures outstrip federal tax receipts:

a. a balanced budget exists
b. a budget surplus exists
c. a budget deficit exists
d. the national debt rises
e. none of the above

Answer: _____

3. The Congress of the United States acts to increase government spending for the intended purpose of stabilizing the economy. This is an example of:

a. discretionary expansionary fiscal policy
b. automatic expansionary fiscal policy
c. discretionary contractionary fiscal policy
d. automatic contractionary fiscal policy

Answer: _____

4. If Jones favors big government over small government, he will favor which of the following acts of discretionary fiscal policy?

a. Higher taxes and less government spending as expansionary and contractionary fiscal policy measures, respectively.
b. Higher taxes and more government spending as contractionary and expansionary fiscal policy measures, respectively.
c. Lower taxes and less government spending as expansionary and contractionary fiscal policy measures, respectively.
d. Lower taxes and more government spending as contractionary and expansionary policy measures, respectively.

Answer: _____

5. Keynesians would propose discretionary contractionary fiscal policy:

a. if the economy is in a recessionary gap
b. if the economy is in an inflationary gap
c. as a stabilizing measure if the economy is in long-run equilibrium
d. if the economy gets stuck below natural real GNP

Answer: _____

6. In the basic Keynesian theory with government, a rise in government spending of $8 billion will increase real national income by how much if the marginal propensity to consume is .80 (80 percent)?

a. $25 billion
b. $40 billion
c. $ 8 billion
d. $30 billion
e. none of the above

Answer: _____

7. In the basic Keynesian theory with government, a rise in taxes of $20 billion will change real national income by how much if the marginal propensity to consume is .80?

a. -$80 billion
b. +$40 billion
c. -$60 billion
d. +$25 billion
e. none of the above

Answer: _____

8. In the basic Keynesian theory with government, an increase in government spending of $14 billion combined with an increase in taxes of $14 billion will change real national income by how much if the marginal propensity to consume is .60?

a. $10 billion
b. $14 billion
c. $ 6 billion
d. $12 billion
e. none of the above

Answer: _____

9. Suppose the government increases spending on X by $1,700 million and individual spending on X drops by $700 million. This is an example of:

a. incomplete crowding out
b. complete crowding out
c. zero crowding out
d. a and c
e. none of the above

Answer: _____

10. Which of the following assures the effectiveness of discretionary expansionary fiscal policy?

a. incomplete crowding out
b. complete crowding out
c. zero crowding out
d. none of the above

Answer: _____

11. Which of the following statements is false?

a. According to new classical theory, consumption will rise as a result of expansionary fiscal policy.
b. According to new classical theory, deficits bring about higher real interest rates.
c. According to new classical economists, individuals do not translate higher deficits into higher future taxes.
d. New classical economists and Keynesians generally have the same view of the effectiveness of expansionary fiscal policy.
e. all of the above

Answer: _____

12. Elaine's taxable income increases by $1.50 and her tax payment increases by $.35. Her marginal tax rate is:

a. 72 percent
b. 28 percent
c. 35 percent
d. 19 percent
e. none of the above

Answer: _____

13. The balanced budget theorem says that:

a. it is better to balance the budget than not (this is pre-Keynesian notion)
b. the change in national income is equal to the change in government spending when government spending and taxes change by the same dollar amount in the same direction
c. the change in goverment spending is equal to real GNP divided by tax receipts
d. budget surpluses generate "too low" unemployment and budget deficits generate "too high" unemployment
e. none of the above
Answer: _____

14. Which of the following economists is known for arguing that current taxpayers will likely leave bequests to their heirs for the purpose of paying higher future taxes?

a. John Maynard Keynes
b. Robert Barro
c. Irving Fisher
d. Robert Solow
e. none of the above

Answer: _____

15. The Laffer curve shows that:

a. as tax rates rise, tax revenues rise
b. as tax rates fall, tax revenues fall
c. as tax rates fall, tax revenues rise
d. as tax rates rise, tax revenues fall
e. all of the above

Answer: _____

True-False

16. Prior to the Keynesian revolution, laypersons   T F
and economists believed that the federal budget
should be balanced except during wartime.

17. The Swedish economist Knut Wicksell argued   T F
that individuals could only make an informed
evaluation of various proposals for government
expenditure if they were presented with a tax bill
at the same time the proposal for additional spending
was made.

18. Walter Heller advised President Kennedy to cut   T F
taxes in the early 1960s.

19. Complete crowding out occurs when the decrease   T F

19. Complete crowding out occurs when the decrease   T F
in one or more components of private spending
completely offsets the increase in government spending.

20. Tax revenues = tax base x (average) tax rate   T F

Fill in the blank

21. Keynesian economists would propose _____ fiscal policy for a recessionary gap.

22. _____ occurs when the decrease in one or more components of private spending only partly offsets the increase in government spending.

23. The _____ theorem holds that there is no difference in effects between raising taxes and issuing debt to finance government expenditures.

24. Arthur Laffer is a _____ economist.

25. The lowest tax rate under tax reform is _____ percent.

Part 5. Answers to Self Test

1. d 2. c 3. a 4. b 5. b 6. b 7. a 8. b 9. a 10. c
11. e 12. e 13. b 14. b 15. e
16. T 17. T 18. T 19. T 20. T
21. discretionary expansionary fiscal policy
22. Incomplete crowding out 23. Ricardian equivalence
24. supply-side 25. 15

Part 6. Answers

Part 2 Review of Concepts
1. c   2. g   3. d   4. e   5. k   6. i   7. h   8. j   9. a   10. f   11. b

Part 3 Key Concepts
1. deficit, exceed
2. wars (or other emergencies), surplus
3. fiscal policy, deficits
4. demand, supply
5. multiplier
6. expansionary, spending, decrease
7. 4=m=1/(1-MPC), so 1-MPC=1/4. This means MPC=3/4 or 0.75.
8. m_T = -MPC x m = -MPC x [1/(1-MPC)] = -MPC/(1-MPC) = -MPC/MPS = -0.75/0.25 = -3
9. rise, $50 mil.
10. discretionary, automatic
11. 91%
12. time (or lag), the White House (the president) and Congress

14. upward, rightward, reduces
15. higher, more, less
16. will not, will not
17. less
18. data, wait-and-see, legislative, transmission, effectiveness
19. Laffer
20. tax, income (or taxable income), $200
21. less, lower, more
22. rightward (increase AS)
23. rate, base
24. base, rate, base, rate
25. 28% (plus a 5% surcharge on some taxpayers, bringing their total to 33%)
26. incentives
27. work, less

Part 4 Problems and Exercises

1. a. 0.5, 2, -1   b. 0.4, 2.5, -1.5   c. 0.75, 4, -3   d. 0.6667, 0.3333, -2
   e. 0.9, 10, -9   f. 0.7778, 0.2222, -3.5
2. confirm
3. a. $20   b. -$50   c. 5   d. 4   e. $720   f. $60
4. a. -$20   b. $30   c. -3   d. -2.5   e. $270   f. -$50
5. 25%
6. $700

7. a. $700
   b. $300, ($700/$300) = 2.333
   c. see grid at right
   d. fall, ($200/2.333) = $85.72,
   $214.28

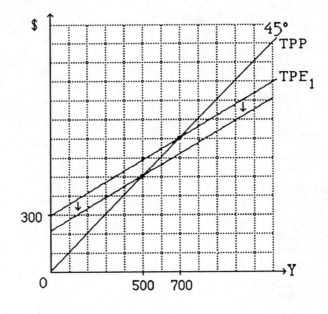

8. a. $0
    b. $9000
    c. $1700
    d. 30%
    e. $2400
    f. $4000
    g. 60%
    h. $1500
    i. $900
    j. $0

9. Laffer curve

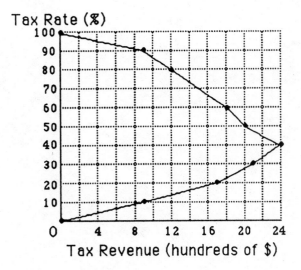

Chapter 18
Monetary Policy

Part 1. Introduction and Purpose
Consider the following points as you read chapter 18 in the text.

Economists have long debated whether monetary policy has a more or less powerful impact on the economy than fiscal policy. Whereas 40 years ago economists were uncertain whether monetary policy had any significant impact whatever, today the question is not *whether* money matters than *how much* money matters in the macroeconomy. Some have suggested that *only* money matters — that is, fiscal policy matters not at all — but that is not a majority opinion at this time.

Monetary policy is less political than fiscal policy and is made by a smaller group of policy makers, so decisions may be made in a few days or weeks and can be put into effect almost immediately. For these reasons, in recent years the Federal Reserve has assumed growing control over the daily conduct of macroeconomic policy. Fiscal policy decisions are few and far between, with most spending and taxing resulting from the automatic operation of legislation passed earlier.

You may recall from chapter 17 that fiscal policy can either affect aggregate demand or aggregate supply. **Monetary policy concentrates on the demand side** of the economy, thereby leaving the supply side to be determined by market (and other) forces. The exception to this rule is the ability of monetary policy makers to influence peoples' expectations about future inflation, which causes the aggregate supply curve to shift by causing workers (and other factor owners) to bargain for higher wages (and prices).

Although there is general agreement that monetary policy can affect the economy — inflation, unemployment, real GNP — there is far less agreement how it is able to do that. Various groups tell different "stories" about how monetary impulses are transmitted to the economy, and each story has different implications regarding the effects of money on the economy. This chapter examines the Keynesian **transmission mechanism** and the monetarist transmission mechanism, which provide the two best known explanations of money's impact.

In the Keynesian model, an increase in the money supply causes the supply of money to exceed the quantity of money demanded. People use the excess money to invest in bonds and make loans of various types, which increases the supply of loanable funds and causes the interest rate to decline. Lower **interest rates** stimulate businesses borrowing to finance capital goods **investments**, which in turn cause total planned expenditures and aggregate demand to increase.

The monetarist transmission mechanism places far less emphasis on interest rates. Beginning in equilibrium, an increase in the money supply leaves most everyone holding **excess money balances**, which they either **spend** or lend to others (who will spend them). Consequently the demand for virtually all goods is increased. Where the Keynesian model indicates that excess money balances flow into the loanable funds market, monetarists believe the dollars flow directly into the market for goods and services.

Policy **activists** — not usually monetarists — prefer to expand the money supply whenever a deflationary gap arises. While this may work up to a point, monetarists point out that rising inflation will eventually cause workers and other factor owners to bargain for higher wages and prices, which in turn will decrease aggregate supply. That prevents real GNP from rising by as much as it otherwise might, and actually makes it very difficult to maintain unemployment below about 6% without causing inflation to accelerate.

An inflationary gap is remedied by reducing the money supply, which will lower aggregate demand. Keynesians, assuming that the aggregate supply curve is fairly "flat," believe that very large reductions in aggregate demand are necessary to reduce inflation. They tend to worry that large reductions in real GNP are necessary to fight inflation. Monetarists believe that real GNP is normally tending toward natural real GNP anyway, so any loss in real output will be relatively small and progress against inflation will be greater than in the Keynesian model. It should come as no surprise that monetarists are more likely to advocate fighting inflation than Keynesians, since they disagree on the relative costs and benefits of that policy. Monetarists tend to believe that Keynesians are biased toward inflation, while Keynesians sometimes say monetarists are biased against full employment and real GNP growth.

One argument against using an activist monetary policy to stabilize the economy is the long and variable **lag** between the time a problem arises and the time something can be done about it. Due to these lags, an activist policy may actually destabilize the economy rather than stabilize it. The lag from money to real GNP is typically in the range of nine months to one year but is often outside this range. The lag from money to prices may be even longer.

Because of the long and variable lags, many non-activists have concluded that the best thing to do is nothing — except provide a stable monetary framework to minimize confusion and permit the economy to equilibrate in the quickest possible way. Many have called for a **money growth rule**, where the money supply increases at a moderate, pre-announced rate (perhaps in the 3-5% range). Another non-activist approach to monetary policy is the automatic **gold standard**, where the U.S. would promise to convert dollars for gold or gold for dollars at a fixed rate — say $400 an ounce. There are practical problems with the gold standard that you will read about in chapter 18.

Part 2. Review of Concepts from Earlier Chapters
Prior to reading chapter 18, match statements at left with the appropriate concept at right.

__1. When real GNP exceeds natural real GNP.	a. M1
__2. Monetary policy makers in the U.S.	b. monetary policy
__3. Currency, traveler's checks, demand deposits, plus OCDs.	c. inflationary gap
__4. Fed purchases of government securities from banks.	d. recessionary gap
__5. When real GNP is less than natural real GNP.	e. expansionary policy
__6. Unemployment in excess of the natural rate of unemployment.	f. money multiplier
__7. Manipulating the money supply to promote macroeconomic goals.	g. Federal Reserve
__8. Multiply this by the monetary base to compute M1.	h. cyclical unemployment

Part 3. Key Concepts in this Chapter
After reading chapter 18 in the text, answer the following questions.

1. According to the demand curve for money, people attempt to hold smaller money balances at higher / lower interest rates.

2. If the money supply increases but the interest rate remains at its original level, the quantity of money people would like to hold is greater than / less than / equal to the quantity of money they do hold.

3. As the prices of goods and services decline, the value (price) of money rises / falls .

4. A liquidity trap is the name given to the horizontal / vertical section of the money demand curve.

5. If the economy is operating in a liquidity trap and then the money supply increases, the extra money balances are spent / are held / are loaned out .

6. In general, monetary policy affects the economy by shifting the aggregate supply / demand curve.

7. In the Keynesian analysis, a decrease in the money supply causes interest rates to rise / fall .

8. The Keynesian model predicts that increases in the money supply cause interest rates to rise / fall , which in turn causes business investment spending to increase / decrease .

9. In both the Keynesian and monetarist analysis, the existence of an inflationary gap suggests that the preferred Fed policy would be to increase / decrease / not change the money supply.

10. An activist / nonactivist monetary policy is one that takes a hands-off approach and maintains a steady policy throughout the business cycle.

11. In the Keynesian model, an increase in the money supply will not stimulate aggregate demand if there is a money / liquidity / bear trap, or if saving / investment does not rise when interest rates fall.

12. Rising interest rates rise imply that bond prices are rising / falling . In general, interest rates and bond prices move in the same / opposite direction.

13. In the monetarist analysis, if the money supply exceeds / is less than money demand, there is an excess supply of money. This implies that aggregate demand will increase / decrease .

14. Those who believe that monetary and fiscal policy should be used to fine-tune the economy are known as monetarists / nonactivists / activists .

15. Suppose that real GNP is less than natural real GNP. One group of economists believe that real GNP will eventually increase to its natural level even without stimulative monetary or fiscal policies. These are monetarist / Keynesian / new classical economists.   Monetarist / Keynesian economists believe the economy can remain in equilibrium even though real GNP is "depressed."

16. Assuming the velocity of money remains unchanged, no long-term inflation could occur if the money supply expanded at the same rate as nominal / real GNP.

17. Keynesian / New classical economists believe that an activist monetary policy cannot successfully stimulate real GNP because people will / will not adjust wages and prices in anticipation of each money supply change.

18. True or false? _____ Because of lags in the effect of policy, activist monetary policies may destabilize the economy.

19. Under a gold standard, the government promises to _buy / sell / both buy and sell_ gold at the _market / official_ price.

20. Under a gold standard, if the market price of gold rises above the official price, people will _buy gold from / sell gold to_ the government. As people do this, the amount of (non-gold) money in circulation will _increase / decrease_.

21. True or false? _____ A gold standard conforms more to a nonactivist point of view than to an activist point of view.

22. Under a monetary rule, the money supply should grow _more / less_ rapidly in years of recession and high unemployment than in a year of high inflation.

23. According to the text, empirical studies _do / do not_ support the existence of a liquidity trap in the demand for money.

24. In the monetarist model, if there is an excess demand for money (or deficient supply of it), people will tend to _increase / reduce / maintain_ their spending. This will cause aggregate demand to _increase / decrease / remain unchanged_.

25. Suppose there is a recessionary gap. Monetarists believe that if monetary and fiscal policies remain neutral, wages will tend to _rise / fall_. This _will / will not_ tend to reduce the gap.

Part 4. Problems and Exercises
After reading chapter 18 in the text you should be able to work the following problems.

1. In the Keynesian economic model, the money supply (M) affects aggregate demand in a roundabout way involving changes in interest rates and planned investment. **Insert up or down arrows ($\uparrow$ $\downarrow$)** in the following transmission "chain" to show what happens following a money supply increase:

$$\uparrow M \rightarrow \underline{}i \rightarrow \underline{}\text{Investment} \rightarrow \underline{}\text{TPE} \rightarrow \underline{}\text{AD}$$
$$\downarrow M \rightarrow \underline{}i \rightarrow \underline{}\text{Investment} \rightarrow \underline{}\text{TPE} \rightarrow \underline{}\text{AD}$$

2. If there is an inflationary gap the unemployment rate is _above / below_ its natural level. This implies that wages and other factor prices will _rise / fall_, which will cause the aggregate supply curve to shift to the _right / left_. This shift in the AS curve will _increase / decrease_ the size of the gap between real GNP and natural real GNP.

3. Use information in the following table to calculate how rapidly the money supply should grow during the year to bring about price stability.

	%ΔV	%ΔQ	%ΔM
a.	1%	2%	___%
b.	3%	3%	___%
c.	-1%	2%	___%
d.	-4%	3%	___%

4. In the graph at right, the current money supply is
$4 billion.

a. The equilibrium interest rate is ___%.

b. Draw a new money supply curve in the grid to show
what happens when the money supply rises by $1 bil.

c. If the interest rate remains at its original level, there will
be an excess money _supply / demand_ amounting to
$___ bil. Show this "gap" in the graph.

d. In the monetarist model the excess money supply is
spent / saved by consumers and others.

e. In the Keynesian model the excess money supply is
mainly used by investors to buy _bonds / land / cars_ .
That drives up their prices _up / down_ and causes interest
rates to _rise / fall_ to ____%.

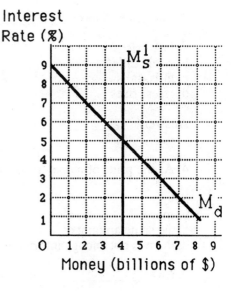

Interest
Rate (%)

Money (billions of $)

Part 5. Self Test
Multiple choice questions

1. The demand curve for money is the graphical representation of the _____ relationship
between the quantity demanded of money and the _____ of money.

a. direct, price
b. inverse, amount
c. direct, amount
d. inverse, price

Answer: _____

2. In a one-good world, the price of money is:

a. the price of the good
b. 1
c. the inverse of the price of the good
d. the price of the good in terms of all other goods

Answer: _____

3. The price of money _____ as the price level rises and _____ as the price level falls.

a. falls, rises
b. rises, falls
c. falls, falls
d. rises, rises

Answer: _____

4. As the price of money rises, people hold _____ money.

a. less
b. more
c. the same amount of
d. there is not enough information to answer the question

Answer: _____

5. Which scenario best explains the Keynesian transmission if the money market is in the liquidity trap?

a. The money market is intially in equilibrium; the money supply rises; there is an excess demand for money; the interest rate rises; investment falls.
b. The money market is initially in equilibrium; the money supply rises; there is an excess supply of money that puts downward pressure on interest rates; investment rises.
c. The money market is initially in equilibrium; the money supply rises; there is an excess supply of money that puts downward pressure on interest rates; investment is unresponsive to the lower interest rate.
d. The money market is initially in equilibrium; the money supply rises; there is no excess supply of money; no money flows into the loanable funds market.

Answer: _____

6. Suppose the price of old and existing bonds are falling. This means that you can expect to see:

a. market interest rates on the decline
b. market interest rates on the rise
c. market interest rates first going up and then coming down
d. market interest rates first coming down and then going up

Answer: _____

7. Compared to the Keynesian transmission mechanism, the monetarist transmission mechanism is:

a. indirect and long
b. direct and long
c. direct and short
d. indirect and short

Answer: _____

8. Which of the following statements is false?

a. In the monetarist transmission mechanism, changes in the money market only indirectly affect aggregate demand.
b. In the monetarist transmission mechanism, there is need for the money market to affect the loanable funds market or the investment market before aggregate demand is affected.
c. In the monetarist transmission mechanism, if individuals are faced with an excess supply of money they spend that money on a wide variety of goods.
d. a and b
e. a, b, and c

Answer: _____

9. Keynesians would not be likely to advocate expansionary monetary policy to eliminate a recessionary gap if they believed:

a. the liquidity trap exists
b. investment spending is interest sensitive
c. monetarists were in favor of such a policy
d. a and b
e. a, b, and c

Answer: _____

10. Read the following statements: (1) The more closely monetary policy can be designed to meet the particulars of a given economic environment, the better. (2) Because of long and uncertain time lags, activist monetary policy may be destabilizing rather than stabilizing. (3) There is sufficient flexibility in wages and prices in modern economies to allow the economy to equilibrate in reasonable speed at the natural level of real GNP. (4) The "same-for-all-seasons" monetary policy is the way to proceed. Which of the statements is likely to be made by an economist who believes in activist monetary policy?

a. Statements 1, 2, and 3
b. Statements 1, and 4
c. Statements 1 and 3
d. Statement 1
e. Statements 1, 3, and 4

Answer: _____

11. Economists who propose a constant money supply growth rule often contend that:

a. setting the annual growth rate in the money supply equal to the average annual growth rate in real GNP maintains price level stability over time
b. setting the annual growth rate in the money supply equal to the average annual growth rate in real GNP is a way to raise investment
c. setting the annual growth rate in the money supply equal to the average annual growth rate in real GNP will cause the price level to fall over time and interest rates to stabilize
d. a and b
e. a, b, and c

Answer: _____

12. The monetary rule Allan Meltzer, a monetarist, has proposed to maintain price stability reads this way:

a. The annual growth rate in the money supply will be equal to the average annual growth rate in real GNP divided by the growth rate in velocity.
b. The annual growth rate in the money supply will be equal to the average annual growth rate in real GNP plus the growth rate in velocity.
c. The annual growth rate in the money supply will be equal to the average annual growth rate in real GNP minus the growth rate in velocity.
d. The annual growth rate in the money supply will be equal to the average annual growth rate in real GNP times the growth rate in velocity.

Answer: _____

13. The quantity demanded of money rises:

a. as the interest rate rises
b. as the interest rate falls
c. as the supply of money falls
d. none of the above, since the quantity demanded of money is unrelated to the interest rate

Answer: _____

14. What does it mean if the investment demand curve is completely insensitive to changes in interest rates?

a. It means that changes in interest rates will lower but not raise investment spending.
b. It means that changes in interest rates will raise but not lower investment spending.
c. It means that changes in interest rates will not change investment spending.
d. It means that changes in interest rates within a certain range will not change investment spending.

Answer: _____

15. When is it best to buy bonds?

a. when interest rates are <u>expected</u> to rise, because this means bond prices will rise
b. when interest rates are <u>expected</u> to fall, because this means bond prices will fall
c. when interest rates are <u>expected</u> to rise, because this means bond prices will fall
d. when interest rates are <u>expected</u> to fall, because this means bond prices will rise

Answer: _____

True-False

16. As the price of money falls people hold more money.   T F

17. The price of old or existing bonds is directly related to the market interest rate.   T F

18. Activists are less likely to advocate fine-tuning the economy than nonactivists.   T F

19. The demand curve for money is usually vertical.   T F

20. As the price level rises, the price of money falls.   T F

Fill in the blank

21. Keynesians would not propose expansionary monetary policy to cure a recessionary gap if investment was interest _____ or the money market was in the _____ .

22. In the monetarist transmission mechanism, changes in the money market _____ affect aggregate demand.

23. Keynesians are less likely to propose _____ monetary policy to eliminate an inflationary gap than _____ monetary policy to eliminate a recessionary gap.

24. Allan Meltzer's monetary rule for price stability sets the annual growth rate in the money supply equal to the average annual growth rate in _____ minus the growth rate in _____ .

25. A gold standard is an example of _____ monetary policy.

Part 5. Answers to Self Test

1. d 2. c 3. a 4. a 5. d 6. b 7. c 8. d 9. a 10. d
11. a 12. c 13. b 14. c 15. d
16. T 17. F 18. F 19. F 20. T
21. insensitive, liquidity trap 22. directly
23. contractionary, expansionary 24. real GNP, velocity
25. nonactivist

Part 6. Answers

Part 2 Review of Concepts
1. c   2. g   3. a   4. e   5. d   6. h   7. b   8. f

Part 3 Key Concepts
1. higher   2. less than   3. rises   4. horizontal   5. are held   6. demand   7. rise
8. fall, increase   9. decrease   10. non-activist   11. liquidity, investment   12. falling, opposite
13. exceeds, increase   14. activists   15. monetarists or new classical, Keynesian   16. real
17. new classical, will   18. true   19. buy or sell, official   20. buy gold from, decrease   21. True
22. equally   23. do not   24. reduce, decrease   25. fall, will

Part 4 Problems and Exercises
1. $\uparrow$ M $\rightarrow$ $\underline{\downarrow}$ i $\rightarrow$ $\underline{\uparrow}$ Investment $\rightarrow$ $\underline{\uparrow}$ TPE $\rightarrow$ $\underline{\uparrow}$ AD
   $\downarrow$ M $\rightarrow$ $\underline{\uparrow}$ i $\rightarrow$ $\underline{\downarrow}$ Investment $\rightarrow$ $\underline{\downarrow}$ TPE $\rightarrow$ $\underline{\downarrow}$ AD

2. below, rise, left, decrease

3. a. 1%   b. 0%   c. 3%   d. 7%

4. a. 5%
   b. See graph at right
   c. supply, $1 bil.
   d. spent
   e. bonds, up, fall, 4%

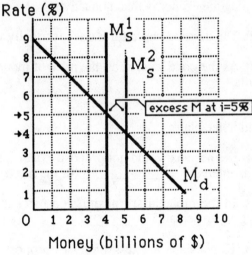

Interest Rate (%)

Money (billions of $)

Chapter 19
Budget Deficits and the National Debt

Part 1. Introduction and Purpose
Consider the following points as you read chapter 19 in the text.

Few economic issues have been debated as much as the national debt. Some people say the national debt is of little concern, others say it stands in the way of our enjoying a more robust economy, while a third group believes the debt postpones the cost of today's government programs and places the burden of paying for them on future generations of taxpayers. Something can be said for each view, as you will see when you read chapter 19.

It is necessary to review a few terms before turning to the analysis of national debt. First, the **national debt** is really the federal government's debt, dollars it has borrowed over the years to finance its spending in excess of tax collections. The national debt is the total outstanding **stock** of federal debt at a point in time

The total stock of debt grows each year that government spends more than its tax collections. Federal government spending *this year* minus taxes collected *this year* equal *this year's* government **budget deficit**. If tax collections are more than government spending, this year's budget will reflect a **surplus**, and the government uses the surplus to retire some of its outstanding debt.

So how does it affect me? you may be asking yourself. Well, since you're a member of the public, then the national debt is partly your obligation to pay interest on and possibly to help pay off. Your share isn't assigned to you personally, but as you earn income and engage in other economic activities the government will be taxing you in various ways for dollars to "service" the debt.

For example if the national debt is $2.8 trillion and there are 113 million employed workers (who pay most federal taxes), then goverment debt is about $24,800 per worker. If the interest rate is 10%, the government would have to collect about $2480 in taxes from each worker annually to pay interest on the debt. (Use your calculator to verify this estimate.)

These kinds of calculations bring many people to conclude that deficits shift the **burden** of current government programs onto **future generations** of taxpayers. If voters and politicians decide to spend $100 bil. more than this year's taxes, future taxpayers will pay higher taxes as a result. How does that affect you? You're one of the future workers whose taxes will increase.

This perspective of the debt burden is the one held by the general public, but some economists argue that the burden of deficits should be measured by the reduced production of private goods that takes place when government spends more. As more resources are used by government, society will immediately have fewer consumption and capital goods available. Consequently the view that the **current generation** suffers the burden of its own spending programs.

Who is right? They are both right, but they are talking about different issues. One looks at the impact of deficits on particular individuals, while the other looks their impact on resource use. Neither analysis really denies the truth of the other, but advocates of each point of view tend to feel that the effects they have identified are more important than those identified by the other school of thought.

Apart from the burden of debt, a number of other issues related to national debt and budget deficits have been discussed in recent years. One is the **real national debt**, and the ability of inflation to reduce it. The U.S. Government is the world's largest debtor, so the real value of its obligation declines whenever prices increase.

The debt and deficit figures have another shortcoming. Government can become obligated to make future payments — which means it can obligate future taxpayers — without actually borrowing money and issuing bonds. For example, a promise to pay retirement benefits to someone who is now 40 years old represents a financial obligation that falls due 25 years from now — not unlike a 25-year bond or bank loan. The federal government has a large number of transactions falling into this category, and the text points out that the national debt would be about three (3) times as large if such promises were included in the official debt figures.

Regardless of the particular position one takes on the national debt, just about everyone agrees that it is too large and should either be held at the current level or reduced. The debt will stop growing if the budget deficit equals zero each year, but budget surpluses are required to actually reduce it.

Recognizing the political difficulty of dealing with the deficit, some believe that the solution must lie outside the ordinary budget process. They advocate changes in **fiscal policy rules** which would bias the budget process toward balance — to offset the current bias toward deficits. One is a **balanced budget amendment** to the U.S. Constitution that would require Congress to balance the budget during "ordinary" (non-war, non-depression) years. Most states have a balanced budget provision in their constitutions, and the proposal calls for a similar debt limit at the national level.

A second proposed change is the **line item veto**. The line item veto would permit a president to block certain parts of a spending bill while accepting the overall bill. Currently the Congress passes major spending laws that authorize dozens to hundreds of specific projects or programs.

A third proposal is to maintain primary control of the budget within Congress, but set budget targets that it must meet until the deficit is reduced to zero. The **Gramm-Rudman-Hollings** (GRH) legislation of 1985 established such targets, and despite many difficulties Congress has made some amount of progress toward the ultimate goal. GRH contains a built-in penalty for not satisfying the deficit targets — an across-the-board spending cut that would affect about two-thirds of all government outlays.

Part 2. Review of Concepts from Earlier Chapters
Prior to reading chapter 19, match statements at left with the appropriate concept at right.

__1. Manipulating gov't. spending & taxes to promote macroeconomic goals.
__2. When government spending exceeds government receipts.
__3. When government receipts exceed government spending.

__4. Price charged for credit.
__5. Along this curve, to get more of one good one must give up another.
__6. This is an amount existing at a point in time, not a flow over time.
__7. The tradition that the budget should be balanced in most years.

a. PPF curve
b. interest
c. Old Time Fiscal
   Religion
d. stock
e. budget surplus
f. budget deficit
g. fiscal policy

Part 3. Key Concepts in this Chapter
After reading chapter 19 in the text, answer the following questions.

1. If the national debt is initially $1300, but this year the federal government runs a deficit of $120, then by the end of the year the national debt will be $_____.

2. The "national debt" is a debt obligation of _individual Americans / US Government / states_. According to the text, in 1988 the national debt was about $ _1 / 2.5 / 5_ trillion.

3. In discussing who bears the burden of the national debt, one group says that the burden is borne by future _consumers / taxpayers_. Another group believes that the current generation bear the burden of government programs when _____ of production are shifted from producing private goods to producing government goods.

4. Exhibit 19-1 shows that the ratio of national debt to GNP peaked in _1946 / 1960 / 1980 / 1988_.

5. The government's fiscal year is _January / July / October_ 1 until _January / July / September_ 30 of the following calendar year.

6. Professor James Buchanan suggests that debt-financed government spending programs impose a burden on _the current / a future_ generation of taxpayers. When the government borrows dollars today and uses them to finance current programs, the people who currently lend dollars and who se'l the ~sources to government _do / do not_ bear a burden in Buchanan's model.

7. A consumption tax would apply to the difference between disposable _income / consumption_ and his and one's annual _consumption / saving_ .

8. A _sales / income / value added_ tax would be levied on businesses against the total value of their sales minus their payments for purchases of _services / material inputs_ .

9. Turning over government activities to private sector firms is called _____.

10. In the interview with Professor Richard Musgrave, he mentions that members of the public argue for _more / less_ government spending and _higher / lower_ taxes. He says that there is a built in tendency for excessive _surpluses / deficits_ .

11. Looking at the increase in federal government expenditures in the 1980s, Professor Musgrave believes that the sharpest increase is in the area of _defense spending / transfer payments_ . These _have / have not_ been particularly successful at improving the situation of low-income groups.

12. Suppose initially the national debt is $1000. During the current year the government borrows another $50 and the inflation rate is 4%. The real value of the national debt _rises / falls_ by $____.

13. A rule that would permit the president to eliminate specific programs from legislation containing a large number of different policies is known as a _pocket veto / spending freeze / line item veto_.

14. A fiscal year that begins Oct. 1, 1998 and ends Sept 30, 1999 will be called fiscal year 19____.

15. The federal government budget has been in deficit each year since _1929 / 1946 / 1960 / 1969_.

16. Gramm-Rudman-Hollings (GRH) legislation establishes _spending / tax / deficit_ targets for the government to meet. In the event of failure, then _____- the -_____ spending cuts would be applied to most programs.

17. In speaking of the national debt, the argument that "We Owe It To Ourselves" suggests that the burden of the national debt falls on _the current / a future_ generation of taxpayers.

18. Those who normally argue that the current generation bears the full burden of government spending agree that the burden falls on future generations of taxpayers if the government borrows funds from _domestic / foreign / young_ lenders and investors.

19. Legislation is "like a bond" when a law promises monetary payments to people in the _past / present / future_. The example discussed in the text is _national defense / Social Security_.

Part 4. Problems and Exercises

After reading chapter 19 in the text you should be able to work the following problems.

1. One of the things bankers consider before granting a loan is the ratio of a person's debts to his or her annual income. For example, if you earn $25,000 annually but have a $60,000 mortgage, a $6,000 car loan, and $1000 worth of assorted consumer credit, then:

        a. your debt equals $_____

        b. your income equals $_____

        c. so your ratio of debt to income is   _____

2. In a recent year the national debt was about $2.3 trillion (= $2,300 bil.) and the government's total receipts were about $900 bil. Use the method from #1 above to calculate the government's debt-to-income ratio: _____.

3. Suppose the national debt is $1,000 billion and there are 100 million taxpayers in the U.S.

    a. This means that debt per worker equals $_____.

    b. If the interest rate is 8%, then the average worker will be taxed $_____ each year on his or her share of the national debt.

Part 5. Self Test
Multiple choice questions

1. The national debt is:

a. larger than GNP
b. approximately equal to GNP
c. smaller than GNP
d. smaller today in absolute dollar terms than it was 1979

Answer: _____

2. Which of the following statements is false?

a. All economists agree that the current generation bears the burden of the debt.
b. Today the entire national debt is held almost exclusively by foreigners.
c. Since the early 1970s, Americans have come to hold a smaller percentage of the (U.S.) national debt.
d. Economist James Buchanan argues that the future generation does not bear the burden of the debt.
e. a, b, and d

Answer: _____

3. Suppose the federal government runs a $100 billion deficit in year 1 that increases the national debt from $1,900 billion to $2,000 billion by year's end. During year 1 the price level rises by 5 percent. What is the real deficit?

a. $100 billion
b. zero dollars ($0)
c. $ 5 billion
d. $ 50 billion

Answer: _____

4. Suppose the federal government runs a $150 billion deficit in year 1 that increases the national debt from $2,000 billion to $2,150 billion by year's end. During
year 1 the price level rises by 1 percent. What is the real deficit?

a. $130 billion
b. zero dollars ($0)
c. $150 billion
d. $ 20 billion

Answer: _____

5. During the period 1983-88, the national debt/GNP ratio:

a. fell consistently
b. grew consistently

c. grew in 1983 and 1984, and then fell in each of the remaining years
d. fell in 1983 and 1984, and then grew in each of the remaining years

Answer: _____

6. The critics of the balanced budget amendment do not argue that:

a. taxes will be lower with a balanced budget amendment
b. Congress can evade the amendment by moving expenditures off-budget
c. the discipline of a balanced budget may cause the government to enact the wrong kind of fiscal policy
d. a and b
e. b and c

Answer: _____

7. Proponents of Gramm-Rudman argue that:

a. it calls for disproportionately large cuts in some spending programs
b. it calls for deep cuts in Social Security
c. it calls for deep cuts in interest payments on the debt and in social welfare spending
d. a and b
e. none of the above

Answer: _____

8. The president submits a budget to Congress in:

a. November of each year
b. January or February of each year
c. July of each year
d. October of each year

Answer: _____

9. Which of the following statements is false?

a. We would expect that conservative presidents would want the presidential line-item veto much more than liberal presidents.
b. In 1985, President Reagan signed into law the act that gave all future presidents (beginning in 1991) the line-item veto.
c. President Carter was the only president in modern times to have the line-item veto.
d. a and c
e. a, b, and c

Answer: _____

10. The base of a valued added tax (VAT) is:

a. wages and salaries
b. tax receipts
c. the value added to a good at each stage of its production
d. the value added to a good at the first and last stage of production
e. none of the above

Answer: _____

True-False

11. The deficit is a stock variable.   T F

12. In 1988, the national debt was approximately   T F
$2.5 trillion.

13. The first day of the fiscal year is November 1.   T F

14. Future bondholders gain nothing, they simply   T F
trade one asset for another of equal value. This
statement is likely to be made by an economist who
believes the current generation bears the burden of
the debt.

15. Richard Musgrave argues that future generations   T F
exclusively pay for the debt.

Fill in the blank

16. The critics of the balanced budget amendment argue that the discipline of a balanced budget may make
it hard to use _____ policy to stabilize the economy.

17. Richard Musgrave argues that to the extent that debt finance diverts saving and reduces
_____ , the future gneration is left with less _____ and this is a burden.

18. Economist _____ believes future generations do bear the burden of the debt.

19. Suppose the government runs a $250 billion deficit in year 1 that increases the national debt from
$2,000 billion to $2,250 billion by year's end. During year 1 the price level rises by 10 percent. The real
deficit is _____ .

20. Since the early 1970s, Americans have come to hold a _____ percentage of the national
debt.

Part 5. Answers to Self Test

1. c 2. e 3. c 4. a 5. b 6. a 7. e 8. b 9. e 10. c
11. F 12. T 13. F 14. F 15. F
16. discretionary fiscal 17. capital formation, capital stock 18. James Buchanan 19. $50 billion
20. smaller

Part 6. Answers

Part 2 Review of Concepts
1. g   2. f   3. e   4. b   5. a   6. d   7. c

Part 3 Key Concepts
1. $1420   2. the US Gov't, $2.5 tril.   3. taxpayers, factors (resources)   4. 1946
5. October, September   6. future, do not   7. income, saving   8. value added, material inputs
9. privatization   10. more, lower, deficits   11. transfer payments, have not   12. rises, $10
13. line item veto   14. 1999   15. 1969   16. targets, across-the-board   17. the current
18. foreign   19. future, Social Security

Part 4 Problems and Exercises
1. a. $67,000   b. $25,000   c. 2.68 (debt equals 268% of income)
2. 2.556 (debt equals 256% of annual government income)
4. a. $1,000 bil.÷0.1 bil people=$10,000 each   b.$800

Chapter 20
The Logic of Consumer Choice

Part 1. Introduction and Purpose
Consider the following points as you read chapter 20 in the text.

Although related topics are also included in the chapter, "the logic of consumer choice" is a theoretical discussion of the behavior summarized as the **law of demand**, which you read about in chapter 3. In the present chapter we will look at the logic underlying a consumer's choice to buy more of a good when its price declines, or to buy less when its price rises.

The chapter begins by introducing several concepts used in the economic analysis of consumer behavior. The first of these is **utility** — or the satisfaction or well-being one gets from satisfying personal wants or needs. Virtually all of microeconomic analysis assumes that people are motivated by a desire to maximize their personal utilities. In this particular the people we are concerned with **consumers**, but we will also rely on the utility maximization assumption in later chapters when we consider company managers, workers, store owners and others.

When a person consumes units of a good it is possible to speak of the **total utility** he or she receives from it. Although utility is really a subjective feeling that is experienced rather than measured (like body temperature), we will use a hypothetical unit of utility — a **util** — in the discussion to make the ideas clearer. If the consumer drinks 10 sodas per week she receives 120 utils of total utility.

There is also a name for the extra utility the consumer receives from one more soda — its **marginal utility**. The 11th soda is the marginal soda, and the extra utility it provides is its marginal utility. If the marginal utility of the 11th soda is 8 utils, then the consumer receives 128 utils of total utility from all 11 sodas. The thing to keep in mind about marginal utility is that it declines as a person consumes more and more units of the same good during a given time period. The **law of diminishing marginal utility** — a famous economic law — tells us that a second unit of some good provides less marginal satisfaction than the first, the third unit provides less marginal satisfaction than the second, etc. The textbook explains why this should be true — namely that people use the first unit of a good to satisfy their most urgent needs (so marginal utility is at its highest), while the second unit is used to satisfy the consumer's second-most urgent need, and so on.

In any case, the law of diminishing marginal utility tells us that consumers place a lower subjective value on additional units of a good during any given time period. With a little imagination you can see how this is related to the law of demand. Additional units provide less marginal utility, so the only way to induce consumers to buy more units is to lower price per unit. Lower prices result in greater consumption.

Price changes actually affect consumers through two conceptually distinct channels. The **substitution effect** of a price change says that when a good's relative price declines, consumers will substitute it for other goods in the market basket; if the good's relative price increases consumers will substitute other goods for it. How large the effect will be depends on the size of the relative price change and on the shape of the consumer's marginal utility curves for various goods.

A second effect of price changes usually tends to reinforce the substitution effect. The **income effect** is based on the fact that the real purchasing power of the consumer's money income will increase whenever the dollar prices of goods decline (and vice versa). With the increase in real income, the consumer will consume more of all normal goods — including the good whose price initially declined. You can see that in most circumstances the income effect will probably be pretty small relative to the substitution effect. Still, the income effect tends to add to the substitution effect: both tend to increase the consumption of a good whose price declines. (Both tend to reduce consumption of a good whose price rises.)

The income effect works in the opposite direction of the substitution effect when the good is an **inferior** good, but since the income effect is predictably smaller than the substitution effect, the net impact of a price change is dominated by the substitution effect. There will be an inverse (opposite) relationship between a good's relative price and the quantity of it people will consume.

The present chapter examines the *direction* of the impact a price change on quantity demanded. The next chapter discusses the *size* of the impact — the responsiveness of quantity demanded to price changes.

Part 2.   Review of Concepts from Earlier Chapters
Prior to reading chapter 20, match statements at left with the appropriate concept at right.

__1. The price of one good expressed in units of another good.   a. marginal
__2. More of this good is consumed as real consumer incomes decline.   b. equilibrium
__3. More of this good is consumed as real consumer incomes rise.   c. ceteris paribus
__4. A situation away from which there is no tendency to move.   d. utility
__5. A change in consumption caused by a change in own price.   e. opportunity cost
__6. What is foregone when a choice is made.   f. relative price
__7. All other things remaining constant.   g. normal good
__8. Another term for happiness or satisfaction.   h. inferior good
__9. Additional or incremental units of something.   i. Δ quantity demanded
__10. Something that provides utility to consumers.   j. good

Part 3.   Key Concepts in this Chapter
After reading chapter 20 in the text, answer the following questions.

1. When Adam Smith spoke of the utility provided by a good, he said it had value in
    <u>consumption / use</u>.   In speaking of the market value of the good, he said it had value in
    <u>trade / exchange</u>.

2. The satisfaction one gains from consuming one additional unit of a good is called _____ utility. _Total / marginal / average_ utility is the benefit from all of the units consumed.

3. Utils are hypothetical units of _____.

4. The law of _rising / diminishing / constant_ _average / marginal / total_ utility says the 6th unit of a good will provide less satisfaction than the 5th unit, but more than the 7th.

5. In the diamond-water paradox, the marginal utility of water is _higher / lower_ than that of diamonds. The total utility of water is _greater/ less_ than that of diamonds.

6. The law of diminishing marginal utility is based on the idea that consumers use units of a good to satisfy their most _____ want. Consequently the fourth unit of a good provides _less / more_ satisfaction than the third unit.

7. According to the law of diminishing marginal utility, who will value a $100 cash prize more?
   a) Rich person   b) Poor person   c) They value it equally   d) Impossible to say which

8. According to the law of diminishing marginal utility, a person who has a monthly income of $1000 will value a $100 cash prize _more_ than she would have if her monthly income had been _____.
   a) $900   b) $999   c) $1100   d) Impossible to say

9. An _____ utility comparison occurs when one compares one person's happiness to another's. This practice _is / is not_ considered to be scientific analysis.

10. The diamond-water paradox suggests that the market price or exchange value of a good depends on the _total / marginal / average_ utility it provides.

11. If the necessities of life were provided free by government, people would desire all units that provide a marginal utility as low as _____.

12. Suppose Juanita receives 500 utils from a morning more doughnut, for which she pays 60¢. The marginal utility per dollar's worth of doughnuts for Juanita is _____ utils.

13. Suppose Juanita receives 11,200 utils from a $14 compact disk recording. The marginal utility per dollar's worth of this CD is _____ utils. In questions 12-13, Juanita receives a higher marginal utility per dollar from _doughnuts / CD recording_.

14. Refer to questions 12-13. If Juanita is a utility maximizing customer, she will tend to substitute more _doughnuts / CDs_ in her market basket and less _doughnuts / CDs_.

15. If a consumer is maximizing utility, then for this person the marginal utility per dollar's worth of good X is _greater than / less than / equal to_ the marginal utility per dollar's worth of good Y.

16. If a person is in consumer equilibrium, that consumer _is /is not / may or may not be_ maximizing his or her utility.

17. If the price of good X rises, then consumers of good X will experience _an increase / a decrease_ in their standard of living. This is called a change in consumer _nominal / real / money_ income.

18. If the price of good X falls, consumers of X will experience _an increase / a decrease_ in their real incomes. This will allow them to buy _more / less_ of all normal goods and cause them to buy _more / less_ of all inferior goods. This chain reaction from price to real income to consumption is known as the _budget / income / substitution_ effect.

19. The substitution effect of a price change is triggered by an inequality in the _____ _____ per dollar spent on various goods. If the relative price of a good rises, then its _____ _____ per dollar _rises above / falls below_ that of other goods.

20. Researchers at Texas A&M University have tested _rats / birds / cows / giraffes_ to see if the law of demand applies to the animal kingdom. They found that it _does / does not / is impossible to say_.

21. For normal goods, the income and substitution effects of a price change _do/ do not_ cause consumers to change their purchases in the same direction. For inferior goods, the income and substitution effects of a price change _do/ do not_ cause consumers to change their purchases in the same direction.

22. William Stanley Jevons is considered to be a father of _marginal utility / demand / microeconomic_ theory. Rather than that term, he spoke of the _____ degree of utility. Jevons _did / did not_ advocate making interpersonal utility comparisons.

Part 4. Problems and Exercises

After reading chapter 20 in the text you should be able to work the following problems.

1. Herman, the white rat, lives in a laboratory at a well-known university. Herman can "buy" a milliliter (ml.) of root beer by pushing a lever in his cage. For the past several weeks Hermie (as his friends call him) has been able to purchase one ml. of "suds" by pushing the lever 30 times, and he has been purchasing 4 ml. per day. For the last couple of days, Hermie's scientist friends have reduced the number of lever pushes to 20 for each ml., and he has been consuming 11 ml. each day.

Plot the two price-quantity combinations in the grid, and sketch Herman's demand curve for root beer.

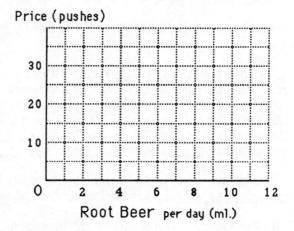

2. The table below contains information about the total utility received from consuming various quantities of good X. Plot these quantity-utility combinations in the grid at right, and connect the points to sketch out a total utility function.

Units of X	0	1	2	3	4	5	6
Total Utility	0	20	38	54	66	76	84

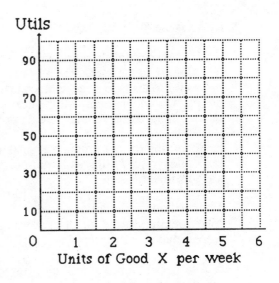

3. a. Use information from problem 2 to calculate the marginal utilities of various units of good X, and write those amounts in the table below.

Unit of X:	1	2	3	4	5	6
Marginal Utility:	__	__	__	__	__	__

b. Plot the marginal utility figures from the table in the grid at right, and connect the points to sketch out a MU curve.

c. The shape of the MU curve indicates that the law of diminishing marginal utility _does / doesn't_ apply to this case.

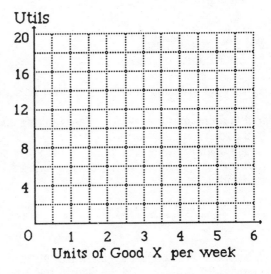

4. The table shows a consumer's marginal utility from consuming various units of good Z. Compute marginal utilities per dollar when good Z's price goes from $1 to $2 to $0.50.

Unit of Z:	1	2	3	4	5	6
Marginal Utility:	100	90	80	70	60	50

Unit of Z:	1	2	3	4	5	6
a. MU per dollar when Price=$1:	100	__	__	__	__	__
b. MU per dollar when Price=$2:	50	__	__	__	__	__
c. MU per dollar when Price=$0.50:	__	__	__	__	__	__

5. Refer to the grid at right.

a. Plot MU per dollar figures from
question #4 in the grid. Plot all of the
points for to a single price, then connect the
points; then do the same for the next price.
When finished you should have 3 curves.

b. According to your graph, marginal utility
per dollar rises / falls as larger quantities
are consumed.

Marginal utility per dollar would
 rise / decline if the quantity consumed
were reduced.

c. The MU/P curve shirts up / down
when price rises.

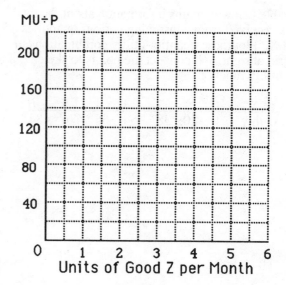

Part 5. Self Test
Multiple choice questions

1. If Fiona says that drinking soda gives her utility, what specifically does she mean?

a. that there are things worse than drinking soda
b. that drinking soda is tasty
c. that drinking soda is something that gives her satisfaction or pleasure
d. that there is nothing better than drinking soda
e. b and d

Answer: _____

2. Suppose Will consumes 5 units of good X and receives 20 utils from the first unit, 18 from the second, 12 from the third, 7 from the fourth, and 1 from the fifth. The total utility Will receives from consuming 5 units is:

a. 50 utils
b. 58 utils
c. 40 utils
d. 45 utils
e. none of the above

Answer: _____

3. Suppose Bob receives 123 utils from consuming one banana and 159 utils from consuming two bananas. What is the marginal utility of the second banana?

a. 282 utils
b. 30 utils
c.   0 utils
d. 36 utils
e. none of the above

Answer: _____

4. The law of diminishing marginal utility says that the marginal utility gained by consuming equal _____units of a good will _____as the amount consumed _____ .

a. successive, decline, decreases
b. successive, decline, increases
c. large, decline, decreases
d. small, decline, increases
e. none of the above

Answer: _____

5. Which of the following is false?

a. It is impossible for total utility to rise as marginal utility falls.
b. Marginal utility is the same as average utility.
c. Marginal utility is greater than total utility for the first unit of a good consumed.
d. a and c
e. a, b, and c

Answer: _____

6. In which of the following settings is an interpersonal utility comparison not being being made?

a. Brady says to Armond, "I get a lot more satisfaction from eating hamburgers than you do."
b. Francis says, "I don't know what he is feeling or thinking; I can't read a person's heart or mind."
c. Ida says to Lucy, "I know you like this course a lot more than I do."
d. a and b
e. a, b, and c

Answer: _____

7. Suppose for a consumer the marginal utility of pickles is 50 utils and the marginal utility of milk is 30 utils; the price of pickles is $1 and the price of milk is $1.25. Given this:

a. the same amount of utility is gained from consuming milk as pickles, per penny
b. more utility is gained from consuming milk than pickles, per penny
c. more utility is gained from consuming pickles than milk, per penny
d. the consumer is in consumer equilibrium

Answer: _____

8. The price of good Y, a normal good, falls from $10 to $8. As a result, the quantity demanded of good Y rises from 125 units to 155 units. Holding real income constant, the quantity demanded of good Y rises 20 units. Which of the following is true?

a. The consumer consumes 20 more units of Y because it has become relatively cheaper; therefore this is the income effect.
b. The consumer consumes 10 more units of Y because he or she has more real income; therefore this is the income effect.
c. The consumer consumes 20 more units of Y because it has become relatively cheaper; therefore this is the substitution effect.
d. The consumer consumes 10 more units of Y because it has become relatively more expensive; therefore this is the income effect.
e. b and c

Answer: _____

9. In the study of the the "buying" behavior of two white rats, as the "relative price" of one beverage was raised:

a. one white rat began to consume more of the higher priced beverage and the other began to consume less
b. both white rats began to consume less of the higher priced beverage
c. both white rats began to consume more of the higher priced beverage
d. both white rats continued consuming the same amount of the beverage as before its price was raised

Answer: _____

10. Which of the following statements is false?

a. If Tracy receives 30 utils from consuming one hamburger and 55 utils from consuming two hamburgers, the marginal utility of the second hamburger is 25 utils.
b. The law of diminishing marginal utility says that the more of a particular good one consumes, the less total utility one receives from the consumption of that good.
c. The consumption of gold probably takes place at relatively high marginal utility since there is little gold in the world.
d. b and c
e. none of the above

Answer: _____

True-False

11. One makes an interpersonal utility comparison if   T F
he or she compares the utility one person receives
from a good with the utility another person receives
from the same good.

12. That portion of the change in quantity demanded   T F
of a good that is attributable to a change in its
relative price is called the substitution effect.

13. A consumer is in disequilibrium if she   T F
receives different marginal utility per dollar for
different goods she purchases.

14. The three fathers of marginal utility theory   T F
are Jevons, Menger, and Walras.

15. The law of diminishing marginal utility should be   T F
used to make interpersonal utility comparisons.

Fill in the blank

16. The _____ states that that which sometimes has great value in use has little value in
exchange and that which has little value in use sometimes has great value in exchange.

17. When the consumer has spent all his income and the marginal utilities per dollar spent on each good
purchased are equal, the consumer is said to be in _____ .

18. That portion of the change in the quantity demanded of a good that is attributable to a change in real
income (brought about by a change in absolute price) is called the _____ .

19. Prices reflect _____ .

20. Income adjusted for price changes is called _____ .

Part 5. Answers to Self Test

1. c 2. b 3. d 4. b 5. e 6. b 7. c 8. e 9. b 10. b
11. T 12. T 13. T 14. T 15. F
16. diamond-water paradox 17. (consumer) equilibrium
18. income effect 19. marginal utility 20. real income

Part 6. Answers

Part 2 Review of Concepts
1. f   2. h   3. g   4. b   5. i   6. e   7. c   8. d   9. a   10. j

Part 3 Key Concepts
1. use, exchange
2. marginal, total
3. utility (satisfaction)
4. diminishing marginal
5. lower, less
6. urgent, less
7. d
8. c
9. interpersonal , is not
10. marginal
11. zero
12. 500/0.6 = 833.3
13. 11,200/14 = 800, doughnuts
14. doughnuts, CDs
15. equal to
16. is
17. a decrease, real
18. an increase, more, less, income
19. marginal utilities, marginal utility, falls below
20. rats, does
21. do, do not
22. marginal utility, final degree, did not

Part 4 Problems and Exercises

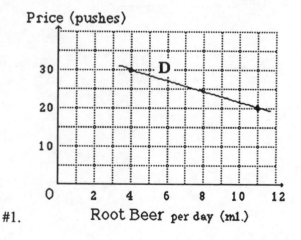

#1.

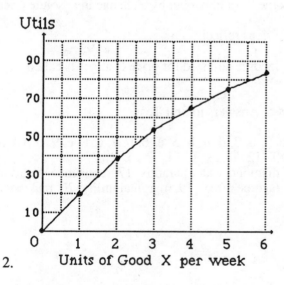

2.

3. a. 20, 18, 16, 12, 10, 8
    b. See graph below
    c. does

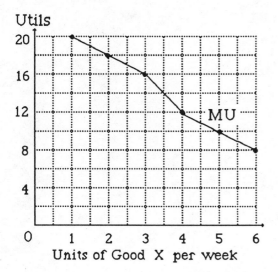

4. a. 100, 90, 80, 70, 60, 50
    b. 50, 45, 40, 35, 30, 25
    c. 200, 180, 160, 140, 120, 100

5. a. See graph below.
    b. declines, rise

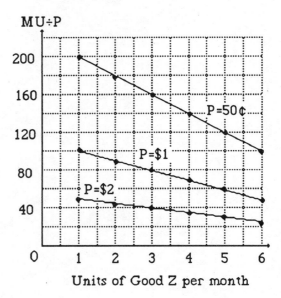

Chapter 21
Elasticity

Part 1. Introduction and Purpose
Consider the following points as you read chapter 21 in the text.

In the jargon of economists, **elasticity** is another term for responsiveness. The price elasticity of demand describes the responsiveness of quantity demanded to price changes, the income elasticity of demand describes the responsiveness of consumer demand to changes in income, an so on.

Elasticity means responsiveness, but it means more than that. Elasticity is a **ratio** of two things. One is the size of original stimulus or event that causes someone to react, and the other is the size of their reaction. **Stimulus** and **response**. If the response is larger than the stimulus, that is an "elastic" (large) response. If the response is smaller than the original stimulus, that is an "inelastic" (small) response. Between these two extremes is the "unit elastic" case, where the stimulus and response are proportional to one another. In the present chapter we're mainly interested in the stimulus associated with a price change, where the response is a changing quantity demanded. This is a movement from one point to another along the demand curve.

Any price change will either attract or repel customers, and can therefore cause total company revenues to rise or fall, depending on how much customers react to the price change. The elasticity coefficient addresses exactly that issue.

To see how, begin by defining a seller's **total revenue** (TR) as product **price** per unit (P) times the number of **units** sold (Q): TR = PxQ. Now, the law of demand says that a price increase causes consumers to purchase fewer units, so the two forces that influence total revenue push in opposite directions. A higher price means TR should rise, but fewer units sold means that TR should fall. Ultimately it will depend on which changes by more — price (the stimulus) or quantity demanded (the response):

$$
\begin{array}{ccccc}
\uparrow & & \uparrow & \downarrow & \text{(demand is inelastic)} \\
\text{TR} & = & \text{P} & \text{x} \quad \text{Q} & \\
\downarrow & & \uparrow & \downarrow & \text{(demand is elastic)}
\end{array}
$$

If demand is *elastic* then the response (↓Q) is larger than the stimulus (↑P), so TR decreases. *Total revenue will change in the same direction as whichever variable (P or Q) changes by more,* so when demand is *elastic* TR will rise and fall with quantity sold. When demand is *inelastic,* price changes are larger than changes in quantity demanded, so TR moves in the same direction as price.

The only thing wrong with all of this is that companies do not usually know in advance the elasticity coefficient for the products they sell. Some technique is needed for estimating the elasticity of demand *before* price is changed, not afterward.

While it will never be possible to know with precision how consumers will respond to a price change, estimates may be made by relying on past experience, buy locating elasticity estimates made by other researchers in similar situations (look in the economics and marketing sections of the library), and by having a general understanding of the determinants of elasticity. The **determinants of elasticity** are real world conditions that influence the size of the elasticity coefficient on any given occasion. These include: a) the **number of substitute goods** available; b) the **percentage of the consumer's budget spent on the good**; and c) the **time** that has passed since price was raised or lowered. Does the seller have a unique product for which there are few or no substitutes? Does the seller's product absorb a large or small proportion of the customer's total budget? Over what time period is the seller hoping to predict the response? The customer's reaction to a price change is determined by answers to these questions.

In addition to price elasticity of demand, a few other elasticity measures are examined in the chapter. The **income elasticity** of demand indicates the percentage change in consumption that results when consumer incomes change by one percent. For normal goods — goods for which demand increases when income increases — the income elasticity coefficient is positive. Income elasticity is negative for inferior goods; positive changes in income cause consumption to decline.

The **cross price elasticity** of demand measures the percentage change in the consumption of one good divided by the percentage change in the price of a different good. This is a measure of the interrelationship between the two goods. In the case of **substitute goods** X and Y, if the price of Y increases then some of the people who formerly bought good Y will purchase X instead. This is represented as a rightward shift in the demand curve for good X. The change in the price of Y is positive and the change in the consumption of X is positive, so the cross price elasticity coefficient is positive, too. If goods X and Z are **complementary goods**, an increase in the price of Z will cause people to buy less Z (due to the law of demand) and also less X, since it is consumed in conjunction with Z. A positive change in Z's price causes a negative change in consumption of X, so the cross price elasticity is negative for complementary goods.

The final elasticity mentioned in the chapter is the price elasticity of supply, defined as the percent change in quantity supplied as market price changes by one percent. The price elasticity of supply ranges from zero (no quantity response to a higher price) to infinity (a huge quantity response to a very small change in price). In general, the elasticity of supply increases as time passes following a price change — just as for the elasticity of demand.

The chapter closes by looking at a few issues that make use of elasticity concepts. The question of **who ultimately pays a sales tax** is a particularly interesting one that economists like to analyze. As you will learn in the text, companies directly pay sales taxes to the government but consumers ultimately must pay some or all of the tax in the form of higher prices. The burden of a sales tax can fall on sellers or buyers. In common sense terms, *the sales tax will fall most heavily on those whose demands or supplies are inelastic; the burden will fall least on those whose demands or supplies are elastic.*

Where else but in an economics book would you have learned this secret?

Part 2. Review of Concepts from Earlier Chapters
Prior to reading chapter 21, match statements at left with the appropriate concept at right.

__1. A regular inverse relationship between price and quantity demanded.

__2. A good that is in greater demand as consumer incomes rise.

__3. A good for which demand falls as consumer incomes rise.

__4. The positive relationship between price and quantity offered for sale.

__5. Change in consumption caused by anything other than price change.

__6. Two goods that satisfy the same desires or needs.

__7. Goods that are used jointly in consumption.

__8. The market clearing price.

__9. Cause a movement along a single demand curve.

a. complements
b. equilibrium
c. law of demand
d. shift in demand
e. law of supply
f. price change
g. normal good
h. substitutes
i. inferior good

Part 3. Key Concepts in this Chapter
After reading chapter 21 in the text, answer the following questions.

1. The price elasticity of demand is a measure of the responsiveness of _demand / quantity demanded_ to changes in price.

2. The coefficient of price elasticity equals the percentage change in _demand / quantity demanded_ divided by the percentage change in _____.

3. If the elasticity coefficient is 3.5, a 1% price increase causes quantity demanded to _increase / decline_ by _35 / 1 / 3.5 / 10_ % .

4. If a 10% increase in price causes quantity demanded to decline by 5%, the price elasticity coefficient equals _5 / 10 / 2 / 0.5_ .

5. Suppose the price of a good rises from $20 to $22. Using the formula provided in the text, compute the percentage change in price: _____%.

6. If the percentage change in quantity demanded is greater than the percentage change in price which caused it, then demand is _elastic/ inelastic_. If the percentage change in quantity demanded is smaller than the percentage change in price, then demand is _elastic/ inelastic_.

7. If demand is elastic, then a 5% price reduction will cause quantity demanded to _rise / fall_ by _more than / less than / exactly_ 5%.

8. Suppose a 7% price increase does not affect quantity demanded at all. Then the elasticity coefficient equals _____. Demand is perfectly _elastic/ inelastic_.

9. If a 1% change in price causes quantity demanded to change in the opposite direction by 1%, then the elasticity coefficient equals ____. In this case demand is _____ elastic.

10. When demand is inelastic, a 3% increase in price will cause quantity demanded to decline by _more than / less than_ 3%.

11. If the price of a good is reduced and demand is elastic, quantity demanded will _rise / fall_ and the seller's total revenues will _rise / fall_ .

12. If the price of a good is increased and demand is inelastic, quantity demanded will _rise / fall_ by a _larger / smaller_ percent than the price change. The seller's total revenues will _rise / fall_.

13. The three most important determinants of the price elasticity of demand are the number of _____ goods, the percentage of the consumer's _____ spent on the good, and the _____ elapsed since a price change.

14. Ceteris paribus, the more substitutes a good has the _larger / smaller_ its elasticity of demand coefficient. The fewer substitutes a good has the _larger / smaller_ its elastiticy of demand

15. There are _more / fewer_ substitutes for Chevrolets than for cars in general. There are _more / fewer_ substitutes for Sony TV sets than for TV sets in general.

16. If consumers consider a particular good to be a necessity, they feel there are _few / many_ substitutes for that good.

17. Other things equal, the elasticity of demand for a good will be greater for a good that absorbs _2% / 5% / 8%_ of the consumer's income than one that absorbs 5%.

18. The elasticity of demand will generally be _larger / smaller_ immediately following a price change than it is after a few days or weeks. The long run elasticity of demand for gasoline is about _____ times the short run elasticity.

19. If the price of good H increases and the consumption of good G decreases, then H and G are _substitute / complementary / unrelated_ goods. If the price of good M decreases and the consumption of good R decreases, then M and R are _substitute / complementary / unrelated_ goods.

20. In the previous question, the cross price elasticity coefficient is _positive / negative / zero_ between G and H; the cross price elasticity coefficient is _positive / negative / zero_ between M and R.

21. The income elasticity of demand for Blah Beer equals -1.2. This means that a 1% rise in consumer real income will cause consumers to consume _____% _more / less_ Blah than before. Blah Beer is a _normal / inferior_ good.

22. The coefficient of elasticity of supply will typically be a _positive / negative_ number. The elasticity of supply equals zero for a _horizontal / vertical / upward sloping_ supply curve.

23. Ceteris paribus, consumers will pay a larger share of a sales tax the _more / less_ elastic their demand. Ceteris paribus, suppliers will pay a larger share of a sales tax the _more / less_ elastic their supply.

Part 4. Problems and Exercises
After reading chapter 21 in the text you should be able to work the following problems.

1. Refer to the demand curve at right.

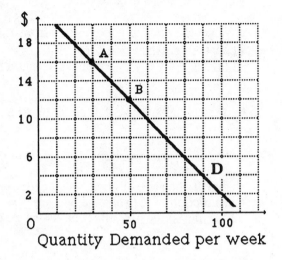

Quantity Demanded per week

a. If the seller charges $20 per unit for the good, how many units a week will be sold? _____ Use information from the demand curve to fill in the following table:

Price ($)	20	18	16	14	12	10	8	6
Units:	__	__	__	__	__	__	__	__

b. To compute the seller's total revenue (TR) it is necessary to multiply the good's _____ by the _____ demanded.

c. Use information in the table above (part a) to compute the seller's total revenues when it sells various quantities:

Units	10	20	30	40	50	60	70	80
TR ($):	__	__	__	__	__	__	__	__

2. Refer to the graph above (question 1). Compute the price elasticity of demand coefficient between points A and B: _____. Over this range of the demand curve, a 1% price change causes quantity demanded to change by ____% in the opposite direction.

3. When Patti Mendez earned $20,000 a year she bought 3 new sweaters annually. Now that she earns $35,000, she buys 8 sweaters a year. Over this income range, Patti's income elasticity of demand equals _____. That is, for each 1% rise in Patti's income her sweater purchases rise by _____%. For Patti, sweaters are _a normal / an inferior_ good.

4. Refer to the diagram at right.

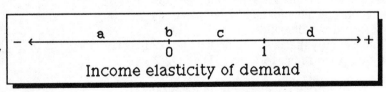

Income elasticity of demand

a. Goods with an income elasticity coefficient falling in range **a** are known as _____ goods.

b. Goods with an elasticity coefficient at **b** are _____ to total income.

c. Goods with an elasticity coefficient in the range **c** are _____ goods, where the effect is an _elastic / inelastic_ one.

d. Goods with an elasticity coefficient in the range **d** are _____ goods, where the effect is an _elastic / inelastic_ one.

5. Refer to the diagram at right. In the case under consideration there are two goods, X and Y. The price of X is $9.

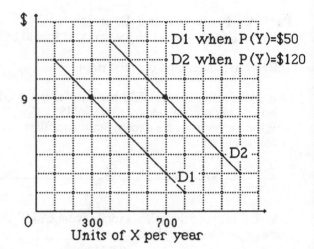

a. When the price of good Y rises from $50 to $120, the demand curve for X shifts to the _right / left_ by _____ units at any given price.

b. Y is a _substitute / complement_ to good X.

c. The cross price elasticity coefficient in this case equals _____. That is, each 1% change in the price of good Y will cause the consumption of X to change by _____% in the _same / opposite_ direction as the ΔP(Y).

6. Refer to the table below. On the left are listed various conditions that may affect the price elasticity of demand for good X. Other things being equal, does the condition imply a higher or lower price elasticity coefficient than otherwise? Place a (√) in the appropriate space at right to indicate your answer.

Condition or circumstance	Elasticity Coefficient Higher	Lower
a. Good X has a large number of substitutes (versus few).	—	—
b. Good X absorbs a small part of the consumer's income.	—	—
c. Good X has no substitutes.	—	—
d. A short period of time has passed since the price of X was changed.	—	—
e. Good X absorbs a large share of the consumer's income.	—	—
f. A long time has passed since the price of X was changed.	—	—
g. Consumers consider good X a necessity and will buy it at any price.	—	—

7. Refer to the diagram at right.

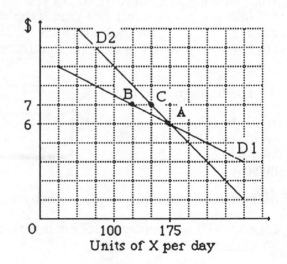

a. If the price rises from $6 to $7 the percentage price change is the same in both cases but the percentage change in quantity demanded is greater along demand curve _D1 / D2_. Consequently the elasticity of demand is greater in this price range for curve _D1 / D2_.

b. The coefficient of elasticity along curve D1 between $6 and $7 equals _____.

c. The coefficient of elasticity along curve D2 between $6 and $7 equals _____.

8. a. How many students currently attend your college? _____ What is the current annual tuition? $_____

b. As a ballpark guess, how many students do you think would decide <u>not</u> to attend your college if the tuition rose by $100? _____ Total enrollments would probably fall to about _____ (the current enrollment minus those who would leave).

c. Use prices and quantities from (a) and (b) to plot the demand curve for an education at your college in the grid provided at right.

d. Compute the price elasticity coefficient for your college over the tuition range considered here: _____. Each 1% change in tuition will cause enrollments to change by _____% in the opposite direction.

e. If tuition does rise, your elasticity estimate in (d) suggests that total tuition revenue should <u>rise / fall</u> .

(write in appropriate quantities & $ amounts)

$

0

Total Student Enrollment per year

Part 5. Self Test
Multiple choice questions

1. In general, elasticity deals with:

a. the responsiveness in one variable to a change in another variable
b. price and quantity demanded
c. income and quantity demanded
d. supply and demand
e. b and c

Answer: _____

2. Price elasticity of demand is:

a. a measure of the responsiveness of quantity demanded to changes in interest rates
b. a measure of the responsiveness of quantity demanded to changes in supply
c. a measure of the responsiveness of quantity demanded to changes in price
d. a measure of the responsiveness of quantity demanded to changes in demand

Answer: _____

3. If quantity demanded rises by 27 percent as price falls by 30 percent, price elasticity of demand equals:

a. 2.4
b. 0.9
c. 1.1
d. 1.7
e. none of the above

Answer: _____

4. Price rises from $12 to $14 and the quantity demanded falls from 80 units to 60 units. What is the price elasticity of demand between the two prices.

a. approximately 1.86
b. approximately .80
c. approximately .53
d. 1.00
e. none of the above

Answer: _____

5. If the percentage change in quantity demand is greater than the percentage change in price, demand is:

a. inelastic
b. unit elastic
c. elastic
d. perfectly elastic
e. perfectly inelastic

Answer: _____

6. If quantity demanded is completely unresponsive to changes in price, demand is:

a. inelastic
b. unit elastic
c. elastic
d. perfectly inelastic
e. perfectly elastic

Answer: _____

7. If the price of good X falls and the demand for good X is elastic, then:

a. the percentage rise in quantity demanded is greater than the percentage fall in price and total revenue rises
b. the percentage rise in quantity demanded is less than the percentage fall in price and total revenue falls
c. the percentage rise in quantity demanded is greater than the percentage fall in price and total revenue falls
d. the percentage fall in quantity demanded is greater than the percentage fall in price and total revenue falls
e. the percentage rise in quantity demanded is equal to the the percentage fall in price and total revenue remains constant

Answer: _____

8. The more substitutes a good has, ceteris paribus:

a. the higher its price elasticity of demand
b. the lower its price elasticity of demand
c. the less elastic the demand for the good
d. the more inelastic the demand for the good

Answer: _____

9. Ceteris paribus, the price elasticity of demand is lowest for which of the following goods?

a. McDonald's hamburgers
b. hamburgers
c. Wendy hamburgers
d. Burger King hamburgers
e. it is between a, c, and d

Answer: _____

10._____ measures the responsiveness of changes in the quantity demanded of one good to changes in the price of another good.

a. Price elasticity of demand
b. Income elasticity of demand
c. Price elasticity of supply
d. Cross elasticity of demand

Answer: _____

11. _____ measures the responsiveness of changes in the quantity demanded of a good to changes in income.

a. Price elasticity of demand
b. Price elasticity of supply
c. Income elasticity of demand
d. Cross elasticity of demand

Answer: _____

12. Income elasticity of demand for an inferior good is:

a. less than zero
b. greater than zero
c. equal to zero
d. none of the above

Answer: _____

13. Suppose someone says that because of the per-unit tax being placed on the producers of good Y, the producers of good Y will end up paying the full tax. This person assumes that the demand curve for good Y is:

a. elastic
b. perfectly inelastic
c. inelastic
d. perfectly elastic
e. unit elastic

Answer: _____

14. If price and total revenue move in the opposite direction, then:

a. demand is elastic
b. demand is inelastic
c. demand is unit elastic
d. supply is elastic
e. supply is inelastic

Answer: _____

15. If price and total revenue move in the same direction, then:

a. demand is elastic
b. demand is inelastic
c. demand is unit elastic
d. supply is elastic
e. supply is inelastic

Answer: _____

True-False

16. The greater the percentage of one's budget   T F
spent on a good, the higher the price elasticity
of demand.

17. The less time that passes (since a change   T F
in price), the lower the price elasticity of
demand.

18. A normal good can be income inelastic but   T F
not income elastic.

19. Supply is elastic if price changes by a   T F
greater percentage than quantity supplied.

20. Total revenue always rises when price rises.   T F

Fill in the blank

21. If the percentage change in quantity demanded is greater than the percentage change in price, the
_____ is greater than 1, and demand is _____ .

22. If price rises and total revenue rises, too, demand is _____ .

23. As we move up a straight-line downard-sloping demand curve from lower to higher prices, price
elasticity of demand _____ .

24. The short-run price elasticity of demand for gasoline is likely to be _____ than the
long-run price elasticity of demand for gasoline.

25. If price falls and total revenue rises, then demand is _____ .

Part 5. Answers to Self Test

1. a 2. c 3. b 4. a 5. c 6. d 7. a 8. a 9. b 10. d
11. c 12. a 13. d 14. a 15. b
16. T 17. T 18. F 19. F 20. F
21. elasticity coefficient, elastic 22. inelastic
23. increases 24. lower 25. elastic

Part 6. Answers

Part 2 Review of Concepts
1. c 2. g 3. i 4. e 5. d 6. h 7. a 8. b 9. f

Part 3 Key Concepts
1. elasticity, quantity, price   2. quantity demanded, price   3. decline, 3.5%   4. 0.5 (one-half)
 5. %ΔP = ΔP ÷ avg. P = 2÷21 = 0.0952 = 9.52%   6. elastic, inelastic   7. rise, more than
8. 0 (zero), inelastic   9. 1, unit   10. less than   11. rise, rise   12. fall, smaller, rise
13. substitute, income (or budget), time   14. larger, smaller   15. more, more   16. few   17. 8%
18. smaller, 3.5   19. complementary, substitute   20. negative, positive   21. 1.2%, less, inferior
22. positive, vertical   23. less, less

Part 4 Problems and Exercises
1. a. 10, 20, 30, 40, 50, 60, 70, 80   b. price, quantity   c. $200, 360, 480, 560, 600, 600, 560, 480
2. 1.75, 1.75%
3. 1.67, 1.67%, a normal
4. a. inferior   b. unrelated   c. normal, inelastic   d. normal, elastic
5. a. right, 400   b. substitute   c. 0.9714, 0.97%, same
6. Higher (a,e,f)   Lower (b,c,d,g)
7. a. D1, D1   b. 2.167   c. 1
8. Answers depend on your particular situation.

Chapter 22
The Firm

Part 1. Introduction and Purpose
Consider the following points as you read chapter 22 in the text.

A **firm** is an organization that **employs** resources for the purpose of **producing** and **selling** an output (goods and services) to buyers. Since firms have been around longer than any of us can remember, we take them for granted and seldom ask why they exist or what role they play in the economy.

If you are an employee of a firm you may think of the organization in terms of commands handed down from upper management — Do this, don't do that. The text observes that people are not forced to work for companies — they agree to be supervised more closely for the higher pay associated with **team production**. Supervision is necessary to ensure that all members of the production "team" contribute the agreed-on share of work. Another way of putting this is to say that managers prevent employees from **shirking**. If the team's output can be increased sufficiently when supervisors reduce shirking, every team member will **earn more** than he or she could in a less-structured organization or by remaining self-employed. In this theory of the firm's origin, firms are formed because team production is **more efficient** than individual production. In the event teams are no more productive than an equal number of individuals working individually, the team (firm) will not exist, shirking will not be a problem, and managerial supervision is unnecessary.

If circumstances justify starting a firm, firm owners may select one of three organization forms. An individual **proprietorship** is owned by an individual who makes all business decisions, receives all profits, and runs all risks in the event of loss. If the company's losses exceed the company's capacity to pay, the owner must sacrifice his or her personal assets to satisfy the firm's obligations. The proprietorship is the simplest form of business organization and affords the greatest managerial flexibility. Large companies are seldom proprietorships however, since funds from many thousands of investors are needed to finance the construction of large factories and other facilities used by major producers.

A **partnership** is a kind of proprietorship with two or more owners. The chief disadvantage of a partnership is that **all partners are personally liable** for any losses incurred by their firm. How would you like to personally stand behind any loss that General Motors might run in a particular year? As long as owners' liability is unlimited, most potential investors are unwilling to take an ownership position — so funds needed for expansion are not forthcoming.

Corporations avoid this difficulty. The corporate form of ownership limits the personal liability of firm owners to the amount they have directly invested in the firm. **Limited liability** makes ownership more attractive, and permits companies to sell ownership shares to thousands and sometimes millions of investors. Access to financial capital is necessary to operate large companies in the U.S. today. The disadvantage of the corporate form of ownership is its treatment under the tax laws. A dollar's worth of **profit is taxed twice**: once when it is earned by the corporation (through the corporate profits tax), and a second time when the corporation distributes profits to shareholders. Shareholders must declare the dividend as personal income, so the profits are taxed again by the income tax.

As a practical matter, most companies are individual proprietorships (about 70% of all companies), while most production and sales originate in corporations (about 90% of total output).

Because corporations tend to have large numbers of owners who are not particularly knowledgeable about the company's operations, corporations are often run by professional managers rather than the owners themselves. This may result in what has been termed the **separation of ownership from control** — a situation where managers use the company's assets to pursue their own goals rather than those of owners (profits).

Although these possibilities are always present — at any point in time it is possible to identify any number of mis-managed companies — over time the market tends to reject such behavior on the part of top managers. Poor management means falling stock prices, and that is likely to cause shareholders to replace the current managers. A second thing that might happen is for outside investors to purchase the company when its share price is depressed, then replace the managers and change their policies. If they are correct, outside investors can later sell their stock for a higher price than they paid once profits have recovered. Third, managers can be given shares of stock or have their bonuses tied to stock performance, so their own interest will coincide with that of shareholders. Fourth, a company that is not being operated efficiently will normally be unable to compete in the marketplace with those at are, and will eventually go out of business if their policies are not altered. When all is said and done, there are strong pressures within the marketplace to limit inefficiencies resulting from the separation of ownership and control.

The control of other types of firms is a final issue examined in the chapter. **Nonprofit firms** lack a **residual claimant** who can claim the difference between firm revenues and costs ("profit"). This situation describes both public nonprofit firms (government firms) and private nonprofit firms (private charitable organizations). Lacking residual claimant status, no owner or manager may be willing to devote the time and effort needed to monitor employee behavior, change policy, or do the other things needed to ensure efficient production. The result may be similar to the inefficiencies that take place in large corporations when ownership is separated from control. Many of the market-oriented solutions that limit inefficiency within the private corporation are not available to the owners and customers of nonprofit firms however, so inefficiencies may actually be worse in many instances than would be tolerated in for-profit corporations.

Part 2. Review of Concepts from Earlier Chapters
Prior to reading chapter 22, match statements at left with the appropriate concept at right.

___1. The act of trading one thing for another.
___2. The generic name for the resources used to produce goods.
___3. Exchanges between buyers and sellers occur here.
___4. Those who produce and sell goods occupy this side of the market.
___5. These signal producers what goods are in greatest demand.
___6. The act of transforming factors into goods and services.

a. market
b. supply
c. factor of production
d. prices
e. production
f. exchange

Part 3. Key Concepts in this Chapter
After reading chapter 22 in the text, answer the following questions.

1. A firm is an organization that employs _____ of production, produces an _____, and _____ it to consumers.

2. The _____ of a firm is responsible for making its policies.

3. One explanation for the firm's existence begins by recognizing that <u>individual / team / mechanical</u> production is more efficient than production by individual workers. The main problem with production under these circumstances is that some workers may <u>dislike / shirk / exceed</u> their work responsibilities.

4. If the person who monitors the firm's workers receives the additional production (profit) that results from his monitoring activities, the monitor is a _____ claimant.

5. Team production combined with monitoring causes workers to earn <u>more / less</u> than they would earn working independently.

6. <u>Proprietorships / Partnerships / Corporations</u> are said to experience difficulties arising out of the separation of ownership from control. The problem is that <u>workers / managers / shareholders</u> may pursue goals that conflict with that of the firm's owners.

7. Satisficing behavior refers to meeting a satisfactory <u>profit / revenue / output</u> target, and then pursuing other goals.

8. Individual proprietorships account for about <u>50 / 70 / 90</u> % of all businesses in the U.S., and about <u>1 / 6 / 30</u> % of the total sales revenues of all businesses.

9. The owners of <u>proprietorships / partnerships / corporations</u> have their liabilities limited to the amount they invested in the company. Owners of _____ and _____ potentially face unlimited liabilities arising out of their investment. A _____ partner faces limited liability.

10. The earnings of a <u>proprietorship / partnership / corporation</u> are subject to double taxation. A <u>proprietorship / partnership / corporation</u> has greater access to financial capital than the other two organization forms.

11. A _____ is similar to a proprietorship, but has two or more owners.

12. If a company buys its own shares from a large investor for more than the market price in order to prevent the investor from controlling the company, the overpayment is called <u>a bribe / blackmail / greenmail</u>. One reason for paying this amount is to protect the jobs of <u>workers / managers</u>.

13. It is said that some investors buy the stock of companies and issue takeover _____ in order to pressure managers into paying _____ -mail.

14. In every balance sheet, total assets equal total _____ plus net _____.

15. To compute net worth or equity, subtract total _____ from total _____.

16. Two ways corporations can attract financial capital are by issuing _stock / bonds / IOUs_, which represents an ownership position in the company, or by selling _stock / bonds / IOUs_, which are promises to repay the debt with regular interest payments on specific dates.

17. If a company adopts a policy that will reduce its efficiency and profitability in future years, the price of the company's stock is likely to _immediately / eventually / never_ change to reflect the new policy. In this instance, the share price will adjust _upward / downward / neither_.

18. According to the theory that prices immediately reflect all of the public information about a company's situation, the only way to regularly make money in the stock market is to possess _inside / outside / expert_ information. This information _is / is not_ available to the public and _can / cannot_ legally be used by stock market investors.

19. A nonprofit firm does not have a _____ claimant. Any revenues over costs remain with the firm. This may cause the manager of a nonprofit to pay _higher / lower_ wages than the market clearing wage for a given quantity and quality of work.

20. Those who provide funds to public nonprofit firms are _taxpayers / donors_. Those who provide funds to private nonprofit firms are _taxpayers / donors_.

Part 4. Problems and Exercises
After reading chapter 22 in the text you should be able to work the following problems.

1. You may recall from the text that one reason firms exist is to overcome a difficulty of team production — shirking. The example given in the text is that of a lightbulb manufacturing operation that employs 5 workers. Row a in the table shows that independently each worker is capable of producing 15 lightbulbs per day. As a team (row b), average output per worker is potentially as high as 28 bulbs per day. Shirking (row c) causes output to fall to 23 bulbs per worker. Monitoring and related activities increase output toward the maximum (row d). Use this information to complete the table.

Situation	Output per Worker	Total Output All 5 Workers	Price per Bulb	$ Value of Output All 5 Workers
a. Work in isolation	10	50	$2	$100
b. Team production (potential)	28	___	$2	$___
c. Team with shirking, no monitor	23	___	$2	$___
d. Team with monitor	28	___	$2	$___

e. According to your calculations, the monitor causes the total value of output produced by the five workers to rise from $_____ to $_____, for an increase of $_____. Can the team afford to pay a monitor $30 and still pay the workers more than they earned in the shirking case? _yes / no_

f. According to your calculations, team production causes the average worker's total output to rise by _____ units, even when shirking occurs. The value of this extra output is $_____ per worker per day.

2. Each year several thousand new U.S. companies begin doing business. The figures below show new business incorporations during the first part of the 1980s. Graph these figures in the grid at right, and connect the points with a line.

Year	New Business Incorporations
1980	533,520
1981	581,242
1982	566,942
1983	600,400
1984	634,991
1985	662,047
1986	702,601

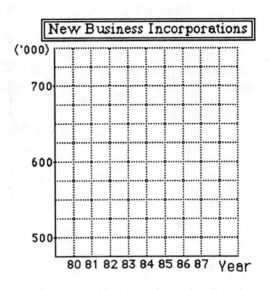

3. Each year several thousand U.S. companies stop doing business due to failures . The figures below show the business failure rate during the first part of the 1980s. Graph these figures in the grid at right, and connect the points with a line.

Year	Business Failure Rate*
1980	42
1981	61
1982	89
1983	110
1984	107
1985	115
1986	120
1987	102

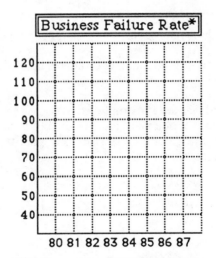

*Failures per 10,000 businesses

4. The table below includes figures for the Dow Jones Industrial Average (DJIA) on Dec. 31 of each year indicated. Plot these observations in the grid at right and connect the points with a line.

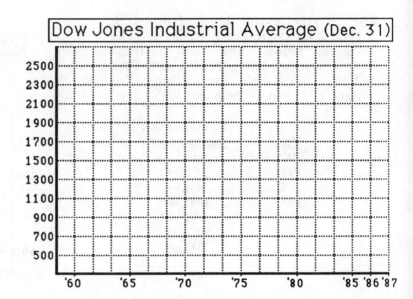

Year	DJIA
1960	618.04
1965	910.88
1970	753.19
1975	802.49
1980	891.41
1985	1328.23
1986	1792.76
1987	2275.99

Part 5. Self Test
Multiple choice questions

1. "The market guides and coordinates individuals' actions." Which of the following is an example of this happening?

a. An employer tells an employee to come to work on Saturday instead of Friday.
b. The manager of a plant issues a directive that there will be no more smoking inside or outside the plant.
c. The price of computers rises, the profits from producing computers rise, and more firms end up producing computers.
d. a and c
e. a, b, and c

Answer: _____

2. Economists Alchian and Demsetz suggest that firms are formed when:

a. people demand goods
b. the sum of what individuals can produce alone is greater than what they can produce as a team
c. capital gains taxes are lowered
d. the sum of what individuals can produce as a team is greater than what they can produce alone
e. c and d

Answer: _____

3. In which setting is there likely to be the least amount of shirking?

a. Fifty individuals decide to work together to produce shoes; they decide to split the proceeds equally.
b. Harrison works for himself producing watches.
c. Nineteen individuals decide to work together to produce book covers; they decide to split the proceeds equally.
d. a and c, since the costs of shirking are equally low in these two settings.

Answer: _____

4. Some persons argue that the monitor-employee relationship is one of the monitor exploiting the employee. The "theory of the firm" proposed in the text, however, comes closer to being one where the monitor-employee relationship is one of:

a. shared residual claimant status
b. mutual trust
c. mutual benefit
d. shared decision-making

Answer: _____

5. Economist _____ has argued that firms seek to maximize sales.

a. Richard Cyert
b. William Baumol
c. James March
d. Herbert Simon

Answer: _____

6. As a percentage of U.S. firms, which type of business firm is most common?

a. proprietorships
b. partnerships
c. corporations
d. nonprofit organizations

Answer: _____

7. Which of the following is not an advantage of the partnership form of organization?

a. ease of organization
b. benefits of specialization
c. unlimited life
d. absence of double taxation of profits

Answer: _____

8. Limited liability is one of the advantages of a:

a. proprietorship
b. partnership
c. corporation
d. b and c
e. none of the above

Answer: _____

9. What does "separation of ownership from control" refer to?

a. It refers to the unlimited liability provision of proprietorships.
b. It refers to some persons in a firm having more decision-making authority than others; for example, the president has more decision-making authority than the vice president of finance.
c. It refers to the owners of the corporation being different persons than the managers who control it on a day to day basis.
d. It refers to the fact that many firms are physically so large that they are impossible to control on a day to day basis.

Answer: _____

10. Which of the following statements is true?

a. A person who buys a bond always pays more than the face value for the bond.
b. If a corporation issues a bond and you purchase it, you become one of the owners of the corporation.
c. A stockholder of firm X does not have an ownership right in firm X.
d. If the coupon rate on a bond is 11 percent this means the owner of the bond receives periodic payments equal to the coupon rate times the price he paid for the bond (whether or not the price he paid for the bond equals the face value of the bond).
e. none of the above

Answer: _____

11. Which of the following is true?

a. There are residual claimants in nonprofit firms.
b. A police force that receives state-appropriated funds is a private nonprofit firm.
c. A charitable organization is considered a profit firm.
d. a and b
e. none of the above

Answer: _____

12. The Dow fell 508 points on:

a. October 12, 1986
b. October 11, 1981
c. October 19, 1987
d. October 30, 1980

Answer: _____

13. Assets minus liabilities equals:

a. net worth
b. net margin
c. net product
d. net profit

Answer: _____

14. A thing of value to which a firm has a legal claim is called:

a. an estate
b. a factor
c. a resource
d. an asset

Answer: _____

15. The major disadvantage of a corporation:

a. is the double taxation of corporate income
b. is its large size
c. are the social pressures placed upon it
d. are the government regulations it must submit to

Answer: _____

True-False

16. The invisible hand of the marketplace refers   T F
to market coordination and not managerial
coordination.

17. The lower the cost of shirking, the more   T F
shirking, ceteris paribus.

18. A residual claimant receives the excess of   T F
revenues over costs as his or her income.

19. Herbert Simon has argued that firms do   T F
not try to maximize profits, but instead try
to achieve some satisfactory target profit level.

20. Inside information is public information.   T F

Fill in the blank

21. _____ is a legal term that signifies that the personal assets of the owner(s) of a firm may be used to pay off the debts of the firm.

22. A _____ is a legal entity that can conduct business in its own name the way an individual does.

23. Nonprofit firms are firms in which there are no _____ .

24. The most widely cited Dow average is the _____ .

25. When the Dow was first calculated in 1884, _____ companies made up the Dow.

Part 5. Answers to Self Test

1. c 2. d 3. b 4. c 5. b 6. a 7. c 8. c 9. c 10. e 11. e 12. c 13. a 14. d 15. a
16. T 17. T 18. T 19. T 20. F
21. Unlimited liability 22. corporation
23. residual claimants 24. Dow Jones Industrial Average
25. 11

Part 6.   Answers

Part 2 Review of Concepts
1. f   2. c   3. a   4. b   5. d   6. e

Part 3 Key Concepts
1. factors, output, sells   2. manager   3. team, shirk   4. residual   5. more
6. Corporations, managers   7. profit   8. 70%, 6%   9. corporations, proprietorships, partnerships, limited   10. corporation, corporation   11. partnership   12. greenmail, managers   13. threats, greenmail   14. liabilities, worth   15. liabilities, assets   16. stock, bonds   17. immediately, downward   18. inside, is not, cannot   19. residual, higher   20. taxpayers, donors

Part 4 Problems and Exercises

1. b.140, $280
   c. 115, $230
   d. 140, $280
   e. $230, $280,
      $50, yes
   f. 13, $26

2. See graph at right

3. See graph at right.

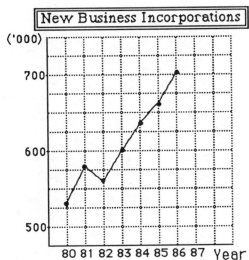

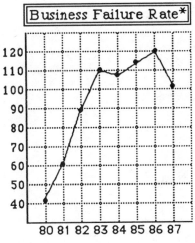

*Failures per 10,000 businesses

4.

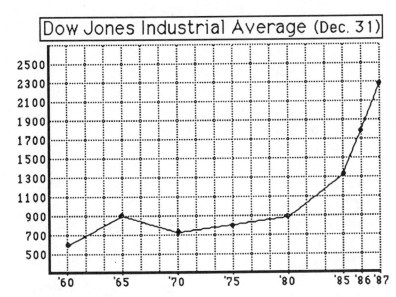

Chapter 23
Production and Costs

Part 1. Introduction and Purpose
Consider the following points as you read chapter 23 in the text.

By the time you have finished this chapter in the text, you will have been exposed to about 15 different cost measures, all of which have something to do with a firm's costs of producing output. In fact, costs are incurred by every decision maker, so the ideas discussed in this chapter can be used in many areas of decision making. Most of the cost examples relate to the costs of operating a business so the analysis of cost can be used in later chapters on the firm. If you have difficulty understanding a particular point, try applying it to some experience of your own. If you aren't sure what the marginal cost of producing X refers to, think about the marginal cost of another ounce of cheese at the supermarket. Individual consumers face the same general types of costs as firms, and because you have had experience as a consumer it may help to recall some of your past experiences from time to time.

Take a good look at the chapter title — **production and costs**. While it is inevitable you will concentrate on the calculations and graphs that correspond to each cost measure, you can avoid many confusions by keeping in mind that costs are related to the firm's production process, and each cost is a measure of what happens when the firm hires factors of production to produce an output.

One of the first ideas discussed in the chapter highlights this point. The **production function** indicates the amount of output produced when a particular combination of inputs is employed. Suppose that when the first worker is hired total production goes up from 0 to 100 units, a second worker increases total output to 250, and a third increases output to 300. This is a typical production function where output rises when more inputs are hired. The **marginal physical product (MPP)** of the first worker is 100 units of output. The second worker adds another 150 units to output, so his marginal product is 150, and the third's marginal product is 50.

The worker's marginal product is related to the **marginal cost (MC)** of producing additional units of output. In the previous paragraph, the first worker contributed 100 units of output. It follows that one unit of output required about 1/100 of the worker's time — so the time cost of production is 1/100 units of labor. Convert this time to dollars and you've got the dollar cost of producing an extra unit of output. For example, if the worker is paid $500 per week, then 1/100 units of labor costs 1/100 of $500, or $5. The marginal cost of producing one more unit of output is $5.

In the foregoing example, the equation we used to calculate marginal cost is: MC = (1/MPP) x Wage. This is equivalent to the expression in the text, MC = Wage / MPP. Because **the law of diminishing marginal product** says that an input's MPP will eventually decline as more units of that input are employed, the MC of producing units of output will eventually rise.

The law of diminishing returns applies to **short run** situations, in which the firm employs more of one input and maintains a constant quantity of all other inputs. It stands to reason that if more and more workers (the variable input) have a fixed amount of capital and other inputs to work with, eventually workers will be hired that don't have enough capital available to permit them to produce as much as other workers could. In this example diminishing marginal returns is the result of having inadequate capital for each worker — which will always happen if one hires additional workers without acquiring more capital and other inputs.

In the **long run** the firm can vary all inputs, so all costs are variable costs. When the firm feels that diminishing returns are substantial with respect to its variable inputs in the current short run period, the decision may be made to employ more capital or other "fixed" inputs once it is possible to do so. The long run has arrived once it is possible to acquire these other inputs — which will vary in each particular situation. By hiring the proper mix of the "variable" and "fixed" inputs, the firm's manager can minimize the total cost of producing any desired quantity of output. Such cost savings translate dollar-for-dollar into profits.

In the long run the firm will employ more of all inputs when expanding its output. This is an expansion in the firm's scale of operations since the firm is growing in every way — more workers, more machines, more office space, and so forth. If the firm experiences **increasing returns to scale** then a 10% increase in the amount of all inputs hired will cause output to rise by more than 10%. With costs rising by 10% and output rising even more rapidly average per-unit costs decline. A firm may also experience constant and decreasing returns to scale. In these cases the LRATC curve is horizontal and upward sloping, respectively.

Finally, the chapter notes that changes in three conditions cause the firm's cost curves to shift. Increases or decreases in output cause a movement *along* the firm's cost curves. Anything else (besides a variation in output) that causes the firm's operating costs to change actually shifts one or more of the curves. Three of these "shift factors" are taxes, input prices, and productivity.

As you read through the text, keep a pencil and some paper handy. Costs are often easier to understand by working an example.

Part 2. Review of Concepts from Earlier Chapters
Prior to reading chapter 23, match statements at left with the appropriate concept at right.

__1. What must be foregone as a result of taking an action.   a. good
__2. Land, labor, capital, and entrepreneurship.   b. firm
__3. Something that gives consumers happiness.   c. factor of production
__4. Organization that employs factors to produce and sell an output.   d. sunk cost
__5. Historical costs or past costs.   e. opportunity cost

Part 3. Key Concepts in this Chapter
After reading chapter 23 in the text, answer the following questions.

1. When costs require dollar outlays, then they are referred to as _explicit / implicit / real_ costs. Implicit costs are costs _do / do not_ require the payment of funds.

2. Accounting profits equal total sales revenue minus _explicit / implicit_ costs. Economic profits equal total sales revenue minus _explicit / real_ and _implicit / total_ costs.

3. Costs were incurred in the past that cannot be changed by current decisions are _____ costs.

4. Factors of production or inputs that a firm is free to hire more or less of during the current time period are _fixed / variable / labor_ inputs. Inputs that cannot be varied in the current period are known as _____ inputs. In the _short / long_ run, all inputs can be varied.

5. The firm's _____ function states the relationship between inputs employed and outputs produced.

6. Some of the firm's costs do not change as it increases or decreases its production level. These are _____ costs, the amount paid to the firm's _____ inputs. The graph for the _VC / TC / FC_ curve is a _horizontal / vertical_ line.

7. To increase production, a firm will hire more of its _fixed / variable_ inputs, so its _____ cost curve will slope upward as the total level of output increases.

8. A firm's total costs equal its total _____ costs plus its total _____ costs. The corresponding equation says that TC = _____ + _____.

9. Total costs divided by total quantity of output is called _marginal/ average total / average variable_ cost. This is abbreviated ___ ___ ___.

10. In the _short / long_ run, some inputs can be varied and some cannot.

11. Total variable costs (VC) equal the quantity of the _____ inputs employed by the firm multiplied by input _____.

12. Total fixed costs (FC) equal the quantity of the _____ inputs employed by the firm multiplied by their _____.

13. Dividing all fixed costs by the quantity of output produced equals _marginal/ average / total_ fixed cost. Dividing all variable costs by the quantity of output produced equals _average / total_ variable costs. These two costs are abbreviated ___ ___ ___ and ___ ___ ___.

14. "Unit cost" is another name for _MC/ AVC / ATC / AFC_.

15. _____ cost is the extra cost associated with producing one more unit of output. Mathematically, this cost equals Δ ___ ___ $\div \Delta$ ___.

16. The law of diminishing marginal returns says that as a firm hires additional units of a single _fixed / variable_ input and continues hiring a constant quantity of _fixed / variable_ inputs, eventually an additional unit of the input will cause _costs/ output / employment_ to expand by less than the previous unit did.

17. If one worker can produce 20 units of output per hour, then 20 is the marginal/ average / total product of an hour's work. At this rate, it takes 1/__ of an hour to produce one unit of output. This part of an hour is _____ minutes.

18. Refer to the previous question. If the worker earns $10 an hour, then it would be necessary to pay the worker 1/___ of that amount to produce one more unit of output, or $_____. The wage rate divided by marginal physical product equals $_____ ÷ _____ units, or $_____ per unit. This is one method of calculating the marginal/ average / total cost of output.

19. Decreases in the marginal physical product of a variable input implies an increase / a decrease in the marginal cost of production. So the law of diminishing marginal returns implies that there should also be a law of increasing / diminishing / constant marginal cost.

20. The average-marginal rule says that if marginal cost is greater than average cost, then average cost will rise / fall as output expands. It also says that if marginal cost is less than average cost, then average cost will rise / fall as output expands.

21. The long run marginal/ average / total cost curve shows the lowest unit cost at which a firm can produce various output levels. This curve touches the lowest possible short run ___ ___ ___ curve at each output level.

22. When the LRATC curve slopes downward, the firm is experiencing economies / diseconomies of scale. This indicates that a 10% increase in output will cause the firm's total costs to rise by more / less than 10%.

23. When the LRATC curve is horizontal, the firm is experiencing increasing / decreasing / constant returns to scale. This indicates that a 10% increase in output will cause the firm's total costs to rise by 1/ 5 / 10 / 20 % .

24. When the LRATC curve slopes upward, the firm is experiencing economies / diseconomies of scale. This indicates that a 10% increase in output will cause the firm's total costs to rise by more / less than 10%.

25. In the long run all of the firm's costs are sunk / fixed / variable .

26. If the minimum efficient scale (MES) of operations is 5% of industry sales, then up to 5 / 10 / 20 / 25 / 50 firms in the industry can take advantage of all possible economies of scale.

Part 4. Problems and Exercises
After reading chapter 23 in the text you should be able to work the following problems.

1. A large part of your success with the material in this chapter depends on understanding the definition and calculation associated with each cost concept. In this exercise, match the descriptions given below (choices a-p) to the appropriate cost concept listed in the box. (For example if <u>statement a</u> describes total cost, write <u>a</u> next total cost.) Assume labor is the firm's only variable input.

a_____Total Cost	_____Average Total Cost	_____Marginal Cost
_____Variable Cost	_____Average Variable Cost	
_____Fixed Cost	_____Average Fixed Cost	

a. The amount paid to all inputs, both fixed and variable.
b. Total cost divided by total output.
c. Additional cost incurred when producing one more unit.
d. Sunk costs.
e. Total amount paid to variable inputs divided by total output.
f. Change in variable costs divided by change in output.
g. Wage rate divided by MPP of labor.
h. Total payment for non-variable inputs.
i. Total cost minus variable costs.
j. Wage x quantity of labor employed.
k. ATC x quantity of output produced.

l. AVC + AFC
m. ATC - AVC
n. VC ÷ Q(output)
o. TC - FC
p. ATC - AFC
q. TC - VC
r. FC ÷ Q(output)
s. ΔTC ÷ ΔQ(output)
t. ΔVC ÷ ΔQ(output)
u. (1/MPP of labor) x Wage
v. TC ÷ Q(output)

2. Imagine a firm with one variable input, labor, producing good X. Workers have access to capital equipment leased for $20 a day. Compute the firm's costs and complete the table below.

	Units of Labor	Units of X	Wage ($)	VC ($)	FC ($)	TC ($)	ATC ($)	AVC ($)	AFC ($)	MC ($)
a.	0	0	$5	$___	$20	$___				
b.	1	10	$5	$___	$20	$___	$___	$___	$___	$___
c.	2	25	$5	$___	$20	$___	$___	$___	$___	$___
d.	3	38	$5	$___	$20	$___	$___	$___	$___	$___
e.	4	49	$5	$___	$20	$___	$___	$___	$___	$___
f.	5	58	$5	$___	$20	$___	$___	$___	$___	$___
g.	6	64	$5	$___	$20	$___	$___	$___	$___	$___
h.	7	67	$5	$___	$20	$___	$___	$___	$___	$___
i.	8	69	$5	$___	$20	$___	$___	$___	$___	$___

3. Use the grid at right to graph
the AFC, AVC, ATC, and
MC values you computed in
the previous problem. Each
cost should be plotted above
the quantity of output to
which it applies (which is
column 2 in the table).

Once you have plotted all of
the cost figures from a
particular column, connect
the points and label the
curve.
Then go on to the next cost
column and do the same.

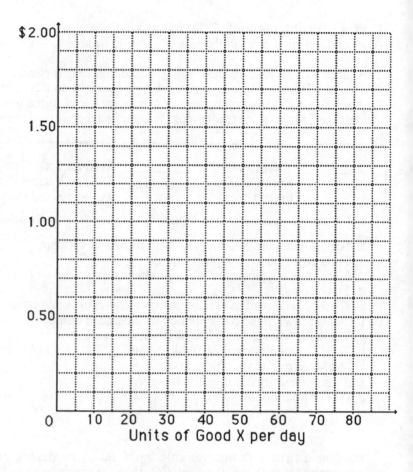

4. Refer to the table in exercise 2 to answer this question. The marginal physical product of labor begins
to decline when the _1st / 2nd / 3rd / 4th_ worker is employed. The marginal cost of output begins to
increase when the _1st / 11th / 26th / 39th_ unit of output is produced. This occurs when the
_1st / 2nd / 3rd / 4th_ worker is employed.

5. Assume the wage rate is $5 per hour. Hiring the fourth worker causes the firm's hourly output to
increase from 56 units to 71 units.

a. The total labor cost associated with producing 71 units of output equals $_____. If labor is the
only variable input, then VC = $_____.

b. The firm's AVC when it produces 56 units is $_____. The firm's AVC when it
produces 71 units is $_____.

c. The marginal cost of producing the 57th unit or other units between 57 and 71 is $_____ per unit.

d. If the firm's fixed costs are $10 an hour regardless of the amount produced, its total costs are
$_____ when it produces 56 units and $_____ when it produces 71 units.

e. When the firm produces the 71st unit its marginal cost is _greater than / less than_ its ATC at 71
units and _greater than / less than_ its AVC at 71 units.

6. In the following cases the firm increases or decreases output as shown in the left-hand column. Assume that each of the cost changes relates to the long run, and indicate whether each example illustrates economies, diseconomies, or constant returns to scale by placing a check mark (√) in the appropriate space at right.

	Change in Output	Change in Total Cost	Economies	Diseconomies	Constant Returns
a.	↑20%	↑15%	_____	_____	_____
b.	↓20%	↓35%	_____	_____	_____
c.	↑10%	↑15%	_____	_____	_____
d.	↓20%	↓15%	_____	_____	_____
e.	↑20%	↑20%	_____	_____	_____
f.	↓15%	↓15%	_____	_____	_____

Part 5. Self Test
Multiple choice questions

1. Which of the following statements is true?

a. Implicit costs are necessarily higher than explicit costs.
b. Explicit costs are necessarily higher than implicit costs.
c. Tammy owns a restaurant; she paid Jack $15,000 for the curtains he installed in the restaurant. The $15,000 for curtains is an explicit cost.
d. An implicit cost is a cost that represents actual monetary payment.
e. none of the above

Answer: _____

2. Which of the following is false?

a. Economic profit is always higher than accounting profit.
b. Accounting profit is the difference between total revenue and explicit costs.
c. Economic profit is the difference between total revenue and implicit costs.
d. a and c
e. a, b, and c

Answer: _____

3. Here is some information that relates to a business Max opened last year (all data relate to a year): price = $5, quantity sold = 15,000, implicit cost $4,500; explicit cost $8,500. What did economic profits equal for the year?

a. $66,500
b. $62,000
c. $52,000
d. $70,500

Answer: _____

4. You purchased a lamb chop from the grocery store yesterday for $5. The store has a no-return policy. The $5 purchase of the lamp chop is best described as:

a. an average cost
b. a normal cost
c. a sunk cost
d. a low fixed cost

Answer: _____

5. Evie recently went into the business of producing and selling greeting cards. For this business, which of the following is likely to be a fixed cost?

a. paper costs
b. labor costs
c. the six month lease for the factory
d. long distance telephone costs
e. a, b, and d

Answer: _____

6. Which of the following statements is true?

a. Since fixed costs are constant as output changes in the short run, it follows that average fixed cost is constant in the short run, too.
b. Marginal cost is the additional cost of producing an additional unit of output.
c. Changes in variable costs are reflected dollar-for-dollar in total cost.
d. b and c
e. a and b

Answer: _____

7. The law of diminishing marginal returns states that:

a. as ever larger amounts of a variable input are combined with fixed inputs, eventually the marginal physical product of the variable input will increase

b. as ever smaller amounts of a variable input are combined with fixed inputs, eventually the marginal physical product of the variable input will increase

c. as ever larger amounts of a fixed input are combined with a variable input, eventually the marginal physical product of the fixed input will decline

d. as additional units of a variable input are added to fixed input, eventually the marginal physical product of the variable input will decline

Answer: _____

8. The production of a good usually requires two types of inputs:

a. variable and fixed
b. long-run and short-run
c. total and unit
d. sunk and fixed
e. none of the above

Answer: _____

Exhibit A

Variable input	Fixed input	Quantity of Output	MPP of Variable input
0	1	0	
1	1	40	A
2	1	62	B
3	1	80	C
4	1	96	D
5	1	106	E
6	1	114	F

MPP = Marginal physical product

9. In Exhibit A, the numbers that go in blanks A and B are, respectively:

a. 40, 22
b. 0, 22
c. 20, 20
d. 1, 2
e. 20, 22

Answer: _____

10. In Exhibit A, the numbers that go on blanks C and D are, respectively:

a. 18, 16
b. 20, 16
c. 40, 184
d. 20, 22
e. none of the above

Answer: _____

11. If the average variable cost curve is falling:

a. the marginal cost (MC) curve must be above it
b. MC must be less than AVC
c. the MC curve is necessarily rising
d. the MC curve is horizontal (neither rising nor falling)

Answer: _____

Exhibit B

Variable input	Price per variable input	Fixed cost	Output	Marginal cost
1	$15	$100	30	
2	$15	$100	31	A
3	$15	$100	33	B
4	$15	$100	36	C
5	$15	$100	38	D

12. In Exhibit B, the dollar amounts that go in blanks A and B are, respectively:

a. $10.00, $ 7.50
b. $10.00, $ 5.00
c. $15.00, $ 7.50
d. $ 5.00, $ 5.00
e. $ 2.00, $12.00

Answer: _____

13. In Exhibit B, the dollar amounts that go in blanks C and D are, respectively:

a. $ 5.00, $ 7.50
b. $10.00, $ 3.33
c. $ 5.00 $10.00
d. $10.00, $10.00
e. $ 9.33, $10.00

Answer: _____

14. If, in the production process, inputs are increased by 18 percent and output increases by more than 18 percent:

a. economies of scale exist
b. diminishing marginal returns exist
c. diseconomies of scale exist
d. constant returns to scale exist
e. none of the above

Answer: _____

15. If, in the production process, inputs are increased by 10 percent and output increases by less than 10 percent:

a. economies of scale exist
b. diminishing marginal returns exist
c. diseconomies of scale exist
d. constant returns to scale exist
e. none of the above

Answer: _____

True-False

16. It is impossible for the marginal cost curve   T F
to be rising if it is below the average variable
cost curve.

17. Accounting profit is the difference between   T F
total revenue and explicit costs.

18. A firm that makes zero economic profit is   T F
earning a normal profit.

19. In the long run, there are only fixed   T F
costs.

20. The average-marginal rule states that if   T F
the marginal magnitude is below the average
magnitude, the average magnitude rises.

Fill in the blank

21. The _____ shows the lowest unit cost at which the firm can produce any given level of output.

22. The _____ is the lowest output level at which average total costs are minimized.

23. If inputs are increased by some percentage and output increases by a smaller percentage, unit costs _____ and _____ are said to exist.

24. Assume labor and some fixed input are used to produce good X. As the marginal physical product of labor decreases, marginal cost _____ .

25. The _____ of a variable input is equal to the change in output that results from changing the variable input by one unit, holding all other inputs fixed.

Part 5. Answers to Self Test

1. c 2. d 3. b 4. c 5. c 6. d 7. d 8. a. 9. a 10. a
11. b 12. c 13. a 14. a 15. c
16. F 17. T 18. T 19. F 20. F
21. long-run average total cost curve (LRATC)
22. minimum efficient scale 23. rise, diseconomies of scale
24. rises 25. marginal physical product

Part 6.   Answers

Part 2 Review of Concepts
1. e   2. c   3. a   4. b   5. d

Part 3 Key Concepts
1. explicit, do not   2. explicit, explicit and implicit   3. Sunk   4. variable, fixed, long
5. production   6. fixed, fixed, FC, horizontal   7. variable, variable cost   8. variable, fixed, VC+FC
9. average total cost, ATC   10. short   11. variable, price(s)   12. fixed, price(s)
13. average, average, AFC, AVC   14. ATC   15. Marginal, MC=ΔTC÷ΔQ or MC=ΔVC÷ΔQ
16. variable, fixed, output   17. marginal physical product, 1/20, 3 min.
18. 1/20, $0.50, $10÷20=$0.50, marginal   19. an increase, increasing   20. rise, fall   21. average,
ATC   22. economies, less   23. constant, 10%   24. diseconomies, more   25. variable   26. 20

Part 4 Problems and Exercises

#1

<u>a, k</u> Total Cost	<u>b, l, v</u> Average Total Cost	<u>c, f,g, s, t,u</u> Marginal Cost
<u>j, o</u> Variable Cost	<u>e, n, p</u> Average Variable Cost	
<u>d, h, i, q</u> Fixed Cost	<u>m, r</u> Average Fixed Cost	

2.

	Units of Labor	Units of Output	Wage ($)	VC ($)	FC ($)	TC ($)	ATC ($)	AVC ($)	AFC ($)	MC ($)
a.	0	0	$5	$0	$20	$20				
b.	1	10	$5	$5	$20	$25	$2.50	50¢	$2.00	$0.50
c.	2	25	$5	$10	$20	$30	$1.20	40¢	80¢	$0.33
d.	3	38	$5	$15	$20	$35	$0.92	39¢	53¢	$0.38
e.	4	49	$5	$20	$20	$40	$0.82	41¢	41¢	$0.45
f.	5	58	$5	$25	$20	$45	$0.78	43¢	34¢	$0.56
g.	6	64	$5	$30	$20	$50	$0.78	47¢	31¢	$0.83
h.	7	67	$5	$35	$20	$55	$0.82	52¢	30¢	$1.67
i.	8	69	$5	$40	$20	$60	$0.87	60¢	29¢	$2.50

3. See graph at right.

4. 3rd, 26th (thru 38th), 3rd

5. a. $20, $20   b. $0.268, $0.282
   c. $0.357   d. $25, $30
   e. less than, greater than

6. a. economies: a & d
   diseconomies: b & c
   constant returns: e & f

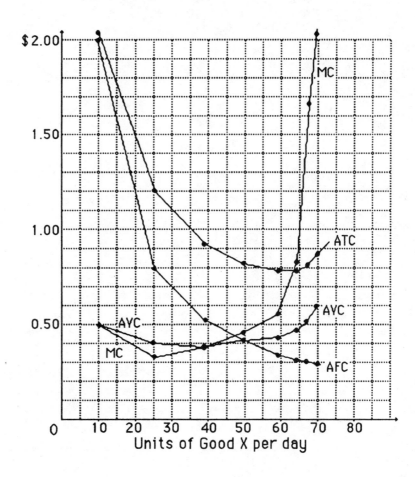

Chapter 24
Perfect Competition

Part 1. Introduction and Purpose
Consider the following points as you read chapter 24 in the text.

Back in chapters 3 and 4 you learned how to analyze the effects of shifting demand and supply curves. Demand increases cause prices to move higher, while supply increases bring price down. The analysis in this chapter and the two which follow examine supply and demand *from the perspective of suppliers*. If demand shifts, how are profits affected? Will the firm respond to the demand shift by increasing or reducing production? Should the firm raise or lower its price? These questions and others can be logically answered by using some ideas presented in previous chapters (particularly the chapter on production and costs) and a couple of new ones introduced in the present chapter.

The present topic is the theory of firm behavior in "perfect competition." The latter phrase isn't meant to describe the firm, but to describe market conditions. In this particular chapter the firm operates in a market which is extremely competitive because certain circumstances have made it that way. First, there are **many buyers and sellers** in the marketplace. Second, all firms sell an **identical product**. Third, buyers and sellers have good **information** about prices, product quality, and so forth. Finally, new firms can **enter** the industry and existing firms can **exit** (leave) it at very low cost.

Being small relative to the market causes one to be a **price taker** rather than a "price maker." In this situation, the firm has its first question answered: **Charge the market price**.

The second problem the firm faces is deciding how many units of output to produce. Since the firm can always produce one more or one less unit than its current output, marginal thinking should be used. The firm can **maximize profit by producing that quantity of output where MR = MC**. Since the firm's marginal revenue from selling a unit equals the price charged, (MR = P), the condition for profit maximization can also be stated as P = MC.

In the typical case, MR > MC for the first units produced. Since MR is the revenue from selling one unit and MC is the cost of producing it, the firm earns a profit on units for which MR > MC. Because MC increases as the firm expands output, eventually MC will equal MR. That signals the firm not to expand output further. If units for which MC > MR are produced, losses are earned on those particular units and total firm profits decline.

In the **short run,** that's about all there is to the theory of the firm. Profit maximization requires the firm to follow the MR = MC rule. If the market price changes, the firm will change its output to restore the P = MR = MC condition.

In the **long run** something else can happen that is impossible in the short run — it is possible for new firms to enter the industry or for existing firms to exit it. Because of entry and exit, the typical firm in the industry will earn zero economic profits. Whenever economic profits are being earned, new firms will enter the industry in search of above-normal returns. The additional supply causes market price to decline, which at some point will be enough to eliminate whatever profits previously existed. If the typical firm is initially earning a loss, some firms will exit the industry. That reduces total supply of the good and causes its price to increase — eventually to the point where losses have been eliminated. In the long run the typical firm will earn zero economic profits.

This analysis is useful for investigating the effects of changes in market demand or changes in production costs. For example, suppose that the average **cost of producing** good X **rises** by $1. Since we know that economic profits will equal zero in the long run, the $1 cost increase will be matched by a $1 increase in the market price of good X. Any other price change would either create economic profits or losses, neither of which can occur in the long run.

Or second, suppose the **demand** for good X **increases** by 1 million units. Assuming that unit production costs do not change, you will learn that in the long run suppliers will increase their output by 1 million units to match the greater demand. This willingness to "please the customer" is strongest when the owners of firms seek to maximize their profits. Theories of the firm typically assume that firm owners attempt to maximize their profits. It may seem paradoxical that in the long run extreme profit maximizing behavior causes suppliers to produce exactly those goods that consumers want most (as expressed by their willingness to pay dollars) but that's the way life is — paradoxical.

While you're thinking about that, here's a suggestion. Keep a pad of paper and a pencil handy when you read the chapter. When the text graphs a particular situation (such as a shift in costs or shift in demand), draw your own graph. Include arrows and short notes with each graph that describes the action being examined. Each step logically follows the one before, so practice walking your way through the analysis.

Part 2. Review of Concepts from Earlier Chapters
Prior to reading chapter 24, match statements at left with the appropriate concept at right.

__1. Higher prices mean reduced consumption.	a. opportunity cost
__2. A change in quantity demanded at each possible price.	b. average variable cost
__3. What must be foregone or given up when an action is taken.	c. average total cost
__4. The additional cost of one more unit of something.	d. total revenue
__5. Variable cost (VC) divided by quantity produced.	e. cost curves shift
__6. Unit cost; total cost divided by quantity produced.	f. marginal cost
__7. Total revenues minus total explicit costs.	g. accounting profit
__8. The process of transforming inputs (factors) into goods.	h. firm
__9. Horizontal demand curve.	i. law of demand
__10. Higher wages and other factor prices cause this.	j. economic profit
__11. Price per unit times quantity sold.	k. shift in demand
__12. Total revenue minus total explicit and implicit costs.	l. production
__13. An organization that hires inputs, produces and sells outputs.	m. perfectly elasatic

Part 3. Key Concepts in this Chapter
After reading chapter 24 in the text, answer the following questions.

1. A perfectly competitive market is one with _many / few_ buyers and sellers, each of whom possess _no / some / very good_ information about the price and availability of goods. In the long run, firms may _____ into and exit from the industry at low cost.

2. A price _maker / taker / breaker_ can buy or sell any desired quantity at the constant market price.

3. If the firm raises its price above the market price, it will lose _some / all_ of its customers to competing firms. Demand is perfectly _elastic / inelastic_ because a small change in price causes a _large / small_ change in quantity demanded.

4. The change in total revenue from selling one more unit of output is the firm's marginal _____. This is abbreviated _____ _____.

5. A _cartel / firm / industry_ is the collection of all firms that produce the same output -- all suppliers.

6. For a price taker, the _price / cost / size_ of a good also equals the marginal revenue from selling it.

7. Profit maximization occurs at the output level where _____ revenue equals _____ _____. Producing one more unit will cause the firm's total profit to _rise / fall_ .

8. The decision to shut down means that the firm will produce ___ units of output. The decision to shut down _does / does not_ mean that the firm has exited the industry.

9. Total revenue equals _price / MR_ multiplied by the quantity sold; total cost equals average _total / variable_ cost multiplied by the quantity produced.

10. (Refer to question 9.) TR = (Px__) & TC = (ATCx___). Consequently TR - TC = ___ x (P - Q).

11. As long as price _exceeds / is less than_ average variable cost, the firm will produce the quantity where price equals marginal cost. Consequently the _MC / ATC / TC_ curve is the firm's supply curve as long as P > AVC.

12. A firm will shut down production if price is _above / below_ the minimum average _total/ variable_ cost of production.

13. Above the point where P=AVC, the horizontal sum of the marginal cost curves of all firms in the industry is the industry's _demand / supply / cost_ curve. This curve _will / will not_ shift as firms enter the industry. If firms exit the industry the curve shifts to the _left / right_ .

14. If the typical firms earns positive economic profits, _entry / exit_ by new firms is likely and supply of the good will _increase / decrease_ .

15. If costs rise for all producers, firms will earn _positive / negative_ economic profits. This will cause existing firms to _enter / exit_ the industry, which will cause market supply to _rise / decline_ .

16. In long run equilibrium, there _is / is not_ a tendency for additional new firms to enter the industry. There _is / is not_ a tendency for existing firms to exit the industry.

17. A _____ cost industry is one where cost curves do not shift as new firms enter the industry and existing firms expand output.

18. In an _____ cost industry, hiring more factors of production will cause their prices to increase. Consequently firms' cost curves shift upward / downward .

19. If an increase in the demand for factors of production cause their prices to decline, then the industry that hires them will be a _____ cost industry. Such an industry has higher / lower unit production costs as it grows larger and expands output.

20. In an increasing cost industry, a decrease in demand will cause market price to rise / fall in the long run compared to its original level.

21. If a particular piece of land is more productive than other farmland, then the rent on that land will be greater / less than the rent on other land. In the long run the farmer who farms this land will/ will not earn an economic profit.

22. If one firm's cost curves shift upward but the costs of all other firms remain unchanged, the market price will rise / fall / not change . If it was originally earning a zero economic profit this firm will now earn positive / negative / zero profits.

23. Resources are allocated efficiently when the value of the last unit produced to consumers equals /exceeds the marginal cost of production. The equation for this condition is ____ = _____.

24. Firms in a perfectly competitive industry do/ do not usually advertise their product.

25. In the interview with Professor George Stigler, he says that adding factual content about the "real world" is will be used to explain makes a theory more/ less powerful.

26. Professor Stigler believes that economists are "awfully good" at microeconomics/ macroeconomics compared to their skill in microeconomics/ macroeconomics .

27. Augustin Cournot is called the father of micro / macro / mathematical economics. He first showed that the firm maximizes profit when marginal _____ equals _____ cost.

Part 4. Problems and Exercises

After reading chapter 24 in the text you should be able to work the following problems.

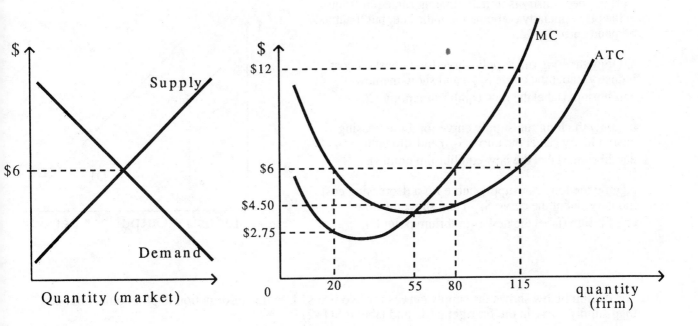

1. Refer to the exhibit above to answer this series of questions.
   a. The equilibrium price of the good is $____.
   b. The firm whose cost curves are drawn will maximize profit by producing ____ units.
   c. The firm will earn profits of $_____.
   d. In the long run do you expect entry or exit in this industry? _____
   e. In the event the market price falls to $4.50 the firm will earn a _profit / loss_ .
   f. Shade in the area in the diagram at right that shows the firm's total profits when P=$4.50.
   g. The firm will produce 115 units if the market price is $_____.
   h. If the firm produces 115 units and charges $6 per unit, its profits will equal $____.
   i. The firm's unit costs are minimized when it produces _____ units.

2. Each row (a-d) of the table below contains a different problem. Use the information provided to fill in missing values.

	Q	P	ATC	AVC	AFC	FC	VC	TC	TR	Profit
a.	50	$6	$5	$____	$2	$____	$____	$____	$____	$____
b.	____	$4	$3	$2	$____	$____	$60	$____	$____	$____
c.	200	$10	$8	$5	$____	$600	$____	$____	$2000	$____
d.	120	$2	$____	$1.50	$____	$180	$____	$____	$____	$____

3. At right the industry is initially in long run equilibrium
   at the price-quantity combination indicated, but thentotal
   demand shifts to D2.

   a. <u>Draw</u> the long run supply curve for a constant cost
   industry (label the curve S_{CC}) and show the new
   equilibrium (label the new equilibrium point C).

   b. <u>Draw</u> the long run supply curve for an increasing
   cost industry (label the curve S_{IC}) and show the new
   equilibrium (label the new equilibrium point I).

   c.<u>Draw</u> the long run supply curve for a decreasing cost
   industry (label the curve S_{DC}) and show the new
   equilibrium (label the new equilibrium point D).

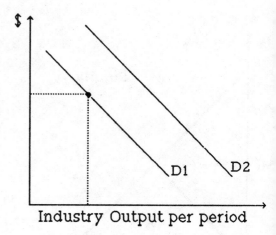

4. The exhibit below shows the supply curves for two firms. Use this information to plot points on their
   <u>total</u> supply curve in the far right grid., and label it S(1+2)

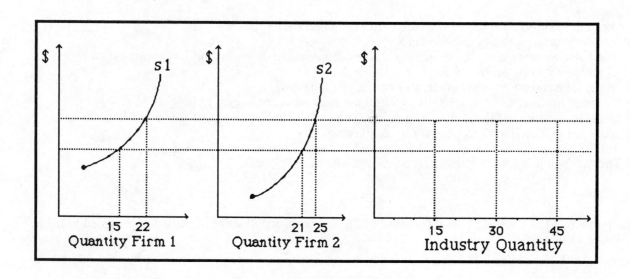

Part 5.   Self Test
Multiple choice questions

1. Which of the following is one of the assumptions of the theory of perfect competition?

a. there are few buyers and few sellers
b. there are many buyers and few sellers
c. there are few buyers and many sellers
d. there are many buyers and many sellers

Answer: _____

2. Which of the following markets comes closest to being a perfectly competitive market?

a. the corn market
b. the cigarette market
c. the insurance market
d. the soft drink market

Answer: _____

3. In a perfectly competitive market there are:

a. neither barriers to entry nor to exit
b. barriers to entry but not to exit
c. barriers to exit but not to entry
d. barriers to both entry and exit

Answer: _____

4. A firm that is a price taker is a firm:

a. that has the ability to control the price of the product it sells
b. that has the ability, albeit limited, to control the price of the product it sells
c. that can raise the price of the product it sells and still some units of its product
d. that sells a slightly differentiated product
e. none of the above

Answer: _____

5. Which of the following statements is true?

a. In the theory of perfect competition the single firm's demand curve is downward-sloping.
b. In the theory of perfect competition the market demand curve is downward-sloping.
c. In the theory of perfect competition the single firm's demand curve is horizontal.
d. In the theory of perfect competition the market demand curve is horizontal.
e. b and c

Answer: _____

6. If the firm produces the quantity of output at which marginal revenue (MR) equals marginal cost (MC) is it guaranteed to maximize profit?

a. Yes, when MR = MC, it follows that total revenue (TR) is greater than total cost (TC), and thus the firm maximizes profit.
b. Yes, since it is always the case that if the MC curve is rising, the average variable total cost curve lies below it and thus profit is earned.
c. No, when the firm produces the quantity at which MR = MC it means that TR - TC = 0.
d. No, at the quantity of output at which MR = MC, it could be the case that average total cost is greater than price. If this is the case, the firm will take a loss not earn a profit.

Answer: _____

7. Consider the following data: equilibrium price = $12, quantity of output produced = 100 units, average total cost = $9, and average variable cost = $6. Given this, total revenue is _____ , total cost is _____, and fixed cost is _____.

a. $1,200, $900, $300
b. $1,200, $700, $100
c. $1,200, $900, $600
d. $1,000, $800, $200
e. none of the above

Answer: _____

8. Consider the following data: equilibrium price = $12, quantity of output produced = 50 units, average total cost = $9, and average variable cost = $8. What will the firm do?

a. shut down in the short run, since it is taking a loss of $150
b. continue to produce in the short run, since firms are always stuck with having to produce in the short run
c. shut down in the short run, since average total cost is greater than average variable cost
d. continue to produce in the short run, since price is greater than average total cost and average variable cost

Answer: _____

9. The perfectly competitive firm's short-run supply curve is:

a. that portion of its average variable cost curve above its marginal revenue curve
b. that portion of its marginal cost curve above its average total cost curve
c. that portion of its marginal cost curve above its average variable cost curve
d. that portion of its average total cost curve above price
e. none of the above

Answer: _____

10. Which of the following conditions does not characterize long-run competitive equilibrium?

a. economic profit is positive
b. firms are producing the quantity of output at which price is greater than marginal cost
c. no firm has an incentive to change its plant size
d. a and b
e. a, b, and c

Answer: _____

11. The following holds: (1) there is no incentive for firms to enter or exit the industry; (2) for some firms in the industry short-run average total cost is greater than long-run average total cost at the level of output where marginal revenue equals marginal cost; (3) all firms in the industry are currently producing the quantity of output at which marginal revenue equals marginal cost; (4) all firms in the industry are producing a homogeneous product. Is the industry in long-run competitive equilibrium?

a. Yes
b. No, because of numbers 1 and 2
c. No, because of numbers 2 and 3
d. No, because of number 2
e. No, because of numbers 1, 2, 3 and 4

Answer: _____

12. An increasing-cost industry has a long-run (industry) supply curve that is:

a. upward-sloping
b. downward-sloping
c. horizontal
d. vertical

Answer: _____

13. Demand increases in a decreasing-cost industry that is initially in long-run competitive equilibrium. After full adjustment, price will be:

a. equal to its original level
b. below its original level
c. above its original level
d. there is not enough information to answer the question

Answer: _____

14. The change in total revenue which results from selling one additional unit of output is called:

a. average revenue
b. median revenue
c. marginal revenue
d. standard revenue

Answer: _____

15. Which of the following conditions about a firm in long-run competitive equilibrium is false?

a. P = AVC
b. P = MC
c. P = SRATC
d. P = LRATC

Answer: _____

True-False

16. A real-world market has to meet all the   T F
assumptions of the theory of perfect competition
before the theory predicts well.

17. In the theory of perfect competition, price   T F
is greater than marginal revenue.

18. A perfectly competitive firm is a price   T F
searcher.

19. A decreasing-cost industry is an industry   T F
in which average total costs decrease as industry
output increases.

20. If price is average total costs, the firm   T F
earns profits and will continue to operate in the
short run.

Fill in the blank

21. A firm that produces the quantity of output at which price equals marginal cost exhibits _____ .

22. In the long run in perfect competition, profits are _____ .

23. Firms attempt to produce that quantity of output at which (the condition) _____ holds.

24. The firm's _____ is that portion of its marginal cost curve that lies above the average variable cost curve.

25. The greater the fixed cost-total cost ratio, the _____ likely the firm will operate in the short run.

Part 5. Answers to Self Test

1. d 2. a 3. a 4. e 5. e 6. d 7. a 8. d 9. c 10. d
11. d 12. a 13. b 14. c 15. a
16. F 17. F 18. F 19. T 20. T
21. resource allocative efficiency 22. zero 23. MR = MC
24. short-run supply curve 25. more

Part 6. Answers

Part 2 Review of Concepts
1. i   2. k   3. a   4. f   5. b   6. c   7. g   8. 1   9. m   10. e   11. d   12. j   13. h

Part 3 Key Concepts
1. many, very good, enter   2. taker   3. all, elastic, large   4. revenue, MR   5. industry   6. price
7. marginal revenue equals marginal cost, fall   8. 0 (zero), does not   9. price, total   10. Q, Q, Q
11. exceeds, marginal cost   12. below, variable   13. supply, will, left   14. entry, increase
15. negative, exit, decline   16. is not, is not   17. constant   18. increasing, upward
19. decreasing, lower   20. fall   21. greater, will not   22. not change, negative   23. equals, P=MC
24. do not   25. less   26. micro, macro   27. mathematical, revenue, marginal

Part 4 Problems and Exercises

1. a. $6   b. 80   c. $1.50x80=$120
   d. entry   e. profit
   f. Rectangle: $4.50-$6, 0-80 units
   g. $12   h. $0   i. 5

2. a. $3, $100, $150, $250, $300, $50
   b. 30, $1, $30, $90, $120, $30
   c. $3, $1000, $1600, $400
   d. $3, $1.50, $180, $300, $240, -$60

#3

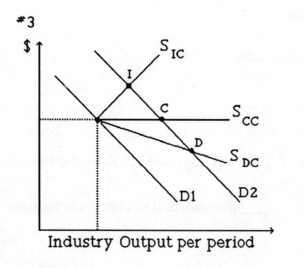

#4

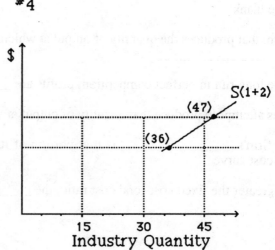

Chapter 25
Monopoly

Part 1. Introduction and Purpose
Consider the following points as you read chapter 25 in the text.

In the previous chapter you learned about the behavior of a firm which had a large number of competitors; in this one you will learn how the same firm would perform if it had no competitors at all. This is the case of monopoly. Differences in the behavior of perfectly competitive firms and monopoly firms arise from the *circumstances* they confront rather than something inherently different about the firms themselves. Firms are assumed to maximize profit in both situations, but in one situation the firm has no real market power and in the other its market power is considerable. Little wonder that a firm behaves differently when the market structure changes.

First the definition: a **monopolist** is the **only producer** of a good with **no close substitutes**. In this case the total market demand is also the demand for firm's product. Where the competitive firm was a price taker, the monopolist is a **price searcher** — it can raise or lower price to search for the level that maximizes profit. (The competitive firm would have lost all of its customers if it had tried that.)

Real-world monopolies are rare, because they can exist only if there are significant **barriers to entry** that prevent other firms from entering the marketplace. Three types of barriers are **legal** barriers resulting from government regulation, **economies of scale** in production which give an existing large firm a significant cost advantage over small firms that might venture to enter the industry, and the firm's (monopoly) ownership of all supplies of a **resource** required for the good to be produced.

Behind a barrier to entry the firm produces and sells the profit maximizing output level. As in the last chapter, that is the **quantity that equates marginal revenue and marginal cost.**

The marginal revenue curve for a monopolist (price searcher) is different than the MR curve for a perfectly competitive seller (price taker). In a perfectly competitive market a firm could increase its unit sales without affecting the market price. A monopolist doesn't have that luxury. Expanding its market means lowering price, and that causes marginal revenue to be less than price for the monopolist.

For example, consider what happens if a company has been selling 100 units of good X for $10 apiece. Total revenues equal $1000. If the company wants to expand sales by one unit (to 101), it has to lower price by enough to attract the new customer. Assume the seller lowers price to $99.90 to make the sale, and *assume that it charges the same price for every unit it sells*. Now the company will receive $99.90 for the marginal unit, but since it has also lowered price by 10¢ on the other 100 units it previously could have sold for $100 apiece it is giving up $10 in potential revenues. The firm's marginal revenue from the 101st unit is price charged on the unit ($99.90) minus the price reductions given to non-marginal buyers ($10) — for $89.90 in the present case.

If it had been necessary to lower price to $99 to attract the marginal sale, the company's marginal revenue would have been $99 (price) minus $100 worth of price reductions ($1 to each buyer of the non-marginal 100 units) for a *negative* marginal revenue! This case in particular shows that the monopolist's price will be higher than marginal revenue. Since marginal revenue equals marginal cost when the firm maximizes profit, the monopolist's price must also be above its marginal cost (P > MC). This represents an **inefficient** use of resources, as you will learn in the text.

After selecting the profit-maximizing level of output (where MR = MC), the monopolist charges the highest price which can be charged and still sell that output. The firm's price is shown by the *height* of the market demand curve above the MR = MC quantity. Profit is the difference between price and average total cost, multiplied by quantity sold.

Due to **barriers** to entry, profits will not attract new firms into the industry as they did in competitive markets. Consequently profits may exist in the **long run** in a monopolized industry. At least they can until people recognize that monopoly profits are being earned. Then others compete for the profits in other ways. One thing investors will do is **buy ownership** of a profitable monopolist. Another thing that can happen is for outsiders to try and convince government officials (regulators) to allow them into the profitable industry. Pursuing profits through political channels is known as **rent seeking**.

Finally, you will learn how price searchers try to practice **price discrimination** to increase their profits. Price discrimination refers to charging different prices for different units of the same good. Price discrimination permits the seller to lower price to sell another unit of output, without simultaneously lowering price on all non-marginal units. By reducing the revenue losses that create a gap between price and marginal revenue, the price discriminating firm will sell more output than the non-discriminating firm and will also earn larger profits.

Part 2. Review of Concepts from Earlier Chapters
Prior to reading chapter 25, match statements at left with the appropriate concept at right.

___1. An organization that hires inputs, then produces & sells an output.
___2. When new firms start producing a particular good.
___3. The extra cost associated with producing one more unit of output.
___4. The additional revenue from selling one more unit of output.
___5. Profit is maximized by following this rule.
___6. Total cost divided equally among all units produced.
___7. Total revenue minus total cost.
___8. Industry where sellers are price takers.
___9. Horizontal summation of demands by all consumers.

a. profit
b. entry
c. average total cost
d. total market demand
e. perfect competition
f. marginal revenue
g. MR = MC
h. firm
i. marginal cost

Part 3. Key Concepts in this Chapter
After reading chapter 25 in the text, answer the following questions.

1. A monopoly firm is one of many sellers/ the only seller of a product with _____ close substitutes. Barriers / Invitations to entry prevent new firms from competing with a profitable monopolist.

2. There are three general types of barriers to entry. First are _____ barriers, which are created by government. Second, substantial _____ of scale can make it impossible for small firms to compete with large firms. Third, the monopolist may be the only owner of a _____ that is required to produce the good.

3. A _____ monopoly results if economies of scale are pronounced enough to make it impossible for a second firm to enter a market.

4. A "_____" monopoly is one created by legal barriers to entry.

5. The demand curve for the monopolist's product is the same as the _____ demand. This curve is / is not downward sloping.

6. True or false? _____ The standard monopoly model assumes that a monopolist charges the same price for all units of output sold.

7. When a monopolist does not charge the same price on all units, it practices price _____.

8. Marginal revenue for a non-discriminating monopolist is greater than / less than the price charged for a given unit.

9. A monopolist maximizes profit by producing an output where P=ATC / P=MC / MR=MC / MR=ATC . Price equals / exceeds marginal cost at that quantity.

10. Other things being equal, a monopoly industry will sell more / fewer units of output than a perfectly competitive industry.

11. Consider a monopolist that can sell 20 units of output for $5 apiece, but would have to lower price to $4.90 to sell another unit. For the 21st unit price equals $_____ while price reductions to customers of non-marginal units equal $_____, so the firm's marginal revenue equals $_____.

12. True or false? _____ Profit maximization is the same as revenue maximization. The profit maximizing output is the one that maximizes the firm's total revenues.

13. Resource allocative efficiency requires the firm to produce that output where _____ = marginal cost. The single-price monopolist will produce more / less than this output.

14. If the price of a company (as expressed in its share price) reflects the monopoly profits a firm is likely to earn in the future, then those profits have been incorporated / capitalized in the current stock price. The buyer of such stock will earn a positive / zero / negative economic profit.

15. If a firm works to influence government officials to grant them monopoly powers in the marketplace, these activities are called profit/ rent seeking. These activities do / do not create value for consumers.

16. Under 1st / 2nd / 3rd degree price discrimination, each unit of output is priced separately. Under 1st / 2nd / 3rd degree price discrimination, customers are separated into various groups and are charged different prices.

17. Buying a good where its price is low to resell where its price is higher is called _____. This activity improves/ limits the ability of monopolists to engage in price discrimination.

18. Suppose hamburgers are 60¢ each for the first burger and 50¢ apiece for each additional one. This is an example of _1st / 2nd / 3rd_ degree price discrimination.

19. Due to a lack of competition, monopolists may not operate at their lowest possible cost. Inefficiencies of this nature are sometimes called _A / B / M / X_ -inefficiency.

20. The allocative inefficiency associated with monopoly power is represented by a _____ cost triangle. Estimates of these inefficiencies suggest that the inefficiency cost of monopoly is about ___% of total output for the economy.

21. In the interview, Professor Gordon Tullock says research suggests that the welfare cost of monopoly is _greater / less_ than that suggested by the welfare loss triangle analysis.

22. Another term for rent seeking is ___ ___ ___, or directly _____ profit seeking. DUP activities _do / do not_ benefit consumers.

Part 4. Problems and Exercises
After reading chapter 25 in the text you should be able to work the following problems.

1. Refer to the diagram.

    a. The profit maximizing firm will produce and sell _____ units.
    b. The firm can charge $_____ per unit and sell the number of units indicated in (a).
    c. The firm's ATC equals $_____ at the chosen output.
    d. The firm will earn profits of $_____ per unit (on average), multiplied by _____ units, for total profits of $_____.
    e. If the firm produces and sells 100 units, the price it can charge _exceeds / equals_ ATC. The firm _would / would not_ earn a profit

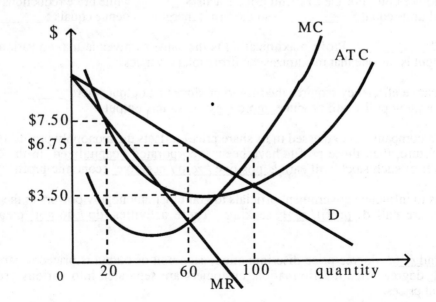

2. Use information in the table to calculate values for total revenue and marginal revenue.

The relevant definitions are:

• TR = ___ x ___
    and
• MR = Δ ___ ÷ Δ ___.

	P	Q	TR	MR
a.	$20	1	$____	$____
b.	$18	3	$____	$____
c.	$16	5	$____	$____
d.	$14	8	$____	$____
e.	$12	10	$____	$____

3. Use numbers from the first two columns of the table in exercise 2 to draw the demand curve for the firm's product. Label the curve D.

Following that, use numbers from columns 2 and 4 to plot the firm's marginal revenue curve. Label the curve MR.

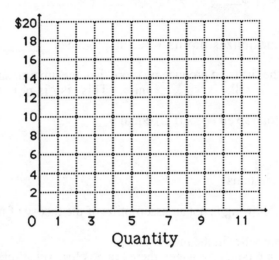

4. In the diagram at right, the firm's marginal cost and unit cost are constant and the monopolist produces a profit maximizing level of output.

a. In this case the firm earns total profits of $_____.

b. Shade in the area that represents the social losses due to resource allocative inefficiency with a pattern of diagonal lines ▨.

c. Shade in the area in the graph that represents the firm's profits with horizontal lines ▤.

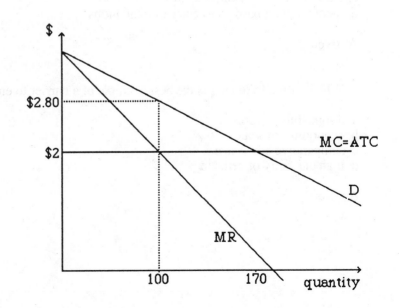

5. The table below provides information on a monopolist's costs of production and the demand for its product. Complete all missing values.

	Demand Qty.	P	TC	MC	ATC	TR	MR	Net Profit
a.	0	$15	$5			$___		$___
b.	1	$14	$8	$___	$___	$___	$___	$___
c.	2	$13	$___	$5	$___	$___	$___	$___
d.	3	$12	$___	$7	$___	$___	$___	$___
e.	4	$11	$___	$9	$___	$___	$___	$___
f.	5	$10	$___	$11	$___	$___	$___	$___

g. The firm maximizes profits when it produces _____ units. Total profit equals $_____.

h. Assuming the firm can produce no more than the amount shown in the table, the firm maximizes total revenue when it sells _____ units. This _is / is not_ the same output that maximizes profit.

i. This firm's total fixed costs (FC) equal $_____.

Part 5. Self Test
Multiple choice questions

1. Which of the following is not an assumption of the theory of monopoly?

a. there is only one seller in the industry
b. the seller sells a product for which there are no close substitutes
c. the seller has high variable costs
d. there are high barriers to entry into the industry

Answer: _____

2. Which of the following is the best example of a barrier to entry into a monopolistic industry?

a. diminishing returns
b. economies of scale
c. comparative advantage
d. high elasticity of demand

Answer: _____

3. In the United States, patents are granted to inventors of a product or process for a period of:

a. 2 years
b. 12 years
c. 17 years
d. 22 years
e. none of the above

Answer: _____

4. A price searcher:

a. faces a horizontal demand curve
b. is a seller that searches for good employees and pays them a low wage
c. is a seller that searches for the best price at which to buy its nonlabor inputs
d. is a seller that has the ability to control to some degree the price of the product it sells
e. a and c

Answer: _____

5. Which of the following statements is true?

a. A price searcher must raise price to sell an additional unit of its product.
b. For a price searcher, price equals marginal revenue for all units except the first.
c. For a price searcher, price is less than marginal revenue for all units except the first.
d. A price searcher, like a price taker, produces that quantity of output for which marginal revenue equals marginal cost.
e. c and d

Answer: _____

6. The marginal revenue curve lies above the demand curve for a:

a. monopoly firm
b. price taker
c. price searcher
d. a and c
e. none of the above

Answer: _____

7. Economic or monopoly rent is:

a. a payment in excess of price
b. a payment in excess of average variable cost
c. a payment in excess of opportuntity cost
d. a payment in excess of explicit cost but not necessarily a payment in excess of implicit cost
e. none of the above

Answer: _____

8. When a seller charges different prices for the product he sells and the price differences do not reflect cost differences, the seller is engaging in:

a. rent seeking
b. arbitrage
c. the capitalization of profits
d. price discrimination

Answer: _____

9. A seller who charges the highest price each consumer would be willing to pay for the product rather than go without it, is practicing:

a. perfect price discrimination
b. disciplined price discrimination
c. ideal price discrimination
d. competitive price discrimination

Answer: _____

10. For a firm that perfectly price discriminates:

a. price equals marginal revenue
b. price is less than marginal cost
c. price is greater than average total cost
d. there is not enough information to answer the question

Answer: _____

11. Which of the following is a rent-seeking activity?

a. Carol produces shoes that will be purchased by the Army.
b. Mick produces blankets that are sold in Egypt.
c. Jackie produces sun tan lotion that is sold exclusively in Hawaii.
d. a and b
e. none of the above

Answer: _____

12. According to Gordon Tullock:

a. monopoly profits or rents are subject to rent seeking
b. the welfare cost triangle is subject to rent seeking
c. X-inefficiency is something that differentiates government monopolies from private monopolies
d. the theory of monopoly is superior to the theory of perfect competition

Answer: _____

13. (Single-price) monopoly firms:

a. produce the resource allocative efficient output
b. produce more than the resource allocative efficient output
c. produce less than the resource allocative efficient output
d. produce where P = MC

Answer: _____

14. The monopolist will maximize profits at a level of output at which marginal revenue equals:

a. average fixed cost
b. average variable cost
c. average total cost
d. marginal cost

Answer: _____

15. Perfect price discrimination is sometimes called:

a. discrimination among buyers
b. discrimination among sellers
c. discrimination among quantities
d. discrimination among units

Answer: _____

True-False

16. If a firm is a price searcher, it necessarily   T F
cannot price discriminate.

17. The revenue-maximizing price is the   T F
profit-maximizing price when there are no
variable costs.

18. A monopoly firm charges a higher price and   T F
produces more output than a perfectly competitive
firm with the same demand and cost conditions.

19. Monopoly profits can turn out to be zero   T F
in the long run through the capitalization
of profits.

20. In perfect competition, P = MC; in monopoly,   T F
P < MC.

Fill in the blank

21. _____ is the condition where economies of scale are so pronounced in an industry that
only one firm can survive.

22. A _____ is a seller that has the ability to control to some degree the price of the product it sells.

23. Buying a good in a market where its price is low, and selling the good in another where its price is
higher, is called _____ .

24. _____ is the increase in costs and organizational slack in a monopoly resulting from
the lack of competitive pressure to push costs down to their lowest possible level.

25. The major developer of the theory of rent seeking is _____ .

Part 5. Answers to Self Test

1. c 2. b 3. c 4. d 5. d 6. e 7. c 8. d 9. a 10. a
11. e 12. a 13. c 14. d 15. d
16. F 17. T 18. F 19. T 20. F
21. Natural monopoly 22. price searcher 23. arbitrage
24. X-Inefficiency 25. Gordon Tullock

Part 6.   Answers

Part 2 Review of Concepts
1. h   2. b   3. i   4. f   5. g   6. c   7. a   8. e   9. d

Part 3 Key Concepts
1. the only seller, no, barriers   2. legal, economies, resource (or factor or input)   3. natural
4. government   5. total (or market), is   6. True   7. discrimination   8. less than
9. MR=MC, exceeds   10. fewer   11. $4.90, $2.00, $2.90   12. False (except when variable costs $0)
13. price, less   14. capitalized, zero economic profit (normal accounting profit)   15. rent, do not
16. first, third   17. arbitrage, limits   18. second   19. X-   20. welfare, 1%   21. greater
22. DUP, unproductive, do not

Part 4 Problems and Exercises

Part 4 Problems and Exercises

1. a. 60   b. $6.75   c. $3.50
d. $3.25, $195   e. equals, would not

2. a. $20, $20
b. $54, $34÷2=$17
c. $80, $26÷2=$13
d. $112, $32÷3=$10.67
e. $120, $8÷2=$4

3. See graph below:

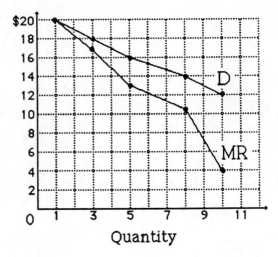

4. a. $80¢ x 100 units = $80
   b. and c. see graph below

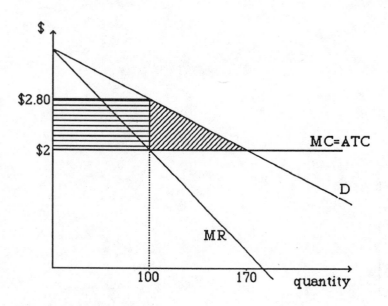

5. a. $0, -$5
   b. $8, $3, $14, $14, $6
   c. $6.50, $13, $26, $12, $13
   d. $6.67, $20, $36, $10, $16
   e. $7.25, $29, $44, $8, $15
   f. $8, $40, $50, $6, $10
   g. 3, $16   h. 5, is not   i. $5

Chapter 26
Monopolistic Competition and Oligopoly

Part 1. Introduction and Purpose
Consider the following points as you read chapter 26 in the text.

This chapter examines the performance of firms operating in markets falling somewhere between perfectly competitive and perfectly monopolistic. Where monopolists produce considerably less output and charge a significantly higher price than firms in a perfectly competitive industry would, the **intermediate cases of monopolistic competition and oligopoly** predict a lower quantity and higher price than perfectly competitive markets, but a larger quantity and lower price than complete monopoly.

Monopolistically competitive markets have a large number of sellers and low costs of entry and exit, as in perfect competition, but in monopolistic competition firms produce similar rather than identical products. As in other market settings, the profit maximizing firm will produce the quantity of output where MR = MC.

Easy **entry** and **exit** mean the typical firm will earn zero economic profits in the long run. Because firms produce similar rather than identical products, some customers will continue to purchase a good even when its price rises relative to the prices of competing products. Although demand is elastic, the **demand** for each supplier's product is **less than perfectly elastic** (as it was in perfect competition), so the monopolistically competitive firm is a **price searcher** rather than a price taker. The firm will charge more for the product than its marginal cost of production, and produce less than the allocatively efficient quantity of output.

Oligopoly markets are characterized by a relatively small number of firms that produce similar or identical products. More firms are prevented from entering the industry because of barriers to entry similar to those discussed in the previous chapter on monopoly. (Legal barriers, economies of scale, and ownership of a unique resource can prevent additional firms from entering an industry.)

Unlike the other market structures we've looked at, a firm in an oligopolistic market does not act independently of other firms. When only a few firms make up an entire industry, the actions of one can have a big impact on the others, and they may respond in unforseen ways. Because of the ultimate unpredictability of the situation, there is **no single oligopoly model** that applies in all situations. There are several oligopoly models, and circumstances dictate which one should be used in a particular application.

In the absence of other information about an industry other than its oligopolistic composition, a basic model of oligopoly recognizes that each oligopolist's output is a **close substitutes** for the output of other oligopolists. Recall from chapter 3 that when the price of a particular good changes, the demand curve for a substitute good will shift. Ceteris paribus, if private colleges raise their tuitions, demand will increase at public colleges.

In oligopoly markets it works pretty much the same. If one steel company raises its price, quantity demanded of that steel declines *and* the demand increases for other companies' steel. Faced with a stronger demand, the other companies are also likely to raise their prices. **Interdependence** between firms is exhibited here, since one company's price increase caused others to respond with price increases of their own. The same model predicts that if the first company had lowered price, the others would have done likewise because of declining demands for their products.

But firms in oligopolistic markets face a complex situation, and sometimes behave in ways that can't be explained with this basic model. The **kinked demand curve** model is applied to situations in which the company under consideration is competing against other companies that are trying to maintain or increase their **market shares**.

Another oligopoly model applies to situations where there is one large firm and many small firms in the industry. Called the **price leadership** by the dominant firm model, this theory predicts that the large firm sets price to maximize its own profits and smaller firms will match the large one's price.

Still another oligopoly model describes the actions of a **cartel**, which is a group of producers who jointly agree to produce a quantity and charge a price that will maximize the **group's profit** rather than their individual profits. By all agreeing to reduce output they can all charge higher prices and earn larger profits — at least in theory. Real-world cartels are plagued by "cheating" among their members, by which is meant producing more or charging less than the cartel quantity and price.

Finally, the chapter examines a new theory of markets. The distinction we have been making between different markets has stressed the *number* of firms in the industry. One firm is monopoly, two or three or five is oligopoly, and a hundred is perfect competition or monopolistic competition.

The theory of **contestable markets** suggests that markets may achieve competitive results if **entry and exit** are approximately **costless**. In such cases, any appearance of profit in an industry will attract additional suppliers into the market and they will compete the profits away. The theory of contestable markets predicts a competitive *outcome* whenever such "hit and run" entry can be practiced, regardless of the actual number of firms.

Part 2. Review of Concepts from Earlier Chapters
Prior to reading chapter 26, match statements at left with the appropriate concept at right.

__1. One firm.	a. MR = MC
__2. Perfectly competitive firm that charges the market price.	b. economies of scale
__3. Small price change causes a huge change in qty. demanded.	c. monopoly
__4. A firm that varies price to sell the desired number of units.	d. price taker
__5. Long run unit costs decline as output increases.	e. price searcher
__6. These prevent firms from entering an industry.	f. substitute goods
__7. Legal obstacles to entering an occupation or industry.	g. marginal revenue
__8. Increase in the price of X increases the demand for Y.	h. perfectly elastic demand
__9. Additional revenue when one more unit is sold.	i. zero
__10. Rule for maximizing profit.	j. barriers
__11. Long run economic profit with zero entry & exit costs.	k. legal barriers

Part 3. Key Concepts in this Chapter
After reading chapter 26 in the text, answer the following questions.

1. A monopolistically competitive firm is one where _one / a few / many_ firms compete for customers, with each producing _identical / similar_ products. There are _high / low_ costs of entry end exit.

2. In the long run, a typical firm in a monopolistically competitive market _will / will not_ earn economic profits.

3. A firm in monopolistic competition is a price _taker / searcher_. Price _equals / exceeds_ MR. The demand for its product is _elastic / inelastic / perfectly elastic / unit elastic_.

4. In the long run firms in monopolistic competition will produce _more / less_ than the output which minimizes its unit cost.

5. Consumers have _more / fewer_ product choices in monopolistic competition than under perfect competition or monopoly.

6. The firm in monopolistic competition maximizes profit by producing the output where _____ = MC. The firm's price _equals / exceeds / is less than_ marginal cost of production at this output.

7. Suppliers that distribute cents-off coupons on their products are practicing something economists call price _____.

8. An industry with only a few firms is called an _____. Suppliers in these industries produce _similar / identical / either similar or identical_ products.

9. One way of measuring the degree to which an industry is dominated by a few large firms is to look at the industry's _____ ratio. This is the percent of total industry sales accounted for by the _largest / smallest_ _4 / 6 / 10_ firms.

10. There _are / are not_ high entry costs into oligopoly industries. Entry costs _are / are not_ barriers to entry. Other than government regulation, most oligopolies probably arise because of economies of scale that make large firms _more / less_ efficient than smaller firms.

11. Each oligopolist's product is a close _complement / substitute_ for the product produced by other oligopolists in the industry. A decrease in the price charged by one will _increase / reduce_ the demand for the output of other firms.

12. A kinked demand curve shows the situation of a firm that faces an _elastic inelastic_ demand when it raises price and an _elastic inelastic_ demand when it lowers price.

13. If a company that faces an elastic demand increases its price, total revenues _rise / fall_. If a company that faces an inelastic demand lowers its price, total revenues _rise / fall_.

14. The kinked demand curve analysis suggests that an oligiopolist whose rivals are trying to increase their market share will be _quick / slow_ to change price in the event its marginal cost curve shifts up or down.

15. In the kinked demand curve model the firm under consideration _is / is not_ a profit maximizing firm. Other (rival) firms in the industry _are / are not_ profit maximizers.

16. A model in which one firm sets price and other firms decide to charge the same price is called a price <u>follower / leadership / parallelism</u> model. The text discussed a situation in which the _____ or largest firm in the industry is the price setter. This firm <u>is / is not</u> a profit maximizer, and it <u>does / does not</u> produce an output where MR = MC.

17. A <u>cartel / oligopoly / monopoly</u> is a group of firms in the same industry that agree to <u>reduce / increase</u> their total output in order to <u>reduce / increase</u> price. If successful, each firm's profits will <u>rise / fall</u> .

18. After a cartel has been formed, its main problem is a tendency by members to <u>live by / cheat on</u> the agreement. Cartel members tend to produce <u>more / less</u> output than the agreed-on amount.

19. OPEC is a cartel of <u>petroleum / diamond / steel</u> producing nations. OPEC greatly increased the price of its product during the 19<u>60s / 70s / 80s</u>, but its price fell in the 19<u>60s / 70s / 80s</u>.

20. The "incredible electrical conspiracy" refers to a <u>monopoly / cartel</u> that functioned between 19___ and 19___. It included several major companies who agreed in advance to "rig" _____ they submitted for contracts to produce electrical equipment (such as large generators). The organization <u>did / did not</u> have problems with cheating by members of the group. Participants in the conspiracy <u>were / were not</u> found guilty of violating the law.

21. Government regulation of the airline industry <u>permitted / prevented</u> cartel-like behavior by the airline industry. Deregulation has caused air fares to <u>rise / fall</u>.

22. A _____ market is one where costs of entry and exit are theoretically zero. There is (are) <u>one / many / a few / any number of</u> firms in this type of industry.

23. In a contestable market, price <u>equals / exceeds</u> average total cost and marginal cost.

24. A contestable market is one with "_____ and run" entry and exit.

25. In the interview with Professor William Baumol, he said that a key insight of the contestable market theory is the suggestion that free _____ can act as a substitute for _____ competition.

26. Professor Baumol <u>does / does not</u> believe that most markets are contestable. Two markets he believes are contestable are _____ and _____.

27. According to Professor Baumol, effective competition or monopoly power in a market <u>is / is not</u> measured by counting the number of firms that currently compete in the market (which he called "incumbents").

28. The theory of monopolistic competition was developed at about the same time by two economists, Joan _____ and Edward _____.

Part 4.   Problems and Exercises
After reading chapter 26 in the text you should be able to work the following problems.

1. The graph at right shows what happens when demand shifts for the product sold by a price searcher.

   Sketch the profit-maximizing quantity and price for the two cases.   Label the prices P1 and P2.

   Label the quantities Q1 and Q2.

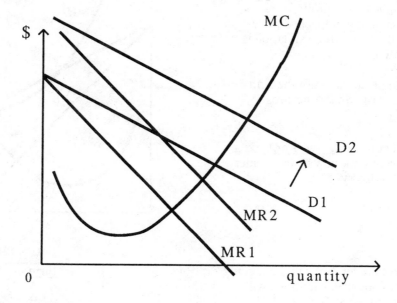

2. In the graph at right,

   a. Indicate the profit maximizing output and price for the firm whose situation is shown.

   b. Indicate the profit the firm will earn.

   c. There will / will not be a tendency for new firms to enter this industry.

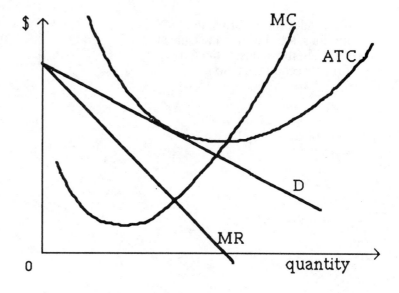

3. In the graph at right,

a. Indicate the profit maximizing output and price for the firm whose situation is shown.

b. Indicate the profit the firm will earn. Shade this area ▨.

c. There will / will not be a tendency for new firms to enter this industry.

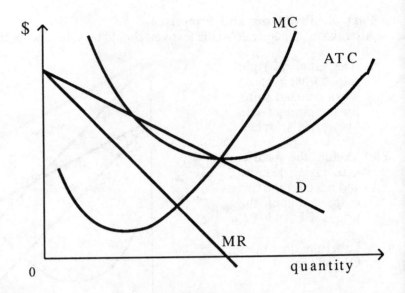

4. There are ten firms in the jogging shoe industry, whom we will refer to as A, B, C, D, E, F, G, H, I, and J.

Total sales for the firms, in millions, are shown in the table at right. In this industry the four-firm concentration ratio is _____%.

Firm	Sales
A	$105
B	70
C	65
D	60
E-J	175
TOTAL	$475

5. See the graph at right.

a. The graph shows the demand curve for a good produced by a firm in an
 monopoly / oligopoly
industry

b. Indicate the profit maximizing quantity and price for this situation.

c. How high could the marginal cost curve shift without causing the firm to raise price? Sketch a new MC curve that shows this amount, and label it MC-high.

d. How low could the marginal cost curve shift without causing the firm to raise price? Sketch a new MC curve that shows this amount, and label it MC-low.

e. The demand curve in the graph is said to be

_____.

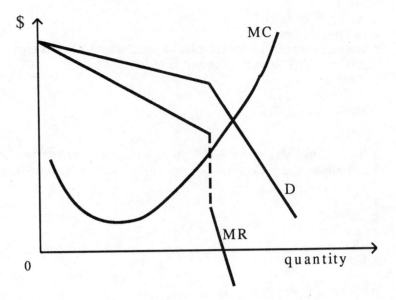

Part 5. Self Test
Multiple choice questions
Part 5. Self Test.

Multiple Choice

1. Which of the following is not an assumption of the theory of monopolistic competition?

a. there are high barriers to entry
b. there are many sellers and many buyers
c. each firm in the industry produces and sells a highly differentiated product
d. a and c
e. all the above

Answer: _____

2. The monopolistic competitor:

a. is a price searcher
b. is a price taker
c. is a mix between a price taker and a price searcher (it has elements of competition and monopoly)
d. produces that quantity of output at which MR > MC
e. a and d

Answer: _____

3. Total industry sales for year 1 are $10 million. The top four firms, A - D, account for sales of $2, $2.5, $3.1 million, and $0.5 million, respectively. What is the four-firm concentration ratio?

a. .91
b. .55
c. .69
d. .81
e. none of the above

Answer: _____

4. Concentration ratios are not perfect guides to industry concentration because:

a. they do not take into account foreign competition and competition from substitute goods
b. they do not adjust for inflation
c. they do not adjust for quality of products
d. they do not adjust for price
e. a and d

Answer: _____

5. If a single firm lowers price, other firms will do likewise, but if a single firm raises price, other firms will not necessarily follow suit. This is the behavioral assumption in the:

a. cartel theory
b. price leadership theory
c. kinked demand curve theory
d. price discrimination theory
e. none of the above

Answer: _____

6. Which of the following statements is true?

a. According to the kinked demand curve theory the marginal cost (MC) curve can shift within a certain region and the firm will continue to produce the same quantity of output but charge a different price.
b. According to the kinked demand curve theory the MC curve can shift within a certain region and the firm will continue to produce the same quantity of output and charge the same price.
c. According to the kinked demand curve theory the demand curve can shift within a certain region and the firm will continue to produce the same quantity of output and charge the same price.
d. According to the kinked demand curve theory the marginal revenue curve can shift with a certain region and the firm will continue to produce the same quantity of output but charge a different price.

Answer: _____

7. The top firm in the industry determines price and all other firms take this price as given. This is the behavioral assumption of the:

a. kinked demand curve theory
b. price leadership theory
c. both the cartel and price leadership theories
d. monopolistic competitive theory

Answer: _____

8. In the price leadership theory, at a price of $5 per unit, the fringe firms supply the entire market. At a price of $4, the (market) quantity demanded is 900 units and the quantity supplied by fringe firms is 430. Given this, which of the following quantity-price combinations is represented by a point on the dominant firm's demand curve?

a. 1,330 units at $5
b. 230 units at $4
c. 470 units at $4
d. 470 units at $5
e.   1 unit at $5

Answer: _____

9. The key behavioral assumption of the cartel theory is that:

a. oligopolists in an industry try to maximize revenue instead of profits
b. oligopolists in an industry act as if they are perfect monopolistic competitors
c. oligopolists in an industry act in a manner consistent with there being only one firm in the industry
d. oligopolists in an industry try manipulate government into subsidizing their activities
e. b and d

Answer: _____

10. Which of the following is an example of an oligopoly?

a. a law partnership
b. a local gas company
c. a dental firm
d. General Motors Company
e. none of the above

Answer: _____

11. Product differentiation is a form of:

a. advertising
b. nonprice competition
c. lowering variable costs
d. lowering the fixed costs to total cost ratio
e. none of the above

Answer: _____

12. Ceteris paribus, the free rider problem is more serious:

a. the smaller the number of potential cartel members
b. the larger the number of potential cartel members
c. the higher total costs
d. the lower total costs
e. b and c

Answer: _____

13. Which of the following statements is true?

a. One of the developers of contestable markets theory is William Baldwin.
b. Orthodox market structure theory places much greater weight than contestable markets theory on the number of firms in an industry as a major factor in determining a firm's behavior.
c. Contestable markets theory emphasizes product differentiation; orthodox market structure theory does not.
d. Contestable markets theory emphasizes nonprice competition; orthodox market structure theory does not.
e. a and b

Answer: _____

14. The prisoner's dilemma game illustrates that:

a. what is good for you and me individually may be bad for us collectively
b. what is good for me is good for you
c. cartels are likely to be stable in the long run
d. what is high is low and what is low is high
e. none of the above

Answer: _____

15. A monopolistic competitor has a demand curve that is:

a. flatter than a perfectly competitive firm
b. less flat than a perfectly competitive firm
c. steeper than a monopoly firm
d. b and c

Answer: _____

True-False

16. There is easy entry but costly exit in   T F
monopolistic competition.

17. In monopolistic competition, the marginal   T F
revenue curve lies below the demand curve.

18. In equilibrium a monopolistic competitor   T F
produces an output smaller than the one that
would minimize its costs of production.

19. Third-degree price discrimination is   T F
sometimes seen in the form of cents-off
coupons.

20. There are few sellers and few buyers in   T F
oligopoly.

Fill in the blank

21. The economist _____ found no evidence that the oligopolists he examined were more reluctant to match price increases than price cuts.

22. A _____ is an organization of firms that reduces output and increases price in an effort to increase joint profits.

23. Once a cartel agreement is made, there is an incentive for cartel members to _____ on the agreement.

24. The _____ states that a monopolistic competitor will, in equilibrium, produce an output smaller than the one at which average total costs (unit costs) are minimized.

25. The tactic of _____ is possible in a contestable market.

Part 5. Answers to Self Test

1. d 2. a 3. d 4. a 5. c 6. b 7. b 8. c 9. c 10. d
11. b 12. b 13. b 14. a 15. b
16. F 17. T 18. T 19. T 20. F
21. George Stigler 22. cartel 23. cheat
24. excess capacity theorem 25. hit-and-run

Part 6. Answers

Part 2 Review of Concepts
1. c   2. d   3. h   4. e   5. b   6. j   7. k   8. f   9. g   10. a   11. i

Part 3 Key Concepts
1. many, similar, low   2. will not   3. searcher, exceeds, elastic   4. less   5. more   6. MR, exceeds
7. discrimination   8. oligopoly, either similar or identical   9. concentration, largest 4   10. are, are,
more   11. substitute, reduce   12. elastic, inelastic.   13. fall, fall   14. slow   15. is, are not
16. leadership, dominant, is, does   17. cartel, reduce, increase, rise   18. cheat, more
19. oil (petroleum), 70s, 80s   20. cartel, 56-59, bids, did, were   21. permitted, fall
22. contestable, any number of firms   23. zero, equals   24. hit   25. entry, actual
26. does not, barges and trucking   27. is not (although that is one factor)   28. Robinson, Chamberlin

Part 4 Problems and Exercises

Part 4 Problems and Exercises

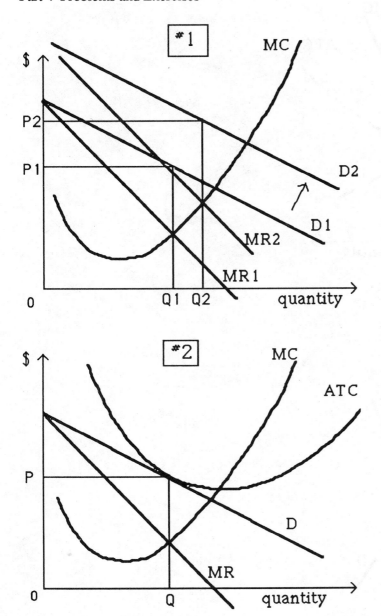

2. b. zero profit since P=ATC
c. will not

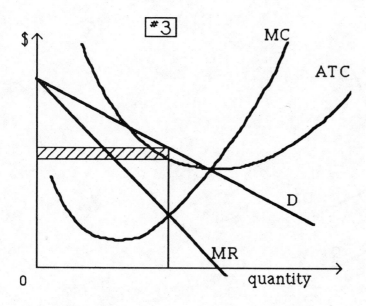

3. c. will

4. 63.2%

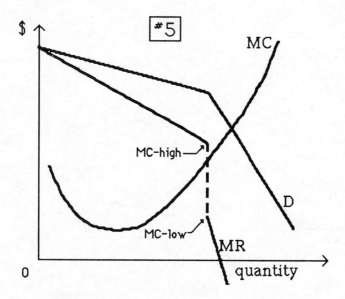

5. a. oligopoly
b-d See graph above.
e. kinked

Chapter 27
Factor Markets: With Emphasis on the Labor Market

Part 1. Introduction and Purpose
Consider the following points as you read chapter 27 in the text.

The past few chapters have examined one side of the firm's operations — the output side. To maximize profit a firm produces every unit of output for which marginal revenue exceeds marginal cost. There is a parallel decision on the other side of the firm's operations regarding the proper quantity and mix of inputs to hire. The general rule is that a firm will hire inputs whose **marginal revenue product** exceeds their **marginal factor cost**. Profit is maximized by hiring units up to the point where MRP = MFC.

There is more than a passing similarity between the MR = MC and MRP = MFC conditions for profit maximization. The two rules have to be **consistent** in the guidance they provide or they are not of much use. The production function states the relationship between inputs hired and the quantity of firm output, so if the MR = MC rule indicates that the firm must produce 1000 units of output to maximize profits, the MRP = MFC approach had better provide sufficient quantities of labor and other inputs to produce the desired 1000 units of output. The MRP = MFC approach will make those inputs available.

Technically, the marginal revenue product curve for labor is the labor demand curve, while the margainal factor cost is the wage rate. Hiring up to the point where MRP = MFC is equivalent to saying the firm should hire the number of units indicated by its demand curve, at the market wage rate.

Rightward **shifts** in the **demand curve** for labor or decreases in the wage rate will cause a profit maximizing firm to hire more workers (and vice versa). Because a changing demand for the seller's final product will affect the firm's demand for factors of production, factor demand is said to be a demand **derived** from the demand for final products.

You may recall that one issue discussed in the chapter on **production and costs** was the difference between short run and **long run** production decisions. We saw that to minimize production cost, in the long run the firm should acquire more or less of the "fixed" input until the firm was operating on the **lowest possible short-run ATC** curve. As you will see in this chapter, to achieve the lowest SR-ATC curve the employer will substitute among factors whenever the MPP÷P for one factor is greater than MPP÷P for others. In words, **MPP÷P** is the **extra output** generated for the firm by hiring **another dollar's worth of a factor**. When a dollar's worth of capital causes total output to rise by more than a dollar's worth of labor, it is appropriate to increase the firm's capital base (plant and equipment) and hire somewhat less labor. By making such **substitutions** the firm's total cost of producing a desired amount of output is minimized and profits are maximized.

The chapter's second major purpose is to examine the **overall market** for labor — total demand and supply rather than just demand and supply from the individual firm's perspective.

The **total demand** curve for labor is found by adding together the labor demand curves by all firms. The law of diminishing returns indicates that hiring more workers will cause MPP and therefore MRP to decline; so the firm's labor demand curve is downward sloping. Therefore the **total demand** for labor curve will be downward sloping as well. The **total supply** of labor curve is upward sloping, indicating that higher wages induce additional people to enter the labor market. In combination the total demand and supply curves determine the market wage rate. This is the wage that companies pay and workers receive when they are small enough to be considered "price takers" in the labor market.

Naturally all workers don't earn the same wage. **Wage differences** may arise in which some workers are paid more than the overall average and others are paid less. For example, wage differences **between different occupations** mainly arise of circumstances on the **supply side** of the labor market. Stress, risk, inclement weather, and other conditions can make certain occupations **less desirable** than others, which will cause workers to reduce the supply of labor to those occupations, which increases wage rates.

Wage differences can also arise **between different workers** when some workers are more productive than others.

Two additional topics remain in the chapter. One is an application of the supply and demand for labor model — showing what happens to wages if a **tax** is imposed on companies in proportion to the amount of labor they employ.

The other is the use of screening procedures in the labor market. While it is easy to discuss hiring the most productive inputs at the least possible cost, in practice it is difficult to know in advance of hiring someone whether they will be productive or not. **Screening** techniques are methods used to **select** the most productive workers at **lowest cost**. If experience shows that high IQs are closely related to career success, then it is cheaper to administer an IQ test than to hire job candidates and check out their performance on the job. In many instances a student's GPA is used as a screening device, as is the academic prestige of the school which the student attended.

Screening may be cost effective, but it may not appear to be "fair." Because almost everyone uses screening techniques at one time or another, it is somewhat arbitrary to say just when screening becomes unfair. Drawing that line is a political decision rather than an economic one.

Part 2.   Review of Concepts from Earlier Chapters
Prior to reading chapter 27, match statements at left with the appropriate concept at right.

___1. Land, labor, capital, entrepreneurship.

___2. A buyer or seller who cannot affect the market price.

___3. An organization that hires inputs and produces an output.

___4. The responsiveness of quantity demanded to price changes.

___5. Relationship between qty. of inputs hired and qty. of output.

___6. Change in total revenue from selling one more unit of output.

___7. Change in total output as one more unit of input is hired.

___8. Change in total cost from producing one more unit of output.

___9. The price of labor.

a. marginal revenue
b. elasticity of demand
c. wage
d. firm
e. inputs or factors
f. price taker
g. marginal cost
h. production function
i. MPP

Part 3. Key Concepts in this Chapter
After reading chapter 27 in the text, answer the following questions.

1. A firm that cannot affect the market price of the good it sells is a product price _taker / searcher_ . A firm that cannot affect the market price of the inputs it hires is a factor price _taker / searcher_. A firm that can affect the market price of the good it sells by producing more or less output is known as a product price _____.

2. The demand for factors _is is not_ derived from the demand for the goods the factors are used to produced. Factor demand is a _____ demand.

3. Marginal revenue product is defined as the additional _cost / revenue_ generated by employing another unit of a factor. Mathematically, MRP = Δ _____ ÷ Δ _____.

4. Marginal _revenue / factor_ cost is the additional cost associated with employing one additional unit of a _____ of production. Mathematically, MFC = Δ _____ ÷ Δ _____.

5. The firm will continue to hire more and more units of a factor if its (abbreviate): ___ ___ ___ exceeds ___ ___ ___. The firm will maximize profit by hiring that quantity of the input where ___ ___ ___ = ___ ___ ___.

6. A profit maximizing firm should not hire an input if its marginal _____ cost exceeds its marginal _____ product.

7. The _____ of marginal product for a factor equals its MPP multiplied by the selling price of the good being produced. The ___ ___ ___ curve and the ___ ___ ___ curve will be identical for a firm that is a product price taker.

8. The _most / least / least_ cost rule shows the combination of factors that permits the firm to produce any desired quantity of output at the least possible cost. The rule says that a firm should hire inputs until the ___ ___ ___ per dollar's worth of one input equals the ___ ___ ___ per dollar's worth of other inputs.

9. Assume a firm hires two factors, L and K. The MPP of L is 10 while the MPP of K is 35; the price of L is $3 and the price of K is $11. Under these circumstances the firm could produce the same amount of output at a lower total cost by hiring more of input _L / K_ and more of input _L / K_. One dollar's worth of L produces _____ units of output, while a dollar's worth of K produces _____ units of output.

10. True or false? _____ The market demand curve for labor is the horizontal summation of the demand curves of individual firms.

11. The _____ of demand for labor tells the percent change in the quantity of labor demanded when the wage rate changes by 1%. If a 12% wage increase causes companies to hire 18% fewer workers, the _____ coefficient equals _____.

12. The more substitutes that are available for labor, the _greater / lower_ the elasticity of demand for labor. The more elastic the demand for the good produced by labor, the _greater / lower_ will be the elasticity of demand for labor.

13. Non-_____ benefits are nonmonetary benefits associated with a particular job. Ceteris paribus, the more benefits of this type associated with an occupation, the _greater / less_ will be the supply of labor to that job and the _higher / lower_ will be the wage rate.

14. To hire a worker, an employer must offer that worker a combined wage plus _____ benefits that equal or exceed that worker's next-best _____ plus _____ benefit package.

15. Ceteris paribus, there will be a _greater / smaller_ supply of labor to jobs with more than average risk. That will cause the wage rate to _rise / fall_ in such jobs compared to the average wage.

16. Ceteris paribus, wages will be _higher / lower_ in cities that are more pleasant to live in, and _higher / lower_ in cities that are less pleasant to live in.

17. According to the text, in 1988 the combined employer-employee social security tax was _____% of wage and salary income up to $45,000. Officially, workers pay a _____% tax on earnings and employers pay a _____% tax on their labor costs. The text suggests that after market adjustments are complete most or all of the tax is actually paid by _workers / employers / taxpayers_.

18. The _average / marginal / total_ productivity theory of wages says that a factor will be paid an amount equal to the value of its contribution to the employer's total _costs / revenues_.

19. According to research on the subject, in the past 15-20 years baseball player salaries have moved _closer to / further from_ the value of player's marginal revenue products.

20. With a military draft a nation _does / does not_ pay military personnel a wage equal to their next-best alternative wage.

21. Employee _____ techniques are used to lower the cost of locating more productive workers. An example of screening devices include college _____'s.

22. The reason for using screening techniques is to lower the cost of _____ productive workers. This _is / is not_ the same thing as discriminating against workers because of their age, race, sex, or nationality.

Part 4. Problems and Exercises
After reading chapter 27 in the text you should be able to work the following problems.

1. Compute the marginal physical product (MPP) of labor in the table at right

   Assume that the firm's product sells for $2 per unit and compute the marginal revenue product (MRP) of labor.

	Units of Labor	Qty. of Output	MPP	MRP
a.	0	0	-	-
b.	1	12	_____	$_____
c.	2	21	_____	$_____
d.	3	27	_____	$_____
e.	4	30	_____	$_____

2. Use the grid to graph MRP values from the table in exercise 1.

Connect the points with a solid line and label the curve MRP.

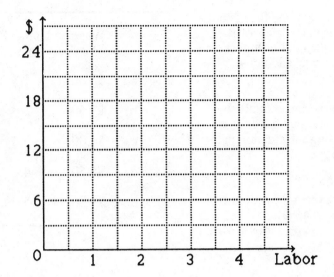

3. Refer to the previous two problems.

a. If the wage rate is $10, the company will employ _____ workers. (Hint: Draw a <u>horizontal line</u> in the graph in #2 to indicate the market wage.)

b. With the number of workers you have selected, the firm's total variable costs = $_____. The firm's total revenue = $_____.

c. If the firm's <u>fixed cost</u> equals $5, total cost = $ _____. The firm's profit equals $_____.

d. If the wage rises to $13 the firm will now employ _____ workers.

4. The table provides information on the MPP and price of two factors of production, L and K.   In each case (a-e) determine whether the profit maximizing firm will substitute toward L and away from K, toward K and away from L, or retain the current mix of factors.

Indicate the proper action to take by checking (√) the appropriate space at right.

	Factor of Production L		Factor of Production K		Substitute Toward		
	MPP	Price	MPP	Price	L	No Sub.	K
a.	15	$4	79	$22	___	___	___
b.	150	$21	50	$7	___	___	___
c.	4	$12	9	$20	___	___	___
d.	200	$25	60	$5	___	___	___
e.	2	$40	10	$200	___	___	___

5. In this problem, the firm is not a price taker in the labor market; instead, it must offer higher wages to attract additional workers.

Compute the firm's total labor cost and marginal factor cost (MFC) using information in the table at right.

f. For all except the first unit of labor, the wage rate is
 above / below labor's MFC.

	Wage Rate	Units of Labor	Total Labor Cost	Marginal Factor Cost (MFC)
a.	$3.00	1	$____	$____
b.	$3.50	2	$____	$____
c.	$4.00	3	$____	$____
d.	$4.50	4	$____	$____
e.	$5.00	5	$____	$____

6. Consider two occupations, A and B. Occupation A pays $30,000 and occupation B pays $40,000. Despite the difference in pay, at the margin workers consider the two occupations to be equally desirable overall.

a. This suggests that occupation A / B has $_____ worth of nonpecuniary benefits more than those in occupation A / B .

b. Assume nonpecuniary benefits remain unchanged from the first part of this problem. If the wage in occupation B is suddenly $15,000 higher than in A, which occupation will be more desirable to the marginal worker? A / B   Given this difference, workers will reduce the supply of labor to occupation A / B and will increase the supply to occupation A / B . The shift in the supply of labor will bring the monetary pay difference between the two occupations to $_____.

Part 5. Self Test
Multiple choice questions

1. A factor price taker is a firm that:

a. can buy all of a factor it wants at the equilibrium price
b. can sell all of a product it wants at the equilibrium price
c. must pay a higher price to buy an additional unit of a factor
d. must lower price to sell an addition unit of the good it produces

Answer: _____

2. A firm that is a price taker in a factor market faces:

a. an upward-sloping factor supply curve
b. a vertical factor supply curve
c. a downward-sloping factor supply curve
d. a horizontal factor supply curve

Answer: _____

3. The demand for factors is:

a. a derived demand
b. an extra demand
c. an indirect demand
d. a distinct demand
e. none of the above

Answer: _____

Exhibit C

Units of Factor X	Quantity of Output	Product Price	Marginal Revenue Product
0	10	$12	
1	20	12	A
2	29	12	B
3	36	12	C
4	41	12	D

4. In Exhibit C, the dollar amounts that go in blanks A-D are, respectively:

a. $120, $108, $84, $60
b. $100, $204, $30, $40
c. $190, $180, $70, $40
d. $105, $140, $40, $30

Answer: _____

5. Suppose a factor price searcher purchases one unit of factor X for $15. What would it purchase the second unit of factor X for, and what would marginal factor cost (MFC) equal?

a. It would purchase the second unit for $15, and MFC equals $15.
b. There is not enough information to know what it would purchase the second unit for, and thus we do not know what MFC equals.
c. It would purchase the second unit for $15, but there is not enough information to know what MFC equals.
d. There is not enough information to know what it would purchase the second unit for, but MFC equals $15.
e. none of the above

Answer: _____

6. The marginal factor cost (MFC) curve is:

a. vertical for a factor price taker
b. horizontal for a factor price taker
c. horizontal for a factor price searcher
d. upward-sloping for a factor price searcher
e. b and d

Answer: _____

7. For a product price searcher:

a. VMP = MRP
b. VMP < MRP
c. VMP > MRP
e. there is not enough information to answer the question

Answer: _____

8. For a price taker in both the product and factor markets, at the profit-maximizing factor quantity:

a. VMP = MRP > MFC = factor price
b. VMP < MRP = MFC = factor price
c. VMP > MRP = MFC = factor price
d. VMP = MRP = MFC = factor price

Answer: _____

9. The wage rate increases 30 percent and the quantity demanded of labor falls by 90 percent. The elasticity of demand for labor is:

a. 1.33
b. 2.40
c. 1.50
d. 3.00
e. none of the above

Answer: _____

10. The lower the elasticity of demand for a product:

a. the higher the ratio of labor costs to total costs
b. the lower the ratio of labor costs to total costs
c. the lower the elasticity of demand for the labor that produces the product
d. the higher the elasticity of demand for the labor that produces the product
e. none of the above

Answer: _____

11. A rise in the wage rate:

a. shifts the supply curve of labor rightward
b. increases the quantity supplied of labor
c. shifts the supply curve of labor leftward
d. decreases the quantity supplied of labor

Answer: _____

12. Employees will end up paying the full Social Security tax:

a. if the aggregate supply curve of labor is perfectly elastic
b. if the aggregate supply curve of labor is unit elastic
c. if the aggregate supply curve of labor is perfectly inelastic
d. if the aggregate supply curve of labor is downward-sloping

Answer: _____

13. Marginal factor cost is:

a. the additional cost incurred by employing an additional factor unit
b. the additional revenue generated by employing an additional factor unit
c. always equal to marginal revenue product
d. constant in the long run
e. a and d

Answer: _____

14. The marginal revenue product (MRP) curve is the firm's:

a. marginal output curve
b. factor supply curve
c. average revenue curve
d. factor demand curve

Answer: _____

15. The more substitutes there are for labor:

a. the more sensitive buyers of labor will be to a change in the price of labor
b. the less sensitive buyers of labor will be to a change in the price of labor
c. the faster costs will rise in the short run
d. the greater marginal revenue will be in the long run
e. none of the above

Answer: _____

True-False

16. The firm minimizes costs by buying factors in   T F
the combination at which the MPP-price ratio for
each factor is the same. (price = factor price)

17. Marginal productivity theory states that firms   T F
in competitive or perfect product and factor markets
pay factors their marginal revenue products.

18. A factor price taker faces a horizontal supply   T F
curve of factors.

19. A firm can be a product price taker and a   T F
factor price searcher, but it cannot be a product
price searcher and factor price taker.

20. If the demand curve for the product that labor   T F
produces shifts rightward, the demand curve for
labor shifts leftward.

Fill in the blank

21. _____ = P x MPP.

22. The process used by employers to increase the probability of choosing "good" employees based on
certain criteria is called _____ .

23. The elasticity of demand for labor is defined as the percentage change in the _____ divided by the percentage change in the _____ .

24. The firm buys and employs the factor quantity at which (the condition) _____ holds.

25. The demand for labor is _____ .

Part 5. Answers to Self Test

1. a 2. d 3. a 4. a 5. b 6. e 7. c 8. d 9. d 10. c
11. b 12. c 13. a 14. d 15. a
16. T 17. T 18. T 19. F 20. F
21. value marginal product (VMP) 22. screening
23. quantity demanded of labor, wage rate 24. MRP = MFC
25. derived

Part 6. Answers

Part 2 Review of Concepts
1. e   2. f   3. d   4. b   5. h   6. a   7. i   8. g   9. c

Part 3 Key Concepts

1. taker, taker, searcher   2. is, derived   3. revenue, $\Delta TR \div \Delta$Factor quantity
4. factor, $\Delta TC \div \Delta$Factor quantity   5. MRP, MFC, MRP=MFC   6. factor, revenue
7. value, VMP, MRP   8. least, MPP, MPP   9. more L and less K, 3.33, 3.18   10. false
11. elasticity, elasticity, 1.5   12. greater, greater   13. Nonpecuniary, greater, lower
14. nonmonetary, wage, nonmonetary   15. smaller, rise   16. lower, higher
17. 15.02, 7.51%, 7.51%, workers   18. marginal, revenues   19. closer to   20. does not
21. screening, GPA's   22. hiring, is not

Part 4 Problems and Exercises
1. b. 12, $24   c. 9, $18   d. 6, $12   e. 3, $6
2. see graph at right

3. a. 3
   b. $30, $54
   c. $35, $19
   d. 2

4. toward L: a
   toward K: c, d
   no substitution: b, e

5. a. $3, $3
   b. $7, $4
   c. $12, $5
   d. $18, $6
   e. $25, $7
   f. above

6. a. A, $10,000, B
   b. B, A, B, $10,000

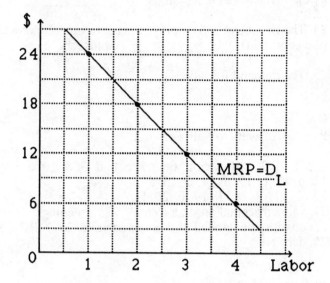

Chapter 28
Wages, Unions, and Labor

Part 1. Introduction and Purpose
Consider the following points as you read chapter 28 in the text.

The supply and demand model of labor markets discussed in previous chapter assumed that labor markets were perfectly competitive — that each buyer and seller of labor services is a price taker that is unable to influence the market wage rate. The present chapter examines the consequences of **dropping the assumption that everyone in the labor market is a price taker**.

For example, workers may gain some monopoly power in the labor market by banding together and forming a **union**. A union is something like a cartel for labor suppliers. Alternatively, an employer may be the only purchaser of labor services in a particular labor market, and insist that workers accept a lower wage if they want to work. A single buyer is known as a **monopsonist** (mo-nop-son-ist). A successful cartel on the supply side of the market will raise the wage rate above that indicated by the supply and demand model in the previous chapter; a successful monopsonist will lower the wage below that benchmark. The first part of the chapter examines unions, while the second part looks at the behavior of monopsonists. The first part of the chapter examines unions, and is followed by a discussion of monopsonists.

Unions are employee organizations that **bargain** on the behalf of workers for **higher wages** and improved working conditions. Although there are different **types of unions** (craft, industrial, public employee) the same model is used to analyze the impact of each one. Stripped to its essentials, we see that unions can increase wages by **restricting the supply of labor** to a firm or industry. This is reinforced when a union withholds (or threatens to withhold) the labor of union members by calling a **strike**. Less direct but more effective in the long run are laws and regulations which a union may be able to convince officials to impose which would limit the entry of new workers into the industry. Occupational licensing is often used for this purpose.

In the event a union isn't able to restrict the supply of labor in its particular market, it will probably have difficulty raising wages above the economy-wide average. With the free movement of labor, any increase in the wage rate in a particular occupation or at a given workplace will attract supplies of labor from the remainder of the economy, which would reduce the wage rate to the average level.

If a union can restrict the flow of labor into an industry and exercise some degree of monopoly power in the labor market, there is still the matter of deciding which **goals** to promote with that power. The text mentions that unions may try to obtain **employment** for all union members, or they may try to maximize the **total earnings** of all union members, or they may try to maximize the total earnings of some segment of the union membership. Since these goals may conflict, it is impossible to predict the specific wage-employment outcome until more is known about the objective chosen in a particular instance.

In addition to achieving their goals by restricting the supply of labor, unions may also improve their bargaining power if they can **increase the demand** for the services of union members. The union may help train members to make them more productive, or it may attempt to get legislation passed that will restrict the supply or increase the wages of non-union labor, or it may help promote sales of products produced by union labor. In practice, unions do all of these things.

On the demand side of the market, a **monopsonist** (or an oligopsonist) may exercise a degree of monopoly power as an employer. That is significant in the present model because it means the employer will have to offer **higher wages to hire more workers**. If all workers are paid the same wage rate, then hiring a new worker at a higher wage rate increases total cost by the amount of the new worker's pay *plus* pay increases to existing employees who expect to earn as much as the new worker.

For example, suppose an employer has 10 employees who each earn $4 an hour. If the company has to raise its wage to $4.05 to hire the 11th employee, the firm's total costs rise by the $4.05 paid to the new worker plus an extra 5¢ each for the other 10 workers (50¢ in all), or a total of $4.55. In technical terms, **marginal factor cost** ($4.55) **is higher than the wage rate** ($4.05) for a monopsonist.

Recall that firms maximize profits by hiring workers up to the point where MRP = MFC. Since we just saw that MFC > wage, then it follows that **MRP > wage** for a monopsonist employer. This means workers are paid less than their dollar contribution to the employer's total revenues. If you think workers are happy when that happens, you are mistaken.

To summarize, this chapter is essentially a refinement of the supply and demand model presented in the last chapter. The part of the chapter about labor unions examines the influence of monopoly power on the supply side of labor markets; the discussion of monopsonists looks at monopoly power on the demand side of the market. Ceteris paribus, market power helps workers or employers increase their own income at the expense of the other.

Part 2.   Review of Concepts from Earlier Chapters
Prior to reading chapter 28, match statements at left with the appropriate concept at right.

___1. The additional output that results when one more worker is hired.
___2. The additional revenue associated with hiring one more worker.
___3. The additional cost associated with hiring one more worker.
___4. Their intersection determines equilibrium price.
___5. A legislated wage.
___6. Responsiveness of quantity demanded to a change in price.
___7. If price changes by a larger percent than quantity demanded.
___8. Demand for factors is linked to the demand for final goods.
___9. The wage rate times the quantity of workers employed.

a. minimum wage
b. inelastic demand
c. elasticity of demand
d. marginal revenue product
e. marginal factor cost
f. total labor costs
g. derived demand
h. supply and demand
i. marginal physical product

Part 3. Key Concepts in this Chapter
After reading chapter 28 in the text, answer the following questions.

1. There are many different types of labor unions. For example a labor / craft / industrial union is made up of workers who all practice the same type of work -- such as plumbers or electricians. An labor / craft / industrial union represents all of the workers or a company or industry, regardless of their particular craft. A _____ employee union is comprised of government workers.

2. An _____ association is an organization whose members belong to a particular profession.

3. Union membership has risen / fallen as a percent of the labor force in the past decade. Union membership reached its peak in the decade of the 19____s.

4. According to the table on union membership in the text (exhibit 1), the unions that have experienced membership increases from 1975 to 1987 were (use their abbreviations): _____, _____, and _____. These are / are not unions made up of government workers.

5. The _____ of Labor was the first major labor union in the U.S. The union was organized in 18____ and collapsed in 19____.

6. In the early 1900s, the Sherman Act made it easy / difficult for unions to strike or picket their employers.

7. The American _____ of Labor was formed in 18____ and its first leader was _____ _____. This union was a craft / an industrial union. The union concentrated on economic / political issues, seeking to end / work within the capitalist economy.

8. The _____ Act of 1935 required employers to bargain in good faith with workers, including unions selected by workers. The act also set up the _____ Labor _____ Board to investigate unfair labor practices.

9. The _____ of _____ Organization was an industrial union begun by John L. _____ in 19____. In 1955 the union merged with the ___ ___ ___ union to form the ___ ___ ___ - ___ ___ ___.

10. The _____ - Hartley act gave states the right to pass right to work laws. It also gave the president the right to issue an _____ to halt strikes that could seriously disrupt the national economy.

11. The _____ - _____ Act was designed to police the internal affairs of labor unions. Ex- _____ and _____ were prohibited from holding high union offices.

12. In 1981 President Reagan ordered the Federal Aviation Administration to fire striking members of the ___ ___ ___ ___ ___ union, whose strike was / was not illegal.

13. The text mentioned that union leaders may want to ensure employment for all members; second, they may want to maximize total _____ earned by union members; or third, they may wish to maximize _____ for a limited number of union members. In general it _is / is not_ possible to pursue all of these goals simultaneously.

14. Ceteris paribus, a higher wage rate means that _more / fewer_ workers will be employed. A 1% rise in wages will cause total worker income to rise if the quantity of workers hired falls by less than ___%. In this case the demand for labor is _elastic / inelastic_.

15. Consider two situations. In one, the demand for labor is elastic; in the other, it is inelastic. In which situation will union leaders be more likely to bargain for higher wages? _elastic / inelastic_

16. When the wage rate falls by 4% the number of workers hired rises by 6%. In this instance the elasticity of demand for labor is _____.

17. The demand for labor will be more elastic the _more / fewer_ substitutes there are for that labor. Other things being equal, the more elastic the demand for a particular output (good X), the _more / less_ elastic will be the demand for the labor that produced the good.

18. Union leaders _would / would not_ like to reduce the elasticity of demand for labor. (Hint: see your answer to #15 above.) Because the elasticity of demand for unionized labor is lower if there are _more / fewer_ substitutes for that labor, union leaders will tend to _support / oppose_ immigration by foreigners into the U.S.

19. If the wage rate rises for non-union workers, the demand for union labor will _increase / decrease_. That is because union and non-union labor are _substitutes / complements_ in the labor market. A higher minimum wage rate will _increase / decrease_ the demand for non-union labor.

20. A _closed / open / union_ shop is one in which workers must join a union before going to work in that shop. A _closed / open / union_ shop in one in which workers must join a union after going to work. A _closed / union_ shop is legal in many states while a _closed / open / union_ shop is illegal throughout the U.S.

21. Unions _do / do not_ like states to adopt right to work laws. Those laws make _____ shops illegal.

22. When union representatives bargain with employers over wages and working conditions on the behalf of their members, the process is called _____ bargaining. In the event no agreement is reached, union members may refuse to work, which means they would go out on _____.

23. A _____ is a buyer's monopoly. An example of this would occur if there were only one _employer / employee_ in a town.

24. A monopsonist _can / cannot_ hire more workers at a constant wage rate.

25. If a firm has to raise the wage it pays from $5 to $5.10 to hire the 40th worker, the firm's total labor bill rises by the amount paid to the 40th worker, $_____, plus a wage increase of ____¢ apiece to the previous _____ workers, or $_____. In total, the additional cost of hiring the 40th worker is $_____. The firm's marginal factor cost (MFC) _equals / exceeds / is below_ the wage rate paid to workers by $_____.

26. The additional revenue associated with hiring one more worker is called _____ _____ _____ (or ___ ___ ___); the additional cost associated with hiring one more worker is called _____ _____ _____ (or ___ ___ ___). When the employer is in equilibrium, ___ ___ ___ will equal ___ ___ ___.

27. A firm maximizes profit by hiring the quantity of labor where MRP=MFC, but if the firm is a monopsonist then MFC is _above / below_ the wage rate. Consequently when the monopsonist firm is maximizing profit its workers earn a wage rate that is _above / below / equal to_ their MRP.

28. Researchers find that the average wage of union members is _above / below_ the average wage of non-union workers by about ____ - ____%

29. As unions successfully bargain for higher wages, the number of jobs in that line of employment _increases / declines_. As a consequence the supply of labor to non-union jobs _increases / decreases_, which causes the wage of non-union workers to _rise / fall_.

30. True or false? a)_____ In the long run, higher wages for unionized workers will come out of employer profits. b) _____ In the long run, higher wages for unionized workers will increase product prices by a comparable amount.

31. The traditional view is that unions promote _efficiency / inefficiency_. A newer view is that unions may also promote _efficiency / inefficiency_.

Part 4. Problems and Exercises
After reading chapter 28 in the text you should be able to work the following problems.

1. In this problem, assume that labor is the only variable input for a firm that produces a product which it sells for $2 per unit. Use information in the following table to complete missing values.

	Units of Labor	Qty. of Output	MRP	Wage Rate	Total Labor Costs	MFC
a.	0	0	-	$6.00	$0.00	-
b.	1	12	$____	$6.50	$____	$____
c.	2	21	$____	$7.00	$____	$____
d.	3	27	$____	$7.50	$____	$____
e.	4	30	$____	$8.00	$____	$____

f. How many units of labor will the profit maximizing employer hire? _____ units

g. Total revenue for this firm will equal $_____; total labor costs will equal $_____.

h. If the firm's _fixed_ costs equal $20 per period, the firm will earn a _profit / loss_ of $_____.

2. Use information from the table in
   exercise 1 to complete this question.

   a. Plot the wage rate paid to attract the
   number of workers in the left-hand
   column of the table. Connect the points
   with a solid line and label the curve S.

   b. Graph the firm's MFC curve in the
   same grid. Connect the points with a
   solid line and label the curve MFC.

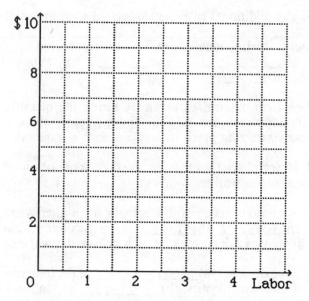

3. In this problem your firm hires only one variable input, labor, and sells its output for $2 per unit. Later
   the price of the product rises to $3. Assume also that your firm is a monopsonist and has to pay higher
   wages to attract more workers. Complete missing values in the table.

	Units of Labor	MPP	Price=$2 MRP-1	Price=$3 MRP-2	Wage Rate	Total Labor Costs	MFC
a.	0	0	-	-	$20.00	$0.00	--
b.	1	20	$40.00	$60.00	$25.00	$_____	$_____
c.	2	18	$_____	$_____	$30.00	$_____	$_____
d.	3	16	$_____	$_____	$35.00	$_____	$_____
e.	4	14	$_____	$_____	$40.00	$_____	$_____

4. Use the grid at right to graph the two separate MRP curves from the table above, and to graph MFC for your firm.

a. You can see in the diagram that when your product's price is $2 per unit, your firm maximizes profits by hiring _____ units of labor. To hire this many workers a wage of $_____ is required.

b. When price is $3 per unit, your firm hires _____ units of labor. To hire this many workers a wage of $_____ is required.

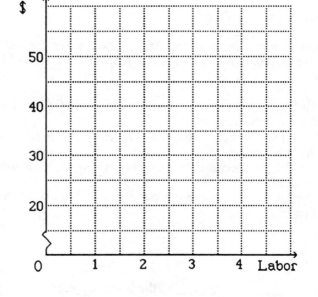

5. The figures below show the annual number of work stopages (strikes) in the U.S. during 1978-86.

a. Graph these figures in the grid at right and connect the data points with a solid line.

Year	Strikes
1978	219
1979	235
1980	187
1981	145
1982	96
1983	81
1984	62
1985	54
1986	69

b. Some people feel that President Reagan's decision to fire illegal PATCO strikers in 1981 made union leaders and members less bold and less willing to strike. Does your chart tend to support this view? _yes / no_

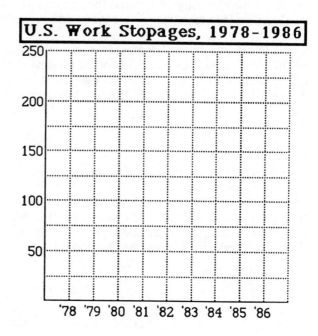

U.S. Work Stopages, 1978-1986

'78 '79 '80 '81 '82 '83 '84 '85 '86

Part 5. Self Test
Multiple choice questions

1. Labor Union A faces an inelastic demand curve for its labor. Labor Union B faces an elastic demand curve for its labor. Which of the two labor unions is less likely to push for higher wages, ceteris paribus, and why?

a. Labor Union A because for A it is more costly (in terms of union memberslosing jobs) than it is for B to push for higher wages.
b. Labor Union B because for B it is more costly (in terms of union members losing jobs) than it is for A to push for higher wages.
c. Labor Union A because the members of it work in the manufacturing sector of the economy and not the service sector.
d. Labor Union B because the members of it work in the service sector of the economy and not the manufacturing sector.

Answer: _____

2. _____, the lower the elasticity of demand for the product, which in turn means the lower the elasticity of demand for union labor, which means the union will have a smaller cutback in employment for higher wages (the wage-employment tradeoff is less pronounced).

a. The fewer substitutes that exist for the product the labor union produces
b. The more substitutes that exist for the product the labor union produces
c. The more workers in the labor union
d. The higher the profits of the firm the labor union works for

Answer: _____

3. Unions may be interested in increasing the productivity of their members because:

a. as their productivity rises, the demand for their labor falls, and their wages rise
b. as their productivity rises, the supply of their labor falls, and their wages rise
c. as their productivity rises, the supply of their labor rises, and their wages rise
d. as their productivity rises, the demand for their labor rises, and their wages rise

Answer: _____

4. The _____ Act prohibited the closed shop.

a. Norris-LaGuardia
b. Taft-Hartley
c. Wagner
d. Reagan
e. none of the above

Answer: _____

5. Which of the following comes closest to being a monopsony?

a. a computer company in California
b. a Burger King in a big city
c. a farmer who hires labor
d. a firm in a small town and there are no other firms for miles around
e. a and b are equally monopsonistic

Answer: _____

6. Which of the following statements is false?

a. A monopsony cannot buy additional units of a factor without increasing the price it pays for the factor.
b. A monopsony can buy additional units of a factor without increasing the price it pays for the factor.
c. The supply curve a monopsony faces is the industry supply of a factor.
d. a and c

Answer: _____

7. During the time labor unions have been in existence:

a. there has been almost no change in the fraction of national income that goes to labor
b. the fraction of national income that goes to labor has decreased
c. the fraction of national income that goes to labor has increased
d. the fraction of national income that goes to rent has increased

Answer: _____

8. In a perfectly competitive industry, do higher wages for labor union members diminish profits?

a. No, higher wage costs can only affect profits if they affect labor morale and this doesn't happen.
b. Yes, in the long run, but not in the short run, since in the short-run profits are (close to being) fixed.
c. Yes, in the short run, but not in the long run, since in the long run some firms will exit the industry because of higher costs and losses and price will rise, reestablishing zero economic profit.
d. No, because higher labor costs usually bring more firms into the industry and this effect dampens price hikes.

Answer: _____

9. The traditional or orthodox view of labor unions holds that they do not:

a. negatively impact productivitiy and efficiency
b. positively impact productivity and efficiency
c. drive an artificial wedge between the wages of comparable labor in the union and nonunion sectors of the labor market
d. a and c
e. b and c

Answer: _____

10. Which of the following is consistent with the new view of labor unions as collective voice?

a. job exiting is increased
b. workers feel less secure in their jobs
c. the turnover rate is increased
d. labor productivity declines
e. none of the above

Answer: _____

11. Which of the following is an example of an employee association?

a. the American Medical Association
b. the International Brotherhood of the Teamsters
c. the Letters Carriers union
d. a and b
e. none of the above

Answer: _____

12. The act that says "every person who shall monopolize, or attempt to monopolize, or combine or conspire with any other person or persons, to monopolize any part of the trade or commerce among the several States, or with foreign nations, shall be deemed guilty of a misdemeanor," is the:

a. McCormick Harvester Act
b. Wagner Act
c. Sherman Antitrust Act
d. Norris-LaGuardia Act
e. none of the above

Answer: _____

13. Which of the following does not directly affect the demand for or quantity demanded of labor?

a. increasing the marginal physical product of labor
b. rising factor prices for labor
c. increasing demand for the product that labor produces
d. a strike

Answer: _____

14. The decline in union membership as a percentage of the total labor force in recent years would have been greater had it not been for the growth in _____ .

a. teamster union membership
b. public employee union membership
c. garment workers membership
d. postal worker membership

Answer: _____

15. In 1988, approximately _____ million workers in the United States belonged to labor unions.

a. 30
b. 24
c. 10
d. 80

Answer: _____

True-False

16. Slightly less than one out of every five   T F
workers in the United States in 1988 was a union
member.

17. The American Federation of Labor was formed   T F
in 1886 under the leadership of Taft Hartley.

18. The Landrum-Griffin act was passed with the   T F
expressed intent of policing the internal affairs
of labor unions.

19. There is evidence that labor unions generally   T F
have the effect of increasing their members' wages
and lowering the wage rates of nonunion labor.

20. Some economists contend that employee   T F
associations are a type of labor union.

Fill in the blank

21. Laws that make it illegal to require union membership for purposes of employment are called _____ .

22. A single buyer in a factor market is a called a _____ .

23. The total wage bill is maximized at that point where the demand for labor is _____ .

24. A _____ occurs when unionized employees refuse to work at a certain wage or under certain conditions.

25. The monopsonist buys the factor quantity at which (the condition) _____ holds.

Part 5. Answers to Self Test

1. b 2. a 3. d 4. b 5. d 6. b 7. a 8. c 9. b 10. e
11. a 12. c 13. d 14. b 15. b
16. T 17. F 18. T 19. T 20. T
21. right-to-work laws 22. monopsony 23. unit elastic
24. strike 25. MRP = MFC

Part 6.   Answers

Part 2 Review of Concepts
1. i   2. d   3. e   4. h   5. a   6. c   7. b   8. g   9. f

Part 3 Key Concepts
1. craft, industrial, government   2. employee   3. fallen, 50s   4. NALC, AFSCME, AFT, are
5. Knights, 1868, 1917   6. difficult   7. Federation, 1886, Samuel Gompers, craft, economic, work within
8. Wagner, National, Relations   9. Congress of Industrial Organization, Lewis, 1938, AFL, AFL-CIO
10. Taft-, injunction   11. Landrum-Griffin, convicts and communists   12. PATCO, was
13. wages, income, is not   14. fewer, <1%, inelastic   15. inelastic   16. 1.5   17. more, more
18. would, fewer, oppose   19. increase, substitutes, increase   20. closed, union, union, closed
21. do not, union   22. collective, strike   23. monopsony, employer   24. cannot
25. $5.10, 10¢, 39, $3.90, $9, exceeds, $3.90
26. marginal revenue product, MRP, marginal factor cost, MFC, MRP, MFC   27. above, below
28. above, 10-15%   29. declines, increases, fall   30. a. False b. True   31. inefficiency, efficiency

Part 4 Problems and Exercises

1. b. $24, $6.50, $6.50
   c. $18, $14, $7.50
   d. $12, $22.50, $8.50
   e. $6, $32, $9.50
   f. 3 (MFC > MRP for unit #4)
   g. $54, $22.50
   h. $11.50

3. b. $25, $25
   c. $36, $54, $60, $35
   d. $32, $48, $105, $45
   e. $28, $42, $160, $55

4. a. 2   b. 3

5. a. See chart below right
   b. yes

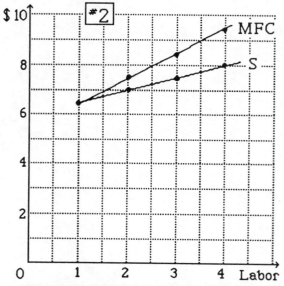

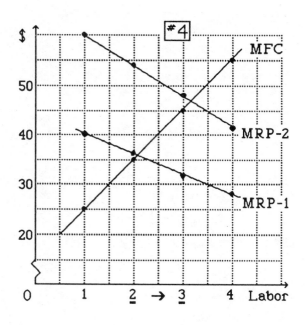

#5

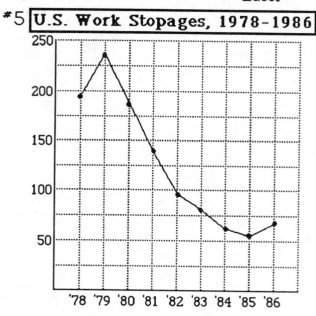

U.S. Wool Shortage, 1976-1990

Chapter 29
Interest, Rent, and Profit

Part 1. Introduction and Purpose
Consider the following points as you read chapter 29 in the text.

As the title suggests, this chapter looks at the market for the non-labor factors of production. Many of the ideas discussed in the "Factor Markets" chapter also apply to the non-labor factors. Consequently the present chapter spends less time presenting extensive supply and demand models and more time discussing some of the **special features** of each factor that make it different from the others.

In general, all factor returns are determined by the interaction of **supply and demand**. The supply and demand for **loanable funds** determines the price of credit — or the **interest rate**. Because some people have a particularly urgent desire to spend dollars now rather than wait until later, they are willing pay for the use of someone else's funds. The interest rate reflects borrower's **time preference** for present over future dollars. It also reflects the time preference of the people who lend. In equilibrium, the rate of time preference for borrowers equals the interest rate, which equals the rate of time preference for lenders.

One important group of borrowers are the businesses that borrow funds to finance investments in capital goods. As long as the rate of return on capital exceeds the interest rate, companies borrow and invest more in productive facilities. Capital goods are subject to diminishing returns, so eventually the rate of return on capital declines until it is no higher than the interest rate. In equilibrium, the interest rate equals the gross rate of return on capital goods.

In practice there are many **different interest rates** rather than one because the terms and conditions of loans can differ. More risky loans are less desirable, and cause lenders to insist on a premium above the normal interest rate, or else they lend their funds only to borrowers with good credit ratings. In the end, more risky borrowers have to pay a higher interest rate than less risky borrowers.

The interest rate quoted daily in the newspaper is the **nominal interest rate**. The nominal interest rate has two components — a **real interest rate** that would exist in a non-inflationary environment and an inflation premium equal to the **anticipated rate of inflation** over the life of the loan. Higher inflation rates typically cause interest rates to rise because lenders demand a larger inflation premium and borrowers agree to pay it.

The second factor income examined in this chapter is **rent**. Technically, rent is the return to land (natural resources). Because nature provided land, those who receive rents are sometimes said to "reap what they did not sow." Rent for the land's use is determined by the intersection of supply and demand. However the supply of natural resources is determined by nature rather than man, so the supply curve is a vertical line. Since the owner of natural resources has no costs, his entire income is **rent**.

Generalizing the use of the term rent, we can apply it to the income of any resource owner who receives more than their opportunity costs. For example if Phred's labor has a market value of $6 but someone hires him for $15, then Phred is receiving **economic rents** valued at $9 an hour. Other factor owners will attempt to move into the market and compete for such rents.

The problem arises if some **artificial barrier** prevents others from entering the market. For example, if government regulations permit others from entering Phred's line of work, then outsiders hopeful of entering the industry will use resources to try and change the existing regulation or find a way of getting around it. Lawyers may be hired, bribes may be paid, letters may be written, and other **rent seeking** activities will be undertaken. Your text explains why this represents an **inefficient** use of resources.

Finally **profits** are the return to entrepreneurs who spot profitable exchange opportunities, organize production, cope with uncertainty, and bring new products and methods to market. Profits are the return to the entrepreneur's **superior ability to move goods and resources from lower- to higher-valued uses**. Although the entrepreneur does not intend it to happen, his profits also signal other resource owners to move resources into the same (profitable) market. The economy grows larger as resources move into more valuable uses.

Part 2. Review of Concepts from Earlier Chapters
Prior to reading chapter 29, match statements at left with the appropriate concept at right.

__1. Land, labor, capital, entrepreneurial skills.	a. stock
__2. Marginal revenue product curve.	b. opportunity cost
__3. What must be foregone when taking an action.	c. profit
__4. Total revenue minus total cost.	d. demand curve for factor
__5. A security that promises to repay debt with interest.	e. zero economic profit
__6. A security that represents ownership of a firm.	f. profit maximization
__7. Value of expected future profits included in stock price.	g. factors
__8. The goal of firm owners.	h. bond
__9. Accounting profit minus implicit cost.	i. capitalization
__10. Additional output from one more unit of input.	j. marginal physical product

Part 3. Key Concepts in this Chapter
After reading chapter 29 in the text, answer the following questions.

1. Those who supply loanable funds require borrowers to pay _____. The _____ _____ is a ratio of the amount of annual interest to the principal amount of a loan.

2. Those who demand loanable funds are borrowers / lenders . Those who supply loanable funds are borrowers / lenders .

3. The primary supply of loanable funds is consumption / saving by households.

4. The quantity supplied of loanable funds _increases / decreases_ when interest rates rise. The supply curve of loanable funds _does / does not_ shift when the interest rate changes.

5. If the expected rate of inflation rises, the demand curve for loanable funds shifts to the _right / left_ and the supply for loanable funds curve shifts to the _right / left_. Together, these cause the equilibrium interest rate to _rise / fall_.

6. Many companies find it necessary to borrow funds so that they can invest in _consumption / capital_ goods. The latter permit the firm to engage in more _intensive / roundabout_ methods of production.

7. In equilibrium, the interest rate equals the rate of _____ on capital investments and the rate of time _____ felt by savers.

8. Some loans will have higher interest rates than others because they subject lenders to _more / less_ credit risk, or they are _long / short_ -term loans, or they have higher processing _____.

9. The inflation-adjusted interest rate is the _nominal / real_ rate of interest. The ordinary unadjusted interest rate is the _nominal / real_ interest rate. The interest rate banks quote to borrowers is the _nominal / real_ rate.

10. If the nominal interest rate is 9% and the expected rate of inflation over the life of the loan is 5%, then the real rate of interest equals ____%.

11. When computing the present value of dollars to be received on a future date, divide the future dollar amount by one plus the _____ rate, raised to the power of **n**, where **n** is the number of _____ in the future when the dollars will be received.

12. Use the present value formula to compute today's value of $100 to be received 2 years from now, if your rate of time preference is 8% (=0.08) per year. PV = $_____

13. Economic rent is a payment in excess of _____ _____. When the supply of a factor is perfectly inelastic, _part / all_ of the factor's income is economic rent.

14. The economist David Racardo _did / did not_ believe that economic rents on farmland caused the price of food to increase. Ricardo _did / did not_ believe that high food prices caused land rents to increase.

15. Land rents are determined by the intersection of the _____ and _____ for land.

16. Suppose a worker earns $6 an hour but her next best opportunity would pay $4 an hour. Then this worker earns economic rent of $____ an hour.

17. Government regulations _can / cannot_ create economic rents. When firms or individuals compete for these rents, the resources they use _are / are not_ socially productive.

18. The profits in newspaper headlines are _accounting / economic / nonpecuniary_ profits.

19. Suppose that owners invest $1000 in a business rather than leaving the money in a bank account that pays a 5% interest rate. Foregone interest income equals $_____ in this case. If the company's accounting profit equals $80 and the firm has no other implicit costs, the firm is earning an economic profit of $_____. The tendency will be for firms to _enter / exit_ the industry that this business is in.

20. _Risk / Uncertainty_ exists when a situation is unpredictable and a probability of success or failure cannot be established. Profits _can / cannot_ be earned in this environment.

21. If you can buy apples from one store for 10¢ apiece and sell them to another store for 15¢, then you are engaging in _____.

22. Those who devise new products, production processes, or marketing techniques are engaged in _innovation / research_ . This _is / is not_ one of the principle tasks of the entrepreneur.

23. A profit is a _reward / signal_ to factor owners that they should move resources from their current uses to other ones.

Part 4. Problems and Exercises
After reading chapter 29 in the text you should be able to work the following problems.

1. The table at right provides information on the nominal interest rate (i), the real interest rate (r), and the expected rate of inflation (π). Fill in the table's missing values.

	i	π	r
a.	4%	___%	3%
b.	8%	3%	___%
c.	___%	5%	2%
d.	3%	0%	___%
e.	___%	11%	3%
f.	18%	___%	5%

2. The graph at right shows the supply and demand for loanable funds.

   a. Suppose a new tax law is adopted that increases the after-tax return on saving.

   Draw a new supply curve to show how the tax law affects the loanable funds market. Label the new curve S2 and label the new interest rate i_2.

   b. The new interest rate (i_2) is _greater / less_ than i_1.

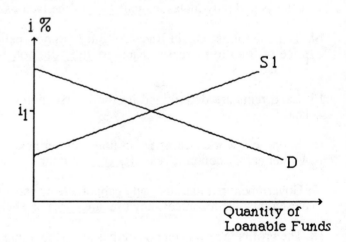

3. Suppose that new technologies reduce the cost of producing electrical motors and lower the cost of electricity. As a result the rate of return on a broad range of capital investments that use electricity will _rise / fall_ . This will cause the demand curve for loanable funds to shift _right / left_ . Other things being equal, this will cause interest rates to _rise / fall_ .

4. Living on your own Caribbean island, you can catch 10 fish per day with a simple fishing pole, and you require this number of fish each day to remain alive. With a fishing net you could catch 20 fish per day, but it will take you four weeks (50 days) to make a net and during that time you wouldn't be catching any fish at all. The net will wear out after 11 months' use, and is made of hemp and other natural materials available on your island.

a. With a pole your annual (365-day) production is _____ fish;

b. After working for 50 days on a net, you would be able to catch _____ fish during the remaining 315 days of the year.

c. In 50 days you could catch _____ fish with your pole (during the time it would take to make the net).

d. If a friend would lend you enough fish to feed yourself while making the net, your total annual catch would rise by _____ fish each year. After repaying your friend the same number of fish she loaned you, you would still have an extra_____ fish.

e. If your friend charges a 100% interest rate on the loan, you will have to repay interest and principal equal to _____ fish. Now your annual income after repaying the loan and interest is _____ fish per year. This is _more / less_ than your original income by _____ fish. It would _raise / lower_ your standard of living to invest in the net.

5. The diagram at right shows the total supply and demand for loanable funds, plus your personal demand curve for funds.

Indicate in the diagram the quantity of funds you would borrow under the circumstances.

This is $_____.

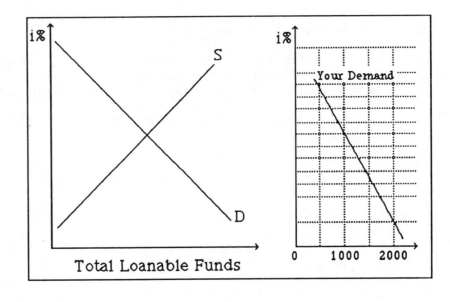

6. In the diagrams at right three suppliers are receiving the price indicated. Indicate how much economic rent is being received in each instance by shading ▨ the area representing rent.

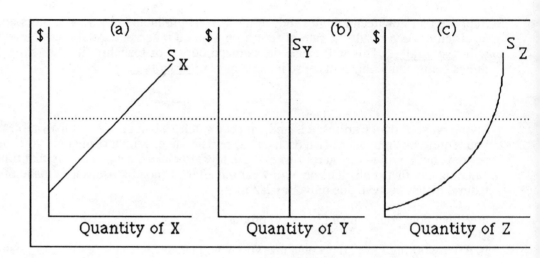

Part 5. Self Test
Multiple choice questions

1. The supply of loanable funds most directly depends on:

a. people's investment activity
b. stock market activity
c. people's savings and newly created money
d. the profits and losses of firms

Answer: _____

2. Which of the following statements is true?

a. The quantity supplied of loanable funds and the interest rate are inversely related.
b. The supply curve of loanable funds is horizontal.
c. One of the reasons the federal government demands loanable funds is that it needs to finance budget surpluses.
d. Savers are people who consume less than their current income.
e. none of the above

Answer: _____

3. If consumers have a positive rate of time preference, this means they:

a. prefer earlier availability of goods to later availability
b. prefer later availability of goods to earlier availability
c. prefer goods to services, since services can be delivered quicker
d. prefer goods to services, since goods are more tangible
e. none of the above

Answer: _____

4. The people least likely to save are those people with a:

a. low rate of time preference since they only slightly prefer present consumption to future consumption
b. low rate of time preference since they greatly prefer present consumption to future consumption
c. high rate of time preference since they greatly prefer present consumption to future consumption
d. efficient rate of time preference since they do not prefer consuming luxury goods to necessities
e. roundabout rate of time preference since they don't really care about consuming

Answer: _____

5. If the price for loanable funds is greater than the return on capital, then:

a. firms will borrow in the loanable funds market and invest
in capital goods, and as this happens the quantity of capital decreases and its return rises
b. firms will borrow in the loanable funds market and invest in capital goods, and as this happens the quantity of capital increases and its return falls.
c. firms will not borrow in the loanable funds market and over time the capital stock will decrease and the return on capital will fall
d. firms will not borrow in the loanable funds market and over time the capital stock will decrease and the return on capital will rise

Answer: _____

6. If a 5 percent instead of a 1 percent inflation rate is expected by both the suppliers and demanders of loanable funds, then:

a. the nominal interest rate will rise, ceteris paribus
b. the real interest rate will fall, ceteris paribus
c. the real interest rate will rise
d. the nominal interest rate will fall, ceteris paribus

Answer: _____

7. If the nominal interest rate is 10 percent and the expected inflation rate is 6 percent, the real interest rate equals:

a. 16 percent
b. 6 percent
c. 10 percent
d. 4 percent
e. none of the above

Answer: _____

8. The present value of $10,000 two years in the future, at a 5 percent interest rate is:

a. approximately $7,789
b. approximately $9,260
c. approximately $8,790
d. approximately $9,070

Answer: _____

9. As interest rates decrease, present values:

a. increase, and firms will buy fewer capital goods
b. decrease, and firms will buy fewer capital goods
c. increase, and firms will buy more capital goods
d. decrease, and firms will buy more capital goods

Answer: _____

10. A payment in excess of opportunity costs is called:

a. price
b. implicit price
c. economic rent
d. excess profits
e. none of the above

Answer: _____

11. The economist David Ricardo argued that grain prices were _____ because land rents were
_____ .

a. high, high
b. low, high
c. high, low
d. low, low
e. none of the above

Answer: _____

12. Uncertainty:

a. is the result of a positive time preference
b. is the same thing as risk
c. exists when the probability of a given event can be estimated
d. is the result of a negative time preference
e. none of the above

Answer: _____

13. Michael can work at job X earning $150,000 a year, or job Y earning $183,000 a year, or job Z earning $195,000 a year. If Michael chooses job C, then economic rent equals:

a. $33,000
b. $45,000
c. $30,000
d. $12,000
e. none of the above

Answer: _____

14. Entrepreneurship differs from the other factors of production in that:

a. the return to it is always negative
b. the return to it is always positive
c. it cannot be measured
d. the return to it is larger than the returns to the other factors of production

Answer: _____

15. A person buys A for $400 and sells it the next day for $450. Which theory of profit is most consistent with this example?

a. the theory that profit is the return to the entrepreneur as innovator
b. the theory that says uncertainty is the source of profit
c. the theory that says profit is the return to being alert to arbitrage opportunities
d. none of the above

Answer: _____

True-False

16. The nominal interest rate is the interest rate   T F
adjusted for expected inflation.

17. Present value refers to the future worth of some   T F
current dollar amount.

18. No factor besides land can receive pure economic   T F
rent.

19. Entrepreneurship is measured in terms of entins,   T F
such that 2 entins = 1 enton.

20. The word interest refers to the price paid by   T F
borrowers for loanable funds and the return on
capital in the production process.

Fill in the blank

21. Investors (or firms) demand loanable funds so that they can invest in productive _____
of production.

22. Over time, the price for loanable funds and the return on capital tend to _____ .

23. If the expected inflation rate is positive, the _____interest rate
is greater than the _____ interest rate.

24. The present value of $1,000 _____ year(s) from now is
$925.92 at an 8 percent interest rate.

25. As present values _____, firms will buy more capital goods, ceteris paribus.

Part 5. Answers to Self Test

1. c 2. d 3. a 4. c 5. d 6. a 7. d 8. d 9. c 10. c
11. e 12. e 13. d 14. c 15. c
16. F 17. F 18. F 19. F 20. T
21. roundabout methods 22. equality 23. nominal, real
24. one 25. increase

Part 6. Answers

Part 2 Review of Concepts
1. g 2. d 3. b 4. c 5. h 6. a 7. i 8. f 9. e 10. j

Part 3 Key Concepts
1. interest, interest rate 2. borrowers, lenders 3. saving 4. increases, does not
5. right, left, rise 6. capital, roundabout 7. return, preference 8. more, long, costs
9. real, nominal, nominal 10. 4% 11. interest, years 12. $100 \div (1.08)^2 = \$85.73$
13. opportunity cost, all 14. did not, did 15. supply and demand 16. $2 17. can, are not
18. accounting 19. $50, $30, enter 20. Uncertainty, can 21. arbitrage 22. innovation
23. signal

Part 4 Problems and Exercises

1. a. 1%   b. 5%   c. 7%
   d. 3%   e. 14%   f. 13%

2. a. See the graph.
   b. less than

3. rise, right, rise

4. a. 3650
   b. 6300
   c. 500
   d. 2650, 2150
   e. 1000, 5300, more, 1650, increase

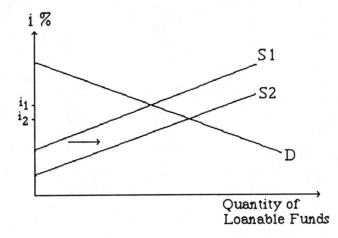

5. Draw a horizontal line from intersection of S&D over to your demand curve. At this interest rate you will borrow $1000

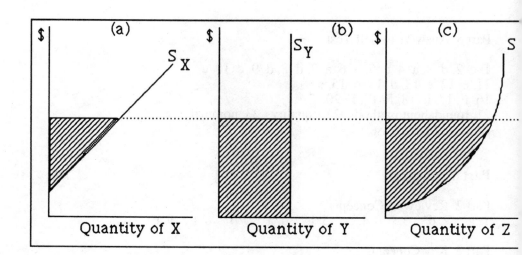

Chapter 30
Agriculture: Problems and Policies

Part 1. Introduction and Purpose
Consider the following points as you read chapter 30 in the text.

The chapter on agriculture is an "application" of economic theory. The market for food is a particularly interesting one to apply economic analysis to. Everyone is a consumer of food products, every taxpayer subsidizes the farm industry, and the government has had so many different farm policies over the years that there's quite a bit to analyze.

The primary model of analysis in this chapter is supply and demand. Because farmers compete in what is essentially a perfectly competitive market (many suppliers, homogeneous products, easy entry and exit), the supply and demand model was practically made for this situation.

What makes things interesting in the market for foodstuffs are two problems, one short-run and one long-run in nature. The short-run problem is that unpredictable weather conditions often cause shifts in the market supply curve. In conjunction with an inelastic market demand for many farm products, this can cause major fluctuations in market prices. For example, if the elasticity of demand is 0.5, a 10% reduction in supply implies a 20% price increase. If good weather causes production to rise by 10%, price falls by 20%.

It appears that farm income has stabilized in the late 1980s after a difficult time earlier in the decade. Low rainfall in 1988 did something that farmers aren't able to do for themselves: reduce farm output and increase food prices. Because demand is inelastic, a 1% decline in production pushes price up by more than 1%, so total farm revenue increases. Because total costs are also lower if less output is produced, farm profits would definitely increase if all farmers would reduce their outputs by some percentage.

That is essentially what cartels do — or attempt to do. Farmers face the same problem other cartels face, namely the tendency of individual producers to "cheat" on the cartel agreement. If the cartel can raise the market price, each profit maximizing firm wants to increase production rather than decrease it. The pursuit of extra profit by individual firms expands total supply and brings price back down to a competitive level.

The second major problem facing farmers is a long run problem. The demand for food products is income inelastic, so over the long run the demand for food doesn't increase as rapidly as consumer income. (If your income triples from its current level would you eat three times as much food as you do now? The average consumer won't.) As a consequence food production is something of a dwindling industry. By itself this doesn't mean that food production will ever decline, only it does mean that demand increases are limited.

This is particularly troublesome in light of another long-term trend. The productivity of the American farmer has tended to rise over the years because of better technology and more capital equipment. These productivity gains increase the supply of food products and drives down their prices. This long-term decline in food prices has been particularly troubling to farmers over the years.

These are the problems of the farm industry: large supply fluctuations and inelastic demand in the short run make farm income unstable; in the long run, productivity-related supply increases outpace demand increases to cause prices to decline.

Understanding the nature of these problems makes it easier to understand the reason for some of the farm policies we've adopted over the years. Too much food supply? Government rewards farmers for taking their land out of production. Too little demand for food? Congress provides food stamps to low-income households to stimulate their demand for food. Not exporting enough food? Government programs have subsidized food exports for the past several years. Not able to form a cartel that would reduce output and raise price? Acreage allotment programs limit the number of acres of certain crops, and marketing quotas limit sales of other products.

One difficulty of farm policies that in practice has limited their effectiveness and probably always will is the long run tendency for price to equal average cost of production in competitive industries. Successful farm policies — those that increase farm income — attract more farmers into producing the most profitable crops, so within a few years the average farm is back to where it started. As of this writing, no "final solution" to the farm problem has gained serious consideration.

Part 2.   Review of Concepts from Earlier Chapters
Prior to reading chapter 30, match statements at left with the appropriate concept at right.

__1. These determine price in a competitive market.
__2. Producers that agree to reduce output and raise price.
__3. %Δ in quantity demanded divided by %Δ in price.
__4. Vertical (fixed) supply curve.
__5. In this case price increases cause total revenues to rise.
__6. %Δ in quantity consumed divided by %Δ in income.
__7. A leftward shift in supply causes this.
__8. Causes a rightward shift in supply.
__9. A seller that is unable to affect the market price.

a. price increase
b. technology improvement
c. cartel
d. supply and demand
e. income elasticity
f. elasticity of demand
g. price taker
h. inelastic supply
i. inelastic demand

Part 3.   Key Concepts in this Chapter
After reading chapter 30 in the text, answer the following questions.

1. Farmers comprise about _____% of the U.S. labor force. Over the years farm productivity has risen / declined , which has increased / decreased the supply of agricultural products.

2. An increase in the supply of farm products should cause food prices to rise / fall . If quantity sold increases / decreases while price increases, then the total revenues of farmers will rise / will fall / may rise or fall .

3. When price declines, then total revenue will rise if the percent change in _price / quantity_ exceeds the percent change in _price / quantity_. In this case, demand is price _elastic / inelastic / unit elastic_.

4. If a 4% rise in consumption is associated with a 6% reduction in price, demand is _elastic / inelastic / unit elastic_. In this case total revenues will _rise / fall / not change_.

5. In practice, as farm productivity has increased over the years, food prices have _increased / declined_ and total revenue by farmers has _risen / fallen_. This _has / has not_ been a problem for the farm sector.

6. The demand for food in the U.S. _does / does not_ expand very rapidly as a result of economic growth and rising family incomes. As incomes rise by 1%, the demand for food tends to rise by _more / less_ than 1%. The demand for food is income _elastic / inelastic_.

7. According to the _____ _____ ratio, the prices of agricultural products have _risen / fallen_ relative to other prices during most of this century. This ratio uses farm prices in the years 19___ - 19___ as the base year for comparison. That was a period of _prosperity / depression_ for farmers.

8. The price elasticity of demand for cattle is _____. The elasticity for potatoes is _____. These figures imply that demand is _elastic / inelastic_.

9. Unpredictable changes in the weather cause the _supply / demand_ curve for food products to shift.

10. There was very little rainfall in several midwestern states in summer 1988, and consequently a large part of that year's crop died. That should have shifted the supply curve to the _right / left_ and should have caused food prices to _increase / decrease_. Because the demand for food is usually _elastic / inelastic_ we predict that this change in price would cause total revenues to _rise / fall_.

11. Because the weather is an important factor in determining the supply of crops, a large part of farm income is _predictable / unpredictable_.

12. Bad weather that destroys a significant part of the year's harvest causes food prices to _rise / fall_. From the point of view of farmers whose crops didn't perish, this is _bad / good_ news.

13. An acreage allotment program _increases / reduces_ farm output.

14. If acreage allotment programs reduce by 10% the number of acres planted in wheat, then according to the text total wheat production is likely to decline by _more than / less than / approximately_ 10%.

15. A marketing quota sets limits on the _____ of a product that a farmer can send to market. The text mentioned that marketing quotas apply to California _____.

16. The _____ bank program compensates farmers for take part of their _____ out of production. This program has been in existence since 19____.

17. A _____ price is the price farmers are guaranteed by government for their product.

18. If the market price of a commodity is $3 per bushel and the government's target price is $5.50, then government programs would provide direct payments to farmers of $_____ per bushel. This payment is called a _____ payment.

19. The ___ ___ ___ program compensated farmers for not producing on certain acres of farmland with grain from government stockpiles (storage). This program was _renewed / phased out_ after its first year. In-kind payments are payments in _money / goods_.

20. The price of sugar in the U.S. is supported by government at about _____ times the world price of sugar. As a result foreign producers try to send their sugar to the U.S. to take advantage of the high prices. To avoid having to subsidize foreign producers, the U.S. applies a _____ to sugar imports.

21. Government policies cost milk consumers between $____ billion and $_____ billion per year. They also cost taxpayers about $_____ per year. These programs _increase / reduce_ the total supply of milk.

22. The traditional _family_ farm has annual sales between $_____ and $_____. _Large_ farms have annual sales of more than $_____.

Part 4. Problems and Exercises
After reading chapter 30 in the text you should be able to work the following problems.

1. Refer to the diagram at right.

a. Of the two demand curves, the one labeled D___ is more elastic, and the one labeled D___ is less elastic (or inelastic).

b. Show the effects of bad weather that destroys 50 million bushels of wheat by drawing the new supply curve. Label this curve S2 and show the new equilibrium prices and quantities.

c. The equilibrium price of wheat will rise by more if _D1 / D2_ is the actual demand curve than it would if _D1 / D2_ is the actual demand curve. The moral of the story is that supply reductions cause price to rise by _more / less_ if consumer demand is elastic than if it is inelastic.

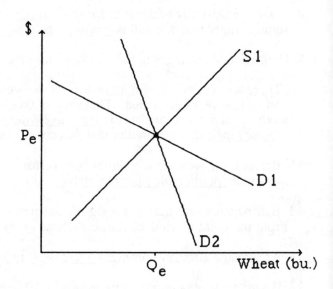

2. a. Experience shows that over the long run the
supply curve of food shifts to the right
 more / less rapidly than the demand curve
shifts to the right.

b. Shift both curves in the accompanying
diagram by the relative magnitudes suggested by
your answer to part (a) above. Label the new
supply and demand curves S2 and D2. Label the
new market price P2.

c. Because of the shifts, will the price of food
rise or fall relative to other prices?

_____

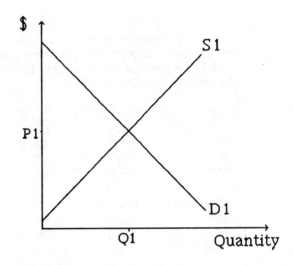

3. The graphs at right illustrate the
effects of various government farm
policies. Match the letter A-D
corresponding to each chart to the
policy it illustrates:

           target price   _____
    marketing quota   _____
          soil bank   _____
       price support   _____

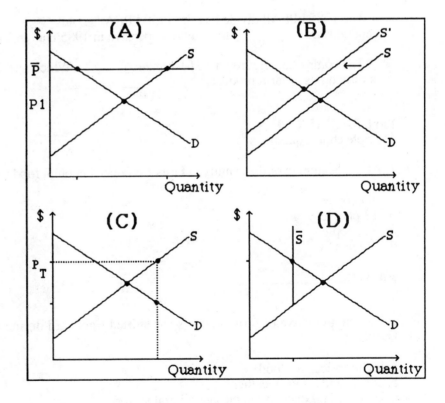

4. The following table contains figures for the producer price index for all commodities (PPI-All) and the producer price index for farm products (PPI-F) for the past several years. In both cases the price index = 100 in 1967.

Year	PPI-All	PPI-F
1950	81.8	106.7
1955	87.8	98.2
1960	94.9	97.2
1965	96.6	98.7
1970	110.4	111.0
1975	174.9	186.7
1980	268.8	249.4
1985	308.7	230.5

a. Plot all PPI data points and then connect them with a solid line; repeat the exercise for PPI-F.

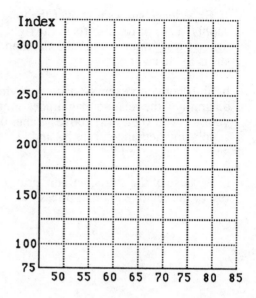

b. The 1985 PPI-All divided by the 1950 PPI-All equals _____. This means that commodities in general were _____ times more expensive in 1985 than in 1950.

___The comparable figure for PPI-F equals _____. Which has risen more in relative terms, all commodities or farm products? _____

Part 5. Self Test
Multiple choice questions

1. At the beginning of the century, a farmer produced enough food to feed:

a. 8 people
b. 17 people
c. 56 people
d. 100 people

Answer: _____

2. The supply curve of farm products has shifted rightward during much of the 20th century principally because of:

a. higher prices for food
b. consistently good weather
c. increased productivity in the agricultural sector
d. more people going into farming

Answer: _____

3. Increased productivity in the agricultural sector is not always a benefit to farmers because with increased productivity comes:

a. higher prices and if demand is inelastic, higher prices mean lower revenues
b. higher prices and if demand is elastic, higher prices mean lower revenues
c. lower prices and if demand is elastic, lower prices mean lower revenues
d. lower prices and if demand is inelastic, lower prices mean constant revenues
e. lower prices and if demand is inelastic, lower prices mean lower revenues

Answer: _____

4. In the United States, studies show that as real income has been rising, the per capita demand for food:

a. has been increasing by as much, which means the demand for food is unit elastic
b. has been increasing by much more, which means the demand for food is income elastic
c. has been increasing by much more, which means the demand for food is income inelastic
d. has been increasing by much less, which means the demand for food is income inelastic
e. none of the above

Answer: _____

5. The ratio of an index of prices that farmers receive to an index of prices that farmers pay is called:

a. parity price ratio
b. farmer index ratio
c. food price index ratio
d. consumer price index ratio
e. none of the above

Answer: _____

6. Suppose the parity price ratio falls below 100. What does this mean?

a. It means that consumers are buying fewer food products than projected.
b. It means that the prices of agricultural products have fallen relative to other prices.
c. It means that more than 100,000 farmers have gone bankrupt.
d. It means that farm mortgage payments are on the decline.

Answer: _____

7. Suppose there are only two goods in the world, soybeans and shirts. In 1910-14 soybeans sold for $3 a bushel and a watch sold for $9. In 1988, let's say a watch sold for $50. If soybean farmers were to get 100 percent parity in 1988, what price would a bushel of soybeans need to sell for?

a. $15.55 a bushel
b. $16.66 a bushel
c. $12.50 a bushel
d. $10.75 a bushel
e. none of the above

Answer: _____

8. Why is good weather sometimes bad news for farmers?

a. Because good weather lowers the demand for and price of agricultural products.
b. Because good weather shifts the supply curve of agricultural products leftward, driving up price and lowering total revenue (assuming demand is elastic).
c. Because good weather shifts the supply curve of agricultural products rightward, driving down price and lowering total revenue (assuming demand is inelastic).
d. Because good weather increases the demand for and price of farm inputs.

Answer: _____

9. Suppose 500 bushels of X are produced at a target price of $7 per bushel but consumers will only buy 500 bushels at $4 a bushel. What is the total deficiency payment to farmers?

a. $1,500
b. $2,000
c. $3,000
d. $1,000

Answer: _____

10. Which of the following statements is false?

a. One of the consequences of the acreage allotment program is that farmers begin to take their least-productive land out of production and farm their remaining acreage more intensively.
b. Under a market quota system, government does not restrict land usage, but instead sets a limit on the quantity of a product that a farmer is allowed to bring to market.
c. In 1956 the Eisenhower administration initiated the soil bank program, under which farmers were paid to take part of their land out of cultivation.
d. With both a target price and a price support, a surplus is generated.

Answer: _____

True-False

11. Today one farmer produces enough food to feed   T F
35 people.

12. Productivity in the agricultural sector has   T F
increased faster than productivity in the economy
as a whole.

13. In the target price program, government sets   T F
a target price for an agricultural product and then
pays farmers the difference between the target price
and the market price.

14. Any farmers' (voluntary) agreement to restrict   T F
output is not likely to hold, because each farmer
will reason that he will be better off if he
increases output while others do not.

15. The parity price ratio uses the years 1901-04   T F
as a base period.

Fill in the blank

16. The demand for many agricultural products is _____, which means if price _____
total revenue _____.

17. Under the _____ , government does not restrict land usage, but instead sets a limit on the
quantity of a product that a farmer is allowed to bring to market.

18. The traditional family farm has annual sales between _____
and _____ .

19. The farm population was approximately _____ million in the 1980s.

20. An agricultural price support is an example of a price _____ .

Part 5. Answers to Self Test

1. a 2. c 3. e 4. d 5. a 6. b 7. b 8. c 9. a 10. d
11. T 12. T 13. T 14. T 15. F
16. inelastic, rises (falls), rises (falls),
17. market quota system 18. $40,000, $100,000 19. 5
20. floor

Part 6. Answers

Part 2 Review of Concepts
1. d   2. c   3. f   4. h   5. i   6. e   7. a   8.b   9. g

Part 3 Key Concepts

1. 3%, risen, increased   2. fall, decreases, may rise or fall   3. quantity, price, elastic
4. inelastic, fall   5. decreased, fallen, has   6. does not, less, inelastic
7. parity price ratio, fallen, 1910-1914, prosperity   8. 0.68, 0.11   9. supply
10. left, increase, inelastic, rise   11. unpredictable   12. rise, good   13. reduces   14. less than
15. quantity, oranges   16. soil, land   17. target   18. $2.50, deficiency
19. P-I-K, phased out, goods   20. 4, quota   21. $1.6, $3.1, $1, reduce   22. $40,000-$100,000,
$500,000

Part 4 Problems and Exercises

1. a. D1, D2
    b. see graph at right
    c. D2, D1, less

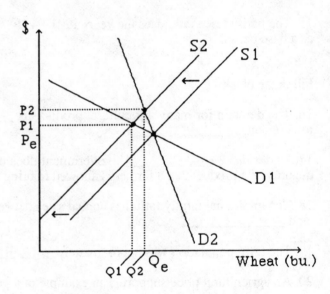

2. a. more
   b. see graph at right
   c. fall

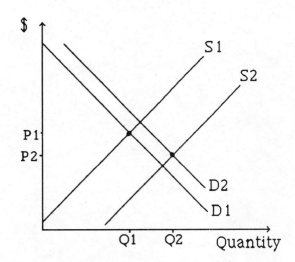

3. C, D, B, A

4. a. see graph at right
   b. 3.77, 3.77, 2.16, all commodities

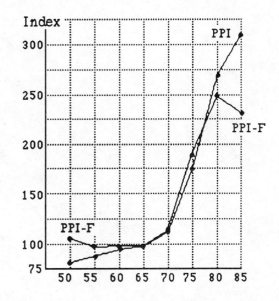

Chapter 31
The Distribution of Income
and Poverty

Part 1. Introduction and Purpose
Consider the following points as you read chapter 31 in the text.

The forces of supply and demand influence each person's standard of living — how much one earns at work, how much one pays for goods and services. Because many people find market-determined standards of living inadequate for some and overly luxurious for others, policies have been implemented to redistribute income and wealth within society. This chapter examines such policies.

The text begins by defining poverty. Under an **absolute standard** of poverty, people are poor if their incomes fall below a certain dollar amount — in the neighborhood of $6000 for a single individual. Under a **relative standard**, the bottom 20% of all people are considered poor regardless of their actual income. In practice, the U.S. Government applies an absolute standard in determining who is "poor" and deserving of assistance.

Although poverty is of considerable interest, the concept focuses attention on one particular group rather than the distribution of income within society as a whole. Fortunately there is a measure of the overall income distribution known as the Gini coefficient. The coefficient is a measure of income equality or inequality, ranging from 0 (everyone has an equal income) to 1 (income is concentrated in the hands of the very richest). The Gini coefficient for the U.S. is about 0.37.

Within a market economy, incomes are unequal because of differing **abilities** acquired at birth, varying amounts of work **effort**, differences in **education** and training, different amounts of **risk** taken, **luck** (including inheritance), and **discrimination**. Some income inequalities may also arise because of **legal barriers** that prevent workers from entering better jobs than they currently hold (such as occupational licensing laws).

Whatever the cause, many people are unwilling to accept the inequalities arising from the operation of market forces. In equilibrium market-based incomes equal the marginal revenue product of the labor service or other factor the individual supplies in the marketplace. That means some people may be especially well paid, while others earn little. This is especially true for children, the handicapped, and the elderly. Through no fault of their own, none of these groups is especially productive. Many people believe that individuals in these groups should not have to suffer with the standard of living the market would provide them in these circumstances.

One way of modifying market determined results would be to adopt a series of taxes and transfers to completely equalize incomes. That is what the **absolute income equality** standard calls for. Critics believe that this approach would eliminate the reward for hard work and would therefore increase the share of the population living in poverty rather than reduce it. John **Rawls** has suggested that a "just" (fair) distribution of income would be the one chosen by people standing behind a **veil of ignorance**. This veil would prevent voters from knowing their own place in society, or their own personal interests. If you were freed of your own personal biases and interests — if you had an equal chance of being rich or poor — what income distribution policy would you vote for? When voters step out from behind the veil of ignorance, their votes may no longer reflect their deeper feelings about poverty and the proper distribution of income.

The poor tend to be very young or old, the handicapped, those born into "unlucky" situations (no inheritance, broken families), or those who face difficult conditions (such as having a large family to raise, or not having an education). Government transfer programs have been developed to deal, to a greater or lesser degree, with each of these difficulties. **Cash transfers** provide a general increase in the recipient's standard of living, while **in-kind transfers** of goods and services increase the recipient's standard of living in a particular area. Food stamps and housing subsidies are two examples of in-kind transfers. In practice, the government spends more for in-kind transfers than for cash transfers.

Because the current welfare system cuts off an individual's transfer payments as he or she earns outside income, it has been said that the current system encourages poverty. One alternative proposal is to guarantee the individual a certain minimum income, and then only very gradually reduce the transfer amount as the individual earns additional income. That is the idea behind the **negative income tax** proposal. Many economists suggest that much of the poverty we observe is the result of **legal barriers** that prevent workers from entering better occupations. From this perspective, less government regulation of the economy would bring about a more equitable distribution of income.

Two **economic arguments** for having government redistribute income rely on the idea that there is a demand for income security, and since no private company can profitably supply that demand, then government should. The first notes that everyone benefits if there is less poverty in society, including those of us who are not poor. In this instance the reduction of poverty is a **public good**. If each of us derives a benefit from the "good" called "reducing poverty," a case can be made for charging us for the cost of providing it. Second, people who are not currently poor may support income transfer programs to **insure** against being poor later in life. Pay taxes today to support a program that you may need later.

Part 2. Review of Concepts from Earlier Chapters
Prior to reading chapter 31, match statements at left with the appropriate concept at right.

___1. Wage equals a worker's marginal revenue product.
___2 A statement that reflects personal values and preferences.
___3. The value of alternatives foregone when taking an action.
___4. In a market, price is determined by these.
___5. Legal limit below which wages may not be lowered.
___6. Risky working conditions affect wages this way.

a. opportunity cost
b. relative increase
c. normative statement
d. minimum wage
e. marginal productivity theory
f. supply and demand

Part 3. Key Concepts in this Chapter
After reading chapter 31 in the text, answer the following questions.

1. Some people consider the top ___% of income recipients as "rich" and the bottom ___% as "poor." By this standard, in 1986 a family would have qualified as rich with an annual income of $_____.

2. Between 1929 and 1986 the distribution of income became _more / less_ equal. The share of total income received by the middle 60% of the population went from _____% to _____%. The share of total income received by the lowest 20% of the population _rose / fell_ from _____% to _____%. Adjusted for in-kind transfers and taxes, the lowest 20% of the population received _____% of total income in 1976.

3. _____ payments do not require the recipient to supply good or service in return. If these payments are not in cash, then they are ____-_____ transfers. Food stamps _are / are not_ cash transfers.

4. (Refer to the text.) Exhibits 1 and 2 in the text _do / do not_ include <u>cash</u> transfers in calculating the distribution of income.   The exhibits _do / do not_ include the effects of <u>in-kind</u> transfers in calculating the distribution of income.

5. Worker earnings typically go through a life cycle. They rise during the workers' 20's through most of their _____'s, then tend to level off. After retirement, worker incomes tend to _rise / decline_.

6. The sources of an individual's income are _____ income, _____ income, _____ payments received, minus _____ paid.

7. Labor income is equal to the _____ rate multiplied by the number of hours worked.

8. A _____ curve graphs the relationship between a cumulative percent of _____ and the cumulative percent of total income they receive. This curve would be a _____ degree line if every family received the same income.

9. If the 10% of the population with the lowest income receives 2% of all income and the next-to-lowest 10% of the population receives 4% of all income, then the lowest 20% of the population receives a cumulative share equal to _____% of total income. If the next 20% of the population receives 12% of all income, then the cumulative share of the bottom 40% equals _____%.

10. As incomes become <u>less equally</u> distributed, the Lorenz curve moves _toward / away from_ the 45 degree line.

11. The larger the area between the Lorenz curve and the 45-degree line, the _higher / lower_ the Gini coefficient will be. A higher Gini coefficient indicates a _more / less_ equally distributed income than a low Gini.

12. The Gini coefficient for the U.S. is about _____; Sweden's Gini equals _____; and France's Gini equals _____. Of the three, _____'s income is most equally distributed.

13. True or false? _____ The Gini coefficient _does / does not_ indicate the share of income going to the poor.

14. People have different incomes because they were born with different abilities and attributes, different decisions regarding _____ and leisure, the amount of _____ they have obtained, the amount of _____ they take, and the degree of _____ they face from employers.

15. The theory of _____ worth says that people who hold comparable (but not identical) jobs should be paid equally. For example clerk-typists are comparable to _____ workers.

16. The State of _Wyoming / Washington / West Virginia_ has a comparable worth policy for state employees. According to that plan, different jobs are rated according to _1 / 2 / 4 / 6_ criteria. Jobs receiving equal _____ earn equal pay.

17. Assume the current equilibrium wage is $6 for clerk-typists. If a comparable wage law indicates that clerk-typists should be paid $8, then a _surplus / shortage_ of workers will develop in this occupation. This is may mean that the _highest / lowest_ skilled clerk typists may be unemployed after the policy has become effective.

18. One normative view is that the distribution of income should be determined purely by competitive market forces. This is the marginal _____ approach.

19. The marginal productivity approach _does / does not_ provide workers with an incentive to work harder than the absolute equality approach to income distribution.

20. Under the absolute income equality approach to income distribution, each person will receive _a different / the same_ slice of the total income "pie."

21. The philosopher John Rawls believes that a fair and just policy toward the redistribution of income is the one people standing behind a _____ of _____ would adopt. This fictional veil would _maximize / minimize_ the degree to which redistribution policy is influenced by voters' personal biases and self interest.

22. There are two ways to define poverty. One is to say that poverty is defined in _absolute / relative_ terms. For example, any family with an income of less than $10,000 is poor. A second approach defines poverty in _absolute / relative_ terms. Here we might say that the 20% of the population with the lowest incomes are poor. The U.S. Government defines poverty in _absolute / relative_ terms.

23. In 1986, the poverty income threshold was $_____ for a family of four. For one person between 15 and 64 years old the poverty level was $_____. In 1986 the share of the population living below the poverty line was _____%.

24. The value of cash transfers made by government is _more / less_ than the value of in-kind transfers. If the value of in-kind benefits is included, the share of the population living in poverty was _____% rather than 13.6%.

25. Overall, a disproportionate share of the poor are from minority groups that live in _small / large_ families headed by a _young / older_ female with _a good / little_ education.

26. The text takes the position that people are poor because _____.
    a) they are victims of circumstances and discrimination
    b) they make choices that result in poverty (such as the choice not to work)
    c) there are many explanations of poverty, and not everyone will agree.

27. The major cash payment program is _____ to Families with _____ _____, or ___ ___ ___ ___ for short. In 1985 this program paid an average monthly payment of $_____ per family served.

28. The major in-kind transfer programs are _____ stamps, public _____, and Medic_____. The first program mentioned pays a family of four up to $_____ per month.

29. Under current programs, if a person who has been receiving public assistance finds a job, then his or her public benefits (transfers) are sometimes reduced by up to _____% for each dollar earned. This is _an incentive / a disincentive_ to work.

30. The _corporate / negative / personal_ income tax proposal examined in the text provided a minimum guaranteed income level amounting to $_____, and reduced transfer payments by _____% of each dollar earned. In theory, that approach would provide _more / less_ incentive to work than today's programs.

31. If a person loses $30 worth of government transfers when his earnings rise by $100, then he faces an _explicit / implicit / hidden_ marginal tax rate of _____%.

32. The market-oriented approach to income distribution says that _unfair / illegal / legal_ barriers to employment are an important cause of poverty, and that taking down those barriers would reduce poverty significantly. Examples are the _____ wage, and _____ procedures that prevent people from moving into various occupations.

33. Assume that most people benefit if there is less poverty around them. This implies that any reduction of poverty is a _public / private_ good. People who enjoy the benefits of such goods without paying their share of the cost are _____ riders. This group will be forced to pay for benefits they receive under a system of welfare assistance and mandatory _____.

34. A person who is financially well off today may want a welfare system to insure against the possibility that some day he may be _____. In this instance welfare assistance is a form of social _____ plan.

35. In the interview with John Kenneth Galbraith, he indicates that two changes he would like to see are: a) an end to the _____ competition with the _____ _____, and 2) more relief for "the _____."

Part 4. Problems and Exercises
After reading chapter 31 in the text you should be able to work the following problems.

1. The information from the following table is taken from an exhibit in the text. It shows the percent of total income received by various income groups <u>before</u> all taxes and transfers and the share received <u>after</u> adjustments for taxes and transfers.

   Your assignment is to fill in the blank spaces at right with the <u>cumulative</u> share of income received by the income group in question plus all groups with lower incomes. See the two examples already worked in the table.

Family Income Group	Income Shares (% of Total) Unadjusted Share	Adjusted for Taxes & Benefits	Cumulative Income Shares Unadjusted Incomes	Adjusted Incomes
a. Lowest 20%	2.6%	6.2%	2.6%	___%
b. Second 20%	8.4	12.0	11.0%	___%
c. Third 20%	15.5	16.9	___%	___%
d. Fourth 20%	23.4	23.0	___%	___%
e. Top 20%	50.1	42.0	___%	___%

2. Use the figures calculated in exercise #1 to graph a Lorenz curve. Plot the cumulative percent of total income received by the (cumulative) total number of families indicated along the horizontal axis of the chart.

a. Plot one Lorenz curve for unadjusted incomes.

b. Plot a second Lorenz curve for adjusted incomes.

c. Draw a 45-degree diagonal line in the graph.

d. The _adjusted / unadjusted_ Lorenz curve lies closer to the diagonal.

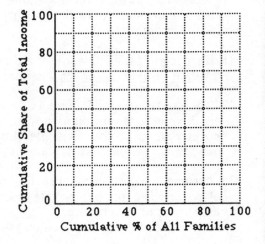

3. The _explicit / implicit_ marginal tax rate referred to in the text is the percent of any income increase offset by a reduction in public welfare received.

The table gives the implicit marginal tax rates and the (explicit) marginal tax rate associated with the tax system for people in different income groups. These two tax rates added together equal the _effective_ marginal tax rate.

Fill in blank spaces in the table with the effective marginal tax rate for each income group.

j. In general, the effective tax rate is highest for _high / low_ income people.

	Income Group	Implicit MTR	Tax MTR	Effective MTR
a.	Bottom 20%	37.1%	14.9%	___%
b.	3rd 10%	36.3	26.2	___%
c.	4th 10%	27.1	27.2	___%
d.	5th 10%	15.4	30.3	___%
e.	6th 10%	10.4	31.3	___%
f.	7th 10%	4.5	33.0	___%
g.	8th 10%	0.7	35.5	___%
h.	9th 10%	0.6	40.8	___%
i.	Top 10%	0.0	45.8	___%

4. Information regarding the distribution of income in six nations is given in the table.

To gauge the financial disparity between "rich" and "poor," subtract the income share received by the bottom 20% from the income share received by the top 20% and write the result in the table.

| | Nation (Year) | Income Group | | |
		Top 20%	Bottom 20%	Difference
a.	Japan (1968)	43.8%	4.6%	____%
b.	France (1962)	53.7	1.9	____%
c.	Britain (1968)	39.2	6.0	____%
d.	W. Germany (1970)	45.6	5.9	____%
e.	Sweden (1970)	42.5	5.4	____%
f.	United States (1970)	38.8	6.7	____%

g. (Refer to the table.) In which nation was the difference between the income shares of "rich" and "poor" families smallest? _____ In which nation is the difference largest? _____

Part 5. Self Test
Multiple choice questions

1. Which of the following statements is false?

a. Between 1929 and 1986, the income distribution in the United States has become less equal.
b. In 1986, the lowest 20 percent of all income earners earned under 10 percent of the total money income.
c. The people that make up the top 5 percent of all income earners are millionaires.
d. a and c
e. a, b, and c

Answer: _____

2. The ex post income distribution is:

a. less equal than the ex ante income distribution
b. more equal than the ex ante income distribution
c. as equal as the ex ante income distribution
d. not adjusted for taxes and transfer payments
e. b and d

Answer: _____

3. The smaller the Gini coefficient, the:

a. greater the degree of income inequality
b. greater the degree of income equality
c. higher the birth rate
d. larger the population
e. none of the above

Answer: _____

4. Which of the following statements is false?

a. Economists agree that it is better for a country to have a lower Gini coefficient than a higher one.
b. Economists agree that it is better for a country to have a higher Gini coefficient than a lower one.
c. There is greater income equality in the United States than Sweden.
d. Because the Gini coefficient is lower in country A than country B, the lowest income group in country A has a greater percentage of total income than the lowest income group in country B.
e. all of the above

Answer: _____

5. One way to increase the degree of income inequality is to:

a. decrease transfer payments going to people with low labor and asset incomes and decrease taxes on people with high labor and asset incomes
b. increase transfer payments going to people with low labor and asset incomes and increase taxes on people with high labor and asset incomes
c. increase transfer payments going to people with low labor and asset incomes by more than you increase taxes on the same people
d. increase transfer payments going to people with high labor and asset incomes by less than you increase taxes on the same people
e. a and d

Answer: _____

6. Which of the following statements is true?

a. If people were alike in terms of their marketable innate abilities and attributes, there would be less income inequality.
b. Some degree of income inequality can be attributed to the fact that some people consume more leisure than others.
c. Schooling is referred to as human capital.
d. a and c
e. a, b, and c

Answer: _____

7. The doctrine that states equal pay for comparable work is called:

a. equal pay doctrine
b. equal work doctrine
c. pay-as-you-go doctrine
d. comparable worth
e. the insurance doctrine

Answer: _____

8. The proponents of absolute income equality sometimes argue that an equal income distribution of income will maximize total utility. Their arguement goes like this:

a. individuals are alike when it comes to how much satisfaction they receive from an increase in income; receiving additional income is subject to the law of diminishing marginal returns; redistributing income from the rich to the poor helps the poor more than it hurts the rich, so total utility rises
b. individuals are alike when it comes to how much satisfaction they receive from an increase in income; receiving additional income is subject to the law of constant marginal costs; redistributing income from the rich to the poor helps the poor more than it hurts the rich, so total utility rises
c. individuals are not alike when it comes to how much satisfaction they receive from an increase in income; receiving additional income is subject to the law of diminishing marginal utility; redistributing income from the rich to the poor helps the poor less than it helps the rich, so total utility rises
d. individuals are alike when it comes to how much satisfaction they receive from an increase in income; receiving additional income is subject to the law of diminishing marginal utility; redistributing income from the rich to the poor helps the poor more than it hurts the rich, so total utility rises

Answer: _____

9. Which of the following is a definition of poverty in relative terms?

a. a family is in poverty if it receives less than $10,000 a year
b. a family is in poverty if it receives an income that places it in the lowest 5 percent of family income recipients
c. a family is in poverty if the majority of families receive more income than it receives
d. b and c
e. a, b, and c

Answer: _____

10. Which of the following leads to an underestimate of the number of persons in poverty?

a. illegal income
b. unreported income
c. some poor persons can't be found, therfore they can't be counted
d. a and b
e. a, b, and c

Answer: _____

True-False

11. The ex ante distribution of income is the before-   T F
tax-and-transfer payment distribution of income.

12. The Lorenz curve is a graphical representation of   T F
the distribution of income.

13. The gini coefficient of the United States is   T F
higher than the gini coefficient of Sweden.

14. John Raws wrote <u>A Theory of Justice</u>.   T F

15. The acceptance of the public good-free rider   T F
argument leads individuals to conclude that
government is justified in taxing all persons
to pay for welfare assistance for some.

Fill in the blank

16. _____ are payments to persons that are not made in return for goods and services currently
supplied.

17. The _____ is a measurement of the degree of inequality in the income distribution.

18. _____ exists when individuals of equal ability and productivity, as measured by their
marginal revenue products, are paid different wage rates.

19. _____ wrote <u>The New Industrial State</u>.

20. The rate at which the negative income tax payment, or any cash grant or subsidy, is reduced as earned
income rises is called the _____ .

Part 5. Answers to Self Test

1. d 2. b 3. b 4. e 5. a 6. e 7. d 8. d 9. d 10. c
11. T 12. T 13. T 14. T 15. T
16. Transfer payments 17. gini coefficient
18. Wage discrimination 19. John Kenneth Galbraith
20. implied marginal tax rate

Part 6. Answers

Part 2 Review of Concepts
1. e   2. c   3. a   4. f   5. d   6. b

Part 3 Key Concepts
1. 20%, 20%, $50,371   2. more, 41.7%, 51.6%, rose, 3.9%, 4.7%, 6.2%   3. transfer, in-kind, in-kind, are not   4. do, do not   5. 40s, decline   6. labor, asset, transfer, taxes   7. wage   8. Lorenz, families, 45 deg.   9. 6%, 18%   10. away from   11. higher, less   12. 0.369, 0.271, 0.417, Sweden's   13. does not   14. work, education, risk, discrimination   15. comparable, warehouse   16. Washington, 4, points   17. surplus, lowest   18. productivity   19. does   20. the same   21. veil of ignorance, minimize   22. absolute, relative, absolute   23. $11,203, $5,701, 13.6%   24. less, 11.6%   25. large, young, little   26. c -- many explanations   27. Aid to Families with Dependent Children, A-F-D-C, $342   28. food stamps, public housing, Medicaid, $264   29. 100%, a disincentive   30. negative, $5000, 50%, more   31. implicit, 30%   32. legal, minimum, licensing   33. public, free, taxes   34. poor, insurance   35. military, Soviet Union, underclass

Part 4 Problems and Exercises

1. a. 6.2%
   b. 18.2%
   c. 26.5%, 35.1%
   d. 49.9%, 58.1%
   e. 100%, 100.1%
      (rounding error)

2. a-c. See graph.
   d. adjusted

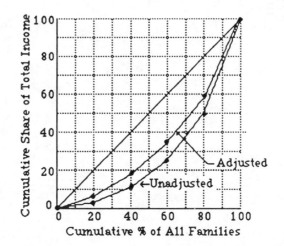

3. implicit
   a. 52.0%   f. 37.5%
   b. 56.5%   g. 36.2%
   c. 54.3%   h. 41.4%
   d. 45.7%   i. 45.8%
   e. 41.7%   j. low

4. a. 39.2%   b. 51.8%   c. 33.2%   d. 39.7%   e. 37.1%   f. 32.1%   g. U.S., France

Chapter 32
Antitrust, Business Regulation, and Deregulation

Part 1. Introduction and Purpose
Consider the following points as you read chapter 32 in the text.

This chapter examines *two important trends in U.S. economic history*. The first began about 100 years ago with the passage, in 1890, of the **Sherman Act** — also sometimes called the Sherman Antitrust Act. Many Americans had been angered by a merger movement where large companies combined to become monopoly sellers that could charge higher prices and earn larger profits. Consequently the Sherman Act made agreements to "restrain trade" or monopolize an industry illegal. In practice this included both monopoly-creating mergers and collusive agreements known today as cartels. A number of additional antitrust laws have been passed over the years, in many cases to clarify issues related to the basic antitrust standards established by the Sherman Act and the 1914 **Clayton Act**. The Clayton Act specified several specific business acts that would be illegal, if the effect would be to "substantially lessen competition."

A different way of controlling the exercise of market power is for the government to **regulate** the monopolist to prevent it from taking full advantage of its monopoly position. In dealing with **natural monopolies** governments often grant firms an exclusive (or semi-exclusive) franchise to operate, and in return the government regulates the firms prices, output, or profits. Natural monopolies are companies whose average total costs continue to decline as they expand output.

Such regulation is typically plagued by two **shortcomings**. First, regulators possess inadequate **information** on firm costs, consumer demands, and other market conditions to regulate firms as the theory proscribes. Second, regulation that prevents "excessive" profits often removes the incentive for firms to minimize **waste**, so in the long run regulated firms have higher costs than a profit-maximizing firm would. In short, regulation has costs that either partially or fully counterbalance the low-price, consumer-oriented approach which regulation was intended to provide.

In addition to this problem with regulation, during the past 25 years economists have increasingly come around to the belief that over the long run the industry subject to government regulation will influence the regulatory body in its rule-making role. The **capture hypothesis** suggests that regardless of the reason the industry was originally regulated, eventually the regulators will come under the influence of the industry. In the limiting case, officials establish rules that create a monopoly situation for existing firms. Because their rules have the force of law, the net effect is to protect firms in the regulated industry from new competition, even when substantial profits are being earned in particular markets.

The capture hypothesis offers one **prediction** that can be tested. If regulators help protect monopoly power rather than prevent its exercise, then deregulation — the removal of regulation — should result in more competition and lower prices. The **public interest theory of regulation** predicts that regulation in the 1960s and '70s held prices down, so under this view deregulation should reduce competition and cause prices to increase.

The result? In industry after industry, deregulation was followed by increasing amounts of **competition**, and consumers paid some 15-25% **lower prices** for the same service. In the case of banking, consumers received higher interest rates on their deposits. These results tend to support the capture hypothesis of regulation.

As economists and policy makers became increasingly convinced that the capture hypothesis was correct, they provided powerful support for a *second major trend in government regulation* that got underway in the late 1970s and has continued into the '80s. This was the trend of **deregulation**, which has had the support of politicians in both political parties. Coming after nearly 90 years of policy geared toward increasing government control of the economy, it is unlikely that the effects of deregulation are fully understood. It is also unlikely that all of the abuses of 90 years of regulation and "trust-busting" have been corrected in a single decade, so deregulation is likely to continue in one form or another for some time to come.

Part 2. Review of Concepts from Earlier Chapters
Prior to reading chapter 32, match statements at left with the appropriate concept at right.

___1. Profit is maximized by following this rule.
___2. One producer of a good with no close substitutes.
___3. Percent of domestic industry sales made by largest 4 firms.
___4. Group of producers agree to reduce output & raise price.
___5. Increases the number of firms in the industry.
___6. A market with low entry costs and potential competition.
___7. A firm will earn zero profits.
___8. If P > MC at the output where profit is maximized.
___9. Graphical representation of allocative resource inefficiency.

a. concentration ratio
b. welfare loss triangle
c. entry
d. MR=MC
e. monopoly
f. allocative inefficiency
g. cartel
h. price = atc
i. contestable market

Part 3. Key Concepts in this Chapter
After reading chapter 32 in the text, answer the following questions.

1. About 100 years ago, an organization formed by combining companies together into a single larger company was called a _____. Laws that prevent such mergers were called anti-_____ laws.

2. The nation's first antitrust law was the _____ Act, enacted in 18____.

3. The Sherman Act made illegal agreements to restrain _____ or commerce among the states. Other provisions of the act _do / do not_ explain which specific acts this refers to.

4. The _____ Act made it illegal for companies to practice price discrimination when the effect was to substantially lessen competetion. This was one of two antitrust acts passed in 19____; the other was the _____ _____ Commission Act.

5. The FTC Act made illegal certain _____ methods of competition.

6. According to the text, the _____ - _____ Act was passed in an attempt to reduce failures among small businesses. In many ways this act was _pro- / anti-_ competitive.

7. The _____ - _____ Act was aimed at reducing false and deceptive acts, including advertising. The ___ ___ ___ was the government agency designated to enforce this act.

8. True or false? _____ The U.S. government successfully prosecuted IBM in a 13-year antitrust case in which the company had been monopolizing the computer equipment industry.

9. A "new" measurement of the degree of competition (or monopoly power) in an industry is the _____ index. This index is the sum of the squared values of the market _____ of each firm in the industry. If an industry is completely monopolized with 100% of industry sales, the index has a value of _1 / 100 / 1000 / 10,000 / 1 million_.

10. The concentration ratio _does / does not_ take into account the existence of foreign competition in U.S. markets.

11. A merger between two firms that does not raise the Herfindahl index by more than _50 / 100 / 200_ points will not bring antitrust action by the government, assuming the index was originally below _100 / 1000 / 5000_.

12. Both the Herfindahl index and concentration ratios implicitly suggest that large firms have _____ power and that they are likely to be _____ it.

13. In 1978 the Civil Aeronautics Board permitted the merger of _____ Airlines and National Airlines even though the Justice Department believed that the merger would make the _New Orleans / New York / New Haven_ air market less competitive. The CAB argued that the market was _competitive / contestable / monopolistic_. This means that the cost of _____ was very low in that market.

14. In 1966, the Supreme Court blocked a merger between Von's Grocery Co. and Shopping Bag Food Stores. The two combined would have had a ____% market share in the _Las Vegas / Los Angeles_ market. Justice Potter Stewart criticized the opinion because it wrongly assumed that the degree of _____ must invariably by proportional to the _____ of competitors.

15. A _legal / government / natural_ monopoly is a firm that enjoys economies of scale in producing a quantity of output sufficient to supply the entire market. The firm has _higher / lower_ unit costs than smaller producers of the product.

16. To prevent a natural monopolist from exploiting its situation, governments often _outlaw / regulate_ such firms. Such policies may include dictating the firm's _____, profit, or _____.

17. By requiring the regulated firm to charge a price equal to _____ _____, the regulator would eliminate allocative inefficiency. If the firm is a natural monopolist however, its marginal cost will probably be _above / below_ the firm's average total cost curve. Following the P = ___ ___ rule would cause the firm to earn _profits / losses_.

18. When regulators maintain the regulated firm's accounting profits at a "normal" level (so that economic profits are zero), the firm _will / will not_ earn losses if waste and inefficiency cause its cost curves to shift upward. As a result, over time its costs will tend to _rise / fall_ .

19. The firm that is required by regulators to produce a certain quantity of output may increase profits by _improving / reducing_ product quality.

20. _____ cost pricing is a regulatory policy that causes the regulated firm to earn zero economic profits.

21. _____ lag refers to the period between which a regulated firm's costs change and its regulated price is adjusted.

22. The trucking industry was regulated by the ___ ___ ___, and the airline industry was regulated by the ___ ___ ___. These two industries _are / are not_ natural monopolies.

23. The _____ hypothesis predicts that regulatory agencies are greatly influenced by the industry they are assigned to regulate. The _____ _____ theory of regulation suggests that regulators will promote the interests of the general public.

24. Members of the general public (including consumers) are _more / less_ likely to attend regulatory meetings than members of the regulated industry. Thegeneral public is _more / less_ likely to become personally acquainted with regulators. Regulators _often / seldom_ have careers in the industry they regulate, either before or after their careers as regulators. These three observations tend to _support / deny_ the relevance of the capture hypothesis.

25. True or false? _____ According to the text, the fact that business executives complain about government regulation indicates that the capture hypothesis is inaccurate.

26. The airline industry was originally regulated by the ___ ___ ___ in 19____. Regulation consisted of setting air _____ and the number of carriers per route. Its successor, the CAB, set fares high enough for most all carriers to meet their _fixed / marginal / average_ costs, so it was possible for _few / inefficient_ firms to survive.

27. The CAB chairman during airline deregulation was Alfred _____. The airline industry was deregulated in 19____. In 1987, _30% / 60% / 90%_ of air travelers received discount fares below the "regular" fare. Between 1979 and 1984, air fares fell by approximately _____% (in real terms).

28. Since airlines were deregulated, the accident rate has _risen / fallen_ and the fatal accident rate has _risen / fallen_ .

29. In the trucking industry the ICC established freight _____, set _____, and created _____ to entry by new firms. The value of a license to operate a truck was worth $_____ in 1976, but by 1981 was worth _more / less_ . These figures suggest that the original ICC rules _favored / imposed high costs on_ trucking companies.

30. In the five years following deregulation of trucking, the number of trucking companies rose from ____,000 to _____,000. Inflation-adjusted trucking rates fell by _5% / 15% / 25%_ over those years.

31. The Federal Communications Commission (FCC) has been gradually deregulating the
_____ industry since 1972. The DID-MCA of 1980 eased some regulations on
_____. For example it permitted the gradual removal of _____ rate ceilings on
deposits.

32. The _wheel / hub / rim_ and _axle / spoke / turnbuckle_ system makes it possible for airlines to
reduce their flying costs and increase profits. The _____ is the center of an airline network;
flights to many smaller cities originate and end there. The flights to smaller cities are called
_____.

33. Although the hub and spoke system makes it possible to reduce air fares, it increases the
_____ cost of traveling.

34. True or false? _____ Professor George Stigler believes that deregulation of the airline
industry proves that airline companies had not captured the regulatory process.

35. True or false? _____ Professor George Stigler believes airline deregulation occurred because
circumstances caused many airlines to desire deregulation, and they influence regulators.

Part 4. Problems and Exercises
After reading chapter 32 in the text you should be able to work the following problems.

1. a. In the situtation
shown in the graph, the
firm _is / is not_ a
natural monopolist.

b. Indicate the price
charged by a profit-
maximizing firm. Label
the price P_1.

c. Indicate the price the
firm will charge if
regulators institute
"marginal cost pricing."
Label the price P_{MC}.

d. Indicate the price the
firm will charge if
regulators institute
"average cost pricing."
Label the price P_{AC}.

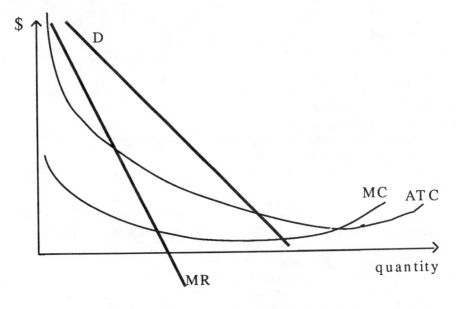

2. (Refer to exercise #1.) When the firm attempts to maximize profit in the case above, its profits are
positive / zero / negative. Under marginal cost pricing its profits are _positive / zero / negative_.
Under average cost pricing its profits are _positive / zero / negative_. (Hint: Compare price to ATC
at the chosen quantity.)

3. The table at right provides market share data for 12 hypothetical firms in a hypothetical industry.

a. The four-firm concentration ratio for this industry equals _____.

b. Square the market share figures and write them in the space provided in the table. Sum that column. The Herfindahl index equals _____.

c. Assume that firm DEF merges with firm STU. Now the 4-firm concentration ratio equals _____.

d. After the DEF-STU merger, the new Herfindahl index for the broom industry equals _____.

e. According to Justice Department guidelines, would the DEF-STU merger be permitted? _____

Firm	Share	(Share)^2	(Merger Share)^2
ABC	10%	_____	_____
DEF	10%	_____	*_____*
GHI	10%	_____	_____
JKL	10%	_____	_____
MNO	9%	_____	_____
PQR	9%	_____	_____
STU	7%	_____	_____
V	7%	_____	_____
W	7%	_____	_____
X	7%	_____	_____
Y	7%	_____	_____
Z	7%	_____	_____
TOTAL		_____	_____

*This is the only "new" number to calculate in the column.

Part 5. Self Test
Multiple choice questions

1. The Clayton Act made:

a. price discrimination illegal
b. price discrimination legal
c. mergers between companies in the same industry illegal
d. union strikes illegal in certain states

Answer: _____

2. Selling to a retailer on the condition that the seller not carry any rival products is called _____ and it was made illegal by the _____ .
a. exclusive dealing, Robinson-Patman Act
b. exclusive dealing, Clayton Act
c. a tying contract, Wheeler-Lea Act
d. price discrimination, Clayton Act

Answer: _____

3. The piece of antitrust legislation which declares illegal "unfair methods of competition in commerce" is:

a. The Sherman Act
b. The Federal Trade Commission Act
c. The Clayton Act
d. The Robinson-Patman Act
e. none of the above

Answer: _____

4. Which of the following statements is true?

a. In the Dupont case in 1956, the market relevant to Dupont was ruled to be the cellophane market rather than the broader flexible wrapping materials market.
b. In 1975, a court ruled that Alcoa was a monopoly.
c. The way a market is defined can have much to say as to whether a firm is viewed as a monopoly or not.
d. a and c
e. a, b, and c

Answer: _____

5. The advantage of the Herfindahl index over the four-firm and eight-firm concentration ratios is that it provides:

a. information about the dispersion of firm size in an industry
b. information about the price effects of industry concentration
c. information about merger acquisitions
d. b and c
e. none of the above

Answer: _____

6. Consider a merger between firm A, with a market share of 19 percent, and firm B, with a market share of 16 percent. Will the Antitrust Division of the Justice Department file suit against these two firms if they enter into a merger?

a. No, because together they have 35 percent of the the market.
b. Yes, because the Herfindahl index is 617 (which is more than 200).
c. Yes, because the difference between the Herfindahl index when the two firms are not merged and when they are is more than 200.
d. No, because neither firm has a market share under 10 percent.
e. No, because the Herfindhal index is 139 (which is more than 100).

Answer: _____

7. When one firm can supply the entire output demanded at lower cost than two or more firms can we have a(an):

a. natural market
b. natural monopoly
c. regulated firm
d. efficient firm
e. none of the above

Answer: _____

Exhibit D

Firm	Quantity	Average total cost
A	200 units	$5
B	400	$4
	600	$7

8. In Exhibit D, the resource-allocative efficient output is 600 units. Currently firm B is the only firm supplying the good; it is supplying 400 units. Based on the data presented in Exhibit D, is firm B a natural monopoly? If so, why?

a. No, because firm A can supply 200 units at a lower average total cost than firm B can supply 400 units.
b. No, because it is not the only firm that can supply the good.
c. Yes, because it can supply the entire output.
d. No, because it cannot supply the entire output (600 units) at lower cost than the two firms together (where firm A produces 200 units at $5 per unit and firm B produces 400 units at $4 per unit).

Answer: _____

9. In margainal-cost price regulation of the natural monopoly firm, the objective is:

a. to set a price that will guarantee zero economic profit
b. to set a price equal to average total cost
c. to set a price consistent with the maximization of profits
d. to set a price equal to the quantity of output corresponding to where the demand curve intersects the marginal cost curve.
e. none of the above

Answer: _____

10. One of the criticisms of average-cost pricing regulation of the natural monopoly firm is:

a. if the natural monopoly firm knows it is guaranteed a price equal to average total cost, it will cut costs and decrease quality
b. the natural monopoly firm is forced into taking a loss
c. the natural monopoly is guaranteed a positive economic profit
d. none of the above

Answer: _____

11. Which of the following is usually noted as a natural monopoly?

a. a firm that builds houses
b. a company that sells electricity
c. a bank
d. a cruise ship company
e. none of the above

Answer: _____

12. Under Civil Aeronautics Board chairman _____ the airline industry began to be deregulated in 1978.

a. Alfred Kahn
b. R.T. McClow
c. Everett George
d. Michael Kennedy
e. none of the above

Answer: _____

13. George Stigler is closely associated with the _____ , which says _____ .

a. public interest theory of regulation, regulators work hard to benefit the public interest
b. capture hypothesis, regulatory agencies are "captured" by the special interests of the industry that are being regulated
c. capture hypothesis, eventually the public "captures" the benefits of regulation through lower prices
d. public interest theory of regulation, the public is dissatisfied with the efforts of the regulatory agencies but can do little about this situation

Answer: _____

14. One of the major criticisms of the antitrust laws is that:

a. certain antitrust acts hinder, rather than promote, competition
b. they do not apply to foreign firms
c. they do not all employ the Herfindahl index
d. they do not all employ the four-firm concentration ratio

Answer: _____

15. What are the ways of regulating the natural monopoly firm?

a. output regulation
b. average-cost regulation
c. marginal-cost price regulation
d. a, b, c
e. none of the above

Answer: _____

True-False

16. The Hart-Scott-Rodino Antitrust Procedural   T F
Improvements Act required that pending mergers be
reported in advance to the Federal Trade Commission
and the Justice Department.

17. The Herfindahl index is equal to the sum of the   T F
squares of the market shares of each firm in the
industry divided by two.

18. Antitrust law is legislation passed for the   T F
stated purpose of increasing monopoly power and
reducing competition.

19. The Wheeler-Lea Act empowered the Federal   T F
Trade Commission to deal with false and deceptive
acts or practices.

20. The Clayton Act made tying contracts illegal.   T F

Fill in the blank

21. The _____ holds that regulators are seeking to do and will do through regulation what is in the best interest of the public or society at large.

22. The _____ declared illegal "unfair methods of competition in commerce."

23. The local gas company is usually cited as an example of a _____ .

24. The way _____ is defined will help determine whether a particular firm is considered a monopoly or not.

25. The Herfindahl index and the four- and eight-firm concentration ratios have been criticized for implicitly arguing from _____ to _____ .

Part 5. Answers to Self Test

1. a 2. b 3. b 4. d 5. a 6. c 7. b 8. d 9. d 10. d
11. b 12. a 13. b 14. a 15. d
16. T 17. F 18. F 19. T 20. T
21. public interest theory of regulation
22. Federal Trade Commission Act 23. natural monopoly
24. market 25. size, market power

Part 6. Answers

Part 2 Review of Concepts
1. d   2. e   3. a   4. g   5. c   6. i   7. h   8. f   9. b

Part 3 Key Concepts
1. trust, antitrust   2. Sherman, 1890   3. trade, do not   4. Clayton, 1914, Federal Trade Commission
5. unfair   6. Robinson-Patman, anti-competitive   7. Wheeler-Lea, FTC   8. false
9. Herfindahl index, share, 10,000   10. does not   11. 200, 1000   12. market, abusing
13. Continental, New Orleans, competitive, entry   14. 7%, Los Angeles, competition, number
15. natural, lower   16. regulate, price, output   17. marginal cost, below, MC, losses
18. will not, rise   19. reducing   20. Average   21. Regulatory   22. ICC, CAB, are not
23. capture, public interest   24. more, more, often, support   25. false
26. CAA, 1938, fares, average, inefficient   27. Kahn, 1978, 90%, 14%   28. fallen, fallen
29. rates, routes, barriers, $500,000, favored   30. 18,000 to 30,000, 25%   31. television, banks,
interest   32. hub and spoke, hub, spokes   33. time cost or opportunity cost or implicit cost   34. false
35. true

Part 4 Problems and Exercises

1. a. is

   b-d. See diagram at right

2. positive, negative, zero

3. a. 40%

   b. $(Share)^2$ = 100, 100, 100, 100, 81, 81, 49, 49, 49,49, 49, 49 -> H.I.=856

   c. 47%

   d. $(Merger\ Share)^2$ = 100, 289, 100, 100, 81, 81, ___,49, 49, 49, 49, 49-> H.I.=996

   e. Yes

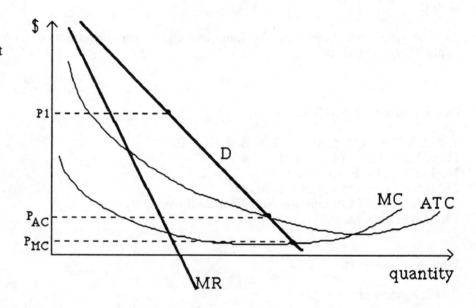

Chapter 33
Market Failure: Externalities
and Public Goods

Part 1. Introduction and Purpose
Consider the following points as you read chapter 33 in the text.

The term market failure really tells the story to this chapter. When private buyers and sellers can trade among themselves and achieve tolerably efficient outcomes — where prices equal marginal cost — then the market "succeeds." When market exchanges have a contrary result, when price is either well above or below marginal cost, then the **market fails** to allocate resources to their highest valued uses. Lost economic value implies a lower standard of living for the average person.

There are thousands of market failures, both great and small, but economists prefer to lump all market failures into a few well-defined categories. First, market failures may result from the exercise of monopoly power, and public policy toward monopoly was examined in the previous chapter.

Second, market failures may stem from externalities. **Externalities** are costs or benefits falling on bystanders as a result of someone else's actions. These effects are *external* to the decision maker, hence the term externality. Because benefits or costs fall elsewhere, the individual who allocates resources on the basis of private benefits and costs probably will not allocate resources in the same way as someone who includes all benefits and costs, both private and social. The efficiency criteria calls for the latter allocation.

A good example of an externality is **smoke** produced as a by-product of burning one's trash. Neighbors are bothered if you burn your trash. From your point of view it is a wise move — you benefit by not having to pay a trash man, and the smoke blows away after a few minutes. Given the zero price of air, you may want to burn all of the trash you generate.

Your neighbors dislike the smoke as much as you do, but receive none of the benefits (lower monthly bills). In short, the **total costs** of burning trash (private plus social) exceed the **private benefits** of the act.

The **Coase Theorem** explains that private agreements among individuals can solve externalities problems — achieve an efficient allocation — if transaction costs are zero. In real life, when a **large number** of people are affected by an externality, transaction costs will be high. Then the market fails and government solutions may be desirable. **Pigou**-type **taxes** and **subsidies** offer one approach, and direct **regulation** of individuals and firms is another.

In addition to monopoly power and externalities, markets may fail to allocate resources efficiently because of the existence of **public goods**. Public goods are goods that provide benefits to many persons simultaneously. Public goods are also commonly subject to another characteristic — nonexclusion difficulties. That is, when a public good is produced it may be impossible to exclude individuals from consuming it.

The best example of this is national defense services. If someone defends most of the U.S. from invasion, then all of us are defended. It is impossible to defend everyone with the exception of one person living in Manhattan, Kansas. Consequently if a private company tried to sell defense services, that guy in Manhattan wouldn't pay. Then each of us would come to the same realization — that we can consume without paying, that we can be free riders. The problem is that when everyone decides to free ride, goods that provide a lot of value compared to their cost are not provided. Consequently the **market fails** to provide an efficient quantity of nonexcludable goods.

Once you understand the nature of externalities and public goods, you will realize that many of the public policy issues debated every day concern these two types of problems. Should people be free to burn their trash? Should people be free to smoke in restaurants? To drive loud or smoky cars? Should property rights be defined in space, 23,200 miles overhead? On the ocean floors?

These are the types of issues examined in the present chapter. (They are examined at greater length in a course in public finance, which is probably offered by your university's economics department.) It can be interesting to look into issues such as these. On the one hand we have very ordinary events or circumstances — someone burning his trash or lighting a cigarette. On the other hand there is an analysis of the individual who produces an externality or decides not to produce a public good, and another analysis which explains why the private behavior is non-optimal. That often suggests solutions — taxes, subsidies, defining private property rights, or whatever — which can reduce the inefficiencies to more reasonable levels. Public policy problems provides rich opportunities for applying economic analysis.

Part 2. Review of Concepts from Earlier Chapters
Prior to reading chapter 33, match statements at left with the appropriate concept at right.

__1. The additional cost of one more unit.	a. opportunity cost
__2. The additional benefit of one more unit of some good.	b. incentive
__3. Value of unit to consumer equals cost of producing that unit.	c. marginal cost
__4. What is foregone as a result of taking some action.	d. marginal benefit
__5. The reason for taking an action, benefits minus costs.	e. P=MC

Part 3. Key Concepts in this Chapter
After reading chapter 33 in the text, answer the following questions.

1. The side-effects of one person's production or consumption activities that affect others are called _3rd party effects / public goods / externalities_ . These are said to be _positive / negative_ when side effects benefit the bystander; they are _positive / negative_ when side effects harm the bystander.

2. The MSC curve measures the _____ cost of some activity. This equals the marginal _private / social_ cost plus the _internal / external_ cost of the activity.

3. The presence of negative externalities (or social costs) implies that private producers who consider only their personal benefits and costs will tend to produce _more / less_ than an efficient quantity of the good. The presence of positive externalities means that private producers will tend to produce _more / less_ than an efficient quantity of the good.

4. It is an _efficient / inefficient_ use of resources to produce a good when marginal social cost exceeds the price customers are willing to pay for it.

5. A person who burns trash generates _positive / negative_ externalities.

6. If a person that generates negative externalities can be influenced to incorporate the external costs of their actions into their private cost-benefit calculations, the externality will be _____ized. This can happen by persuading the externality creator that his actions have harmful effects, or the courts may _____ private property rights, which would cause resources to be _more / less_ protected than under common property arrangements, or parties may reach voluntary _____ to lower external effect to an efficient level.

7. The _____ theorem suggests that market exchanges will result in an efficient allocation of resources if transaction costs are _positive / zero / negative_. This result _does / does not_ depend on the original assignment of property rights.

8. A.C. Pigou believed that a _tax / subsidy_ should be applied to activities that generate negative externalities. Pigou believed that a _tax / subsidy_ should be applied to activities that generate positive externalities.

9. The theories of _Pigou / Coase_ suggest that private negotiations can internalize externalities in cases involving small numbers of people.

10. Some pollution _is / is not_ preferred to zero pollution, once we take account that _more / fewer_ goods will be produced if there is zero pollution.

11. A _____ good can simultaneously provide benefits to more than one consumer. Another way of putting this is to say that this kind of good is _nonexcludable / nonrival in consumption_.

12. A hamburger _is / is not_ a nonrival good. National defense _is / is not_ a nonrival good.

13. A good is non-_____ if it is impossible to exclude someone from consuming it. When a good has this characteristic, private companies _are / are not_ likely to supply it in the market.

14. When a good is nonexcludable, some people will attempt to obtain the benefits it provides without paying anything. These people are _____ _____. Their actions _contribute to / eliminate_ the incentive for private companies to produce the good.

15. A lighthouse provides a service (a warning that nearby rocks endanger ships) that _is / is not_ nonrivalrous among consumers. The service _is / is not_ excludable. Condequently in the 18th and 19 centuries lighthouses were _privately / governmentally_ owned and operated.

16. Traffic congestion occurs when the quantity of road space demanded is _greater / less_ than quantity supplied. This problem could be reduced by charging a _higher / lower_ price to use road space during rush hour. Road space _is / is not_ an excludable good. In _London / Hong Kong / Tulsa_ the government charges a price to drive on some city streets.

17. If someone is smoking in a restaurant, she creates _a public good / an externality_. Rather than having customers negotiate with each other on where to sit and whether to smoke, in practice these decisions are made by the _____ owner.

18. In a society of four people -- A, B, C, and D -- person B is poor. When person A provides assistance to B, then person A probably creates a public _____ for C and D. The tendency will be for C and D to be free _____.

19. Free riding becomes _more / less_ of a problem as the size of the relevant group enjoying a public good increases.

20. Satellites that remain in geosynchronous orbits around the earth are about _____ miles overhead. The amount of space available for such purposes is _a scarce good / virtually unlimited_.

21. A.C. Pigou distinguised between _____ costs and _____ costs.

22. According to the interview with Professor Murray Weidenbaum, the right reason for government regulation is to limit important _____. The best examples are _____ and _____ pollution.

23. According to Professor Murray Weidenbaum, the wrong reason for government regulation is to interfere with _____. The regulation of the interstate _____ industry is one example, and _____ restriction is another.

24. According to Professor Weidenbaum's estimates, the overall cost of complying with federal government regulations is in excess of $_____ billion each year.

Part 4.   Problems and Exercises
After reading chapter 33 in the text you should be able to work the following problems.

1. The graph at right contains a demand (D) and marginal private cost (MPC) curve for a private good. The production of this good results in external costs, shown in the graph.

   a. Label the marginal social cost curve MSC.

   b. Indicate the quantity of the good produced in a competitive industry if only private costs are considered. Label this quantity Q_1.

   c. Indicate the quantity of the good produced if all costs are considered. Label this quantity Q_2.

   d. Shade in the "triangle" that shows the net social cost of being at Q_1 rather than Q_2.

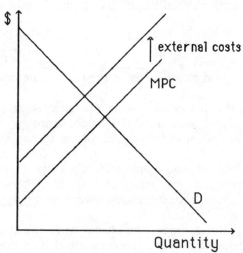

2. The graph at right contains a demand curve labeled
   MPB (=marginal private benefit) and a marginal
   cost (MC) curve for a private good. The
   production of this good results in positive
   externalities.

   a. Draw a marginal social benefit (MSB) curve to
   illustrate this case. Label the curve MSB.

   b. Indicate the quantity of the good produced in a
   competitive industry if only private benefits are
   considered. Label this quantity Q_1.

   c. Indicate the quantity of the good produced if all
   benefits are considered. Label this Q_2.

   d. In the presence of positive externalities, a
   market economy produces _more / less_ than the
   socially optimal quantity.

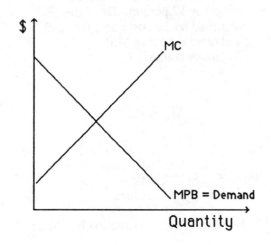

3. The diagram at right shows the hourly supply of
   runway space at your local airport. D1
   represents the peak demand for runway spaces,
   while D2 represents the off-peak (ordinary)
   demand. Assume the landing fee is P_0 at all
   times.

   a. Indicate the quantity of runway spaces desired
   at various times. Label the peak quantity Q_1 and
   the off-peak quantity Q_2.

   b. Will the airport ever be "congested" in the
   sense that more planes want to take off and land
   than the airport's capacity? _yes / no_ At that
   point consumption is _rival / nonrival_ .

   c. In what sense are the airport's runways similar
   to a public good during off-peak hours?

   _____

   _____

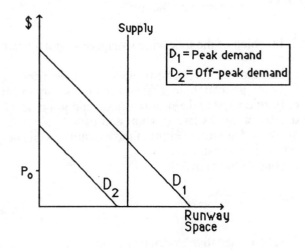

4. Assume that steel production results in negative externalities in the form of air pollution. The value placed on these external effects is $2 per ton. Draw the marginal social cost curve for steel and label the curve MSC. Accuracy counts!

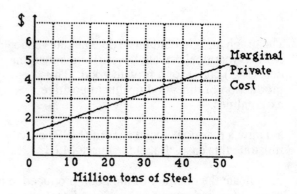

Part 5.   Self Test
Multiple choice questions

1. Market failure is a situation in which:

a. prices are so low that producers will not produce goods
b. there are too many buyers but not enough sellers
c. the market does not provide the ideal or optimal amount of a particular good
d. prices are so high that buyers won't buy the quantity of goods that sellers want to sell

Answer: _____

2. In which of the following situations could a negative externality potentially be involved?

a. Patricia is sitting at home waiting for her friend to call. He never calls.
b. Frank got caught in a rainstorm on his way to Miami.
c. Bergie went to the beauty saloon and got a new hairdo. She hates it.
d. Xavier works late at night and tries to sleep late in the morning. Every Tuesday and Thursday he is awakened at around eight in the morning by his neighbor's television set. His neighbor is slightly deaf and turns the television up loud.
e. none of the above

Answer: _____

3. When a negative externality exists:

a. social costs are greater than private costs
b. social costs equal private costs
c. external costs are greater than private costs
d. external costs are less than private costs
e. none of the above

Answer: _____

4. When a positive externality exists:

a. external benefits are greater than private benefits
b. external benefits are less than private benefits
c. social benefits are less than private benefits
d. social benefits equal private benefits
e. social benefits are greater than private benefits

Answer: _____

5. There are numerous ways of adjusting for externalities. One way is to persuade persons or groups that they ought to consider others when they act. Which of the following scenarios is consistent with this method of adjusting for (internalizing) externalities?

a. The government stipulates how much pollution (over some period of time) a factory can emit into the air.
b. Katrina is sitting at a restaurant when cigarette smoke drifts her way. She asks the manager to ask the person smoking if he would be considerate enough not to smoke. (The restaurant does not have designated smoking and nonsmoking areas.)
c. Mark's next door neighbor is having a loud party at 1 a.m. in the morning. Mark calls his neighbor up on the telephone and asks him to be more considerate.
d. b and c
e. a, b, and c

Answer: _____

6. The Coase theorem states that:

a. private property rights evolve when the costs of defining property rights are less than the benefits
b. in the case of trivial or zero transaction costs, negative externalities are more likely to appear
c. when transaction costs are high, negative externalities are more common than positive externalities
d. in the case of trivial or zero transaction costs, the property rights assignment does not matter to the resource allocative outcome

Answer: _____

7. Which of the following statements is true?

a. One way to internalize negative externalities is for government to subsidize to the activity that generates the externalities.
b. A subsidy is used to adjust for a positive externality, a tax is used to adjust for a negative externality.
c. Simply because taxes and subsidies are sometimes used to adjust for negative and positive externalities, it does not necessarily follow that the socially-optimal level of output will be reached.
d. b and c
e. a, b, and c

Answer: _____

8. When a good is nonexcludable:

a. it is impossible for individuals to obtain the benefits of the good without paying for it
b. it is possible for individuals to obtain the benefits of the good without paying for it
c. it is a government-provided good
d. the benefits of producing it outweigh the costs
e. none of the above

Answer: _____

9. Most economists contend that the market will fail to produce public goods because of the:

a. rivalry problem
b. Coase problem
c. Demsetz problem
d. free-rider problem

Answer: _____

10. Much of the air is polluted. We would expect this natural resource to be less polluted if:

a. there were stiff fines for polluting the air
b. private property rights were established in the air
c. both a and b
e. neither a nor b

Answer: _____

True-False

11. National defense is a public good.   T F

12. A public good is the same as a government-   T F
provided good.

13. A good is excludable if it is possible, or not   T F
prohibitively costly, to exclude someone from
obtaining the benefits of the good once it has
been produced.

14. Economists believe that there is an optimal   T F
amount of pollution and that this probably isn't
zero.

15. Coase discussed the reciprocal nature of   T F
externalities.

Fill in the blank

16. _____ is a situation in which the market does not provide the ideal or optimal amount of a particular good.

17. An externality is _____ if the person(s) or group that generated the externality incorporate into their own private cost-benefit calculations the external benefits of costs that third parties bear.

18. A good is _____ if its consumption by one person does not reduce its consumption by others.

19. In The <u>Economics of Welfare</u>, the economist _____ distinguished between private costs and social costs.

20. When either negative or positive externalities exist, the market output is different from the _____ .

Part 5. Answers to Self Test

1. c 2. d 3. a 4. e 5. d 6. d 7. d 8. b 9. d 10. c
11. T 12. F 13. T 14. T 15. T
16. Market failure 17. internalized 18. nonrivalrous in consumption 19. Pigou 20. socially-optimal

Part 6.   Answers

Part 2 Review of Concepts
1. c   2. d   3. e   4. a   5. b
Part 3 Key Concepts
1. externalities, positive, negative   2. marginal social cost, private, external   3. more, less
4. inefficient   5. negative   6. internalized, assign, more, agreements
7 Coase theorem, zero, does not   8. tax, subsidy   9. Coase   10. is, fewer   11. public, nonrival
12. is not, is   13. non-excludable, are not   14. free riders, eliminate   15. is not, is, privately
16. greater, higher, is, Hong Kong   17. an externality, restaurant   18. good, riders   19. more
20. 22,300, scarce   21. private, social   22. externalities, air and water
23. competition, trucking, import   24. $100 bil.

Part 4 Problems and Exercises

Part 4 Problems and Exercises

1.

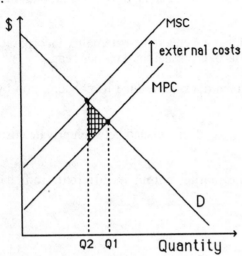

2. a-c.
See the
graph
at right

d. less

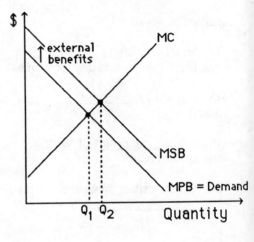

3. a. See graph at right.

b. yes (Q_1 > capacity), rival
c. consumption is non-rival
(many can benefit simultaneously
from the airport's existence)

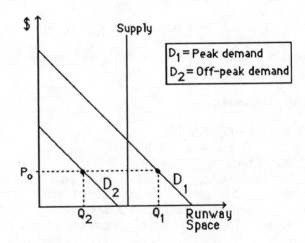

4.

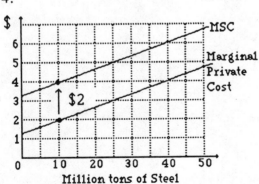

Chapter 34
Public Choice: Economic
Theory Applied to Politics

Part 1. Introduction and Purpose
Consider the following points as you read chaper 34 in the text.

Most of the time microeconomic theory is used to analyze situations in the private (market) economy. Then, consumers attempt to maximize their utility and suppliers attempt to maximize profits.

Although it may seem strange to you at first, economic theory can also be used to analyze the behavior of individuals and groups in the public (government) sector. People vote, candidates run for office, interest groups contribute to political campaigns, and bureaucrats request larger budgets — and in each instance economic incentives may influence the decision taken by the voter, candidate, interest group, or bureaucrat. used to analyze his or her actions Economic theory can be applied whenever self-interest motivates individual behavior. Self-interested behavior means balancing benefits against costs, and that is what is involved in the economic way of thinking.

The chapter actually discusses three major public choice theories. **Public choice** is a sub-discipline within economics that analyzes factors that influence the public's choice of representatives, policies, and constitutional rules. The first major theory examines one of the most important decision made by political candidates — namely what positions to take on various issues to ensure that they are elected (or reelected) to office.

This problem is similar to the decision faced by a company trying to pick a location for its place of business. In fact, the analysis presented in the text — where candidates locate themselves at various positions along the political spectrum — was first developed in an article on the optimum location for a vendor (seller) whose interest is to attract the largest number of customers possible. The conclusions of that analysis can be applied to political candidates. To attract the largest number of customers (supporters), locate in the center of the group. In politics, this means candidates will take positions on many issues that appeal to the **middle** (or median) **voter**. Candidates will not locate at either extreme of the the political spectrum any more than grocery stores will locate away from population areas.

The second group of public choice theories contained in the chapter discuss the **incentives** facing each citizen to **become informed** and to **vote**. One important thing distinguishes your private decisions from decisions you make as a voter. When you as a private individual decide to buy good X for $10, then you get good X. If you vote for candidate X or for policy X however, it is **unlikely that your vote will make a difference** in the outcome. The candidate or policy may win, but would have won even without your vote. Or it may lose, and your vote couldn't keep that from happening. Because of the very low probability that an individual voter's choices will prove decisive — maybe only one chance in millions — then it is not economically rational for the average citizen to gather information relevant for voting. Consequently people exhibit **rational ignorance**. The same analysis helps explains why many people don't spend the time to go **vote** on election day.

When citizens are uninformed and choose not to participate in the political process, then **special interest legislation** can pass fairly easily. For example, a policy that takes $1 from every working person in America would generate about $113 million. Now give that money to 5,000 people — about $22,600 apiece.

Because of rational ignorance, the "silent majority" will not even know that the policy exists. Even if they do find out about it, there is a good chance that they won't vote in the next election. And even if they do vote, very few people are going to be swayed by their feelings regarding a $1 tax. Consequently politicians who support the special interest policy seldom lose votes for giving away taxpayer dollars.

On the other hand, those who hope to receive the $22,600 will be more than happy to vote for politicians who support the program, and may also be willing to contribute to their reelection campaigns. **Thus special interest legislation is "profitable"** for legislators and interest groups. **Logrolling** makes the legislative process work more smoothly and permits an increase in the total supply of legislation. When special interests dominate the process, logrolling mainly increases the supply of special interest laws.

The third public choice theory in the chapter concerns the behavior of government employees other than those who run for political office — bureaucrats. A **bureau** is an organization whose operations are financed with by **funds from the legislature** rather than from private customers. Because bureaus are financed by someone other than consumers, they have less incentive than profit-seeking firms to try to satisfy customer desires. Bureaus also tend to have **higher costs** than a for-profit company producing the same service would have, since no employee or supervisor can receive a monetary reward for making the bureau operate more efficiently.

The conclusion that bureaus are less efficient or less responsive to their customers than private companies follows from an analysis of the incentives created by **institutional arrangements** found in bureaus. This is does not imply that bureau employees (bureaucrats) are somehow different than other people — in fact, by assuming that they are utility maximizers we have assumed that they are like everyone else. Public choice theory examines incentives rather than personalities.

Part 2. Review of Concepts from Earlier Chapters
Prior to reading chapter 34, match statements at left with the appropriate concept at right.

__1. Private suppliers are assumed to maximize this.	a. tax
__2. Mandatory charge levied by government.	b. profit
__3. What must be foregone as a result of taking an action.	c. stock
__4. Consumers and others try to maximize this.	d. utility
__5. Benefits minus costs; the payoff from taking an action.	e. exchange
__6. Government limits on supply have this impact on price.	f. incentive
__7. Certificate of ownership in a private company.	g. cost
__8. Corporate profits move in this direction when costs increase.	h. decline
__9. Giving something in return for something else.	i. increase

Part 3. Key Concepts in this Chapter

After reading chapter 34 in the text, answer the following questions.

1. According to public choice theory, people in the _private / public / both_ sector are motivated to maximize their personal utility. _Personalities / Incentives_ differ between the two sectors, causing differences in behavior.

2. Candidates for elective office tend to move to the _right / left / middle_ of the political spectrum. After two candidates have adjusted their positions, they will tend to support _similar / widely different_ policies. As a general rule, extreme views on an issue attract _more / fewer_ votes for a candidate.

3. True or false? _____ With majority voting, the only projects that will be adopted are those that provide more benefits than costs.

4. If a government project imposes a tax of $10 on someone who would receive $15 worth of benefits from the program, then that person's economic incentive is to vote _for / against_ the program.

5. Majority voting _does / does not_ take into account the intensity of voter preferences.

6. If you vote in the next presidential election, the outcome will _probably / probably not_ be affected by your decision to vote. This fact _increases / reduces_ your incentive to vote. It _increases / reduces_ your incentive to gather information relevant to voting.

7. If the benefits of gathering political information are less than the costs, it _is / is not_ economically rational to gather that information. The result is a phenonen known as rational _____.

8. A _____ _____ group is a subset of the population that holds intense preferences about particular policies that affect them most. These groups _do / do not_ exert a strong influence on the political process.

9. If the taxes to pay for a government program amount to $1 per person, then the average voter _is / is not_ likely to vote against a candidate in opposition to the policy. If a government program provides benefits of $10,000 apiece for people in a particular group, members of that group probably _will / will not_ actively campaign for the program.

10. _____ is the exchange of votes to gain support for legislation.

11. True or false? _____ People living in a congressional district can be a special interest group.

12. True or false? _____ Interest groups often claim that programs are beneficial to the general public even if they are special interest programs.

13. The British factory acts of the 19th century _increased / reduced_ the supply of labor to manufacturing jobs, and thereby caused wages to _rise / fall_. The main supporters of the legislation were _men / women_.

14. A _____ is an unelected government employee.

15. A government bureau receives its operating budget from _consumers / the legislature_.

16. Since a government bureau _is / is not_ attempting to maximize profits, it _will / will not_ work hard to eliminate waste and keep costs down.

17. A government bureau _does / does not_ have shareholders (similar to shareholders of a corporation).

18. In bureaus there is _a strong / no_ monetary incentive to those who reduce operating costs and improve quality.

19. It is _common / uncommon_ for a government bureau to have unspent funds in its budget at the end of the year. If it does have unspent funds, then funding in later years is likely to be _greater / less_ than in the current year.

20. In the interview with Professor James Buchanan, he reveals that his work represents an application of _____ theory to the political process, particularly to the choice of _____ rules.

21. After _____ states pass resolutions (laws) calling for a constitutional amendment to balance the budget, a constitutional convention will be called for that purpose. At the time of the interview with James Buchanan, _____ states had called for the amendment.

22. Professor Buchanan believes that public choice theory teaches us to be _more / less_ skeptical of government and politics.

Part 4. Problems and Exercises
After reading chapter 34 in the text you should be able to work the following problems.

1. Refer to the exhibit. It shows the number of people who favor various positions on an issue -- more or less defense spending, more or less education spending, etc.

Each • represents one person and one vote.

Use this information to answer the next few questions.

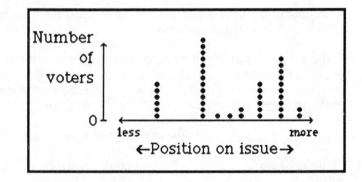

a. How many voters are there? _____

b. If a person were in the "middle" of a group of this size, there would _____ people on one side and _____ people on the other side.

c. Circle the middle or median vote among the voters above. Indicate the median voter's policy preference along the position spectrum with an **X**.

d. If a slightly _smaller_ program is proposed than the middle voter prefers, how many votes will be cast in support of the proposal? _____ How many votes are needed for a proposal to pass? _____

2. In a community of three voters it has been proposed that a road be paved. Voter 1 will receive $120 worth of benefits from the pavement, Voter 2 will receive $110, and Voter 3 will receive $50. Road improvements will cost voters $100 apiece.

   a. The road will provide total benefits of $_____.

   b. The total cost of paving the road equals $_____.

   c. It is / is not an efficient use of resources to pave the road.

   d. Given the choice, Voter 1 will vote yes / no .

   e. Given the choice, Voter 2 will vote yes / no .

   f. Given the choice, Voter 3 will vote yes / no .

   g. If an election is held, a majority will / will not vote to pave the road.

3. Consider a proposal to construct a new highway in the midwest. Because the highway is in a remote area, the main beneficiaries are 30,000 travelers, property owners, and construction workers in that area. Assume that the highway costs $60 million, and will be paid for by taxing every one of 120 million cars in the country by an equal amount.

   a. If the proposal is adopted, $_____ will be spent for the benefit of _____people, which amounts to $_____ apiece.

   b. The average car owner will pay $_____ if this proposal is adopted.

   c. What is the maximum amount the average car owner would be willing to spend to defeat the proposal if he could be certain that his contribution would be decisive? $_____ If there were a 1-in-50 chance that his contribution would be decisive, he would be willing to spend up to $_____ to defeat the proposal.

   d. In this situation it appears that the typical citizen / those who want the highway will be more politically active when the issue is debated in Congress.

4. There are five people in the room -- A, B, C, D, and E. Each prefers that the thermostat be set on a different temperature. Their preferred temperatures are 68, 74, 69, 67, and 73 degrees, respectively.

   a. The average temperature desired by the five is _____ degrees.

   b. The middle or median temperature is _____ degrees.

   c. If majority rule determines the thermostat setting, it will be at _____ degrees.

Part 5. Self Test
Multiple choice questions

1. Which of the following statements would a public choice theorist have some difficulty accepting as true?

a. The way to genuine reform in this country is to elect really good and moral people to government.
b. The people who work for a large government bureaucracy are fundamentally different people than those who work for a private firm.
c. People respond to the costs and benefits of different institutional settings.
d. a and b
e. a, b, and c

Answer: _____

2. In the second presidential debate between George Bush and Michael Dukakis on October 13, 1988, Bush occcassionally referred to Dukakis as "the governor from Massachusetts."
Bush probably did this because:

a. Dukakis was the governor of Massachusetts
b. Massachusetts is generally thought of as being a liberal state, and Bush wanted the viewing audience to consider Dukakis a liberal
c. Massachusetts is the state John F. Kennedy was from and Bush wanted everybody to think of Dukakis as another John F. Kennedy
d. there was proably no good reason for this

Answer: _____

3. In the second presidential debate between George Bush and Michael Dukakis on October 13, 1988, Dukakis would occasionally preface his remarks by saying, "I don't know which George Bush I am listening to tonight." Dukakis probably said this because:

a. he wanted voters to think that the George Bush they know is positioned somewhere differently on the political spectrum than the "real" George Bush
b. he truthfully did not know which George Bush he was listening to since there were at least two running for president
c. he has a hearing problem and usually hears double
d. it was just a spur of the moment thought

Answer: _____

4. Public choice is:

a. a branch of political science that deals with the presidential elections and how they affect the economy
b. a branch of sociology that deals with human behavior in group settings
c. a branch of economics that deals with the theory of the firm
d. a branch of economics that deals with the application of economic principles and tools to public-sector decision making
e. none of the above

Answer: _____

5. A public choice theorist would be most likely to say that government failure is a consequence of:

a. the ineptitude of bureaucrats
b. the rational behavior of the participants of the political process
c. the ignorance of voters
d. the greed of special interest groups
e. b, c, and d

Answer: _____

6. The model that predicts the candidate in a two-person race that comes closer to occupying the center of the voter distribution will win, is built on the assumption:

a. that people vote for the democratic candidate if they are democrats and they vote for the republican candidate if they are republicans
b. that people don't vote in close elections
c. that people vote for the candidate who comes closer to matching their own views
d. that people vote their pocketbooks
e. c and d

Answer: _____

7. In the second presidential debate between George Bush and Michael Dukakis on October 13, 1988, Dukakis repeatedly said that George Bush wanted to give a tax break to the rich. Dukakis probably said this because:

a. he wanted to push Bush to the right, away from the middle of the political spectrum
b. he wanted to push Bush to the left, away from the middle
c. he wanted to push Bush toward the middle
d. he wanted the voters to perceive Bush as a big spender

Answer: _____

8. Rational ignorance refers to:

a. the honeymoon period that every president experiences soon after he is elected
b. the fact that some voters are not smart enough to be informed on some things
c. the state of not acquiring information because the costs of acquiring the information are greater than the benefits
d. political candidates criticizing each other based on something other than the facts
e. none of the above

Answer: _____

9. The "average" member of the public is likely to know less about government agricultural policies than a farmer. The reason for this is:

a. a farmer is smarter than the "average" member of the public
b. government agricultural policies are more likely to directly affect a farmer than the "average" member of the public, and so a farmer has a sharper incentive to be informed about them
c. a farmer is a member of a special interest group and a member of a special interest group is more informed on all issues than the "average" member of the public
d. a and c
e. none of the above

Answer: _____

10. An elected representative may vote for a piece of special-interest legislation without fear of retaliation from the general public because:

a. many voters are rationally ignorant
b. people forgive quickly
c. all politicians do it, so in relative terms one politician is no worse for doing it than another
d. b and c
e. none of the above

Answer: _____

True-False

11. James Buchanan and Gordon Tullock are the   T F
founders of public choice.

12. Public choice economists contend that people   T F
exhibit different behavior in the private sector
than they do in the public sector.

13. The simple majority decision rule does not   T F
take into account the intensity of individuals'
preferences.

14. Logrolling is the exchange of votes to gain support for legislation.   T F

15. It is irrational not to vote in a presidential election.   T F

Fill in the blank

16. _____ is said to exist when government enacts policies that produce inefficient and/or inequitable results as a consequence of the rational behavior of the participants in the political process.

17. Many potential voters will not vote because the _____ of voting -- in terms of time spent going to the polls and so on -- outweigh the _____of voting measured in terms of the probability of their single vote affecting the election outcome.

18. Candidates for political office will speak more in _____ terms than _____ terms.

19. Near the end of a political campaign, we would expect two candidates running for the same office to be _____ to each other in terms of their policy positions than at the beginning of the campaign.

20. _____ won the Nobel Prize in Economics in 1986 for his work in public choice theory.

Part 5. Answers to Self Test

1. d 2. b 3. a 4. d 5. b 6. c 7. a 8. c 9. b 10. a
11. T 12. F 13. T 14. T 15. F
16. Government failure 17. costs, benefits
18. general, specific 19. closer 20. James Buchanan

Part 6. Answers

Part 2 Review of Concepts
1. b 2. a 3. g 4. d 5. f 6. i 7. c 8. h 9. e

Part 3 Key Concepts
1. both, Incentives 2. middle, similar, fewer 3. false 4. for
5. does not (a strong yes is cancelled by a weak no) 6. probably not, reduces, reduces
7. is not, rational ignorance 8. special interest, do 9. is not, will 10. Logrolling 11. True
12. true 13. reduced, rise, men 14. bureaucrat 15. the legislature 16. is not, will not 17 does
not 18. no 19. uncommon, less 20. economic, constitutional 21. 34 (2/3rds), 32 22. more

Part 4 Problems and Exercises

1. a. 41
   b. 20, 20
   c. see chart at right
   d. 20, 21

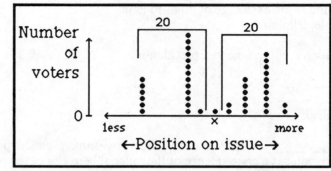

2. a. $280   b. $300
   c. is not   d. yes
   e. yes   f. no   g. will

3. a. $60 mil., 30,000, $2000   b. $0.50   c. $0.50, $0.01   d. those who want the highway

4. a. 70.2   b. 69   c. 69

Chapter 35
International Trade

Part 1. Introduction and Purpose
Consider the following points as you read chapter 35 in the text.

In many respects international trade is "nothing special" to economists. Americans trade with people in other countries for the same reason they trade with other Americans — to buy goods at prices lower than their own production cost, or to sell goods for higher prices than the value they place on the goods themselves. **Self interest** motivates such behavior, so it can be analyzed with the same **supply and demand** model that we use for domestic trade.

What makes international trade different than domestic trade is the way it is treated by political institutions. While trade within the U.S. is relatively free and unrestricted, governments in most nations have special policies for goods crossing their borders. **Tariffs and quotas** are two well-known trade policies, and there are a number of lesser known policies as well.

Most economists support free trade policies. They do so because economic theory demonstrates that trade should benefit the nation, and because there is a considerable body of empirical evidence showing that it does. That was one of the major points demonstrated by Adam Smith about 200 years ago in the first modern economic work, the *Wealth of Nations*.

The benefits of trade — whether local, national, or international — occur because workers and other resources can **specialize** in the production of just a few goods and **trade** with others who specialize in producing different goods. Specialization by everyone increases total production, and trade permits each person to consume goods produced by the most efficient producer. If you aren't convinced that specialization lowers the cost of things, try making your own pencil or coat rather than buying one from someone who specializes in producing those goods.

All of these ideas are contained within David Ricardo's **Law of Comparative Advantage**. Ricardo showed that a nation fares best if it specializes at producing those goods in which it has a **relative** advantage (or where its relative disadvantage is least). Put differently, a nation should produce and export goods for which its **opportunity cost** of production is lower than in other nations.

Even if **free trade promotes the nation's best interests**, it is not necessarily best for each and every person within the nation. It may sound good to say we should specialize in steel production and import computers, but that is not what the people working for or investing in the U.S. computer industry want to hear. They want to have their foreign competitors closed out of the market. **Trade restrictions help** the **specific industries** being protected, and impose costs on domestic consumers. We adopt such policies when protected industries are more effective than customers when it comes to manipulating the political process.

The arguments for restricting trade that economists find most appealing are those to protect strategically important industries that contribute to the **national defense, infant industries** until they are large enough to compete internationally, and domestic industries injured by dumping and other **unfair trade practices** in other nations. Because these are respectable arguments for restrictive trade laws however, virtually everyone seeking protectionist laws claims that one or more of these special cases apply to themselves.

The main policies used to restrict international trade are tariffs and quotas. A **tariff** is a tax on imported goods and a **quota** is a numerical limit on the number of units that can be imported. Both policies **limit** the **supply** of foreign goods in this country, so prices paid by U.S. consumers must increase. These price increases help domestic producers in two ways: companies receive more for each unit, and they produce more units than before. Trade restriction can often provide larger profits (or rents) than investment and invention, and is less risky. Nowadays almost all large companies routinely establish offices in Washington, hire former Congressmen or bureaucrats to promote their causes, and give campaign contributions and other assistance to key members of Congress. Experience shows that it pays to invest in rent seeking, so companies and other interest groups do it.

A number of published **studies** show that such policies accomplish very little in the way of jobs saved, and impose very **high costs on consumers**. For example, each job saved in the U.S. automobile industry following Japan's forced acceptance of export restraints costs American consumers well over $100,000 each year, which is many times the salary earned by those whose jobs were saved. Similar findings apply to other industries including carbon steel, textiles, and shoes. By almost any standard, the economic benefits of trade restrictions are less than the costs. The political benefits are evidently high enough to justify trade restrictions however, so tariffs and quotas exist for a wide range of U.S. imports.

Part 2. Review of Concepts from Earlier Chapters
Prior to reading chapter 35, match statements at left with the appropriate concept at right.

___1. The additional cost of producing one more unit.
___2. Used to produce goods and services.
___3. These determine market price.
___4. What must be foregone as a result of taking an action.
___5. Output of 2 goods produced with all available resources (curve).
___6. Additional producers cause this shift in market supply.
___7. A reduction in market supply has this effect on price.
___8. Giving units of one good in return for another.

a. supply & demand
b. trade/exchange
c. marginal cost
d. resources
e. rightward
f. increase
g. PPF frontier
h. opportunity cost

Part 3. Key Concepts in this Chapter
After reading chapter 35 in the text, answer the following questions.

1. In 1986, ____% of the U.S. gross national product was exported. Imports amounted to _____% of GNP.

2. The dollar value of U.S. exports plus imports was $_____ bil. in 1986.

3. The U.S.'s two largest trading partners are _____ and _____.

4. Major U.S. exports listed in exhibit 2 in the text include diamonds / corn , clothing / computers , and aircraft / petroleum .

5. Americans trade with people in other nations to make themselves better / worse off.

6. Country ABC can produce a maximum of 100 units of wheat or 600 units of steel; country JKL can produce a maximum of 150 units of wheat or 610 units of steel. In this instance ABC has a comparative advantage in wheat / steel / neither / both . In this instance JKL has a comparative advantage in wheat / steel .

7. A nation has a comparative / an absolute advantage in the production of a good if it can produce more of that good than the other nation.

8. Nation ABC can produce 10 units of wheat and 40 units of steel, or it can produce 20 units of wheat and 25 units of steel. For this nation, 5 / 10 / 20 additional units of wheat require enough resources to produce 15 / 25 / 40 units of steel. The opportunity cost of one unit of wheat is ____ units of steel. The opportunity cost of one unit of steel is ____ units of wheat.

9. It is / is not possible for one nation to have a comparative advantage in both goods.

10. International trade does / does not make it possible for a nation to consume at a point beyond its production possibilities frontier (PPF).

11. The economist David _____ originally stated the law of comparative advantage.

12. A nation that obeys the law of comparative advantage does / does not specialize in production. It does / does not trade with other nations.

13. True or false? _____ When a nation has an absolute disadvantage in the production of all goods, then it cannot gain by specialization and trade.

14. International trade does / does not benefit the nation that trades. International trade does / does not benefit every individual in the nation that trades.

15. The maximum amount a consumer is willing to pay for a unit of X minus the price actually paid is known as consumer profit / surplus . This equals _____-cents if you would be willing to pay up to 95-cents for a beer but only have to pay 60-cents.

16. If you produce something at a marginal cost of $2 and sell it for $3, then you receive a producer _____ of $____ on that unit.

17. Suppose an item is produced at a marginal cost of $5, which a consumer values by $9, and the producer sells the unit to the consumer for $7.50. Then producer surplus equals $_____ on the unit and consumer surplus equals $_____.

18. Suppose initially that U.S. companies are not allowed to export their products to foreign consumers. Now assume that law is removed. In the new situation, the total demand for the company's output will be _greater / less_ than before, which implies that the price of the producer's product will _rise above / fall below_ its previous level. This price change is good from the perspective of U.S. _producers / consumers_, but it is bad from the perspective of U.S. _producers / consumers_.

19. Suppose initially that it is illegal to import foreign goods into the U.S. Now suppose that law is removed. In the new situation, the total supply of goods available to consumers is _greater / less_ than before, which implies that product prices will _rise / fall_ compared to previous levels. From the perspective of U.S. _producers / consumers_ this price change is good, but it is bad from the perspective of U.S. _producers / consumers_.

20. Some of the arguments for government policies that interfere with free trade flows are the National _____ argument, the _____-industry argument, and the anti-_____ argument.

21. A _____ is a tax on imports. A _____ is a numerical limit on the amount of a good that can be imported into the country.

22. In this century U.S. tariff rates were highest after the _____-_____ tariff was enacted by Congress in 19_____. These tariffs _did / did not_ help end the depression of that decade.

23. A tariff _increases / reduces_ the total volume of trade. A quota _increases / reduces_ the total volume of trade. A tariff causes price paid by consumers to _rise / fall_. A quota causes price paid by consumers to _rise / fall_.

24. A _mandatory / voluntary_ export restraint was adopted by _Britain / Japan / Germany_ in 1981, whereby that nation agreed to reduce its exports of _electronics / watches / cars_ to the U.S.

25. A voluntary export restraint has an impact similar to the impact of a _tariff / quota_.

26. As a result of the voluntary export restraint on automobiles, U.S. car companies raised their prices by about _$100 / $500 / $1000_ per car. The U.S. International Trade Commission estimated that _____ U.S. jobs were saved by the export restraints, at an annual cost to consumers of $_____ per job saved.

27. Protection of the carbon steel industry in the U.S. has saved an estimated _____ domestic jobs in that industry. The annual cost to consumers was $_____ per job saved.

28. Tariffs and quotas are usually advocated for their _____ effects rather than their aggregate or overall effects. The idea is to pass a law that will protect _me / everyone_, not one that will help _me / everyone_.

29. The interview with Professor Thurow suggests that the pluses from free international trade are probably _larger / smaller_ than the minuses, overall. He believes that the pluses from free trade represent _large / small_ amounts for very many people; while the minuses fall on a small number of people, each of whom suffer _large / small_ losses.

30. In Japan, M ___ ___ ___ runs that nation's industrial policy. Professor Thurow suggests that the policy is / is not effective.

Part 4. Problems and Exercises
After reading chapter 35 in the text you should be able to work the following problems.

1. The tables show combinations of two goods, steel and cloth, that can be produced in two nations, ABC and RST.

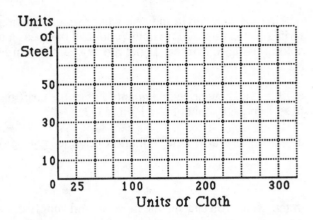

In ABC

Steel:	0	10	20	30	40
Cloth:	100	75	50	25	0

In RST

Steel:	0	20	40	60
Cloth:	300	200	100	0

a. Use figures from the table to plot each nation's production possibilities frontier (PPF). Label the curves PPF-abc and PPF-rst.

b. Which nation has an <u>absolute</u> advantage in the production of cloth? _____ In steel? _____

c. Which nation has a <u>comparative</u> advantage in the production of cloth? _____ In steel? _____

d. According to the law of comparative advantage, nation _____ will export cloth and import steel. Nation _____ will export steel and import cloth.

2. Refer to the figures given in the previous exercise regarding production in ABC and RST.

a. For ABC to increase production of steel by 10 units, it has to reduce production of cloth by _____ units. Accordingly each one unit of steel costs ___ units of cloth in ABC.

b. For RST to increase production of steel by 20 units, it had to reduce production of cloth by _____ units. Accordingly each one unit of steel costs ___ units of cloth in RST.

c. The opportunity cost of steel is less in nation ABC / RST .

3. The graph at right shows the supply and demand for good X, at a time when units of X can be imported into the U.S. without any restriction whatever.

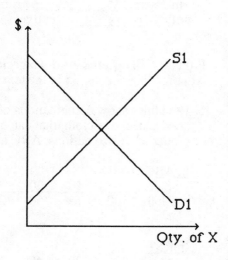

a. Indicate the market price and quantity. Label them P1 and Q1.

b. Alter the diagram to indicate what happens when a tariff (tax) is imposed on units produced overseas and sold in the U.S. market. Label the new supply curve S2.

c. Show the new price and quantity after the tariff has been imposed. Label them P2 and Q2.

d. An import tariff causes market price to rise / fall .

4. In the graph you can see the demand and supply curve for good X.

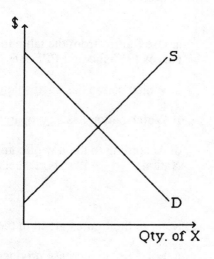

a. Indicate the market price by drawing a solid horizontal line from the equilibrium point to the price axis. Label this price P1 and the quantity Q1.

b. Shade in the amount of consumers' surplus in this particular case with a 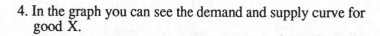 pattern. Shade in the amount of producers' surplus in this particular case with a ▨ pattern.

c. Assume a regulation limits total production of X to one-half its original Q1 level. Draw a vertical supply curve at this new quantity and label it Q2. Label the new equilibrium price P2.

d. Following the new regulation (see c above), consumer surplus is now greater / less than before. Producer surplus is now greater / less than before.

Part 5. Self Test
Multiple choice questions

1. The major single-country trading partners of the United States are:

a. Egypt and Libya
b. the Soviet Union and the People's Republic of China
c. Canada and Japan
d. France and West Germany
e. Belgium and Great Britain

Answer: _____

2. In 1987, which of the following was a major import for the United States?

a. wheat
b. diamonds
c. coal
d. soybeans
e. none of the above

Answer: _____

3. A country has an absolute advantage in the production of a good if it can:

a. with the same quantity of resources produce the same quantity of a good as another country
b. with fewer resources produce the same quantity of a good as another country
c. with the same quantity of resources produce less of a good than another country
d. with more resources produce more of a good than another country
e. none of the above

Answer: _____

Exhibit E

United States		Japan	
Good X	Good Y	Good X	Good Y
120	0	30	0
80	10	20	10
40	20	10	20
0	30	0	30

4. In Exhibit E, the opportunity cost of one unit of Y for the United States is _____ whereas the opportunity cost of one unit of Y for Japan is _____ .

a. 2X, 5X
b. 10X, 2X
c. 4X, 1X
d. 6X, 5X
e. none of the above

Answer: _____

5. In Exhibit E, the United States has an absolute advantage in the production of _____ and Japan has an absolute advantage in the production of _____ .

a. both goods, neither good
b. good X, neither good
c. good Y, good X
d. neither good, both goods

Answer: _____

6. In Exhibit E, the United States is the lower opportunity cost producer of _____ and Japan is the lower opportunity cost producer of _____ .

a. good X, good Y
b. both goods, neither good
c. neither good, both goods
d. good Y, good X

Answer: _____

7. Considering the data in Exhibit E, which of the following terms of trade would both countries agree to?

a. 5.5X = 1Y
b. 0.5X = 1Y
c. 5X = 1Y
d. 2X = 1Y

Answer: _____

8. Which of the following statements is true?

a. It is possible through specialization and trade for a country's inhabitants to consume at a level beyond its production possiblities frontier.
b. A country has a comparative advantage in the production of a good when it can produce the good at higher opportunity cost than another country.
c. If a country has an absolute advantage in the production of two goods in a two-good world, it may still benefit by specializing and trading.
d. a and b
e. a and c

Answer: _____

9. Jack paid $40 for good X and gained $10 consumers' surplus. What is the highest price Jack would have paid for the good?

a. $50
b. $30
c. $60
d. $65
e. there is not enough information to answer the question

Answer: _____

10. Producers' surplus is the difference between the price _____ receive for a good and the _____ price for which they would have _____ the good.

a. sellers, minimum, sold
b. buyers, maximum, bought
c. sellers, maximum, sold
d. buyers, minimum, bought

Answer: _____

11. The national defense argument for trade restriction contends that:

a. the president should have the authority to erect trade barriers in case of war or national emergency
b. free trade makes a country dependent on other countries and this weakens the national defense
c. a country should produce those goods necessary for national defense purposes even if it doesn't have a comparative advantage in them
d. if your enemy erects trade restrictions so should you
e. b and c

Answer: _____

12. Dumping refers to:

a. buying goods at low prices in foreign countries and selling them at high prices in the United States
b. expensive goods being sold for low prices
c. government actions to remedy "unfair" trade practices
d. the sale of goods abroad at a price below their cost and below the price charged in the domestic market

Answer: _____

13. A tariff is a:

a. restriction on the number of people that can work in an export business
b. legal limit on the amount of a good that may be imported
c. business fee incurred to ship goods abroad
d. tax on imports
e. none of the above

Answer: _____

14. Under a policy of prohibiting exports:

a. domestic consumers have greater consumers' surplus than under a policy of permitting exports
b. domestic consumers have less consumers' surplus than under a policy of permitting exports
c. domestic producers have greater producers' surplus than under a policy of permitting exports
d. a and c
e. b and c

Answer: _____

15. Under a policy of prohibiting imports:

a. domestic consumers have greater consumers' surplus than under a policy of permitting exports
b. domestic consumers have less consumers' surplus than under a policy of permitting exports
c. domestic producers have greater producers' surplus than under a policy of permitting exports
d. a and c
e. b and c

Answer: _____

True-False

16. Major U.S. exports include automobiles,   T F
computers, and corn.

17. There is an overall net loss from of a policy of   T F
permitting exports over a policy of prohibiting
exports.

18. The effects of a quota are a decrease in   T F
consumers' surplus, an increase in producers' surplus,
and an increase in total revenue for the importers
who sell the quota.

19. Consumers' surplus is the difference between the   T F
price buyers pay for a good and the maximum price
they would have paid for the good.

20. In this century, tariff rates were at their   T F
highest during the Smoot-Hawley tariff.

Fill in the blank

21. The _____ argument states the domestic producers should not have to compete (on an unequal basis) with foreign producers that sell products below cost and below the prices they charge in their domestic markets.

22. _____ gain more than _____ lose from a policy that permits imports.

23. _____ gain more than _____ lose from a policy that permits exports.

24. _____ lose more than _____ gain from a policy that prohibits exports.

25. _____ lose more than _____ gain from a policy that prohibits imports.

Part 5. Answers to Self Test

1. c 2. b 3. b 4. c 5. b 6. a 7. d 8. e 9. a 10. a
11. c 12. d 13. d 14. a 15. e
16. T 17. F 18. T 19. T 20. T
21. anti-dumping 22. Consumers, producers
23. Producers, consumers 24. Producers, consumers
25. Consumers, producers

Part 6. Answers

Part 2 Review of Concepts
1. c   2. d   3. a   4. h   5. g   6. e   7. f   8. b

Part 3 Key Concepts
1. 5.1%, 8.8%   2. $587.3 billion   3. Canada, Japan   4. corn, computers, aircraft   5. better
6. steel, wheat   7. an absolute   8. 10, 15, 1.5, 0.67   9. is not   10. does   11. Ricardo
12. does, does   13. false   14. does, does not   15. surplus, 35¢   16. surplus, $1   17. $2.50,
$1.50   18. greater, rise, producers, consumers   19. greater, fall, consumers, producers
20. defense, infant-industry, anti-dumping   21. tariff, quota   22. Smoot-Hawley, 1930, did not
23. reduces, reduces, rise, rise   24. voluntary, Japan, cars   25. quota   26. $1000, 44,000,
$193,000   27. 20,000, $85,272   28. distributional, me, everyone   29. larger, small, large   30.
MITI, is

Part 4 Problems and Exercises

1. a. See graph at right.
   b. RST, RST
   c. RST, ABC
   d. RST, ABC

2. a. 25, 2.5
   b. 100, 5
   c. ABC

3. a-c. See graph below, left.
   d. rise

4. a-c. See graph, below right.
   d. less, less

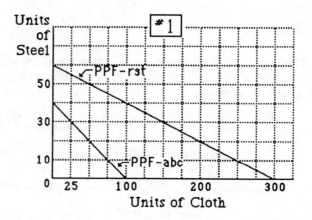

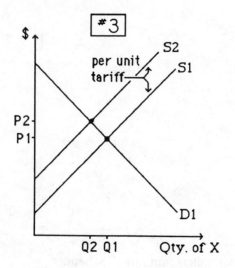

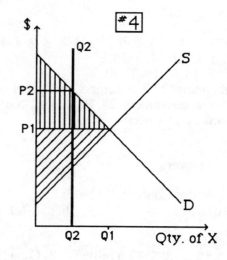

Chapter 36
International Finance

Part 1. Introduction and Purpose
Consider the following points as you read chapter 36 in the text.

This chapter is about international financial arrangements, or the monetary side of international economic transactions. The previous chapter just examined some of the reasons people have for buying and selling goods across national borders, and the present chapter discusses the monetary aspect of those transactions.

Why do dollars and other currencies cross national borders? In the private sector, currency flows out in exchange for foreign-produced goods and services, as gifts, and for the purpose of making investments or loans in foreign nations. If more dollars flow out of a nation than in, then it stands to reason that more goods, services, foreign stocks, and so forth enter the U.S. than leave it during the same time period. A net outflow of funds represents a **deficit** in the international accounts, while a net inflow of funds is a **surplus**. As just noted however, these deficits are in currency units only; the deficit nation also has a net inflow of goods and assets from abroad. To say that the deficit is too large is also to say that one is importing too many foreign goods, or buying too many foreign stocks and bonds.

The **merchandise trade balance** (or **balance of trade**) is one indicator of what is going on in the international markets for merchandise (not including services). The merchandise trade balance equals the value of the nation's merchandise exports minus its merchandise imports. A trade surplus means that the nation's foreign sales exceeds its own imports of foreign goods. This is often interpreted as a sign that the nation's producers are particularly efficient and can produce at lower cost than producers in other nations. A trade deficit may be a sign that the nation's production costs are higher than those overseas.

The **current account** is a somewhat broader measure of the nation's trade position than the merchandise balance. It also includes services exports and imports and net unilateral transfers (gifts, pensions, etc.) made to foreigners. In effect, the current account includes all of the international currency flows of a *non-financial* nature. The **capital account** records the effects of currency flows made for principally financial purposes — loans and investments overseas. If U.S. residents lend and invest more overseas than foreigners lend and invest here, then the overall situation is one where currency is leaving this nation — and there is a **deficit** in the U.S. capital account. For the capital accounts to be in **surplus**, more funds must flow in than leave; foreigners must be buying domestic stocks and bonds, and so forth.

Among the most-watched accounts is the **combined current and capital account**. This represents the overall situation with respect to all non-official flows of currency into or out of the nation. A deficit in the combined account suggests that more funds are leaving the nation than are entering it. This means the value of the nation's currency — the exchange rate — will decline relative to other currencies (unless governments intervene in currency markets and prevent that from happening).

Here's why. It is a key part of the analysis to realize that when Americans buy something from foreigners (goods, bonds, services), *foreign sellers want to be paid in their own (home) currency*. Consequently when you buy a Korean television set for $300, at some point along the line someone has had to hand over Korean *won* to the TV manufacturer. Someone had to sell your dollars to buy *won*. Consequently there is an increase in the **supply** of dollars in currency markets and an increase in the **demand** for *won*. Applying supply and demand analysis, you will recognize this situation as one where the dollar's value declines and the *won* 's value increases.

If we are originally at a point of equilibrium where the combined capital and current account sum to zero, your desire for the Korean television set created a deficit in the trade balance and in the combined current and capital account. Dollars had to be sold to buy *won*, and as a result the dollar **depreciates** in currency markets while the *won* **appreciates**. The same thing would have happened if you had purchased Korean stocks, sent a cash gift to someone in Korea, and so forth. Decisions by consumers, investors, companies, and others affect the flow of goods, services, and assets; and in doing so, affect the exchange rates of various currencies.

The exception to this occurs when governments pledge to maintain **fixed exchange rates**. That pledge means governments plan to buy and sell various currencies to maintain the official exchange rate.

The **gold** standard (1870s-1930s) and the **Bretton Woods** gold-dollar standard (1944-1970s) were two examples of fixed exchange rate systems. To maintain fixed exchange rates over the long run, it is necessary for governments to restrain themselves from following inflationary monetary and fiscal policies. Few governments have been willing to do to that in recent years. Consequently governments have permitted exchange rates to be more flexible during the last 15 years than any time in the past century.

Part 2. Review of Concepts from Earlier Chapters
Prior to reading chapter 36, match statements at left with the appropriate concept at right.

__1. When domestic consumers buy goods from foreign producers.   a. tariff
__2. Selling U.S. goods to foreign consumers.   b. quota
__3. Tax on imports.   c. shortage
__4. Limit on quantity of imports.   d. surplus
__5. These set market price.   e. export
__6. When quantity supplied exceeds quantity demanded.   f. import
__7. When quantity demanded exceeds quantity supplied.   g. supply & demand

Part 3. Key Concepts in this Chapter
After reading chapter 36 in the text, answer the following questions.

1. This chapter examines the _real / monetary_ side of international transactions.

2. If a transaction is recorded as a _credit / debit_ in a nation's international accounts, then its currency is flowing out of the nation is and being supplied in foreign exchange markets. Other things being equal, this will cause the value of the nation's currency to _rise / fall_ relative to other nation's currencies.

3. If a transaction is recorded as a _credit / debit_ in a nation's international accounts, then currency is flowing into the nation from people who have purchased it in foreign exchange markets. Other things being equal, this will cause the value of the nation's currency to _rise / fall_ relative to other nation's currencies.

4. If an American wholesaler purchases 10,000 Korean-produced television sets, then the American _demands / supplies_ dollars in foreign exchange markets. If the American _demands / supplies_ Korean won, that nation's standard currency unit, in foreign exchange markets, the result is that dollars will _rise / fall_ in value relative to the won.

5. The nation's _current / capital / merchandise trade_ account includes all payments related to the imports and exports of goods and services.

6. Exports of merchandise (not including services) minus imports of merchandise equals the merchandise _____ balance, or the balance of _____. There will be a _surplus / deficit_ in this account if imports exceed exports.

7. If an American gives money to a relative or friend in Australia, then this transaction is reflected in the account known as net _____ transfers abroad. Each transfer abroad is recorded as a _credit / debit_ in the U.S. _current / capital_ accounts.

8. The current account includes the balance on exports and imports of _____ and _____ plus the balance of net _____ transfers abroad.

9. The _current / capital_ account includes the effects of payments related to investments and loans that cross national borders. A deficit in this account means that U.S. loans and investments to foreigners _exceed / equal / are less than_ foreign loans and investments in the U.S.

10. Government official reserves include foreign currencies, _____, and deposit balance in the _____ _____ Fund.

11. The balance of payments equals the balance on _____ account, the capital account balance, the _____ reserve balance, and the statistical _____. Including all of these accounts, the balance of payments must sum to _zero / a positive amount / a negative amount_.

12. The value of one currency in terms of another currency is a _trade / official / exchante_ rate. For example, if one dollar exchanges for 2 German marks, then each mark has a value of $_____. If one dollar exchanges for 2.5 marks, the mark has a value of $_____.

13. In a _fixed / constant / flexible / gold_ exchange rate system, exchange rates for currencies are determined by supply and demand.

14. Under a system of flexible exchange rates, it _is / is not_ possible to have a continuing surplus of a currency. It _is / is not_ possible to have a continuing shortage of a currency.

15. If there is currently a shortage of dollars in currency markets, then the quantity of dollars _supplied / demanded_ is greater than the quantity of dollars _supplied / demanded_. As a result the dollar's value will _rise / fall_ relative to other currencies.

16. If the overall price level in the U.S. rises relative to that in other nations, then foreign goods appear relatively _more / less_ expensive than before. This will cause the U.S. to import _more / fewer_ goods from that nation than before. The result will be for Americans to supply _more / fewer_ dollars in currency markets than before. The dollar's value will _rise / fall_ relative to other currencies.

17. If real interest rates fall in the U.S. relative to those in other nations, then foreign loans will look relatively _more / less_ rewarding than before to U.S. banks. This will cause U.S. bankers to loan _more / less_ funds (capital) to that nation than before. The result will be for Americans to supply _more / fewer_ dollars in currency markets. The dollar's value will _rise / fall_ relative to other currencies.

18. The _____ _____ parity suggests that an equilibrium exchange rate is one where one dollar's worth of something in the U.S. could be purchased in a foreign nation with a dollar's worth of that nation's currency. For example, if a pair of shoes is $30 in the U.S. and the dollar is worth 2 German marks, then the shoes would sell for _____ marks in Germany.

19. According to the text, the purchasing power parity theory of exchange rates is most accurate in the _short / long_ run.

20. The dollar will tend to appreciate in currency markets if the _combined_ current and capital account balance is in _surplus / deficit_. It will tend to depreciate if the _combined_ balance is in _surplus / deficit_.

21. If there is a surplus of pounds (£), then the quantity of £ supplied is _greater / less_ than the quantity demanded. The excess suggests that the combined current and capital account is in _surplus / deficit_. That is, the British are buying _more / less_ overseas than they are selling, and are supplying _more / fewer_ £ to currency markets than foreigners currently require to purchase British goods and investments.

22. Suppose there are two currencies, dollars and pounds. The demand for dollars in currency markets _is / is not_ the mirror image of the supply of pounds. The supply of dollars in currency markets _is / is not_ the mirror image of the demand for pounds.

23. International exchange rates were _flexible / fixed / variable_ between 1944 a nd the early 1970s.

24. If the Federal Reserve else wants to increase the value of the £ in foreign exchange markets, it could _buy / sell_ pounds with _dollars / pounds_. In this instance the Fed would be demanding _£ / $_ and supplying _£ / $_.

25. Under a system of fixed exchange rates, the rate maintained by government policy makers is known as the _legal / official_ exchange rate. If this rate is above the rate which supply and demand would establish, then the currency is _over / under / correctly_ valued. If the government lowers the currency's official exchange rate, then the currency has been _revalued / devalued_.

26. Under fixed exchange rates, a nation that faces a persistent deficit in its combined current and capital account can _devalue / revalue_ its currency, _adopt / eliminate_ tariffs and quotas, or tighten its _____ policy.

27. It is commonly believed that fixed exchange rates result in _more / less_ international trade than flexible exchange rates.

28. Someone who has contractually agreed to pay a certain amount of foreign currency at a later date can arrange to purchase the foreign currency ahead of time (today) in the _____ market. This market _increases / reduces_ the risk that the individual faces due to the possibility of fluctuating exchange rates.

29. The _____ standard prevailed from the 1870s to the 19____s. During this period the U.S. stood ready to buy or sell _____ at a fixed price of $_____ per ounce.

30. Under the gold standard, if gold flows into the U.S. from overseas the U.S. money supply would _increase / decline_. The foreign money supply would _increase / decrease_.

31. Under the gold standard, if a nation has a deficit in its combined current and capital account, then gold flows _into / out of_ that nation. As a result the nation's money supply _rises / falls_. That change in the money supply causes the nation's price level to _rise / fall_ in that nation. The price change _increases / reduces_ the nation's exports, which causes the original deficit to _grow / shrink_.

32. True or false? _____ The gold standard represents one type of fixed exchange rate system.

33. The _____ _____ Fund is a kind of international central bank designed by negotiators at Bretton Woods (N.H.) in 19_____. Under the plan, nations pledged to maintain a system of _fixed / flexible_ exchange rates.

34. On August 15, 19_____, President Nixon said that the U.S. would no longer agree to buy and sell _____ at a price of $_____. A short while later exchange rates _were / were no longer_ fixed as they had been before.

35. The _current_ international monetary system can be described as a _____ flexible exchange rate system. Governments do not control exchange rates, but they moderate major _____ in exchange rates.

36. The ____-curve analysis suggests that if a nation's currency depreciates, then the nation's trade deficit will _improve / worsen_ in the short run. The trade deficit will _improve / worsen_ in the long run.

37. The J-curve analysis assumes that demand for imports is price _elastic / inelastic_ in the short run.

38. During President Reagan's two terms, the dollar rose in foreign currency markets during 1981-19_____. The dollar generally fell in value from 19_____ to mid 1988.

Part 4. Problems and Exercises

After reading chapter 36 in the text you should be able to work the following problems.

1. At various times in the text, turning points are mentioned when major changes were made in international financial institutions and policies.

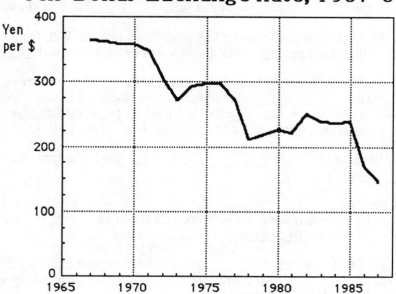

Yen-Dollar Exchange Rate, 1967-87

a. The Bretton Woods system was an arrangement whereby interest rates would be _fixed / flexible_. The Bretton Woods system effectively came to an end in 19 _65/ 71 / 80_.

b. In 19_____, the Group of 5 nations met at the New York Plaza Hotel and agreed to _raise / lower_ the value of the dollar in currency markets.

c. Draw solid <u>vertical</u> lines in the chart to indicate the two important dates in your answers above (a-b).

d. With respect to the Yen-dollar exchange rate, were exchange rates basically fixed prior to 1971? _____

e. Did the value of the dollar fall after the G-5 meeting? _____

2. The table provides information on U.S. merchandise exports and imports, in billions of dollars. Calculate the merchandise balance of trade and plot your results in the grid at right.

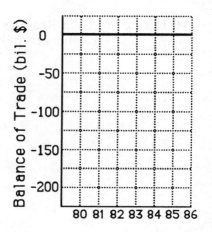

	Year	Merchandise Exports	Imports	Balance of Trade
a.	1980	$224.3	-249.7	$_____
b.	1981	237.1	-265.1	$_____
c.	1982	211.2	-247.6	$_____
d.	1983	201.8	-268.9	$_____
e.	1984	219.9	-332.4	$_____
f.	1985	215.9	-338.1	$_____
g.	1986	224.4	-368.7	$_____

3. Refer to the graph at right, which shows the supply and demand for British pounds (£).

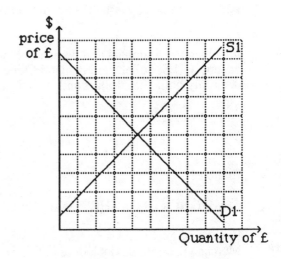

a. Indicate the exchange rate that will prevail if a flexible exchange rate system is in effect. Label this rate P1.

b. Show how the graph will be affected if British consumers suddenly develop a strong preference for imported goods. Label the new supply curve S2. Label the new exchange rate P2.

c. Show how the graph will be affected if American investors suddenly develop a strong preference for British investments. Label the new demand curve D3. Label the new exchange rate P3 (Assume the relevant supply curve is S1).

4. Refer to the graph at right.

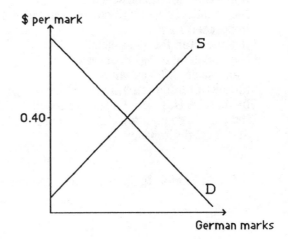

a. The equilibrium exchange rate is one mark per _____ cents.

b. Suppose the U.S. Government (including the Federal Reserve) agrees to stabilize the mark's exchange rate at 50-cents. At that exchange rate, there would be a _shortage / surplus_ of marks in the marketplace. The U.S. would be called on to _buy / sell_ marks in currency markets.

c. Draw a horizontal line at the official exchange rate and show the actual quantity of marks associated with the foreign exchange policy you prescribed above (b).

Part 5.   Self Test
Multiple choice questions

1. An international transaction that supplies the nation's currency:

a. also creates a supply of foreign currency and is recorded as a credit in the balance of payments
b. also creates a demand for foreign currency and is recorded as a credit in the balance of payments
c. also creates a demand for foreign currency and is recorded as a debit in the balance of payments
d. also creates a supply of the nation's currency is recorded as a debit in the balance of payments

Answer: _____

2. If the French buy American computers they:

a. demand U.S. dollars and supply French francs
b. demand U.S. dollars and demand French francs
c. supply U.S. dollars and demand French francs
d. supply both U.S. dollars and French francs

Answer: _____

Exhibit F

COMPONENTS OF THE BALANCE OF PAYMENTS ($ billions)

Exports of goods and services	+ 330
Merchandise exports (including military sales)	+ 150
Export services	+ 40
Income from U.S. assets abroad	+ 140
Imports of goods and services	- 390
Merchandise imports (including military sales)	- 220
Import services	- 80
Income from foreign assets in U.S.	- 90
Net unilateral transfers abroad	- 21
Outflow of U.S. capital	- 46
Inflow of foreign capital	+ 60
Increase in U.S. official reserve assets	- 21
Increase in foreign official assets in U.S.	+ 23
Statistical discrepancy	+ 65

3. Using Exhibit F, the merchandise trade balance equals _____ billions of dollars.

a. - 80
b. +100
c. - 70
d. + 60
e. none of the above

Answer: _____

4. Using Exhibit F, the current account balance equals _____ billions of dollars.

a. -111
b. - 81
c. - 60
d. + 63
e. none of the above

Answer: _____

5. Using Exhibit F, the capital account balance equals _____ billions of dollars.

a. +15
b. - 10
c. +14
d. - 14
e. none of the above

Answer: _____

6. Using Exhibit F, the official reserve balance equals _____ billions of dollars.

a. +2
b. - 1
c. +10
d. +17
e. none of the above

Answer: _____

7. The three major components of the current account are:

a. exports of goods and services, imports of goods and services, and statistical discrepancy
b. outflow of U.S. foreign capital, inflow of foreign capital, statistical discrepancy
c. merchandise exports, merchandise imports, and net unilateral transfers abroad
d. exports of goods and services, imports of goods and services, and inflow of foreign capital
e. none of the above

Answer: _____

8. The lower the dollar price per yen, the _____ Japanese goods are for Americans and the _____ Japanese goods Americans will buy; thus _____ yen will be demanded.

a. more expensive, more, fewer
b. more expensive, fewer, fewer
c. less expensive, more, more
d. less expensive, more, fewer
e. none of the above

Answer: _____

9. An American computer is priced at $5,500. If the exchange rate between the U.S. dollar and the British pound is $1.70 = 1 pound, how many pounds will a British buyer pay for the computer?

a. approxomately 3,235 pounds
b. approximately 3,052 pounds
c. approximately 2,543 pounds
d. approximately 6,599 pounds

Answer: _____

10. If the dollar price per pound moves from $1.90 = 1 pound to $1.40 = 1 pound, the pound is said to _____ and the dollar to have _____ .

a. depreciated, appreciated
b. appreciated, appreciated
c. appreciated, depreciated
d. depreciated, depreciated

Answer: _____

11. The U.S. dollar has appreciated relative to the French franc if:

a. it takes fewer francs to buy a dollar
b. it takes fewer dollars to buy a franc
c. it takes more dollars to buy a franc
d. a and c
e. none of the above

Answer: _____

12. Suppose the current exchange rate between the dollar and pound is $1.70 = 1 pound. Furthermore, suppose the price level in the United States rises 25 percent at a time when the British price level is stable. According to the purchasing power parity theory, what will be the new equilibrium exchange rate?

a. $2.72 = 1 pound
b. $1.55 = 1 pound
c. $1.86 = 1 pound
d. $2.13 = 1 pound
e. none of the above

Answer: _____

13. The purchasing power parity theory predicts less nearly accurately:

a. in the long run, and when there is a small difference in inflation rates across countries
b. in the short run, and when there is a large difference in inflation rates across countries
c. in the long run, and when there is a large difference in inflation rates across countries
d. in the short run, and when there is a small difference in inflation rates across countries

Answer: _____

14. Under a fixed exchange rate system, if the British pound is overvalued then there exists:

a. a shortage of pounds
b. a surplus of pounds
c. the equilibrium level of pounds
d. there is not enough information to answer the question (we need to know the actual exchange rate)

Answer: _____

15. One of the things a nation must do if it is on an international gold standard is:

a. link its money supply to its gold holdings
b. increase taxes
c. declare itself to be on a flexible exchange rate system
d. revalue its currency
e. none of the above

Answer: _____

True-False

16. From the 1870s to the 1930s, many nations tied   T F
their currencies to gold.

17. Under the Bretton Woods system, nations were   T F
expected to maintain fixed exchange rates (within a
narrow range) by buying and selling their own
currency for other currencies.

18. Any transaction that supplies the nation's   T F
currency is recorded as a debit in the balance of
payments.

19. The current account balance is the summary   T F
statistic for exports of goods and services,
imports of goods and services, and the statistical discrepancy.

20. Any transaction that supplies a foreign currency   T F
is recorded as a credit in the balance of payments.

Fill in the blank

21. The _____ is the difference between the value of merchandise exports and the value of merchandise imports.

22. The _____ predicts that changes in the relative price levels of two countries will affect the exchange rate in such a way that one unit of nation's currency will continue to buy the same amount of foreign goods as it did before the change in the relative price levels.

23. When nations adopt the gold standard they automatically _____ their exchange rates.

24. A _____ occurs when the official price of currency (under the fixed exchange rate system) is lowered.

25. Central banks play a much larger role under a _____ exchange rate system than under a _____ exchange rate system.

Part 5. Answers to Self Test

1. c 2. a 3. c 4. b 5. c 6. a 7. e 8. c 9. a 10. a
11. b 12. d 13. d 14. b 15. a
16. T 17. T 18. T 19. F 20. T
21. merchandise trade balance 22. purchasing power parity theory 23. fix 24. devaluation 25. fixed, flexible

Part 6. Answers

Part 2 Review of Concepts
1. f   2. e   3. a   4. b   5. g   6. d   7. c

Part 3 Key Concepts
1. monetary   2. debit, fall   3. credit, rise   4. supplies, demands, fall   5. current
6. trade, trade, deficit   7. unilateral, debit, current   8. goods and services, unilateral
9. capital, exceed   10. gold, International Monetary Fund   11. current, official, discrepancy, zero
12. exchange, $0.50, $0.40   13. flexible   14. is not, is not   15. demanded, supplied, rise
16. more, more, more, fall   17. more, more, more, fall   18. purchasing power parity, 60   19. long
20. surplus, deficit   21. greater, deficit, more, more   22. is, is   23. fixed   24. buy, dollars, £, $
25. official, over, devalued   26. devalue, adopt, monetary   27. more   28. futures, reduces
29. gold, 1930s, gold, $20.67   30. increase, decrease   31. out of, falls, fall, increases   32. true
33. International Monetary, 1944, fixed   34. 1971, gold, $35, were no longer
35. managed, swings (changes)   36. J-curve, worsen, improve   37. inelastic   38. 1985, 1985

Part 4 Problems and Exercises

1. a. fixed, 1971   b. 1985, lower
   d. basically yes   e. yes

2. a. -25.4   b. -28.0   c. -36.4
   d. -67.1
   e. -112.5   f. -122.2   g. -144.3

3. a-c. see graph at right

4. a. 40-cents
   b. surplus, buy
   c. buy quantity supplied minus
      quantity demanded at the
      official price

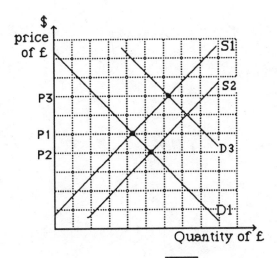

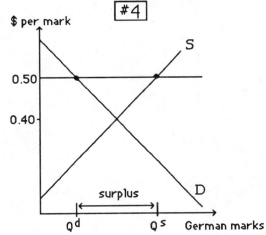

Chapter 37
International Impacts on the Macroeconomy

Part 1. Introduction and Purpose
Consider the following points as you read chapter 37 in the text.

A couple of decades ago international trade (imports and exports) a very small percentage of economic activity for the U.S. Today much of that has changed. Exports and imports run to hundreds of billions of dollars apiece every year, and substantial trade deficits were recorded after the economy recovered from the 1982 recession.

It is a relatively simple matter to incorporate the international sector into the macroeconomic models discussed in earlier chapters. Two models are of particular interest here — the **income-expenditure model** (total planned expenditures equal total planned production) and the **aggregate supply-aggregate demand model**. **Net exports** are an injection into the circular flow of income, and accordingly are able to increase total planned expenditures and aggregate demand. Reductions in net exports reduce TPE and AD.

Much of the remainder of the chapter is devoted to showing what economic conditions might cause net exports to increase or decrease. One possibility is that **prices** rise in this country relative to prices overseas. That would result in more imports and fewer exports for the U.S. — a reduction in net exports. Or **relative incomes** might change. Since consumption spending rises at higher incomes, an increase in national income implies a reduction in the nation's net exports.

The third possibility is a change in **exchange rates**. If the dollar appreciates (grows stronger) against other currencies, then foreigners have to pay more of their own currency to buy dollars — or to buy goods priced in dollars. Consequently an appreciating dollar has an impact comparable to an increase in all U.S. prices, namely to reduce U.S. exports and to increase U.S. imports. Net exports decline, when the dollar appreciates.

What originally caused the dollar to appreciate? One possibility is that **real** (inflation adjusted) **interest rates** rose in the U.S. relative to rates in other nations. Increases in the real interest rate give foreign lenders more incentive than before to lend their funds to U.S. borrowers. When foreigners sell their own currencies to buy the dollars they can lend to American borrowers, the dollar appreciates relative to foreign currencies.

So you see how an event in the **capital market** (higher real interest rates in the U.S.) can affect **exchange rates** (the dollar strengthens), which influences **trade** in goods and services (net exports decline), which in turn is transmitted to **real output** and employment for the entire economy (the decline in net exports lowers aggregate demand).

Changes in the exchange rate can also affect the **aggregate supply** side of the economy. If the dollar depreciates relative to other currencies, then U.S. companies will have to pay more dollars for foreign steel, raw materials, computer chips, and all of the other things they use as inputs in the production process. Higher production **costs** cause aggregate supply to shift leftward, so equilibrium real output will be lower than before. However other things do not remain unchanged. A depreciating dollar also means that U.S. net exports increase (as we saw just a minute ago), so aggregate demand and national income tend to rise. The overall impact on the economy depends on the **relative magnitude** of the two shifts.

It is a good idea to practice with the TPE-TPP and AD-AS models as well as the supply and demand for foreign exchange. Your understanding of these issues is directly related to your ability to manipulate all three models, so it is a good idea to keep some paper and a pencil handy as you read the text.

Part 2.   Review of Concepts from Earlier Chapters
Prior to reading chapter 37, match statements at left with the appropriate concept at right.

__1. Consumption + planned investment + gov't purchases + net exports.   a. aggregate demand curve
__2. Aggregate demand equals aggregate supply.   b. exchange rate
__3. Total quantity of goods produced at various price levels.   c. real interest rate
__4. Total quantity of goods purchased at various price levels.   d. aggregate supply curve
__5. Exports minus imports of goods and services.   e. tariff
__6. The interest rate minus the expected inflation rate.   f. net exports
__7. The value of a currency in terms of another currency.   g. equilibrium
__8. Market value of all final goods & services produced during year.   h. quota
__9. A tax on imports.   i. GNP
__10. A limit on the quantity of imports.   j. total planned expenditure
__11. Rise in a currency's value relative to other currencies.   k. depreciation
__12. A decline in a currency's value in foreign exchange markets.   l. appreciation

Part 3.   Key Concepts in this Chapter
After reading chapter 37 in the text, answer the following questions.

1. If the U.S. imports $10 billion worth of goods and services and exports $8 bil. worth, it has net exports amounting to _positive / negative_ $_____ bil. This is known as a trade _surplus / deficit_.

2. The U.S. will export more goods to Japan if the yen _appreciates / depreciates_ relative to the dollar. The U.S. will import more goods from Japan if the dollar _appreciates / depreciates_ relative to the yen.

3. If Japan's real GNP rises, then it will import _more / fewer_ goods and services from the U.S. This will cause the U.S. trade balance to move toward _surplus / deficit_.

4. If U.S. real GNP declines, then it will import _more / fewer_ goods and services from Japan. This will cause the U.S. trade balance to move toward _surplus / deficit_.

5. Japan's net exports will _increase / decrease_ if U.S. real income rises.

6. If the dollar rises relative to the yen, U.S. companies will sell a <u>larger / smaller</u> quantity of goods to Japanese buyers. Japanese companies will sell a <u>larger / smaller</u> quantity of goods to U.S. buyers. Consequently net exports by the U.S. should _____ and net exports by Japan should _____.

7. If net exports increase, then the total planned expenditure curve shifts <u>up / down</u>. If net exports decrease, the TPE curve shifts <u>up / down</u>. In the latter instance, equilibrium real GNP will tend to <u>rise / decline</u>.

8. Due to international trade, if Japan's real GNP rises then the TPE curve for the U.S. will shift <u>up / down</u>. If U.S. real GNP declines, then the TPE curve for Japan shifts <u>up / down</u>.

9. If there is an increase in the overall level of U.S. prices, then American consumers will be <u>more / less</u> willing to buy British products than before. This implies that U.S. imports will <u>rise / fall</u>. Higher U.S. prices also imply that British consumers will be <u>more / less</u> willing to buy American products. This implies that U.S. exports will <u>rise / fall</u>. In all, the higher price level means that U.S. net exports will turn toward <u>surplus / deficit</u>.

10. If the overall level of prices goes up by 5% in Germany and 3% in the U.S., then the value of net exports by the U.S. should turn toward <u>surplus / deficit</u>.

11. In the J-curve analysis, if the dollar depreciates relative to the French franc, then U.S. net exports will <u>decline / increase</u> in the short run and will <u>decline / increase</u> in the long run.

12. An upward shift in the TPE curve implies a <u>rightward / leftward</u> shift in the aggregate demand curve. This could have been caused by <u>an increase / a decrease</u> in net exports. If net exports decline then the TPE curve will shift <u>up / down</u>, which in turn will cause the aggregate demand curve to shift <u>rightward / leftward</u>.

13. If the dollar depreciates relative to the Swiss franc, then U.S. goods become <u>more / less</u> expensive relative to Swiss goods.. As a result U.S. net exports to Switzerland will <u>rise / fall</u>, which will cause the U.S. TPF curve to shift <u>upward / downward</u>. The latter implies a <u>rightward / leftward</u> shift in the the U.S. aggregate demand curve.

14. If there is an increase in Japan's real GNP then U.S. net exports will <u>rise / fall</u> and U.S. aggregate demand will shift to the <u>right / left</u>. Consequently U.S. real income will <u>rise / fall</u>.

15. If the U.S. dollar appreciates relative to other currencies, then raw materials and other productive inputs purchased by U.S. companies from overseas suppliers will cost <u>more / less</u> than before. This will shift the U.S. aggregate supply curve toward the <u>right / left</u>. As a result of this single effect, U.S. real income will <u>rise / fall</u>.

16. If foreign raw material suppliers lower their prices, then the U.S. aggregate supply curve will shift to the <u>right / left</u>. As a result U.S. real income will <u>rise / fall</u>.

17. Suppose the dollar appreciates relative to other currencies. On the one hand this will cause U.S. net exports to <u>rise / fall</u>, so aggregate demand will shift <u>rightward / leftward</u>. On the other hand this exchange rate change will make raw materials and other productive inputs <u>more / less</u> costly than before, so the aggregate supply curve will shift <u>rightward / leftward</u>.

18. If real interest rates rise in the U.S., then the return from lending money in the U.S. rather than Japan <u>increases / declines</u>. Consequently financial capital will flow <u>into / out of</u> the U.S.

19. Suppose the U.S. government's budget deficit increases from $20 bil. to $200 bil. As a result of this increase in the _demand for / supply of_ credit, real interest rates in the U.S. will tend to _rise / fall_. Consequently financial capital will flow _into / out of_ the U.S. The capital flow will cause the dollar to _appreciate / depreciate_ relative to other currencies, which will cause the nation's net exports of goods to _rise / fall_.

20. An _open / closed_ economy is one that trades with other nations. A _____ economy is one that does not trade with other nations.

21. Assume that saving minus investment in the U.S. remains constant. Now, a $10 billion increase in the U.S. federal budget deficit means that the U.S. trade deficit must _increase / decrease_ by $_____ bil.

22. If the budget deficit equals $30 billion and domestic saving exceeds investment by $40 bil., then exports _exceed / are less than_ imports by $_____ bil. There is a trade _surplus / deficit_.

23. Ways to reduce a nation's trade deficit are: reduce the federal budget _surplus / deficit_, encourage foreign policy makers to _stimulate / slow down_ economic growth in their nations, _increase / reduce_ national saving, and use _____ or quotas to _increase / reduce_ imports of foreign goods.

24. When the U.S. imposes tariffs or quotas, foreign nations may _____ by imposing their own trade restrictions.

25. If the Federal Reserve reduces the U.S. money supply, there will be an _increase / decrease_ in the U.S. supply of loanable funds, so the U.S. real interest rate will _rise / fall_. The change in the real interest rate will cause capital to flow _into / out of_ the U.S. The capital flow will cause the demand for dollars in foreign exchange markets to _rise / fall_, so the dollar _will / will not_ appreciate relative to other currencies. The lesson is that a "tight" money policy implies a dollar that is _strong / weak_ relative to other currencies.

Part 4. Problems and Exercises
After reading chapter 37 in the text you should be able to work the following problems.

1. Assume the dollar-yen exchange rate changes from 150 to 120 yen to the dollar.

a. With respect to the yen, the dollar has _appreciated / depreciated_.

b. Due to the exchange rate change, U.S. exports to Japan should _rise / fall_. U.S. imports from Japan should _rise / fall_. U.S. net exports should turn toward _surplus / deficit_.

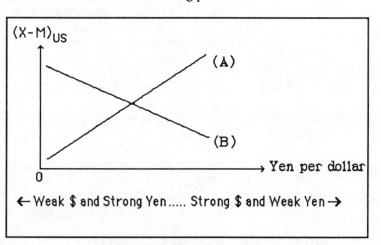

c. Which curve in the diagram (A or B) expresses the correct relationship between the exchange rate and U.S. net exports? ____

2. Assume real incomes rise in Canada and
Mexico while U.S. real income remains
constant or rises less rapidly.

a. Now consumers in Canada and Mexico
will purchase _more / fewer_ imported
goods than before. U.S. net exports
should _increase / decrease_ as a result of
rising foreign incomes.

b. Which curve in the diagram (A or B)
expresses the correct relationship between
foreign income and U.S. net exports? ___

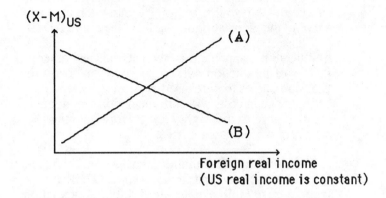

3. Assume the U.S. dollar appreciates with
respect to foreign currencies.

a. Due to the exchange rate change, the
prices of U.S. goods will _rise / fall_ in
terms of foreign currencies. This means
that foreigners will be _more / less_
willing to buy American goods than
before.

b. The diagram at right shows what has
happened to total planned expenditures
(TPE) in the U.S. economy following the
dollar appreciation. Label the pre-
appreciation TPE curve TPE-1 and the
post-appreciation TPE curve TPE-2.

c. Initially the equilibrium level of income
was $_____; after the dollar
appreciated it is $_____.

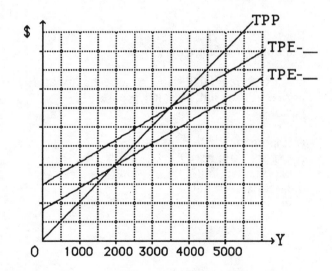

4. (This continues exercise 3 on previous page.)

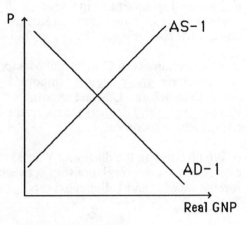

a. If the dollar appreciates, then the aggregate demand curve will shift to the _right left_. Draw the new AD curve in the graph at right, and label the curve AD-2.

b. If the dollar appreciates, raw materials and other factors of production will be _more / less_ costly for U.S. companies to purchase from foreign suppliers. This change in costs will shift the nation's aggregate supply curve to the _right / left_. Draw the new supply curve and label it AS-2.

c. Show the original equilibrium real income and label it Q1. Label the new equilibrium income Q2. Real income _rose / fell_ as a result of dollar appreciation.

d. In your graph, which curve shifted the most (measured horizontally)? _AD / AS_

Part 5.   Self Test
Multiple choice questions

1. As U.S. real GNP rises, Americans import more goods from Japan, causing Japan's _____ to rise. As a result, U.S. net exports _____ and Japan's net exports _____ , ceteris paribus.

a. imports; fall; rise
b. exports; fall; rise
c. exports; fall; fall
d. imports; rise; fall
e. none of the above

Answer: _____

2. A depreciation in the value of the dollar against the yen will cause the U.S. to import _____ goods from Japan and Japan to import _____ goods from the U.S. As a result, U.S. net exports _____ and Japan's net exports _____ .

a. fewer; more; fall; rise
b. more; fewer; fall; rise
c. fewer; more; rise; fall
d. more; fewer; rise fall

Answer: _____

3. The J-curve phenomenon places doubt on which of the following occurrences (at least in the short run)?

a. If a nation's currency depreciates, it will buy fewer imports and sell more exports, thus its net exports rise.
b. If a nation's currency appreciates, it will buy fewer imports and sell more exports, thus its net exports rise.
c. If a nation's currency depreciates, neither exports nor imports will change and therefore net exports remain the same.
d. If a nation's currency appreciates, it will buy more imports and sell fewer exports, thus its net exports fall.

Answer: _____

4. Suppose Americans buy inputs from foreigners. When the prices of foreign inputs fall, the U.S. aggregate supply curve _____ and when the prices of foreign inputs rise, the U.S. aggregate supply curve _____ .

a. shifts rightward, shifts leftward
b. shifts leftward, shifts rightward
c. shifts leftward, remains constant
d. remains constant, shifts rightward
e. none of the above

Answer: _____

5. Suppose the dollar appreciates in value on foreign exchange markets. What is the effect on U.S. real GNP?

a. It rises, since dollar appreciation shifts the U.S. aggregate demand (AD) curve leftward.
b. It falls, since dollar appreciation shifts the U.S. aggregate supply (AS) curve rightward.
c. There is no effect on real GNP since dollar appreciation does not affect either the U.S. AD or AS curve.
d. It depends on whether the U.S. AD curve shifts leftward by more or less than the AS curve shifts rightward.

Answer: _____

6. Expansionary fiscal policy is less effective at raising real GNP in:

a. inflation-prone countries
b. recession-prone countries
c. a closed economy than in an open economy
d. an open economy than in a closed economy
e. b and d

Answer: _____

7. The budget deficit equals:

a. the amount of saving plus investment plus the trade deficit
b. the amount of saving plus investment minus the trade deficit
c. the amount of saving over investment minus the trade deficit
d. the amount of saving over investment plus the trade deficit

Answer: _____

8. Which of the following scenarios best describes the effects of expansionary monetary policy?

a. interest rates fall; there is an outflow of foreign capital from the United States; the supply of dollars rises on foreign exchange markets; the dollar depreciates; U.S. exports rise, U.S. imports fall, and U.S. net exports rise; the U.S. aggregate demand curve shifts rightward; a depreciated dollar shifts the U.S. aggregate supply curve shifts leftward
b. interest rates rise; there is an inflow of foreign capital into the United States; the supply of dollars rises on foreign exchange markets; the dollar depreciates; U.S. exports rise, U.S. imports fall, and U.S. net exports rise; the U.S. aggregate demand curve shifts rightward; a depreciated dollar shifts the U.S. aggregate supply curve shifts leftward
c. interest rates fall; there is an outflow of foreign capital from the United States; the demand for dollars rises on foreign exchange markets; the dollar depreciates; U.S. exports rise, U.S. imports fall, and U.S. net exports rise; the U.S. aggregate demand curve shifts rightward; a depreciated dollar shifts the U.S. aggregate supply curve shifts leftward
d. interest rates fall; there is an outflow of foreign capital from the United States; the supply of dollars rises on foreign exchange markets; the dollar appreciates; U.S. exports fall, U.S. imports rise, and U.S. net exports rise; the U.S. aggregate demand curve shifts rightward; a depreciated dollar shifts the U.S. aggregate supply curve shifts leftward

Answer: _____

9. Do lower input prices abroad affect the U.S. price level under a fixed exchange rate system? (Assume that Americans use foreign inputs.)

a. No, the only things that affect the U.S. price level are changes in either U.S. aggregate demand, aggregate supply, or both.
b. No, since foreign input prices affect foreign aggregate supply curves and domestic input prices affect domestic aggregate supply curves.
c. Yes, since as foreign input prices fall, the U.S. aggregate supply curve shifts leftward and this raises the U.S. price level.
d. Yes, since as foreign input prices fall, the U.S. aggregate supply curve shifts rightward and this lowers the U.S. price level.

Answer: _____

10. A change in the yen-dollar exchange rate affects:

a. both U.S. exports and imports
b. neither U.S. exports or imports
c. only U.S. exports
d. only U.S. imports

Answer: _____

True-False

11. Suppose there are only two countries in the   T F
world, the United States and Japan, and the two
countries trade with each other. As U.S. real GNP
rises, Americans import more goods from Japan,
causing Japan's exports to rise. As a result,
U.S. net exports fall and Japan's net exports rise.

12. If the dollar appreciates and the yen   T F
depreciates, this makes U.S. goods cheaper for Japan
and Japanese goods more expensive for the United
States.

13. If the U.S. dollar depreciates, the U.S. AD curve   T F
shifts rightward and the AS curve leftward.

14. The budget and trade deficits are sometimes   T F
known as the twin tower deficits.

15. A change in the exchange rate can change a   T F
country's net exports.

Fill in the blank

16. Expansionary fiscal policy raises real GNP more in a(an) _____ economy than in a(an) _____ economy.

17. The budget deficit equals the amount of saving over investment plus _____ .

18. In a four-sector economy, _____ , _____, _____, and _____ add up to total otput.

19. Expansionary monetary policy raises real GNP more in a(an) _____ economy than in a(an) _____ economy.

20. Restrictive monetary policy lowers real GNP more in a(an) _____ than in a(an) _____ economy.

Part 5. Answers to Self Test

1. b 2. c 3. a 4. a 5. d 6. d 7. d 8. a 9. d 10. a
11. T 12. F 13. T 14. T 15. T
16. closed, open 17. the trade deficit 18. C, I, G, X-M
19. open, closed 20. open, closed

Part 6. Answers

Part 2 Review of Concepts
1. j   2. g   3. d   4. a   5. f   6. c   7. b   8. i   9. e   10. h   11. 1   12. k

Part 3 Key Concepts
1. negative $2 bil., deficit   2. appreciates, appreciates   3. more, surplus   4. fewer, surplus
5. increase   6. smaller, larger, decline, increase   7. up, down, decline   8. up, down
9. more, rise, less, fall, deficit   10. surplus   11. decline, increase
12. rightward, an increase, down, leftward   13. less, rise, upward, rightward   14. rise, right, rise
15. less, right, rise   16. right, rise   17. fall, leftward, less, rightward   18. increases, into
19. demand, rise, into, appreciate, fall   20. open, closed   21. increase, $10 bil.
22. exceed, $10 bil., surplus   23. deficit, stimulate, increase, tariffs, reduce   24. retaliate
25. decrease, rise, into, rise, will, strong

Part 4 Problems and Exercises

1. a. depreciated
    b. rise, fall, surplus
    c. curve B

2. a. more, increase
    b. curve A

3. a. rise, less
    b. the top curve is TPE-1 and
       the bottom curve is TPE-2
    c. $3500, $2000

4. a. left, see graph at right
    b. less, right, see graph at right
    c. may rise or fall, depending on which shift is greater
    d. The answer varies. Income rises in the graph at
       right, but it would have fallen if the AD had shifted
       as far as point H.

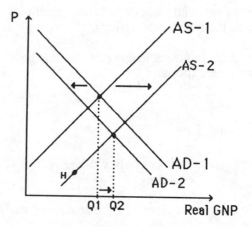

Chapter 38
Economic Growth and Development

Part 1. Introduction and Purpose
Consider the following points as you read chapter 38 in the text.

The chapter on economic growth and development examines a topic you may have thought about before, namely why some nations "get ahead" and others get left behind. To some degree luck probably helps explain why some nations' economies grow and develop. But it takes more than luck. When a national economy experiences sustained growth extending over several generations, of a magnitude that puts it far ahead of its neighbors, it is a sure bet that laws, policies, and customs have played a role too. The present chapter examines each of these factors.

The United States experience provides a few clues about the forces that work toward economic growth. For example, many people believe that economic growth is largely a matter of having ample **natural resources**. This country's vast natural reources seem to support that belief — until you consider that native Americans living in North America when the pilgrims came had even more abundant natural resources than we have today, yet had a very low material standard of living. New methods, new laws, and different cultures combined to raise the American standard of living to its present level, not the resources that have been here all along.

The American experience also suggests that national economies grow and develop slowly and according to a kind of **pattern**. Less advanced nations tend to have a lot of farms and not many factories, so as a practical matter the farm sector is where most growth occurs.

Economic growth is a matter of **increasing national output** from one year to the next, represented by an outward shift of the **production possibilities frontier** (PPF) over time. The PPF curve shifts out as a result of **investments** in capital goods (both physical capital and human capital) and as **technology** advances. Investments are sensitive to incentives, so private investment will be greater in nations that **protect private property** and levy only **moderate taxes** on profit and income. Rising oil prices, inflation-induced tax increases, low investment, price controls, and government regulation combined to limit U.S. economic growth during the 1970s.

Economic development refers to more than increasing national output. It also implies changing the **nature of the economy** so it is capable of producing a more "advanced" basket of goods and services. At about the turn of this century, the U.S. economy was transformed from a farm economy to a manufacturing economy; in the past generation it has become a service economy.

Although there is less agreement regarding the causes of economic development than on the causes of economic growth, experience suggests that many of the policies that encourage long-term economic growth also lay a foundation for economic development — for example, protecting the property of investors and workers, or encouraging work and investment with moderate (not high) tax rates.

To the degree **cultural differences** account for differences in economic development between nations, economic policy makers may be powerless to affect change. One feature of the U.S. cultural landscape has been the "Puritan work ethic," which says that work is good and non-work is bad. Several million people sharing this attitude or one like it can be the most powerful stimulus of all for economic development. Many rapidly growing Pacific nations have a similar **work ethic** and have experienced many notable successes in the past couple of decades.

An increasing number of analysts are now asking what might cause a nation to stop growing or even to move backward. One interesting view advanced by Mancur Olson is that governments in "mature" nations that have lived in peace and prosperity for long enough eventually come to be dominated by **special interest groups**. These groups seek policies to insulate themselves from the fluctuations and uncertainties of a market economy. One by-product of such policies is for the economy to become **rigid and unable to respond to changing market conditions**. Economic decline is the inevitable result. You will learn about Olson's theory and others in the text.

Part 2. Review of Concepts from Earlier Chapters
Prior to reading chapter 38, match statements at left with the appropriate concept at right.

__1. C+I+G+(X-M)   a. saving
__2. Combinations of goods that can be produced with all available resources.   b. per capita
__3. Inflation-adjusted national output of goods and services.   c. production
                                                                           inputs
__4. Take-home income that is not spent on consumption.   d. GNP
__5. The accumulation of capital goods.   e. private property
__6. The right to use a good or to sell it.   f. real GNP
__7. Land, labor, and capital.   g. PPF curve
__8. Per-person measurements.   h. investment

Part 3. Key Concepts in this Chapter
After reading chapter 38 in the text, answer the following questions.

1. Economic growth refers to increases in real _____.

2. Economic development refers to economic growth plus _____ changes that lead to improvements in the standard of living.

3. If a small nation produces 100 million bushels of bananas in year 1 and in year 10 produces 300 million bushels, this would be a sign of economic <u>growth / development</u> but not of economic <u>growth / development</u>.

4. Most economists consider per _day / mile / capita_ increases in real _____ to be economic growth. Real economic growth _has / has not_ been experienced by most nations throughout most of history. Per capita GNP is about _____ times as great in Norway as in India.

5. True or false? _____ If per capita real GNP is $2000 in one nation and $2000 in another nation, then the average person is equally well off in both nations.

6. Over the longer term, economic growth requires an outward shift of a nation's _____ _____ frontier. This is a _necessary / sufficient_ condition for economic growth.

7. For the past 30 years, the U.S.'s production possibilities frontier has shifted _outward / downward_ at a rate _faster than / slower than / equal to_ Japan's PPF curve.

8. Experience suggests that the _higher / lower_ the ratio of investment to GNP, the more rapidly its economy will grow. This requires that a nation devote a _larger / smaller_ percent of its output to producing consumption goods. Japan's saving rate is _greater / less_ than the U.S. saving rate.

9. True or false? _____ In practice, it is difficult if not impossible for a nation to experience high economic growth unless it has abundant natural resources.

10. The two types of capital are physical and _____. While you attend college you are investing in _____ capital.

11. Secure private property rights _encourage / discourage_ investment. Nations that protect private property experience _more / less_ economic growth than other nations.

12. _Technological / Cultural_ advances make it possible to obtain more output from the same amount of inputs. Such advances _do / do not_ shift the PPF curve outward.

13. According to the rule of 72, if a nation's economy grows at an annual rate of 6%, then real GNP will double in _____ years. If the economy grows at a 4% rate, it will take _____ years for real GNP to double.

14. Of the four expenditures on GNP, the one that contributes most to economic growth is _____ spending.

15. In the 1970s, the ratio of capital to labor hours in the U.S. economy _rose / fell_. Also during this period worker productivity _accelerated / slowed down_ in the U.S.

16. Some economists believe that as an increasing number of "baby boomers" and women entered the labor force in the 1970s, the quality of the labor force _improved / declined_. This was because they lacked work _motivation / experience / ability_.

17. It has been suggested that increases in the price of _oil / computers / labor_ in the 1970s caused businesses to acquire a smaller quantity of energy-using capital goods. This _would / would not_ be consistent with the slowdown in labor productivity that was experienced during the period.

18. Government regulation of business _increased / decreased_ through most of the 1970s. This trend caused businesses to invest _more / less_ in standard plant and equipment.

19. Economist Mancur Olson believes that special _____ groups reduce national productivity. They support laws and regulations that make the economy _more / less_ flexible in its ability to adjust to changing market conditions.

20. Julian Simon points out that the quantity of arable land (fit for crops) has _increased / decreased_ in recent years, while the incidence of world famine has been _increasing / decreasing_.

21. In the interview with Professor Robert Solow, he states that Japan's rapid growth in recent years is due to Japan's ability to use _____ already established in the U.S. and Japan's high fraction of national income devoted to _____ and investment. In future years Solow expects the difference between Japan's growth rate and the U.S.'s to _widen / narrow_.

22. Professor Solow suggests that over the long term the economy would grow more rapidly if the nation provided incentives for research and _____ activities and for _____ in capital goods.

23. Professor Solow _does / does not_ believe that economic growth will be greater if the U.S. would adopt tariffs, quotas, and other protectionist policies.

24. An LCD is a _____ _____ _____. LDCs have _high / low_ per capita GNPs.

25. Ignoring the possibility of population migration, if a nation's birth rate is 3% and its death rate is 1%, then the nation's population will _grow / shrink_ at an annual rate of ___%. At this annual rate, the rule of 72 suggests that the population will double once every ____ years.

26. Less developed nations often have _rapid / slow_ population growth, a _high / low_ savings rate, a _stable / unstable_ political system where private property _is / is not_ protected, and _high / low_ tax rates.

27. The _____ circle of poverty refers to the inability of some nations to grow unless they first _____, and the inability to _____ until incomes rise above current levels.

28. In a study of LDCs by A. Rabushka, high-tax nations experienced per capita income growth of ____% per year while low-tax nations experienced per capita income growth of ____% per year.

29. In the 1980s, LDCs had difficulty repaying their foreign _____. In 1987, Mexico offered to exchange $_____ billion worth of new _stocks / bonds_ for $_____ bil. worth of existing loans held by banks in the U.S. and elsewhere.

30. According to a table in the text ("Ten Biggest U.S. Bank Lenders to Mexico"), the four largest U.S. lenders to Mexico held $_____ bil. worth of that nation's debt in late 1987.

31. If one barrel of oil is indistinguishable from another (and can be used for the same purposes), then oil is _____. The same term _does / does not_ applied to dollars.

Part 4. Problems and Exercises

After reading chapter 38 in the text you should be able to work the following problems.

1. In the diagram, two nations (May and Nay) had <u>identical</u> production possibilities frontiers in 1985. This was curve AA'.

Points M and N correspond to actual production conditions in May and Nay, respectively.

a. Which nation has a higher ratio of saving to income? <u>May / Nay</u>

b. Over time nation _____ will experience more rapid economic growth than the other nation.

c. Curve BB' is nation _____'s PPF curve for 1990; curve CC' is nation _____'s PPF curve for 1990.

d. A tax incentive program that moves Nay's allocation from <u>point N</u> to <u>point M</u> would cause Nay to experience <u>more / less</u> rapid economic growth than before, ceteris paribus.

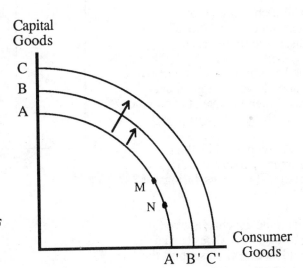

2. A table in the text (exhibit 2) contains information about the rate of economic growth fir the U.S. and Japan in the 1980s.

a. Plot growth figures for the U.S. in the grid at right, connect the points with a solid line, and label the curve US.

b. Repeat the above procedure (see a) for Japan.

c. The diagram suggests that the U.S. experienced an economic recession in 19____.

d. For the first 3 years in the chart which nation grew most rapidly? _____ Which nation grew most rapidly for the following 4 years?

_____

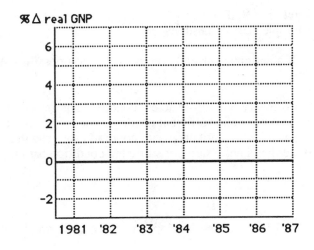

3. The exhibit at right shows two possible relationships between the marginal income tax rate and the rate of economic growth.

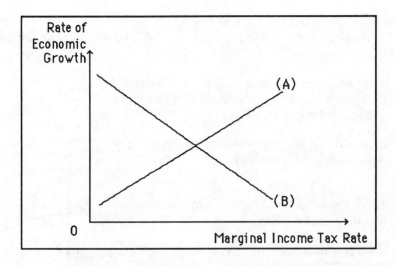

a. Which curve (A or B) represents the relationship discussed in the text? _____

b. According to this theory, if a nation lowers marginal tax rates, then the rate of economic growth should _rise / fall_.

c. A law passed in 1981 gradually reduced U.S. marginal tax rates during 1982-84.

Examine the chart above (in exercise #2). Does casual evidence seem to support the relationship between tax rates and economic growth discussed in the text? _____.

Part 5. Self Test
Multiple choice questions

1. If a nation is currently on its production possibilities frontier (PPF), a shift outward (rightward) in the PPF is a:

a. necessary but not sufficient condition for growth to occur
b. necessary and sufficient condition for growth to occur
c. sufficient but not necessary condition for growth to occur
d. neither a necessary nor sufficient condition for growth to occur

Answer: _____

2. In 1986, the less developed nations, as a group, accounted for approximately:

a. 20 percent of the world's GNP
b. 35 percent of the world's GNP
c. 60 percent of the world's GNP
d. 42 percent of the world's GNP

Answer: _____

3. A less developed country is usually defined as a country with a:

a. high saving-to-investment ratio
b. high unemployment rate
c. low per-capita GNP
d. low-quality public school system
e. none of the above

Answer: _____

4. Which of the following statements is true?

a. The population growth rate is lower in the less developed countries (LDCs) than in the developed nations.
b. About three-quarters of the world's people live in the developed nations.
c. The population growth rate is equal to the birth rate minus the death rate.
d. The birth rate tends to be lower in LDCs than in developed nations.
e. b and d

Answer: _____

5. Which scenario best illustrates the vicious circle of poverty?

a. agricultural incomes are low when the weather is bad, the weather is bad in certain parts of the world, nothing can change the weather, so agricultural incomes will continue to be low
b. incomes are low, thus investment is low, because investment is low, interest rates are high, because interest rates are high, people can't buy homes, without homes people are not satisfied enough to work
c. incomes are low, thus saving is low, because saving is low investment is low, because investment is low income is low
d. if you can't spend, you can't buy, if you can't buy, you can't spend

Answer: _____

6. In the 1970s, the ratio of capital to labor hours worked:

a. began to rise
b. began to decline
c. remained at the same level it was at in the 1960s
d. began to rise faster than national income

Answer: _____

7. Economist Mancur Olson argues that:

a. powerful special-interest groups enhance the economy's flexibility and speed up its ability to adapt to changing circumstances
b. special-interest groups enhance economic growth because they give people an avenue down which to vent their frustrations
c. Germany and Japan, having lost World War II, have less powerful special-interest groups than the United States (which has enjoyed a long period of political stability)
d. a and c
e. b and c

Answer: _____

8. Robert Solow expects the difference between the growth rates in the United States and Japan to:

a. narrow in the future
b. grow in the future
c. not change in the future
d. grow around the year 1998

Answer: _____

9. Real economic growth is an increase from one period to the next in:

a. nominal GNP
b. national income
c. population
d. quality of goods produced and consumed
e. none of the above

Answer: _____

10. Using the rule of 72, how many years will it take a country with a 6 percent growth rate per year to double in size?

a. 10 years
b. 12 years
c. 18 years
d. 24 years

Answer: _____

True-False

11. Martin Feldstein argued that inflation and a tax   T F
system that did not adjust for inflation gains
combined to overtax savings and led to the decline
of the capital stock in the 1970s.

12. The dependency ratio is the sum of the number of children under a certain age plus the number of the elderly (age 65 and over) divided by the total population.   T F

13. Money is not fungible.   T F

14. The Baker plan called for heavily indebted nations to restructure their economies in order to continue to receive loans from commercial banks and the World Bank.   T F

15. The United States had a higher growth rate in real GNP during the 1970s than Japan.   T F

Fill in the blank

16. Some economists have argued that per-capita real economic growth first appeared in those areas where a system of institutions and _____ had involved that encouraged individuals to direct their human capital and energy to effective economic projects.

17. Of the four spending components of GNP, most economists argue that _____ is the major component that promotes economic growth.

18. To accumulate capital it is necessary to _____ : to lower one's current consumption so that resources may be released for _____ .

19._____ comes from the Latin term that means "such that any unit is substitutable for another."

20. Most economists prefer to measure economic growth in _____ terms than absolute terms.

Part 5. Answers to Self Test

1. a 2. a 3. c 4. c 5. c 6. b 7. c 8. a 9. e 10. b
11. T 12. T 13. F 14. T 15. F
16. property rights 17. investment 18. save, investment
19. Fungibility 20. per-capita

Part 6. Answers

Part 2 Review of Concepts
1. d   2. g   3. f   4. a   5. h   6. e   7. c   8. b

Part 3 Key Concepts
1. GNP   2. institutional   3. growth, development   4. capita, GNP, has not, 50   5. false
6. production possibilities, necessary   7. outward, slower than   8. higher, smaller, greater   9. false
10. human, human   11. encourage, more   12. Technological, do   13. 12, 18   14. investment
15. fell, slowed down   16. declined, experience   17 .oil, would   18. increased, less   19. interest,
less   20. increased, decreasing   21. technology, saving, narrow   22. development, investments
23. does not   24. less developed country, low   25. grow, 2%, 36   26. rapid, low, unstable, is not,
high   27. vicious, save, save   28. 0.7%, 3.7%   29. debts, $10, bonds, $20   30. $8.923 bil.   31.
fungible, does

Part 4 Problems and Exercises

1. a. M   b. M   c. Nay, May   d. more

2. a-b. see graph at right
   c. 1982
   d. Japan, approximately equal

3. a. curve B
   b. rise
   c. yes (but this not final "proof")

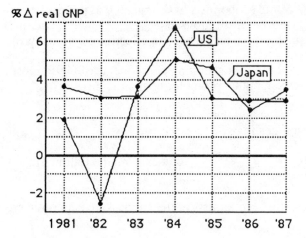

Chapter 39
Alternatives to Mixed Capitalism

Part 1. Introduction and Purpose
Consider the following points as you read chapter 39 in the text.

The U.S. has what may be called a mixed capitalist economy. That is an economy where most economic decisions are made by private individuals rather than government, but where the government's role is significant in many areas. In our particular case the mix is about two-thirds private sector to one-third public sector.

By contrast, a few economies are more purely **capitalistic** — free-market oriented — than our own. Under pure capitalism, virtually all resources are owned and managed (allocated) by **private** individuals. The government does little more than protect the nation from external attacks and provide a system of justice (police, courts, jails) to protect the life and property of its citizens. It is presumed that all private actions are acceptable that do not violate the **non-aggression axiom**. In real life, the Hong Kong economy has perhaps been closest to adopting this approach over the past decade, and the U.S. economy was organized around these principles during most of the 1800s and early 1900s. Experience suggests that laissez faire economies grow very rapidly.

On the other end of the spectrum, the Soviet Union and Yugoslavia represent **socialist** economies where productive resources and other property are owned by **government**. The Soviets use an elaborate central planning bureaucracy to allocate resources, set production targets, control prices, and so forth. The main problem with the Soviet system appears to be the lack of economic incentives it provides to workers and managers. With little or no personal reward for hard work and initiative, worker output has grown very slowly in recent years and companies have failed to adjust their output to satisfy consumer desires.

In Yugoslavia the government owns capital and other non-labor resources, but firms are actually managed by worker-elected teams. The Yugoslavian firms react to market conditions and can earn larger profits by being attentive to consumer demands. Worker-managers also decide whether to distribute the firm's profits as worker bonuses or instead to invest in capital equipment, new product development, and so forth. Bonuses predominate, so firms tend to underinvest and to grow slowly in the long run.

Although the U.S. and all other nations have economic difficulties that deserve attention, in recent years it has grown increasingly apparent that the absence of personal incentives in socialist (and communist) nations is a major threat to their prosperity. Many people believe that the Soviet Union, China, and other command-economy nations will be unable to experience further growth and development unless they substantially reorganize their economies around some of the principles associated with market economies — private property, price flexibility, decentralized decision making, profits, unemployment, and bankruptcy. Both nations have instituted significant but limited changes in that direction, and have indicated a wish to move further. Because such policies are at odds with orthodox communism, someday people may look back on this period as a major turning point in history. Keep your eyes, ears, and mind open and one of these days you'll have quite a story to tell.

Part 2. Review of Concepts from Earlier Chapters

Prior to reading chapter 39, match statements at left with the appropriate concept at right.

__1. These determine price in a market economy.   a. productive resources
__2. No tendency to move away from this point.   b. private property
__3. If price is above equilibrium price.   c. equilibrium
__4. If price is below equilibrium price.   d. inflation
__5. Land, labor, capital.   e. scarcity
__6. Owned by individuals, not government.   f. opportunity cost
__7. When most all prices rise.   g. supply & demand
__8. Production possibilities fall short of satisfying all wants.   h. incentive (gain)
__9. What must be foregone if an action is taken.   i. surplus
__10. The benefits minus costs associated with taking an action.   j. shortage

Part 3. Key Concepts in this Chapter

After reading chapter 39 in the text, answer the following questions.

1. _____ capitalism is an economic system in which most property is privately owned but government plays a substantial role. In a _____ system of capitalism, the government's role is minimal.

2. In socialism, most property is owned by private individuals / government / nonprivate clubs . If resources are allocated by local decision makers responding to market conditions, this is a system of _____ socialism. Resources are allocated by the central government under _____-economy socialism.

3. The law of demand holds in capitalist / socialist / all economies. If the price of Russian television sets rises, Russian consumers will want to buy more / fewer television sets.

4. Human desires exceed production capacity in all nations, so all nations must deal with _____.

5. Libertarians / Socialists / Communists advocate a very limited role for government. The believe government's role is mainly that of protecting _____ rights, enforcing _____, and providing national _____.

6. The libertarian approach to government rests on the non-_____ axiom. This axiom says that no person may _____ the person or property of others.

7. Libertarians approve / disapprove of the minimum wage; they approve / disapprove of tariffs and quotas to help U.S. companies compete against foreign competitors.

8. The libertarian approach is criticized because it _encourages / discourages_ even those government activities that would benefit large groups within society.

9. The economist Karl _____ played a major part in the development of socialism. He was influenced by Ricardo's _____ theory of _____. This theory says that the value of a good is determined by the amount of _____ that went into producing it.

10. According to the labor theory of value, if product X requires 8 hours to produce and product Y takes 2 hours to produce, then a unit of X is _____ times as valuable as a unit of Y.

11. If a worker produces 5 units of X per hour and is paid 2 units of X, Marx said the worker produces a surplus _____ of 3 units. If the employer keeps this amount, the worker _is / is not_ exploited.

12. In Marx's terminology, workers are members of the _proletariat / bourgeoisie_. Those who own businesses are members of the _proletariat / bourgeoisie_. Socialism would represent a dictatorship of the _proletariat / bourgeoisie_.

13. In Marx's theory of pure communism, individuals produce according to their _____ and receive goods according to their _____. People _are / are not_ selfish or greedy, and there _is / is not_ a need for a formal government.

14. Marx predicted that class conflict in the U.S. and Britain _would / would not_ lead to revolutions.

15. Marx believed that history was characterized by an ongoing struggle between social _____ over the division of social _____.

16. In the Soviet Union most property _is / is not_ privately owned. The Soviet economy is an example of _command / decentralized / harmony_ -economy socialism.

17. The central planning agency that manages the Soviet economy is _____. This organization supervises the operation of about _100,000 / 200,000 / 500,000_ different enterprises.

18. Gosplan _does / does not_ establish production targets for firms. Gosplan _does / does not_ provide the resources to companies required to produce output. Companies _are / are not_ supposed to react to changing market prices by reducing output of some goods and increasing that of others.

19. A command economy tend to produce goods _consumers / planners_ believe should be produced.

20. Soviet central planners set prices for about _100,000 / 200,000 / 500,000_ different goods. If planners set price below the market clearing price, there will be a _surplus / shortage_. As a result consumers _will / will not_ stand in line to purchase the good.

21. If the demand for toasters increases in a nation with a centrally planned economy, the official price of toasters _does / does not_ rise. Consequently _a / no_ shortage of toasters occurs.

22. The Soviet Union uses a _____ tax, which is similar to a sales or excise tax in the U.S.

23. Workers are _more / less_ mobile in the Soviet Union than in the U.S. In other words, it is _more / less_ difficult to move to jobs in other communities. Wages are determined by _central planners / market conditions_.

24. The most productive farms in the Soviet Union (output per acre) are large / small farms of approximately _____ acres each. These farms absorb about ____% of total farmland, and account for _____% of total farm output in the nation.

25. In the Soviet Union the 20% of the population with the highest incomes received _____% of all income in the 1970s, while the comparable figure for the U.S. was _____%. The bottom 20% of the population received _____% of all Soviet income, while the bottom 20% in the U.S. received _____%.

26. The GNP of the U.S. is about half / twice / equally as large as that of the Soviet Union.

27. Glasnost / Perestroika is the Soviet term for more open discussions of political and social issues, while Glasnost / Perestroika is the term for market-oriented economic reforms.

28. There are approximately _____ million government bureaucrats in the Soviet Union. The text notes that they probably do / do not support economic reform of the economy.

29. By early 1988, about 100,000 / 200,000 / 500,000 Soviet citizens had gone into business for themselves. Common businesses are _____ repair, _____, and _____.

30. The _____ brigade system in Soviet agriculture permits a group of farmers to manage a productive _____ and keep a share of the _____. This has / has not resulted in higher incomes for farmers.

31. In China, two major reform movements were the Great _____ _____ in 1958 and the _____ Revolution which began in 1966. Both / Neither / The latter proved to be a major encouragement to economic growth and development.

32. The policies mentioned in the previous question were advocated by _____ Tse-tung. Economic liberalization has been pursued under _____ Xiaoping.

33. China's collective farms are organized so that each collective is given land and a specific prodution _____ (quantity target). Individuals contract with the collective / government for a small plot of land. Once individuals have produced enough to fulfill their contract for the land, then any additional production is turned over to government / theirs to keep or sell .

34. True or false? _____ Chinese policy makers no longer interfere with agricultural sector.

35. In 19_____, six enterprises were partially freed from China's central planning system. These enterprises were first obligated to meet a production _____, after which they could produce according to demands in the _____.

36. In Yugoslavia, companies are managed by central planners / workers ; the capital used by firms is owned by _____. Firms do / do not react to market conditions. Yugoslavia's economy is a case of _____ socialism.

37. If a Yugoslavian firm earns a profit, the profit can either be paid to _____ or be used to _____ in expanding the company, buying more capital goods, etc. Workers do / do not hold shares of stock (ownership) in their companies which they can sell.

38. Given the choice between awarding themselves bonuses and investing in capital goods that will be productive in later years, Yugoslavian workers tend to favor _bonuses / investing_. As a result, Yugoslavian firms tend to have _adequate / inadequate_ amounts of capital goods. There _is / is not_ a tendency among worker managed firms to invest in new businesses and new products that may eventually earn a profit.

39. According to the interview with Professor Robert Lekachman, a system of libertarian socialism is one where economic power would shift from its present location to cooperatives, _____ groups, and _____ managements. Government _would / would not_ redistribute wealth as a part of this program.

40. Professor Robert Lekachman believes that an important element missing from standard economic theory is the issue of _____, and its ability to influence markets. He believes that _____ist economics brings this issue into the economic model.

Part 4. Self Test
Multiple choice questions

1. Which of the following policies would a libertarian not favor?

a. an interest rate ceiling
b. a price floor placed on milk
c. the elimination of the Federal Reserve
d. a and c
e. a and b

Answer: _____

2. According to the labor theory of value:

a. direct labor equals indirect (embodied) labor times the price of the product labor produces
b. all value in produced goods is derived from direct and indirect (embodied) labor
c. capitalists are in competition for labor, and over time labor will be in shorter supply
d. labor's value is computed by dividing the quantity of output produced by the quantity of labor used to produce it

Answer: _____

3. Karl Marx argued that the value of labor power tends toward:

a. a comfortable living wage
b. the price of the product it goes to produce
c. below subsistence
d. a "revolutionary wage," by which Marx meant that revolutions are basically economic in nature
e. none of the above

Answer: _____

4. According to Marx, the six stages of economic development are:

a. Adam and Eve farming, modernized farming, urbanization, the move to services, capitalism, socialism
b. capitalism, slavery, landlord aristocracy, dictatorship of the proletariat, primitve communism, pure communism
c. feudal times, renaissance times, colonialism, urbanization, city life, and communal living
d. primitive communism, slavery, feudalism, capitalism, dictatorship of the proletariat, pure communism
e. none of the above

Answer: _____

5. The central planning agency in the Soviet Union is called:

a. Xenoplan
b. Gosplan
c. Centrex
d. Eoplan
e. none of the above

Answer: _____

6. In the Soviet Union, the tax that is used to finance many of the heavily-subsidized goods is the:

a. capital gains tax
b. turnover tax
c. ruble tax
d. property tax
e. turndown tax

Answer: _____

7. Which of the following statements is true?

a. One's absolute standard of living cannot be higher in a nation where one receives a lower percentage of the total income than in a nation where one receives a higher percentage of the total income.
b. The income distribution in the United States is more equal than in the Soviet Union.
c. Income inequality is not always an accurate measure of economic inequality.
d. The poor in the Soviet Union receive a slightly smaller slice of a smaller economic pie, while the poor in the United States receive a slightly bigger slice of a bigger economic pie.
e. none of the above

Answer: _____

8. The Soviet policy of greater openness in public discussions and the arts is called:

a. gorbahlo
b. perestroika
c. mixatent
d. glasnost
e. none of the above

Answer: _____

9. In Yugoslavia, the state owns the assets of the firms and:

a. Gosplan manages the firms
b. state-appointed officials manage the firms
c. the workers manage the firms
d. the Council of Ministers manage the firms

Answer: _____

10. According to Hegel, knowledge and progress occur through a process of:

a. picking and choosing
b. opposing ideas or forces
c. chaos
d. random choice
e. none of the above

Answer: _____

True-False

11. In Marxist terminology, surplus value refers to   T F
the difference between what a buyer pays for a good
and the highest price he or she would have paid.

12. Marx argued that the value of labor power tends   T F
to an above-subsistence wage.

13. Critics of central planning contend that central   T F
planning cannot satisfy consumer demand as well
as market forces.

14. In 1987, the Soviet Union per-capita GNP was   T F
approximately 90 percent of U.S. per-capita GNP.

15. In 1958, Mao Tse-tung instituted an economic   T F
plan known as bao gan dao hu.

Fill in the blank

16. _____ is an economic system characterized by government ownership of the nonlabor factors of production, largely market allocation of resources, and decentralized decision making, in which most of the economic activities take place in the public sector and government plays a major overseer role in the economy.

17. Marx argued that the "labor power" capitalists purchase is itself a commodity and that its value is determined by _____ .

18. The last stage of development according to Marx is _____ .

19. In 1987, U.S. trade with the Soviet Union largely consisted of sales of _____ .

20. _____ is an economic system characterized by purely private ownership of the factors of production, market allocation of resources, and decentralized decision making, in which most of the economic activities take place in the private sector and government plays a small or no role in the economy.

Part 4. Answers to Self Test

1. e 2. b 3. e 4. d 5. b 6. b 7. c 8. d 9. c 10. b
11. F 12. F 13. T 14. F 15. F
16. Decentralized socialism 17. labor time
18. pure communism 19. grain 20. Pure capitalism

Part 5. Answers

Part 2 Review of Concepts
1. g   2. c   3. i   4. j   5. a   6. b   7. d   8. e   9. f   10. h

Part 3 Key Concepts
1. mixed, pure   2. government, decentralized, command-economy   3. all, fewer   4. scarcity
5. Libertarians, property, contracts, defense   6. non-aggression, aggress (injure)
7. disapprove, disapprove   8. discourages   9. Marx, labor, value, labor   10. four   11. value, is
12. proletariat, bourgeoisie, proletariat   13. ability, need, are not, is not   14. would
15. classes, product   16. is not, command   17. Gosplan, 200,000   18. does, does, are not
19. planners (and their bosses)   20. 200,000, shortage, will   21. does, a   22. turnover
23. less, more, planners   24. small, 1 acre, 1.5%, 25%   25. 37.5%, 40.6%, 7.5%, 6.9%   26. twice
27. Glasnost, Perestroika   28. 18 million, do not   29. 200,000, watch, clothing, taxi
30. contract, asset, profits, has   31. Leap Forward, Cultural, neither   32. Mao, Deng
33. quota, the collective, theirs to keep or sell   34. false   35. 78, target (or quota), marketplace
36. workers, government, do, decentralized   37. workers, invest, do not
38. bonuses, inadequate, is not   39. community, worker, would   40. power, Marxist